Facebook®
ALL-IN-ONE
FOR
DUMMIES®
A Wiley Brand

2nd Edition

by Jamie Crager,
Scott Ayres,
Melanie Nelson,
Daniel Herndon,
and Jesse Stay

FOR
DUMMIES®
A Wiley Brand

Facebook® All-in-One For Dummies,® 2nd Edition

Published by
John Wiley & Sons, Inc.
111 River Street,
Hoboken, NJ 07030-5774,
www.wiley.com

Contents at a Glance

Introduction 1

Book I: Creating a Timeline 5

Chapter 1: Deciding to Join 7

Chapter 2: Creating Your Account.......................................15

Chapter 3: Touring the Interface..49

Chapter 4: Customizing Your Privacy Settings 63

Chapter 5: Finding Help...83

Book II: Connecting with Others 91

Chapter 1: Creating Your Social Media Persona.................93

Chapter 2: Posting and Interacting....................................105

Chapter 3: Sharing Photos...117

Chapter 4: Sharing Videos 133

Chapter 5: Participating in Groups.....................................145

Chapter 6: Going Mobile 157

Chapter 7: Keeping Up with Events 171

Chapter 8: Having Private Conversations 187

Chapter 9: Games and Gifts 197

Chapter 10: Professional Networking.................................209

Chapter 11: Managing Connections Gone Awry.................221

Book III: Connecting to Other Social Media.............. 233

Chapter 1: What Is Social Media?.......................................235

Chapter 2: Connecting Facebook to Everything Else 245

Chapter 3: Flying on Autopilot 259

Book IV: Building a Business Page........................... 267

Chapter 1: Creating a Business Page 269

Chapter 2: Customizing Your Business Page 283

Chapter 3: Touring Your Business Page 295

Chapter 4: Building Your Community 319

Book V: Marketing Your Business.............................. 337

Chapter 1: Building a Network of Influence.................................339
Chapter 2: Running a Social Marketing Campaign......................349
Chapter 3: Using Insights to Track Your Success.......................363
Chapter 4: Ads, Promotions, and Offers.....................................377
Chapter 5: Identifying Your Target Audience 407

Book VI: Developing Facebook Apps.......................... 415

Chapter 1: Custom Apps for Business Pages 417
Chapter 2: Building Canvas Apps and Page Tabs.......................429
Chapter 3: Creating Your Own Apps 445
Chapter 4: Tour of the Facebook API 459

Index 475

Table of Contents

Introduction *1*
About This Book 1
Foolish Assumptions...2
Icons Used in This Book 2
Beyond the Book 3
Where to Go from Here..3

Book I: Creating a Timeline *5*

Chapter 1: Deciding to Join 7
Describing Facebook..7
Enjoying the Benefits of Facebook 8
    Embracing Facebook as an extension of your world 8
    Finding your community on Facebook....................................9
    Using Facebook for news and marketing..................................9
Avoiding the Timesuck 10
Agreeing to the Terms of Service 11

Chapter 2: Creating Your Account............................15
Signing Up..15
    Completing step 1: Finding friends 15
    Completing step 2: Filling in profile information 16
    Completing step 3: Choosing interests 16
    Completing step 4: Uploading a profile picture 17
Finding Friends 17
    Understanding what it means to be friends on Facebook.............17
    Searching for people you know..18
    Sending, receiving, and responding to friend requests 20
Finding and Customizing Your Account Settings 22
General Account Settings 23
    Name setting...23
    Username setting 23
    Email setting 25
    Password setting...26
    Networks setting...26
    Language setting 27
    Download a copy of your Facebook data 27

Security Settings 28
   Secure Browsing setting...29
   Login Notifications setting...29
   Login Approvals setting 29
   Code Generator setting 31
   App Passwords setting...31
   Trusted Contacts setting 32
   Recognized Devices setting 32
   Active Sessions setting...33
   Deactivate Your Account setting 33
Timeline and Tagging Settings...34
   "Who can add things to my timeline?" setting...............35
   "Who can see things on my timeline?" setting................35
   "How can I manage tags people add and tagging
      suggestions?" setting 35
Notifications Settings 36
Mobile Settings 37
Followers Settings 39
Apps Settings 40
Ads Setting..43
Payments Settings 43
   Account Balance setting 43
   Subscriptions setting...44
   Purchase History setting..44
   Payment Methods setting 44
   Preferred Currency setting 45
   Shipping Addresses setting 45
Facebook Card Setting 46
Support Dashboard Setting...47
Deleting Your Facebook Account 48

Chapter 3: Touring the Interface **49**

Navigating Your News Feed Page 49
   Top navigation 50
   Left navigation..51
   News feed 53
   Right navigation 54
   Ticker and Chat panes 55
Navigating Your Timeline..57
   Familiarizing yourself with the timeline........................57
   Hiding a story from your timeline...................................61
   Adding a past event to your timeline 62

Chapter 4: Customizing Your Privacy Settings **63**

Understanding Online Privacy..63
Taking Responsibility for Your Own Privacy...........................64
Managing and Customizing Your Privacy Settings...................65
   Blocked People and Apps settings 67

Understanding How Privacy Settings Affect What Others See 68
How people can find you 68
How friend requests work 69
How your updates are shared..69
Utilizing Lists So You Don't Miss a Thing...71
Creating a list...73
Making a list a favorite 73
Managing your lists 74
Discovering Interest Lists...76
Creating or following an interest list..76
Managing your interest list..78
Sharing your interest list with others 80

Chapter 5: Finding Help 83

Using Help Center...83
Searching Help Center...84
Searching specific help topics...85
Using the community forum..86
Getting additional tips...87
Expecting a response from Facebook 87
Finding Important Facebook Documents 88
Finding Additional Facebook Resources 89

Book II: Connecting with Others 91

Chapter 1: Creating Your Social Media Persona 93

Understanding News Feed..93
Finding Your Voice on Facebook...95
Lifecasting..95
Embracing differences...97
Knowing what people read 97
Using humor and provoking controversy...................................98
Speaking to your audience 98
Using Graph Search..98
Building a Brand 100
Building your personal brand 100
Building a business brand 101
Planning Content for a Page 102
Being a Resource 103
Avoiding Inflammatory or Spammy Behavior.................................104

Chapter 2: Posting and Interacting 105

Creating a Status Update 105
Adjusting how you share content...107
Adjusting individual privacy settings.....................................108
Using hashtags to make content discoverable 108
Tagging friends and business pages.......................................109

Allowing Replies to Business Pages 110
Removing and Editing Updates and Comments 111
Interacting with Other People's Updates 113
Understanding How the Follow Feature Works 114
    Adjusting the follow feature settings for your account 115
    Following other people's updates 115

Chapter 3: Sharing Photos **117**

Uploading Images from Your Computer 117
Adding Photos with Instagram 119
Adding a Photo to Your Comments 120
Creating and Editing Albums 120
    Uploading new photos to an existing album 124
    Moving photos from one album to another 125
    Editing privacy settings for albums 126
Editing Pictures 128
Using Smartphone Apps to Share Photos 131

Chapter 4: Sharing Videos **133**

Benefits of Using Video 133
Uploading Video to Facebook 135
    Sharing video from your computer 135
    Sharing video from your phone 136
    Sharing video from another social media channel 137
Customizing Your Video 140
    Finding your video on Facebook 140
    Editing your video 141
Using Facebook Apps to Share Video on Your Business Page 143
Producing Great Video Clips 144

Chapter 5: Participating in Groups **145**

Discovering Groups 145
Creating a Group 146
Personalizing Your Group's Image 148
Establishing the Settings for Your Group 150
Inviting People to Join Your Group 152
    Adding members when you create a group 152
    Adding members to a group any time 152
    Accepting a request to join your group 152
Posting to a Group 153
Sharing Documents in a Group 154
Leaving a Group 155
Deleting a Group 156

Chapter 6: Going Mobile **157**

Going Mobile 157
Using the Facebook Smartphone App 158
    Features of the smartphone app 159
    Updating your status on the Facebook app 162
    Understanding the limitations of the Facebook app 164
Accessing Facebook on a Smartphone or Tablet 164
Using Facebook on a Cellphone 165
    Setting up your Facebook account to accept text messages 166
    Updating your status via text 166
    Changing your mobile number 167
    Using your cellphone to text pictures and posts
        to Facebook 167
Checking In to Places 168
    Using Places to connect 168
    Using Location Services 168
    Finding your place 169
    Finding friends on Places 170

Chapter 7: Keeping Up with Events **171**

Introducing Events 171
Understanding Events Basics 172
    Getting the lay of the land 173
    Kinds of events 174
Finding and Interacting with Events 175
    Searching events 175
    RSVP to an event 176
    Checking out who is attending the event 177
    Interacting on the event wall 178
Synchronizing Events and Birthdays with Your Online Calendar 179
    Synchronizing all your events 179
    Synchronizing a single event 180
Creating an Event 181
    Adding a picture to your event 182
    Inviting friends 183
    Making changes to an event 184
Promoting Events on Facebook 185

Chapter 8: Having Private Conversations **187**

Introducing Facebook Messaging Options 187
Sending Messages 189
    Messaging friends 189
    Messaging nonfriends 191

Chatting with Friends...192
    Initiating a chat message 192
    Chatting with more than one friend 193
    Going offline or limiting your availability 193
Making a Video Call 194
Your Facebook E-Mail Address..196

Chapter 9: Games and Gifts **197**

Facebook Games 197
Playing Games 199
    Finding the games your friends are playing 200
    Allowing games to access your information and timeline...........200
    Inviting friends to a game 202
    Accepting invitations from friends.....................................203
    Blocking unwanted games 203
Making In-Game Purchases 203
Changing a Game's Privacy Settings 204
Games on Facebook Mobile 205
Facebook Gifts and Gift Cards...206
    Gifts...206
    Gift cards 208

Chapter 10: Professional Networking **209**

Before You Begin Networking...209
    Customizing your profile photo for networking 209
    Getting to know the space 210
Using Facebook for Professional Networking 210
    Having personal and professional conversations 212
    Building connections with professional contacts 212
Expanding Your Network...215
    Providing exclusive content to friends and followers 215
    Establishing yourself as an authority.................................215
    Rocking the boat 216
Building Stronger Engagement 216
Networking via Your Business Page...217
    Sharing a business page with a friend................................217
    Inviting e-mail contacts to Like your business page 219

Chapter 11: Managing Connections Gone Awry. **221**

Unfriending or Hiding..221
    Hiding updates from a friend or business page...........................222
    Removing someone as a friend 223
Blocking Someone 224

Leaving Groups 225
Unliking Business Pages 226
Blocking Apps 227
Removing Content from Your Timeline 228
Avoiding Facebook Viruses 228
  Spotting a virus 228
  Fixing your account 230

Book III: Connecting to Other Social Media 233

Chapter 1: What Is Social Media? 235

Defining Social Media 235
Making the Internet Friendly 237
Getting to Know Other Social Media Platforms 238
  Introducing Twitter 238
  Introducing LinkedIn 239
  Introducing Google+ 241
  Introducing Pinterest 242
  Introducing Instagram 242
Understanding What Social Media Means to Marketers 242

Chapter 2: Connecting Facebook to Everything Else 245

Understanding the Basics of Facebook Platform 245
Finding Common Uses for Facebook Platform 247
Connecting to Facebook 249
  Connecting your blog to Facebook 250
  Connecting your Twitter account to Facebook 250
  Connecting Google+ to Facebook 251
Using Facebook Social Plugins 252
Using Facebook Badges for Social Proof 255
Integrating Facebook with Marketing Efforts for Your Business 256
  Business cards 256
  Website or blog 257
  Sign or QR code in store or print materials 257
  Wherever you had your phone number in the year 2000 258

Chapter 3: Flying on Autopilot 259

Automating Facebook to Achieve Marketing Goals 259
Scheduling Updates with Post Planner or HootSuite 260
Setting Up Notifications for Business Pages 263
Connecting Your WordPress Blog to Facebook 264

Book IV: Building a Business Page 267

Chapter 1: Creating a Business Page 269
Deciding to Create a Business Page 269
Creating Your Business Page 271
Creating a Vanity URL 274
Understanding the Importance of Cover and Profile Pictures............ 276
    Choosing a profile picture 277
    Choosing a cover picture 280

Chapter 2: Customizing Your Business Page 283
Adding Information about Your Business Page....................................... 283
Customizing Your Business Page Settings 285
    Page Visibility option 286
    Posting Ability option.. 286
    Post Visibility option 286
    Post Targeting and Privacy option 287
    Messages option 287
    Tagging Ability option.. 287
    Notifications option 287
    Country Restrictions option.. 288
    Age Restrictions option... 288
    Page Moderation option.. 288
    Profanity Filter option... 288
    Similar Page Suggestions option 288
    Replies option 289
    Merge Pages option 289
    Remove Page option 289
Creating Admin Roles.. 289
All about Apps... 290
Suggestions from Your Followers... 293
Choosing Featured Business Pages.. 293
Sending Updates on the Go 294

Chapter 3: Touring Your Business Page. 295
Reviewing the Overall Business Page 295
The Admin Panel... 295
The Admin Panel Toolbar.. 297
Page Info Section 300
Apps Navigation... 303
    Changing the order of displayed apps 304
    Using your own images for displayed apps.................................... 305
    Choosing highlighted apps 305
Your Timeline.. 307
    Status update box.. 307
    Creating a milestone update... 308

Editing updates and milestones...310
Finding friends who Like this page 311
Finding recent posts by others 311
Reviewing liked pages 311
Managing third-party posts 312
Reviewing the Right Sidebar 313
Using Facebook as Your Business Page or Personal Timeline 313
Switching from one to the other...314
The Facebook toolbar when using Facebook as your
business page 315

Chapter 4: Building Your Community **319**

Determining Your Goals and Objectives 320
Establishing Your Authority..321
Establishing Social Proof 322
Creating Shareable Content 323
Sharing instead of broadcasting 323
Sharing links 324
Using photos and video to encourage sharing 326
Asking questions..326
Using calls to action 328
Creating content only for followers...330
Targeting Updates 332
Handling Customer Service 334
Interacting regularly with followers 334
Addressing negative comments and reviews..............................334

Book V: Marketing Your Business *337*

Chapter 1: Building a Network of Influence **339**

The Importance of Engagement...339
Building friends and followers for your business.......................341
Connecting with your friends and followers 342
Integrating Facebook in Marketing Campaigns 344
Promoting Facebook via traditional advertising 344
Having a memorable URL...346
Using apps to build influence 346
Outsourcing your Facebook management....................................346

Chapter 2: Running a Social Marketing Campaign **349**

Understanding What Makes Social Marketing Campaigns Work..........349
Types of Facebook Campaigns 351
Implementing Sharing Contests 352
Getting a good response 354
Avoiding a flopped contest...355

Marketing a Facebook Contest 355
The Power of Crowdsourcing 357
   Using crowdsourcing to create a new product 357
   Using crowdsourcing to determine your Facebook content 357
Preparing Your Business Page for the Campaign 358
   Your cover photo 358
   A custom tab 358
   Contact forms 359
   Canvas apps 359
   The ticker 360

Chapter 3: Using Insights to Track Your Success **363**

Tracking Your Facebook Stats with Insights 363
   Reviewing the main Insights page 364
   Exporting your data 365
   Checking out your settings 366
Touring the Likes Page 366
Understanding Reach Page Data 368
Finding Friends by Using the Visits Page 369
The All-Important Posts Page 370
Understanding the People Page 371
Getting to Know the News Feed Algorithm 372
   Understanding how the News Feed Algorithm works 373
   Using rank to improve your news feed position 374

Chapter 4: Ads, Promotions, and Offers **377**

Finding Facebook Ads 377
Deciding Whether Facebook Ads Are Right for You 378
   Choosing an ad: Facebook ads 379
   Choosing an ad: sponsored stories 380
   Knowing what you can't do with ads 381
Creating Your Facebook Ad 382
   What Kind of Results Do You Want for Your Ads? section 383
   Select Images section 384
   Text and Links section 385
   Audience section 386
   Account and Campaign section 387
   Bidding and Pricing section 388
   Review 389
Finding and Using the Facebook Ads Manager 390
   Understanding the left navigation options 390
Generating a Report 392
Adding or Deleting an Ads Account Administrator 393
Closing Your Facebook Ads Account 394

Using Facebook Promotions to Market Your Business 395
  Getting the word out 396
  Using a strong call to action 397
  Understanding the promotions guidelines....................................398
Using Apps to Create Customized Giveaways and Contests 401
  ShortStack..401
  Wildfire..402
  Strutta..402
Creating Best Practices for Your Facebook Promotion........................403
  Know the goals of your promotion..403
  Keep hoops to a minimum..403
  Provide the what, why, and how 404
  Go beyond your current followers 404
Using Facebook Offers to Reach New Customers 405

Chapter 5: Identifying Your Target Audience **407**
Using Insights to Identify Your Audience...407
Understanding Why Online and Traditional
  Marketing Are Necessary...408
Marketing Facebook Offline...409
  Direct mail marketing 409
  TV ads focused on Facebook...410
  Radio ads focused on Facebook 411
Online Marketing Resources 411
  E-mail marketing 412
  Search marketing with PPC 413
Integrated Campaigns 414

Book VI: Developing Facebook Apps............................ 415

Chapter 1: Custom Apps for Business Pages **417**
Using Apps for Facebook Marketing 417
Extending the Facebook Experience 419
  Screen real estate...419
  Social channels..420
  Analytics 421
Discovering iframes..421
Increasing Engagement with Apps 422
  Draw people in with requests 422
  Publishing stories 423
  News feed discovery stories..423
  Users' permissions with apps 424
  Apps that don't require user permissions....................................426
  Features that encourage sharing with friends 426
Avoiding the Reinvention of the Wheel 428

Chapter 2: Building Canvas Apps and Page Tabs **429**

Finding the Differences between Canvas Apps and Page Tabs 429
Page tab features 430
Canvas app features 431
Choosing between a page tab and a canvas app 432
Creating Your App 432
Getting to Know App Settings 435
App Details page 438
Open Graph 439
Defining roles for your app 441
Insights in Facebook Apps 442

Chapter 3: Creating Your Own Apps **445**

Creating and Deploying a Facebook App 445
At Facebook's core 445
A basic app 446
App, app — who has the app? 447
Installing the Facebook app 449
Authenticating Your App 453
The App Details 453
Request permission 456

Chapter 4: Tour of the Facebook API **459**

Finding Technical Information 459
Facebook's online API documentation 460
Helpful tutorials 461
Understanding Facebook's Core Concepts 462
Open Graph versus Graph API 462
Requesting access to and accessing objects 464
Cool core tools for creating advanced apps 465
Developing Apps More Easily with SDKs 466
Web-scripting SDKs 466
Mobile app–scripting SDKs 468
Placing Facebook Objects on Your Web Pages with Social Plugins 470

Index *475*

Introduction

Facebook is the most prolific social media platform so far, with over 1.19 billion active users at the time this book went to press. If Facebook were a country, it would be the third largest in the world, edged out by China (1.36 billion) and India (1.29 billion).

Facebook itself can be overwhelming. Some people worry about their privacy, while others can't share enough. Some worry that Facebook is getting too big, while others appreciate the innovation that comes from a growing user base. We hope that you focus first on the sections that will help you the most. Don't get bogged down with details. Most people use Facebook to keep up with friends and family, meet new people, and network with colleagues across the world. You'll find that these tasks are easy to perform.

About This Book

Maybe you are not on Facebook yet and are wondering about the hype. Or maybe you're on Facebook, but you have questions and need some answers. We've written this book with the beginner and intermediate social media user in mind. As you work with Facebook, we're confident you'll discover why it's so popular.

Our goal in writing this book is to introduce you to Facebook, explain how you can use it personally and professionally, and show you some tips and tricks along the way. We cover a wide range of topics — this is an *All-in-One* book, after all — and you may or may not want to read everything we offer. This book isn't meant to be read cover to cover like a novel. Use it as a reference when you get stuck and need help.

Social media changes almost daily, and Facebook is no exception. Although Facebook likes to change things up here and there, it generally doesn't change much more than the location of tabs and the size of ads. However, sometimes Facebook does make a drastic change — usually by making the site more useful overall. We kept up with changes as they were happening, and we've documented all the new stuff that's come out of Facebook HQ since December 2013, but new features continue to roll out. You can keep up with the most recent changes to Facebook by checking www.facebook.com/help/whats-new-on-facebook periodically.

Throughout this book, we're consistent in how we present certain information. You find these conventions throughout the book:

- Whenever you need to type something, we put what you need to type in **bold** so it's easy to see.

- When we introduce a new word that you may not be familiar with, we put it in *italics* and define it.

- When we share website addresses (URLs) with you, they look like this: www.dummies.com. If you're reading this book as an e-book, URLs are clickable links.

Facebook is a website, so it's not specific to PCs or Macs. If you can surf the web, you can get on Facebook. However, if we share instructions for tasks that are specific to a Windows PC or Mac, we tell you. For example, if you need to copy text, press Ctrl+C (Windows) or ⌘+C (Mac).

Foolish Assumptions

It would be impossible to consider every single type of reader for this book, so we've had to make some assumptions:

- You have a computer and know how to use it.

- You know what a web browser is and can surf the web.

- You have an e-mail address and know how to use it.

- You know what a mobile device is.

Icons Used in This Book

To make your experience with the book easier, we use various icons in the margins of the book to indicate particular points of interest.

When we share something we think is useful or will make life easier for you, we use the Tip icon.

If we want to reinforce a point or a concept, we use the Remember icon. The information we present here is worth committing to memory.

If we need to warn you about something that could give you problems, we use the Warning icon. Pay close attention when you see a Warning, because when we use it, we mean it!

Information tagged with the Technical Stuff icon gets, well, technical. Technical Stuff isn't essential to your understanding of Facebook, so you can skip these paragraphs if you're not interested.

Beyond the Book

We have written extra content that you won't find in this book. Go online to find the following:

✔ **Online articles covering additional topics at**

> www.dummies.com/extras/facebookaio

Here you'll find some guidelines for customizing your business page, suggestions for increasing your security and privacy online, tips for creating a Facebook ad, and more.

✔ **The Cheat Sheet for this book is at**

> www.dummies.com/cheatsheet/facebookaio

Here you'll find an explanation of Facebook lingo, information on customizing your Facebook browsing, links to important Facebook documents, and more.

✔ **Updates to this book, if we have any, are at**

> www.dummies.com/extras/facebookaio

Where to Go from Here

You can always start by turning the page and reading the first chapter (Book I, Chapter 1). Or look over the table of contents and find something that catches your attention or a topic that you think can help you solve a problem. Or peruse the index to find a specific item or topic you need help with.

We encourage you to Like our business pages on Facebook:

✔ **Post Planner:** http://facebook.com/postplanner
✔ **Crowdshifter Media:** http://facebook.com/crowdshifter

Book I
Creating a Timeline

getting started

with

Facebook

In this part. . .

- ✔ Examine the benefits of using Facebook.

- ✔ Set up your account, and find friends on Facebook.

- ✔ Understand the ins and outs of your news feed and personal timeline.

- ✔ Read about the different ways you can protect your online privacy.

- ✔ Get help from Help Center, online documents, and more.

Chapter 1: Deciding to Join

In This Chapter

✔ Answering the question, "What is Facebook?"

✔ Discovering the benefits of being part of the crowd

✔ Using Facebook efficiently

✔ Understanding the statements of rights and responsibilities

*B*efore considering whether or not to join Facebook, you probably want to know what it is, how you use it, and whether it's going to be invasive in your life. Those concerns are all fair, and the purpose of this chapter is to address them. First, we explain what Facebook is and how it fits into the scheme of social media. Then we discuss the benefits of joining Facebook, the basic rules of doing so, and how you can customize your experience.

Describing Facebook

Facebook is a social networking platform where people share their thoughts, actions, photos, and videos with friends, family, and (in some cases) the public at large.

By setting up a personal *timeline* (sometimes referred to as a *profile*), you can create status updates and keep others up-to-date on what you're doing. Facebook is where you can hang out with friends, even when you're not in the same location. Through status updates and shared applications, you can listen to the same music your friend is listening to or see where your friend had lunch if he or she checked in (in Book II, Chapter 5 we discuss what it means to check in to a place).

Facebook is becoming more than just a way to keep up with friends or family — it's a new way of marketing as well. Brands create business pages to connect with their customers on a more personal level and may offer marketing campaigns, coupons, or special deals to Facebook fans. Some brands have gone so far as to launch new products or services to their Facebook fans first.

Enjoying the Benefits of Facebook

When we tell people that we love Facebook, we get all kinds of reactions. Some people don't get it because they are Twitter or Google+ diehards. Others don't get it because they think Facebook is fine, *thankyouverymuch,* but they're not passionate about it. And some people don't get it because they would never think of sharing their life in the public realm. Luckily, others understand that when we say "we love Facebook," we mean we love the opportunities it brings.

Facebook is not just a way to share photos of the new baby, your lunch, or Saturday's party. It's an integral way of interacting with others — personal friends, colleagues, businesses, and even celebrities. It's a way to research your interests and learn new things. Facebook offers you a way to broaden your social circle with people you've never even met (indeed, they could be a world away), though many people start by finding and reconnecting with old friends (say, friends from high school, college, or even old workplaces).

A benefit of being on Facebook is that you have the opportunity to be heard. Until social media truly became mainstream, we were broadcast to as a whole. News outlets, businesses, and celebrities all shouted their information to you to further their interests. The crux of social media is that broadcasting is frowned upon and conversations are encouraged. You have a chair at the table and an opportunity to have your say. We don't mean to imply that all voices are equal. Obstacles still exist, but social media has opened new avenues that make it more likely for your voice to have an effect if you use it wisely.

When you join Facebook, you have the opportunity to customize how you interact, who you interact with, and how often you interact overall. Your Facebook timeline is a record of your voice. As you interact with other users and businesses, you build your online persona. Others begin to create a perception of you, based on what you share on Facebook. Throughout Books I and II, we emphasize how you can bring your personality into your online persona by choosing your friends, sharing photos and videos, controlling your privacy settings, and creating a stellar cover photo for your timeline. (Your timeline allows you to share all the milestones of your life in one place.)

Embracing Facebook as an extension of your world

You may have seen the commercials or comics poking fun at Facebook. The message is similar to this: "All my friends live in my computer." The message is funny because it contains a grain of truth, but it's also an exaggeration.

If you're using Facebook as a tool, it's unlikely to take the place of your "real" life, where you're out and about doing things. Rather than thinking of Facebook as a *zero-sum game* (that is, you're either in or out), we think of Facebook as a way to extend relationships. So much of "real" life is mimicked on Facebook. When you connect with people at a conference, you can continue networking on Facebook. If you meet someone at a party, you can keep the social relationship going on Facebook. If you go to a family reunion and catch up with everyone but that one weird uncle (we all have one), you can still catch up with the family you love and filter out the crazy uncle.

When you meet someone new and then connect with them on Facebook, you can see what else you have in common. You may find that you're even more *simpatico* than you originally thought! Think of Facebook as a way to keep the conversation going.

Facebook can be an extension of your daily life also because it's always available. Apps on your smartphone or tablet device (such as an iPad) allow you to quickly check for breaking news, updates from friends, and so on. You can use your mobile device to check in with friends to let them know where you are or what you're doing. You can even check in to a specific venue. (See Book II, Chapter 5 for information on check-ins.)

Flipboard is one of our favorite apps because we get a nice overview (with lots of pictures) of what's going on without spending a lot of time sifting through content.

Finding your community on Facebook

When most people start their Facebook accounts, they're doing it to keep tabs on what everyone else is doing. You start by connecting with people you know (this is called *friending* in the world of Facebook). Then you start connecting with people you meet around town, at work, or at conferences. Your circle of friends starts to grow. And as it does, you start to find your groove. You may notice that friends of friends share your interests, so you either friend or follow them. Or you may find a group that shares your passion for whatever it is you're passionate about. Your news feed becomes fine-tuned to your interests and interactions.

Each community you join produces a ripple effect. Those communities build other communities (and when those communities grow too large, they splinter into more specialized groups, and you're once again interacting with people who share your philosophies). Suddenly, Facebook isn't an anonymous place with too much information; it's your customized news feed that gives you the scoop on the things that matter to you most.

Using Facebook for news and marketing

When news breaks, people don't flock to their TVs to see what's happening anymore; they turn to Twitter, Google+, and Facebook for real-time information from the people who are already there. You don't have to wait for the news crew to get there; someone on the ground is already reporting what's happening. When the Boston Marathon bombings happened, you could find information about it on Facebook immediately, and follow the tragedy and subsequent manhunt.

Because the news stories on Facebook aren't filtered through a news agency, the information you gather may or may not be accurate. At the very least, you can see varying points of view and piece together a more complete picture of what's happening.

If you're a small business owner, Facebook can provide a new marketing option for you. We're sure you're aware of the importance of tapping into targeted communities — and Facebook is where you'll find those communities. If you're considering using Facebook as part of your marketing strategy, be sure you read Book IV to get the scoop on building your business page. In that minibook, we explain the importance of understanding social media before jumping in and broadcasting your message, and we give you pointers on how to build your community from the ground up. Then flip over to Book V to discover how Facebook ads and Insights (Facebook analytics software) can help you further target your audience and position you or your company as an authority in your niche.

An interesting benefit of using Facebook is its capability to reach a wide audience for little or no money. You can spread the word about a cause, a movement, or a memoriam and reach hundreds or thousands of people. Looking for an answer about something? Ask the crowd on Facebook (this is called *crowdsourcing*). If you want to know what your audience wants from you, just ask them.

Avoiding the Timesuck

What we often hear as a reason to avoid Facebook is that it's a timesuck. We get that. You could log on to Facebook during your morning coffee and turn around and realize it's noon.

When you use Facebook efficiently, however, it becomes less of a detriment and more of a tool. But using Facebook as a tool doesn't come naturally to everyone. We too have spent hours following a rabbit trail. And we've killed time doing the Trifecta of Timesuck: switching from e-mail to Twitter to Facebook to see what's new in the five minutes since we last checked. It's true that part of using Facebook as a tool requires self-control (we're not judging — we've been there).

You can do several things to help you get the most out of Facebook without wasting time:

✦ **Use lists.** Facebook allows you to group your connections based on criteria that you determine. (For example, Scott has created lists of Facebook experts, social media resources, friends, family, and more.) With lists, you can easily check out what everyone's doing without missing updates that may have slid by in your news feed. See Chapter 3 of this minibook to find out how to set up lists.

✦ **Use your navigation wisely.** Your main Facebook page shows your navigation options in the left sidebar. You can move lists and groups you visit most frequently to your favorites at the top of the sidebar so you can easily access them. See Chapter 4 of this minibook to find out how to organize your navigation sidebar.

✦ **Follow businesses you like.** Just about every website out there has a link to its business page. The next time you visit your favorite website, check for a Facebook link. Clicking it takes you to the business page for that site, and from there, you can click the Like button to follow the page. Many people use Facebook as a *feed reader* (a way to know when a website publishes new content). When you Like a business page, any time it updates, you can see it in your news feed (though you need to interact regularly with those posts to continue seeing them; see Book V, Chapter 3 for details).

✦ **Follow public figures.** Public figures can be athletes, celebrities, or even social causes. When we say "public figure," we're talking about not just Lady Gaga but also people like Chris Brogan, an American author, a journalist, a marketing consultant, and a social media leader (www.facebook.com/broganchris), and George Takei, the actor who played Sulu in the original *Star Trek* series (www.facebook.com/georgehtakei) — both of whom update their Facebook statuses regularly in interesting ways. You can also find just about any bigwig from any industry on Facebook. See Book II, Chapter 2 to find out how to use the Follow feature.

✦ **Create a group and invite people with whom you like to interact.** We're in a few or more groups on Facebook (Scott is in hundreds of groups!), and we've made some wonderful personal and professional connections with people because of them. Groups start out with a common thread. That thread may be that you know all these people or that you're all passionate about a particular subject. You invite people, and those people suggest adding people they know. In no time, you're meeting new people who share your interests. See Book II, Chapter 5 for instruction on how to start or find a group.

Agreeing to the Terms of Service

So you decided to try out Facebook (yay!). Before you begin, you must agree to or meet the following requirements:

✦ You're 13 years old or older.

✦ You use your real information (name, e-mail, birthday, and so on).

✦ You maintain a single account.

Facebook's goal is to "make the world more open and transparent, which we believe will create greater understanding and connection." To do that, Facebook relies on each user to create an account based on real information.

Besides, how can people find you if you make a fake account? Two important parts of social media are authenticity and trust. You can set the foundation for them with your Facebook account.

Facebook is an interesting beast. On the one hand, it's a place where you can send out messages and updates to others when and how you choose. On the other hand, other users can choose how they receive your updates. Facebook allows everyone to control their own privacy and customize their interactions — as long as you adhere to the Statements of Rights and Responsibilities (the terms of service).

Facebook has developed a set of principles it uses as a basis for all other Facebook rules, terms, and guidelines. You can find those principles spelled out at www.facebook.com/principles.php. In general, Facebook strives to provide a free platform where people can connect and share information and experiences while owning their personal space and content. You can share what you want, with whomever you want, as long as both parties consent — which means don't bother, bully, or harass someone. The principles also support the following:

✦ **You own your content, and you control your privacy settings.** You can remove your content from Facebook any time you like, and you can set your privacy settings to reflect how you want to share your content and protect it from others.

Although you own your content on Facebook, if you lose access to your account (for a violation of terms, for instance), you no longer have access to that content. Although it's unlikely that you'll run into that issue, we highly recommend backing up your content (especially photos and video) weekly or even monthly so you have a separate copy. See Chapter 2 of this minibook for instructions on downloading your Facebook data.

✦ **Everyone's equal on Facebook.** We all follow the same rules, whether we're using Facebook for fun or business. Facebook users can build their own reputation on Facebook and won't be excluded unless they violate the terms of service. In other words, Facebook has to have a good reason to lock you out.

The Facebook Statements of Rights and Responsibilities (https://www.facebook.com/legal/terms) are based on the Facebook principles. When you create your Facebook account, you agree to those terms. The following list highlights a few of those agreements (again, we encourage you to read the terms yourself for a full understanding of what Facebook expects):

✦ You're in charge of your privacy on Facebook.

✦ You own your original content on Facebook.

✦ You won't spam other users or collect their information without their consent.

✦ You won't promote pyramid schemes, upload malicious code or viruses, or post hateful content.

When you agree to the Facebook terms of use, you agree that you will not

✦ Engage in bullying, harassment, or hate speech

✦ Sell your status updates

✦ Post pornographic content

The preceding list is just an overview and is not exact nor inclusive.

Facebook has guidelines and terms of service for every aspect of the platform. We encourage you to read each set for yourself so you know exactly what the expectations are. Here's a list for your reference:

✦ **Facebook principles:** www.facebook.com/principles.php

✦ **Statement of Rights and Responsibilities:** www.facebook.com/legal/terms

✦ **Family Safety Center:** www.facebook.com/help/safety

✦ **Terms of service for pages:** www.facebook.com/terms_pages.php

✦ **Data use policy:** www.facebook.com/about/privacy

✦ **Community standards:** www.facebook.com/communitystandards

✦ **Promotions guidelines:** www.facebook.com/promotions_guidelines.php

✦ **Facebook brand permissions:** www.facebook.com/brandpermissions

✦ **Facebook ad guidelines:** www.facebook.com/ad_guidelines.php

✦ **Nonprofits on Facebook:** www.facebook.com/nonprofits

Chapter 2: Creating Your Account

In This Chapter

✔ **Creating your Facebook account**

✔ **Finding friends on Facebook**

✔ **Understanding your account settings**

✔ **Setting up your cellphone to receive Facebook updates**

✔ **Deactivating or deleting your account**

Creating your Facebook account is easy: Fill out a short form, and you're on your way. And when customizing your account, Facebook walks you through the three most important steps: finding friends, filling out your profile information, and uploading a profile picture. But you'll want to know about a few other features, such as where to find your account settings so you can manage your password, username, and security options. This chapter discusses all these tasks, as well as how to connect your cellphone to your account and how to deactivate or delete your Facebook account.

Signing Up

It's easy to create a new Facebook account! Just point your browser to www.facebook.com to get started. You begin by completing the form on the front page. You need to provide your first and last names, your e-mail address, the password you want to use, your sex, and your date of birth. Facebook then sends you an e-mail with a confirmation link. When you receive the e-mail, click the link to complete your Facebook signup. Facebook has this step to ensure that the e-mail account you're using is real.

You can have only one Facebook account, and you should be at least 13 years old to create an account. Be sure to use real information (including your birth date, which you can hide from the public later).

When you've completed the form, click the Sign Up button. At this point, Facebook wants to walk you through some steps to get you started.

Completing step 1: Finding friends

In step 1, you find friends who are already on Facebook by using your e-mail account's contacts list. Facebook offers options for Outlook (Hotmail), Gmail, Yahoo!, and other e-mail services. Click the Find Friends link next to the type of e-mail account you have, type your e-mail address in the text box, and click the Find Friends button. A dialog box may appear, asking you to allow Facebook to access your e-mail account and contacts list. You need to grant this access for Facebook to cross-check the e-mail addresses in your contacts list with the addresses registered on Facebook.

You can find friends associated with multiple e-mail accounts. For instance, if you have three Gmail accounts, you can type any of those addresses to find friends who are already on Facebook. Or if you have a Gmail account and a Yahoo! account, find your Gmail friends and then repeat the process for your Yahoo! account.

After you allow Facebook to access your e-mail account, you're presented with a list of friends who are currently on Facebook. Or, if you're a Gmail user, you see instructions for uploading your contacts.

If you see a list of friends, select the check box next to each friend you'd like to connect with on Facebook. If you want to connect with all your contacts, select the Select All Friends check box. When you've selected your friends, click the Add Friends button to continue.

If Facebook finds e-mail addresses for people who are not on Facebook yet, you're asked if you'd like to invite those people to connect on Facebook. If you choose to do that, Facebook sends a message to those people on your behalf, asking them to join Facebook. You can instead click Skip This Step if you don't want to add contacts right now.

Completing step 2: Filling in profile information

In step 2, you start filling out personal profile information, beginning with the name of your high school, your college or university, your current place of employment, and your current city and hometown. When you're done, click Save & Continue.

You don't have to complete this information right now or ever if you so choose. You can click the Skip link to move directly to step 3.

Based on the information you've shared so far, Facebook pulls a list of recommended friends for you. In general, these people may be in your address book or may have attended the same high school, college, or university while you were there. You can choose to add any of these people as a friend on Facebook simply by clicking the Add Friend link under the person's name. When you do, Facebook sends a friend request to that user and alerts you if he or she accepts your friend request.

Completing step 3: Choosing interests

In step 3, Facebook wants to know as much about you as you'll allow so that it can determine what ads are best to show you and to figure out additional pages that might interest you, such as pages for musicians, news sources, public figures, and actors. You'll be able to immediately Like these pages.

When you Like these pages, you'll see updates from them in your news feed. You may find that some pages update too often or the content is offensive, so choose wisely when Liking a page. (To Unlike a Page, see Book II, Chapter 11.)

Completing step 4: Uploading a profile picture

Your profile picture is one of the most important aspects of your Facebook account because people associate it with your updates. In step 4, Facebook offers you the option of uploading an existing image from your computer or taking a new photo with your computer's webcam. (See Book II, Chapter 3 for tips on taking pictures with your webcam.) After you choose your photo, click Save & Continue. Your personal timeline appears, and you can start using Facebook.

It's best to choose a picture that clearly shows your face so friends and family will recognize you immediately. (This is *Face*book, after all!) We suggest using a picture of yourself, not a picture of your child, pet, favorite team, and so on. Because so many people scan their Facebook news feed quickly, it's easier for them to spot your updates if they can clearly see *your* picture. In addition, using logos or other found pictures you don't own yourself may be in violation of copyright. Contrary to what you may have heard, just because you find something interesting on the Internet doesn't mean it's free to use.

Finding Friends

Because Facebook is all about being social, it makes sense that you'll want to connect with your friends, family, and colleagues. In fact, as you become more comfortable with Facebook, you may interact with friends of friends, see that they're good fits, and send friend requests to them. Facebook says the average number of friends is 130, but just about everyone we know has many, many more. The following sections aim to help you understand what it means to be friends on Facebook and how to find people you want to connect with.

Understanding what it means to be friends on Facebook

In the real world, the term *friend* has different meanings to different people. If you ask an extrovert how many friends she has, she may say hundreds, because to her, everyone she meets is a friend. If you ask an introvert how many she has, she may say three, because her definition of a friend is much different from her extrovert counterpart's. Neither answer is wrong, but you can see how perspective can change what it means to be friends.

Along those same lines, the term *friend* is a little different in the world of social media than in the real world. Online, you may find that you're friends with people you've never even met in person but have interacted with online through the comments on a mutual friend's status updates or through other social media (such as Twitter or blogs). Or maybe someone you met at a party sends you a friend request on Facebook, and you accept. Your circle is widening in a way it may not in the real world.

Consider how you want to connect with others and your criteria for requesting and accepting Facebook friend requests. And respect how others deal with online friends. Understand that some people like to keep their Facebook timelines private and limited to real-life friends and family. Other people are an open book and accept requests from just about anyone. The key is not to take it personally if someone doesn't accept your friend request. (Sometimes easier said than done.)

Social media is interesting because, on one hand, it's a public forum where you can be heard by thousands. On the other hand, it's a private place where you can establish your own space and determine who you interact with. We suspect that your idea of how to relate with others will change as you become more comfortable interacting on Facebook and other social media platforms.

We suggest starting slowly and building a group of Facebook friends you know and are comfortable with, and then expanding your community as you become more familiar with Facebook (and possibly other social media). In particular, pay attention to your privacy settings (see Chapter 3 of this minibook) and how and what you share in your status updates (see Book II, Chapter 2).

Searching for people you know

When you first set up your account with Facebook, it walks you through finding friends who may already be on Facebook. The platform allows you to use your existing e-mail contacts to see whether any of those e-mail addresses are registered with accounts on Facebook and then lets you send a friend request to people you know. (See the previous section "Completing step 1: Finding friends.") If you skipped that step or decided to wait to find friends later, that's not a problem. You can find friends in several ways:

✦ **Check out Facebook's suggestions.** When you visit your personal time-line (by clicking your name or profile image anywhere in Facebook), click the Friends link. To the right of the profile picture, click the +Find Friends button to see a list of people Facebook thinks you may know. (When you first sign up for Facebook, a Find Friends link appears in the Facebook navigation but will eventually disappear.) Facebook draws this list from accounts that have shared information similar to your own (for example, hometown, education, or mutual friends). When you click the +Find Friends button, the People You May Know page appears, as shown in Figure 2-1. If you see someone you'd like to connect with, click the 1+ Add Friend button. (If you have pending friend requests, you can confirm or delete the request.)

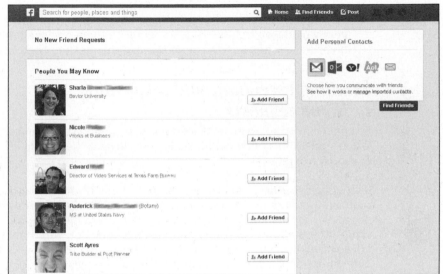

Figure 2-1:
Facebook suggests friends you can connect with.

You may also see friend suggestions from Facebook on the right side of your news feed page.

✦ **Use Facebook's list features.** Lists are a handy way to keep groups of friends together so you can see their updates any time you like. Facebook has a few lists it creates for you based on information you shared when you created your account (such as where you live or where you went to school). Facebook takes that information, tries to find other Facebook accounts that have similar information, and adds them to your lists (you can remove anyone from those lists if you like). See Chapter 3 of this minibook for further information on creating and managing friends lists.

✦ **Use the Graph Search box.** At the top of every Facebook page is a blue toolbar containing a text box for searching called the Graph Search box. Start typing a name in the text box, and check the list that appears. The name may not appear in the initial list, so be sure to click the See More Results option to view a longer list of possible matches. You can also search previous companies you worked for, your hometown, alma maters, and so on.

✦ **Look at friends of friends.** As you build your friends list, you can click over to someone's timeline and view his or her friends. If you spot someone you know, you can click over to that person's timeline and send a friend request.

✦ **Search for topic pages.** Do a search for your high school, college or university, favorite sports team or hobby, and more. If you see someone you know, send that person a friend request or follow the person if he or she has enabled others to follow public updates. (See Book II, Chapter 2 for information on the Follow feature.)

✦ **Look on the sidebar of a website or blog.** Many businesses and bloggers would love to have you connect with them on Facebook. See if your favorite websites have a Facebook logo that links to their business page.

Sending, receiving, and responding to friend requests

To connect with someone on Facebook, you need to send him a friend request. When you visit his personal timeline, you can click the 1+ Add Friend button to send him a request.

If you don't see the 1+ Add Friend button or any option to send a friend request, that person may have his privacy set in a way that doesn't allow people he doesn't know to send a request. For example, Scott's personal privacy settings allow everyone to request a connection with him. His wife, however, allows only friends of friends to make requests. If you don't know her or her friends, you can't send her a friend request.

If you don't know someone but would like to follow his public updates, you can click the Follow button on his personal timeline (if he's enabled it). When you follow someone, you aren't Facebook friends with that person, but you can see any public updates he shares. Following is a good way to follow leaders in your line of work or someone you're interested in. For example, Scott isn't Facebook friends with Mark Zuckerberg (the founder of Facebook), but he follows Mark's public updates. Likewise, Scott has over 24,000 people following him on Facebook, but he's not friends with them all.

When you receive a friend request, Facebook alerts you by highlighting a number next to the friend requests icon, which appears to the right of the search box at the top of the page. If you aren't sure whether you have pending friend requests, click the friend requests icon to see a list similar to the one in Figure 2-2.

You can see from Figure 2-2 that you have two choices: Confirm or Not Now. When you confirm a friend, Facebook adds that person to your friends list. In Figure 2-3, you can see the Friends button, which indicates that the person was added to the list. (Facebook also asks you whether you know this person away from Facebook; we don't know what Facebook does with this feedback.)

Figure 2-2:
Check
your pend-
ing friend
requests.

Figure 2-3:
When you
confirm a
Facebook
friend, the
person goes
into your
friends list.

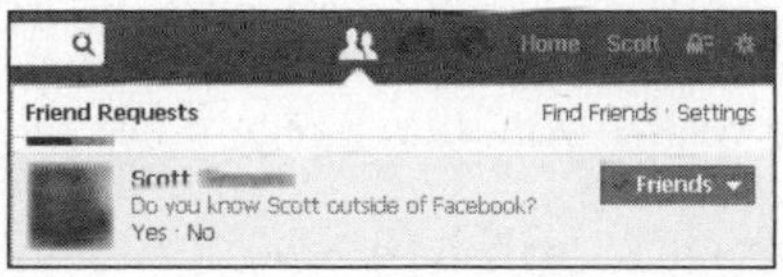

If you click the Friends button, you see the options shown in Figure 2-4. You
can add that person to any of your lists, get notifications when that person
makes a post, and display or hide the person's posts in your news feed.

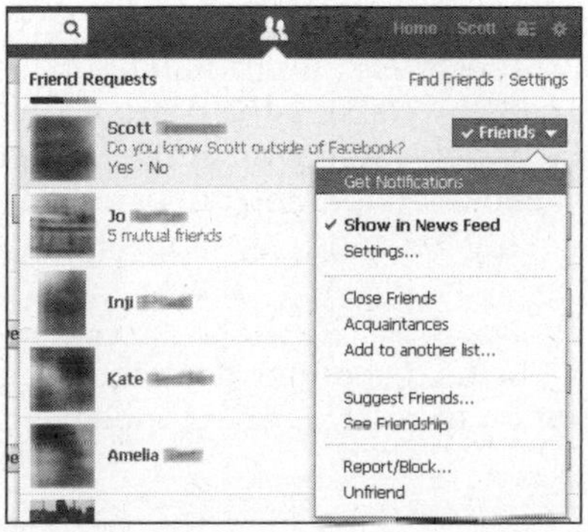

Figure 2-4:
You can add
your new
Facebook
friend to
any list
for easier
access.

If you choose to ignore a friend request or click the Not Now button, Facebook wants to know whether you know the person, as shown in Figure 2-5.

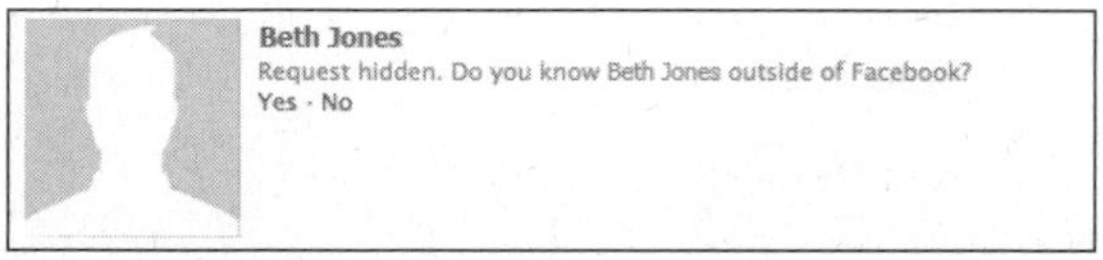

Figure 2-5:
Do you know the person who tried to friend you?

Beth Jones
Request hidden. Do you know Beth Jones outside of Facebook?
Yes · No

Facebook asks if you know the person to help cut down on spam and unwanted requests. If you click Yes, Facebook thanks you for your feedback, and that person can send another friend request. If you click No, Facebook won't allow that person to send you another friend request.

If you don't accept a friend request, Facebook doesn't tell the person who sent the request. However, the person can figure it out. For instance, if she looks at her own list of friends and you aren't there, or if she looks at your personal timeline and sees the +1 Add Friend button instead of the Friend Request Pending button, she'll realize you didn't accept her request.

If you ignore a friend request or click the Not Now button, that person can still see any public updates you post. If you're the one who initiated the friend request, you can see public posts by the person to whom you sent the request. As mentioned, the Follow feature is a great alternative if you aren't ready to be Facebook friends with someone.

Finding and Customizing Your Account Settings

You can control the information you share on Facebook in three areas: General Account Settings, Privacy Settings, and Timeline. The last two are described in Chapters 3 and 4, respectively, of this minibook. You can find your General Account Settings page by clicking the down arrow or the gear (depending on the version of Facebook you have), at the far-right end of the blue toolbar at the top of any Facebook page, and choosing Account Settings from the menu. The General Account Settings page appears, as shown in Figure 2-6.

The options appear on the left. The next sections describe each option and show you how to control the option to suit your Facebook needs.

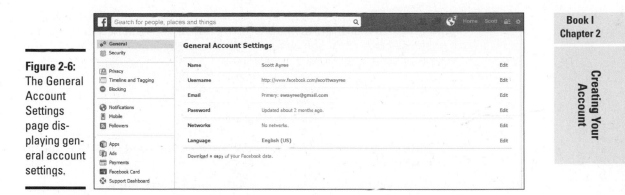

Figure 2-6:
The General
Account
Settings
page dis-
playing gen-
eral account
settings.

General Account Settings

Your General Account Settings page (refer to Figure 2-6) lists the basics of your account and allows you to edit that information. You see options for editing your name, username, e-mail, password, networks, and language. You also have the option to download a copy of your Facebook data. We explain each of these options in the following sections.

For details about the Privacy and Blocking settings, see Chapter 4 of this minibook.

Name setting

The Name row shows the name you registered when you created your Facebook account. This name is what others see when you share content. If you click the Edit link, you can change your first and last names and add your middle name if you like. You can also use the drop-down list to choose how your name appears on your timeline.

Most people display their name as First, Last. The alternative-name option lets you include a nickname or maiden name to help others find you. If you make any changes here, you need to confirm them by typing your Facebook password in the Password text box and then clicking the Save Changes button. You can change your name only three times.

Username setting

A *username* is a customized URL for your Facebook account and is some-times referred to as a *vanity URL*. Facebook assigns a unique number to all new accounts and uses that number in the address for your personal timeline. For example, click over to your personal timeline and look in the address bar of your browser. You probably see something like this:

```
http://www.facebook.com/profile.php?id=1018974455
```

The long string of numbers following `id=` is your account ID. That ID is pretty hard to remember and more than a little inconvenient to include on a business card. When you choose a username, the numbers in the URL for your timeline are replaced. For example:

```
https://www.facebook.com/scottwayres
```

To set your username, follow these steps:

1. **Navigate to your General Account Settings page and click the Edit link next to Username.**

2. **Verify your account via your mobile phone (if it's not already verified).**

   If you've just established your Facebook account, it may not be verified yet (even if you clicked the link in the e-mail that Facebook sent you when you signed up). If that's the case, you can wait a little longer until Facebook confirms your verification, or you can click the Verify via Mobile Phone option. To verify via your phone, do this:

   a. *Click the Verify via Mobile Phone link.*

   b. *Use the drop-down list to choose the correct country code for your cellphone's number.*

   c. *In the Phone Number text box, type your cellphone number.*

   d. *Some users will be given the option to select whether they prefer to receive a text or an automated phone call. Most users will not have a choice and will be sent a text message.*

   e. *Click Continue.*

      The Enter Your Confirmation Code dialog box appears. If, after five minutes, you haven't received the code, click the Resend Code link to try again.

   f. *After you receive your verification code via text, type the code in the text box, and click Confirm.*

      A dialog box appears.

   g. *Select whether you want text notifications turned on and your phone number to be Public, Only Seen by Friends, or Only Me. Then click Save Settings.*

      If you activate text messages, Facebook texts your notifications to you. Normal text messaging charges apply, so be sure you know what your phone's data plan is — you could be receiving a lot of texts.

      When your account is verified, the Username option changes as shown in Figure 2-7.

If the Username option doesn't change right away, click another option (for example, Name) and then click back to Username.

Figure 2-7:
The Username option looks like this if you've verified your account.

> **Username**
>
> Your public username is the same as your address for:
> • Timeline: facebook.com/**your.username**
> • Email: **your.username@facebook.com**
>
> Username: [   ]
>
> Note:
> • Your username can only be changed once and should include your real name. [?]
> • Friends will be able to see your new email address on your timeline. [?]
>
> To save these settings, please enter your Facebook password.
>
> Password: [   ]
>
> [Save Changes] [Cancel]

3. **In the text box, type your desired username.**

If your username isn't available, Facebook suggests a username for you.

You can change your username only one time. It's best to use your real name if you can. (You may have to include your middle name or at least your initial if you have a fairly common name.) Choosing something like PartyBill may be fun now but probably won't be quite as impressive when work colleagues look you up.

4. **In the Password text box, type your Facebook password and then click Save Changes.**

Email setting

The Email row displays the e-mail address you used when you created your Facebook account. When you click the Edit link, you have these options:

✦ **Add another e-mail address to your account.** If you have multiple addresses associated with your account, you must choose one to be your primary address. Facebook uses your primary e-mail to send notifications to you. You can remove an address from your account by clicking the Remove link.

✦ **Activate your Facebook e-mail.** You need to have a username associated with your account to activate your Facebook e-mail. Your username is your Facebook e-mail address (for example, scottwayres@facebook.com). Any messages sent to that address appear in your Facebook messages. You can check for new messages by clicking the messages icon (labeled in Figure 2-6) in the blue toolbar at the top of all Facebook pages.

If your account is new, you may have to wait a few days before e-mail is available.

✦ **Allow friends to include your e-mail in the information that's downloaded when they back up their accounts.** When Facebook users download a copy of their Facebook data (explained in a moment), all sorts of
information is included: status updates, comments, pictures, video, and
even contact information for their Facebook friends. If you don't want
your e-mail address to be included in that download, deselect the check
box next to this option.

If you make any changes to your e-mail settings, be sure to type your
Facebook password in the text box and click the Save Changes button for
those changes to take effect.

Password setting

It's a good idea to periodically change your account password. You can do
that by first clicking Password in the General Account Settings screen. Then
in the text boxes that appear, type your current password in the Current text
box, type your new password in the New box, and retype your new password in the final box. Click the Save Changes button, and your password is
updated. You'll need to use the new password the next time you log in to
Facebook.

We provide tips on choosing a password and protecting your privacy in
Chapter 4 of this minibook.

Networks setting

Facebook has networks associated with high school, college, and some supported companies. To join a specific network, you need to have an official
e-mail address associated with the college or work network you're trying to
join so you can confirm your affiliation. If you're trying to join a high school
network, a classmate in the network must approve you.

You can join up to five networks. If you join more than one, you're prompted
to choose your primary network. Your primary network appears next to
your name and is public. Your primary network also affects your search
results in Facebook. If you do a search, results associated with your network
appear at the top of the results.

To join a network, click Networks in the General Account Settings screen,
and then click Join a Network. Type the name of the network in the Network
Name text box and type your associated e-mail address in the Network Email
text box. Click Save Changes. You need to check that e-mail account for your
confirmation message and follow the instructions to join the network.

To remove a network from your account, click the Remove link beside the
network you want to leave. Then click Save Changes.

Facebook no longer accepts requests for new networks, so if your work doesn't have an approved network, you can create a group and invite people to join that way.

Language setting

Because Facebook is an international social media platform, it's available in myriad languages. To change your primary language, click Language in the General Account Settings screen, and then use the drop-down list to make your selection. Click Save Changes.

Download a copy of your Facebook data

Always remember that you don't own your space at Facebook. If you violate Facebook's terms of service, you may find yourself locked out of your account. If that were to happen, you'd lose access to all the content you've added to Facebook: status updates, pictures, video, comments, friends and their contact information, and so on.

Facebook makes it so easy to use your smartphone to upload pictures and updates that many people use their phones to record and share important life events directly to Facebook. We suggest making a habit of backing up your data on a regular basis if you're consistently keeping important content (for example, vacation photos) on Facebook rather than somewhere else. Your download will include everything you've uploaded to Facebook, including status updates, pictures, video, private messages, chats, and a list of Facebook friends and their contact information (if they've enabled that on their account).

To back up your data, follow these steps:

1. **On the General Account Settings page, click the Download a Copy of your Facebook Data link.**

   The Download Your Information page appears.

2. **Click the green Start My Archive button.**

3. **Enter your password (if requested to do so) and click Submit.**

   The Request My Download dialog box appears and explains that it will take some time to create the backup file.

4. **Click the Start My Archive button.**

   Facebook tells you that it will send a message to the primary e-mail associated with your account when your archive is ready.

5. **Click Okay.**

6. **When you receive the e-mail stating that your archive is ready, click the link to download the file to your computer.**

When you open the archive file, you find the following information:

✦ Your biographical timeline information (your contact information, interests, work history, and so on)

✦ All your status updates and comments by you and your friends

✦ All photos and video you uploaded to your account (and the comments associated with them)

✦ Your friends list

✦ All the notes you wrote and shared

✦ All your sent and received private messages

It's great that you've backed up your Facebook information, but we encourage you to go a step further and save the file to your computer as well as another source (for example, Dropbox or an external hard drive). That way, if something happens to your computer, you'll still have your content.

Security Settings

Facebook states that it takes your personal privacy and security seriously. To that end, Facebook provides many options so you can control how and what you share (see Book I, Chapter 4 for more information on privacy). The Security tab on your Account Settings page, shown in Figure 2-8, is where you find many of the options for securing your account, as you discover in this section.

Figure 2-8: The Security Settings screen.

Security Settings		
Secure Browsing	Secure browsing is currently enabled.	Edit
Login Notifications	Text message notifications are enabled.	Edit
Login Approvals	Use your phone as an extra layer of security to keep other people from logging into your account.	Edit
Code Generator	Code Generator is enabled.	Edit
App Passwords	You have 1 app password.	Edit
Trusted Contacts	You've chosen 3 trusted contacts	Edit
Recognized Devices	You have 16 recognized devices.	Edit
Active Sessions	Logged in from Killeen, TX, US and 6 other locations.	Edit
Deactivate your account.		

General
Security
Privacy
Timeline and Tagging
Blocking
Notifications
Mobile
Followers
Apps
Ads
Payments
Facebook Card
Support Dashboard

Search for people, places and things

Home   Scott

Secure Browsing setting

By default, Facebook uses secure browsing on laptops, desktop computers, and most mobile devices while you're logged into Facebook. We highly recommend leaving this feature turned on. *Secure browsing* encrypts your Facebook activity so it's harder for others to access it without your permission (you grant permission through your share setting, tags, and so on).

If you want to turn off secure browsing, click the Edit link on the far right of the Secure Browsing row, and then deselect the check box labeled Browse Facebook on a Secure Connection (https) When Possible. Then click the Save Changes button.

To make sure secure browsing is enabled, see whether the address bar of your browser begins with `https://` (for example, `https://www.facebook.com`). If you see `http://` instead of `https://`, revisit your settings to be sure you still have this option enabled. You may have turned off secure browsing to access a noncompliant app but then forgot to turn it back on.

Secure browsing is available on most mobile devices.

Login Notifications setting

If you're concerned that someone may access your account without your consent, we suggest enabling the login notifications option. This option notifies you via e-mail or text message when your account is accessed from a device that you haven't used before. So if you usually use your desktop computer to access your account, but one afternoon you use your laptop, Facebook sends you a note (either an e-mail or a text message) to let you know that your account was accessed from a new device. If you were the one logging in from the new device, no problem. If you weren't, you can investigate.

To turn on login notifications, click the Edit link in the Login Notifications row. Then select the E-mail check box or the Text Message/Push Notification check box, or both. Keep in mind that charges for text messages apply here. Click Save Changes to complete the process.

Login Approvals setting

The Login Approvals entry adds another layer of protection to login notifications. Each time you (or someone else) logs into your account from a device that you haven't used before, Facebook sends you a text message with a code that you have to use to complete your Facebook login. For example, if you usually log into your Facebook account with your desktop computer but decide to log in with your laptop, Facebook texts you a code that you must type when prompted to access your account.

Obviously, to use this option, you need to be sure you have a cellphone number associated with your account. You can associate a cellphone number with your account via the Mobile tab on your Account Setting page or when you verify your account by using your phone (see the "Username" section, earlier in this chapter).

To turn on login approvals:

1. **Click the Edit link in the Login Approvals row.**

2. **Select the check box that appears.**

   The check box is labeled Require Me to Enter a Security Code Each Time an Unrecognized Computer or Device Tries to Access My Account.

   The Set Up Login Approvals dialog box appears, with an explanation of how login approvals work.

3. **Read the overview of login approvals, grab your cellphone, and then click Get Started.**

4. **Select the device you are using and then click Continue.**

5. **When the Security Codes box appears, click Continue.**

6. **Activate Code Generator as follows:**

   a. *On your phone, open the Facebook app.*

   b. *Tap the menu button.*

   c. *Scroll down the screen and tap Code Generator.*

   d. *Tap Activate.*

   You need to activate Code Generator so you can receive security codes on your phone.

7. **Back at the Account Settings screen, click Continue.**

8. **Type the code in the text box and click Confirm.**

   If the code doesn't work, you are given the option of having Facebook simply text you a code.

9. **In the text box, type a name for the device you're using (for example,** home computer**) and click Next.**

   The Success dialog box appears, with information about what to do if you get a new phone, lose your phone, or use Facebook apps.

10. **Click the Close button to complete the process.**

Now that login approvals are set up, every time you log in from a new device, Facebook texts a login code to your phone. You see the message shown in Figure 2-9.

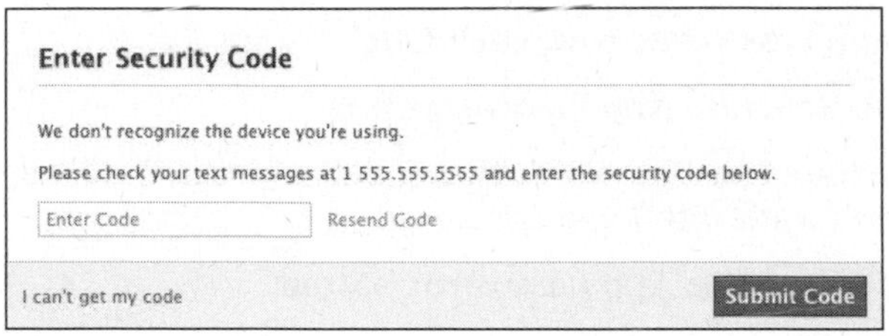

Figure 2-9:
Use the
security
code
Facebook
texts you
to log
in to your
account.

Enter Security Code

We don't recognize the device you're using.

Please check your text messages at 1 555.555.5555 and enter the security code below.

Enter Code | Resend Code

I can't get my code | Submit Code

Type the login code in the text box and click Submit Code to start using Facebook.

Code Generator setting

You can use Code Generator in your Facebook mobile app to reset your password or to generate login approval security codes.

To enable Code Generator, follow these instructions:

1. **In the Code Generator row, click Edit.**
2. **Click Enable.**
3. **Activate Code Generator as follows:**
   a. *On your phone, open the Facebook app.*
   b. *Tap the menu button.*
   c. *Scroll down and tap Code Generator.*
   d. *Tap Activate.*
4. **Back at the Account Settings screen, click Continue.**

   If the code doesn't work, click Continue to have Facebook text you a code.

App Passwords setting

Some Facebook applications don't work with Facebook login approval codes, so if you have that option enabled, you may not be able to use all your apps. Facebook has fixed it so you can use app passwords instead of your account password to log in to certain apps (for example, Skype). According to Facebook's Help section, "when you use an app password you won't have to wait to receive a [login approval] code. Instead, you can skip login approvals and log in immediately." You can read more about app passwords at `http://on.fb.me/FBAppPasswords`.

To generate an app password, follow these instructions:

1. **In the App Passwords row, click Edit.**
2. **Click the Generate App Passwords link.**

   The Generate App Passwords dialog box appears and explains that some apps don't work with login approvals.

3. **Click the Generate App Passwords button.**
4. **In the text box, type the name of the app you want to approve and then click Generate Password.**

   A window appears, with the choice of creating another password (click Next Password) or finishing (click Finish).

5. **To complete the process, click Finish.**

   If you want to create another password instead, click Next Password and repeat Step 4.

You can remove a password by clicking App Passwords and then clicking the Remove link next to the password you want to delete.

Trusted Contacts setting

Trusted contacts are friends who can securely help you if you have trouble accessing your account.

To set up a trusted contact, follow these steps:

1. **In the Trusted Contacts row, click Edit.**
2. **Click Choose Trusted Contacts.**

   A window appears, explaining more about trusted contacts.

3. **Click the Choose Trusted Contacts button.**
4. **Type the names of at least three friends that you can call for help if you have a problem with your account.**
5. **Click Confirm.**
6. **Enter your password, and then click Submit.**

Recognized Devices setting

Recognized devices are those you've used to log into your Facebook account. For instance, if you activated the Login Notifications option discussed earlier, you named your primary device. That device is listed under Recognized Devices. As you use other devices to log in, and they are confirmed as belonging to you, you can name those devices as well, and they appear in Recognized Devices too.

Any device listed under Recognized Devices doesn't require secure login confirmation. You can remove a device from this section simply by clicking the Edit link in the Recognized Devices row and then clicking the Remove link next to the name of the device. Be sure to click Save Changes to complete the removal process.

Active Sessions setting

Click the Edit link to the right of the Active Sessions row to display a list of your recent active sessions on Facebook. You see the name and type of device used to log in and where the login occurred. If you see a location that doesn't look familiar, be sure to check to see whether the session is linked to your smartphone, because those sessions don't always reflect an accurate location.

If you see an active session and you think someone may be accessing your account without permission, click the End Activity link next to the questionable active session. Facebook suggests you also change your account password, as well as your e-mail password, as an added measure to ensure no one can access your account at this point.

Deactivate Your Account setting

Deactivating your account is not the same as deleting your account. When you deactivate your account, it's still around but it's not in use. People can't find your timeline or view previous content you've shared, but friends can still tag you and invite you to events and groups. You also lose your admin status in groups, events, and business pages. You can choose to reinstate your account at any time, and Facebook will restore your timeline to the way it looked before you deactivated your account.

Deleting your account will erase your information and content from Facebook. At the end of this chapter, we explain how you can delete your Facebook account.

To deactivate your Facebook account, follow these steps:

1. **Click the Deactivate Your Account link at the bottom of the Security Settings screen.**

   A new page appears, asking if you're sure you want to deactivate your account.

2. **Select a reason for leaving.**

3. **(Optional) In the text box, type an extended explanation of why you're deactivating your account.**

   This optional step helps Facebook pinpoint areas that may need work.

4. **Select the Opt Out of Receiving Future Emails from Facebook check box.**

   When you deactivate your account, your friends can still tag you in updates, photos, and videos, and invite you to Events and groups. If you choose to opt out of future e-mails from Facebook, you won't receive notifications about those tags and invitations.

   If you've created any apps and you're the only developer, Facebook gives you the option to edit or delete those apps before you deactivate your account.

5. **Click Confirm.**

   A password confirmation window appears.

6. **Type your password in the text box, and then click the Deactivate Now button.**

   Another security check window appears. (Facebook really wants you to think about your decision!)

7. **Type the CAPTCHA in the text box and click the Submit button.**

   Your account is deactivated.

To reinstate your account, go to www.facebook.com and log in with your e-mail and password. Facebook sends you a confirmation e-mail (so be sure you can access the e-mail address you originally used to set up your Facebook account). After you confirm that you own your account, Facebook reinstates your timeline as it was before you left. However, you still won't have any admin privileges for groups, events, or business pages that you had before you left. You need to have someone add you as an admin if that's something you're interested in.

If you're the only administrator for a business page, we urge you to add another administrator to the page before you deactivate your account. If you don't, you lose all administrative rights to your page timeline. You won't be able to access the Admin panel of your business page, and you won't be able to regain your administrative status. When you add another person as an admin and later decide to reinstate your business page, the other admin can grant you admin capabilities again.

Timeline and Tagging Settings

Facebook has added several settings to give you more control over your timeline and who can tag you around the site. Click the Timeline and Tagging entry in the Account Settings pane, and you see the three options shown in Figure 2-10.

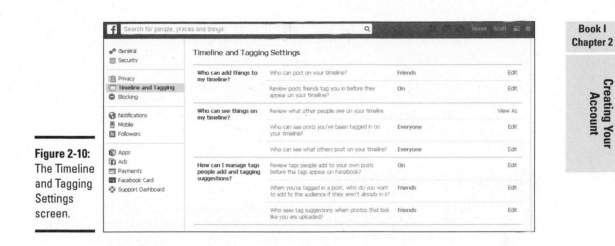

Figure 2-10:
The Timeline
and Tagging
Settings
screen.

"Who can add things to my timeline?" setting

In the first section, you decide whether friends can add posts to your time-line. To change the setting, click the Edit link to and make a selection from the drop-down list. If you do allow friends to add items to your timeline, you can also enable a feature that lets you review the post before it goes live.

"Who can see things on my timeline?" setting

In the second section, you can view your timeline as other people see it by clicking View As. On the screen that appears, you can also enter a person's name in the text box and view the timeline as that person sees it.

The next setting, Who Can See Posts You've Been Tagged In, lets you control who can see posts you've been tagged in on your timeline. For example, you might not want your public following seeing the naked baby picture of you that your mother tagged. Click the Edit link and make a selection in the drop-down list.

The final setting in this section enables you to choose who can see what others post on your timeline. As with the previous option, click the Edit link and make a selection in the drop-down list.

"How can I manage tags people add and tagging suggestions?" setting

In the final section, you can turn on tag review to review tags that friends add to your content before the tags appear on Facebook. When someone you're not friends with adds a tag to one of your posts, by default you'll always be asked to review it. When you approve a tag, the person tagged and his or her friends will likely see it.

Next choose if you want your friends, only yourself, or people on a custom list to be added as the audience of the post you're tagged in if they aren't already in it.

Finally, when a photo that looks like you is uploaded, Facebook will suggest adding a tag of you to the photo. This feature saves time when people add tags to photos, especially from events. You can allow Facebook to show tag suggestions to your friends or to no one.

Notifications Settings

Notifications are messages that alert you when someone tags you in an update, a photo, or a video or comments on one your posts (or comments on someone else's post that you commented on). Some people like to enable notifications because they remind them to visit Facebook and respond to what's happening. On the other hand, if you're on Facebook quite a bit, notifications may be overkill. The Facebook team understands that everyone uses the platform a little differently, so you can determine how you receive notifications.

When you first create your account, your Notifications Settings page looks similar to the one shown in Figure 2-11.

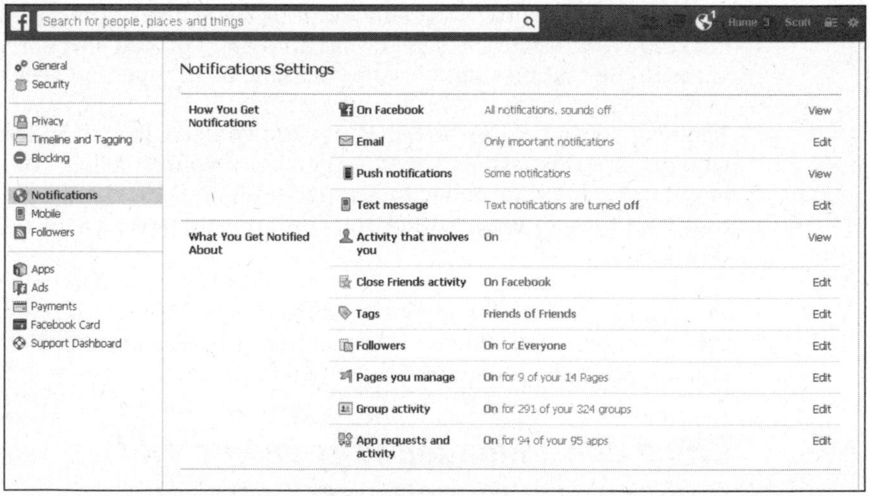

Figure 2-11:
Your
Notifications
Settings
page allows
you to
choose how
you receive
updates.

The Notifications Settings page lists all the different types of notifications you can set. To determine which notifications you receive, click the Edit link or the View link next to each option. That option expands to show a list of further options. You can select or deselect the items about which you want to be notified. Remember to click Save Changes for each category so your changes will take effect.

As you use Facebook regularly, you'll receive more notifications because people will be interacting with you regularly. If you find that you receive too many e-mail notifications from Facebook regarding updates and comments, return to the Notifications Settings screen and choose Email. A screen similar to Figure 2-12 appears.

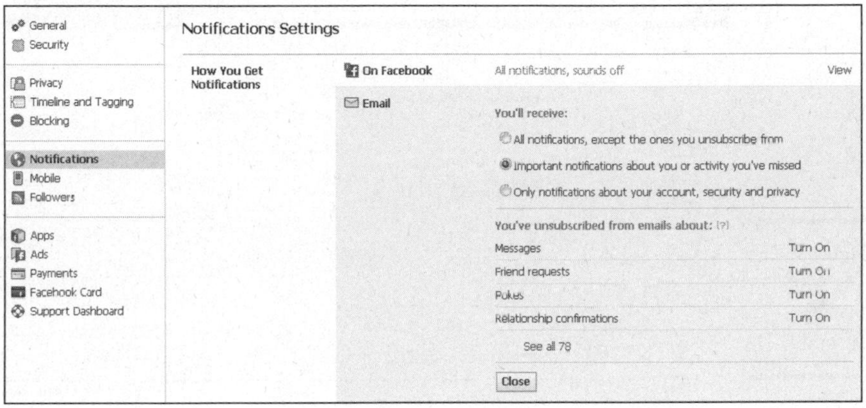

Figure 2-12:
The Email
option
has these
settings.

You can choose to receive all notifications, except ones you have unsubscribed from (in Figure 2-12, you can see that Scott has unsubscribed from 78 items). You can choose to receive important notifications about you or an activity you've missed. Or you can choose to receive notifications only about your account, security, and privacy.

Consider setting up an e-mail address that you use solely for Facebook. That way, all your Facebook correspondence is in one place, and you can check as you like without cluttering your primary e-mail inbox. As a bonus, if your Facebook account is ever hacked or you click a bad link, you have a single e-mail address to deal with (and it doesn't affect your other accounts).

Mobile Settings

Enabling your mobile settings allows Facebook to text you when you have friend requests or other notifications. Additionally, you can text updates (including photos and video) from your phone directly to your Facebook Timeline.

However, if you have a smartphone, you can do all these things directly from the Facebook app for your phone. We explain mobile Facebook options more thoroughly in Book II, Chapter 6; you can also point your browser to www.facebook.com/mobile to find out more.

To set up your Facebook mobile settings, follow these instructions:

1. **On the Account Settings page, click Mobile in the left navigation pane.**

   The Mobile Settings page appears, as shown in Figure 2-13.

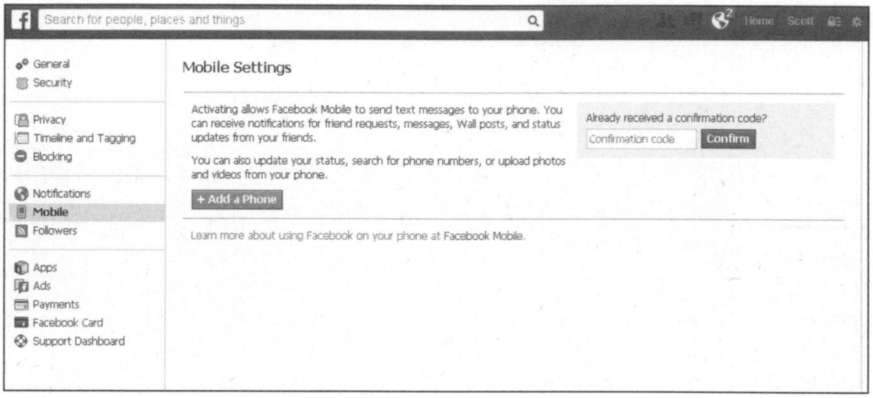

Figure 2-13: The Mobile Settings screen.

2. **Click the green +Add a Phone button.**

   The Add Mobile Phone dialog box appears.

3. **Type your password in the text box and click Confirm.**

   The Activate Facebook Texts (Step 1 of 2) dialog box appears.

4. **Select your country and mobile carrier from the drop-down lists and click Next.**

   The Activate Facebook Texts (Step 2 or 2) dialog box appears.

5. **Text the letter** F **to the number** 32665.

   You receive a text from Facebook with a confirmation code.

6. **In the text box, type the confirmation code.**

7. **Select whether you want to share your phone number with your friends and whether you want to allow friends to text you from Facebook.**

   If you activate text messages, Facebook texts your notifications to your mobile phone.

   Normal text messaging charges apply, so be sure you know the details of your phone's data plan — you could be receiving a lot of texts if you're active on Facebook.

8. **Click Next to complete the process.**

   The Facebook for Mobile page appears, and you can read more about your mobile options. You'll receive a text message from Facebook to let you know that the number has been confirmed.

To remove a phone number from your account, simply click the Remove link beside the number on the Mobile Settings page.

After you confirm a phone number, the Mobile Settings page displays additional options:

✦ **Text Messaging:** If more than one mobile phone is associated with your profile, you can click Edit and choose which phone receives text messages. Although Facebook doesn't charge you for texting, your mobile carrier may. Be sure you understand the details of your data plan.

✦ **Facebook Messages:** Control when Facebook can text you. Click Edit and use the drop-down list to choose the option that works for you.

✦ **Daily Text Limit:** Control how many texts you receive from Facebook each day. You can choose 1, 5, 100, all the way to Unlimited. Remember that your mobile carrier's texting rates apply.

✦ **Post-by-Email Address:** Facebook gives you a unique e-mail address to which you can use to post updates. You could, for example, e-mail a video or photo from your phone and it will automatically be posted to Facebook. Note that posting by using the Facebook mobile app is easier.

Followers Settings

The Followers option (previously called Subscribe) on the Account Settings page has changed how many use Facebook. You can now allow people to follow your public posts, just like in Twitter or Google+, without having to become their friend. For many, especially journalists, celebrities, athletes, artists, and bloggers, this feature has also eliminated the need to run a Facebook business page.

Click the Followers entry in the left sidebar to turn on and off the Follow feature. When you turn on the feature, a new set of options appears, as shown in Figure 2-14.

A description of each option follows:

✦ **Follower Comments:** Determine who can comment on posts (everybody, friends of friends, or friends). If you have a large number of followers, you may not want to deal with the amount of spam you'd get by leaving comments open, but you will also miss out on the connections made.

✦ **Follower Notifications:** Determine whether you want to get notifications when people who aren't your friends start following you and share, Like, or comment on your public posts.

✦ **Username:** You might want to change your username so that people can find and follow you more easily.

✦ **Twitter:** If you have a Twitter account, you can connect it to your profile. Then each time you make an update, your Facebook account will send a Tweet.

✦ **Follow Plugin:** Make it easy for people visiting your website to follow you on Facebook. Add a Follow button on your website by copying and pasting the supplied code.

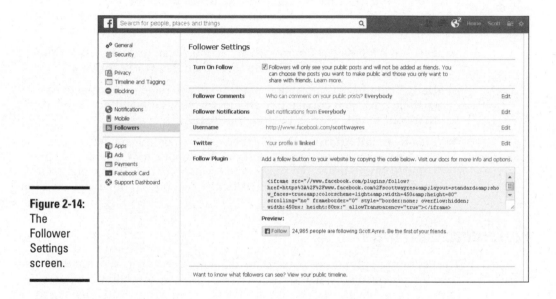

Figure 2-14:
The Follower Settings screen.

Apps Settings

As you interact on Facebook, you'll find that it's nearly impossible to avoid Facebook applications. (We explain applications and how they work in Book VI.) Apps allow you to interact more fully on Facebook. When you play a game, share photos via Instagram (http://instagram.com), update your status via apps such as Post Planner (www.postplanner.com) or HootSuite (https://hootsuite.com), or even enter a giveaway, you utilize a Facebook application. With the release of timeline for personal profiles in late 2011, Facebook applications are becoming even more prevalent because they're a primary way people choose to share an activity (for example, listening to music via Spotify or watching a movie via Netflix).

Each time you click an activity related to an application, Facebook checks to see if your account is already associated with that app. If it is, you move forward and complete the action. If your account isn't associated with the app, you get an alert asking if you'd like to allow the app to have access to your account. And that's where people new to Facebook start to get concerned (rightfully so; your privacy and protecting your account are important).

By their nature, apps must have access to your account in order to function properly. For instance, when you play Words with Friends (it's like mobile Scrabble), you probably want to find out if any of your other Facebook friends are playing so you can start a game with them. By allowing Words with Friends to access your account, the app can look at your list of Facebook friends, compare it with the people who have Words with Friends accounts, and let you know who is already playing. Then, after you play Words with Friends, you can choose to post your wins to your timeline and let people know you are the king or queen of word strategy (or not).

If you don't want to use applications or are uncomfortable allowing them to access your account information, you don't have to install or allow the application on your account. The trade-off is that you'll miss out on some functionality of Facebook and interacting with your friends on a different level. If you decide to allow an app, you can always remove it later.

To see which apps you currently have associated with your account, click Apps on the Account Settings page. A list similar to the one in Figure 2-15 shows you the name of the application, when you last accessed or used the application, the option to edit the application, and the option to remove the application.

Figure 2-15:
Your App
Settings
page lists
the apps
associated
with your
Facebook
account.

We recommend that you check your App Settings page periodically just to clean out apps you no longer use. There's no use having extra apps hanging around.

If you want to see what permissions a particular app has for your account, click the Edit button next to the application name. The app window expands, as shown in Figure 2-16.

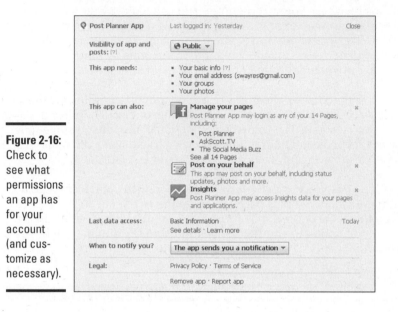

Figure 2-16: Check to see what permissions an app has for your account (and customize as necessary).

Figure 2-16 shows several options for working with this app:

✦ Remove the app by clicking the Remove App link, at the bottom of the page.

✦ Remove nonessential functions such as Manage Your Pages and Post on Your Behalf.

✦ Check to see when the app last accessed you data.

✦ Customize which of your friends or lists can see when and how you use the application.

If you choose to remove an application, you can always add it back to your account later.

Applications will become much more integral to Facebook than they already are. In general, people don't like to leave Facebook to complete other actions. That's why you can watch videos in your news feed instead of clicking over to YouTube, and why you can click a photo and see a lightbox with a larger version of the image. Facebook offers secure browsing and applications that allow payments inside the application. As product sales on Facebook grow, so will the use of applications that can connect third-party websites to Facebook and share inventory.

Ads Setting

The Facebook Ads option on your Account Settings page, shown in Figure 2-17, isn't referring to how to create Facebook ads (which we discuss in Book V, Chapter 4). Instead, this option explains how Facebook ads work with your personal timeline account, what the ads can and can't do, and how your information and your friends' information is (or isn't) used with ads.

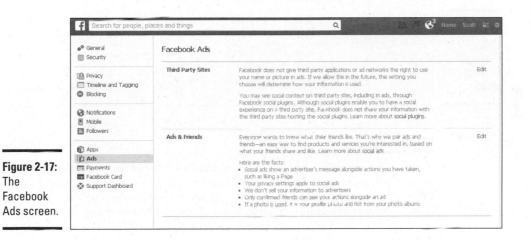

Figure 2-17:
The
Facebook
Ads screen.

Take a moment to read Facebook's explanation and familiarize yourself with how ads work. In a nutshell, Facebook is reminding you that third-party apps and networks don't have the legal right to use your information (including your picture) in their advertisements. You can control third-party ad settings by clicking the Edit link and using the drop-down list to choose who can see your information if Facebook makes changes to its ad policies in the future. Be sure to click the Save Changes button to ensure that your preference is saved.

Payments Settings

The Payment Settings page, shown in Figure 2-18, enables you to view and manage purchases you've made in Facebook. These purchases are conducted in games, apps, when purchasing a gift for someone, or when using promoted posts.

Account Balance setting

If you've previously purchased credits, you'll see an account balance. As of September 2013, the credits system has been dissolved and you can now simply make app purchases in your country's currency.

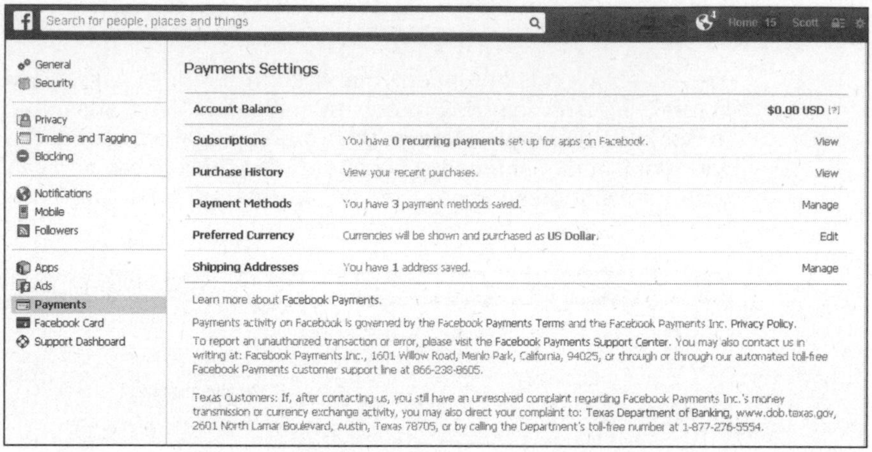

Figure 2-18:
The
Payments
Settings
screen.

Subscriptions setting

You can set up monthly recurring payments to subscribe to your favorite games and apps. Subscriptions are available only on select apps and the offer will vary depending on the app. If you've subscribed to a recurring payment, you'll see that information in the Subscriptions setting.

Purchase History setting

If you've ever made a purchase in Facebook, you can see your purchase history by clicking the View link in the Purchase History row. You might want to use this handy resource to keep track of how much you're spending.

The following details are listed: order date, item purchased, purchase location, and amount. Click the dollar amount to display a new window with the time of the purchase, the payment ID, and the purchase method. You can also dispute the purchase if you don't recognize it.

Payment Methods setting

Facebook offers many payment methods. You can use your credit card, PayPal, or even a Facebook gift card. If you use PayPal to pay for Facebook ads (see Book V), your PayPal information is saved, and you can edit it in the Payment Methods row.

To add a credit card to your payment methods, follow these steps:

1. **In the Payment Methods row, click the Manage link.**

A new page appears, asking for your Facebook account password.

2. **Type your password in the text box, and then click Continue.**

The Payment Methods box expands and lists payment options, as shown in Figure 2-19.

Add a credit card:

First Name:	
Last Name:	
Credit Card Number:	
Credit Card Type:	VISA MasterCard AMERICAN EXPRESS DISCOVER JCB
Expiration Date:	Month ▾ / Year ▾
Security Code (CSC):	[?]
Billing Address:	
Billing Address 2:	
City/Town:	
State/Province /Region:	
Zip/Postal Code:	
Country:	United States ▾
	Add

Facebook will save your payment information for future purchases.
You can always remove or manage this information in your
account settings.

Figure 2-19:
Choose your
payment
method.

3. **Complete the form, and then click the Add button.**

   Facebook saves your information so you don't have to resubmit the
   same information each time you want to buy credits.

You can remove credit card or payment information any time by clicking the
Manage link next to Payment Methods and then clicking Remove for the
information you want to delete.

Preferred Currency setting

The Preferred Currency option is pretty much what it sounds like. You can
choose the currency that you use the most from the drop-down list. The
currency you choose determines how Facebook displays pricing to you (for
example, either in American dollars or euros). If you make changes to your
preferred currency, remember to click Save Changes for those to take effect.

Shipping Addresses setting

With the addition of Facebook Gifts (for details, see Book II, Chapter 9),
you'll want to add a shipping address to Facebook should someone purchase
you a gift card or other item for your birthday.

To add an address, follow these steps:

1. **In the Shipping Addresses row, click the Manage link.**

   A new page appears, asking for your Facebook account password.

2. **Type your password and click Continue.**

   (Any addresses you have entered previously will appear.)

3. **Click the Add an Address link.**

4. **Fill out your address information, and then click Add.**

5. **When you're finished, click Close.**

Note that you can't edit an existing address. To remove an address, click Remove next to the address you'd like to remove. A warning box appears, asking you to confirm. Click Remove and the address is removed.

Facebook Card Setting

The Facebook card is a way for anyone to buy you a gift card and have the balance automatically added to your card. The first time someone sends you a Facebook card, you'll be sent a reusable Facebook-branded card in the mail that looks like any other gift card. When you receive your card, you can use it to make purchases at the store or restaurant with which you have a balance. Then the next time you receive a Facebook card gift, the amount is simply added to your existing card.

You will see the Facebook Card setting only if someone has sent you a Facebook card.

The Facebook Card settings screen is shown in Figure 2-20. If your card is lost or stolen, click the Report Lost or Stolen Card link and follow the onscreen instructions.

The Current Balances row displays any gift cards you have at specific stores, as well as the current balance. Click View in this row to see who sent money to your card and when you spent the money.

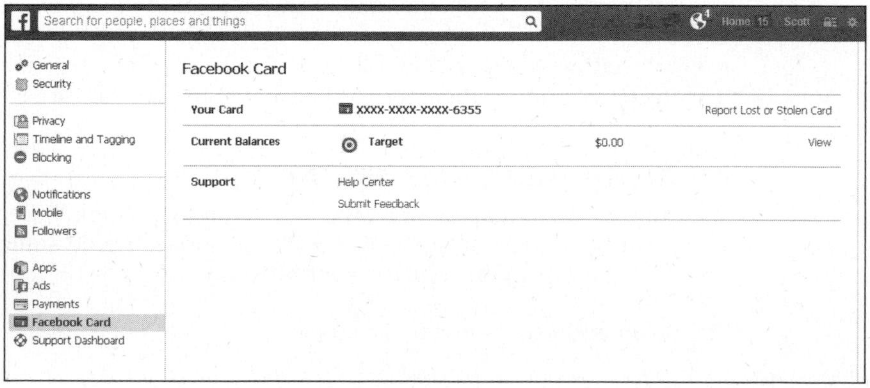

Figure 2-20:
The Facebook Card Settings screen.

Facebook Card			
Your Card	XXXX-XXXX-XXXX-6355		Report Lost or Stolen Card
Current Balances	Target	$0.00	View
Support	Help Center		
	Submit Feedback		

Support Dashboard Setting

The Support Dashboard screen, which is shown in Figure 2-21, enables you to see the status of your reports and inquiries. The following options are available:

+ **Notifications:** Use the Notifications drop-down list on the right to turn notifications off and on.

+ **Pending:** When you report a photo, comment, video, or post from another user or page, the report is placed in Pending. You'll be able to see what you reported as well as be given the opportunity to cancel the report.

+ **History:** When Facebook has reviewed your report, you'll see a list of recent items and Facebook's decision.

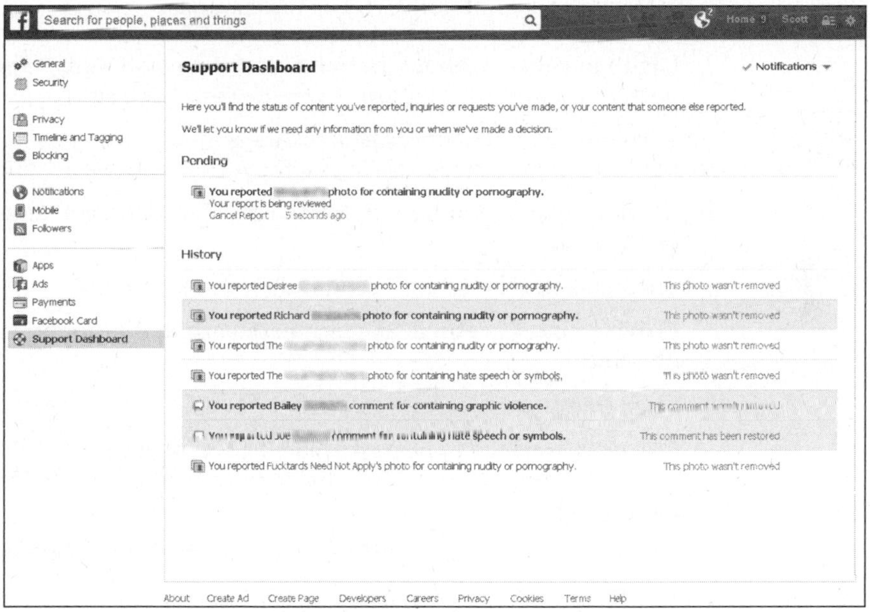

Figure 2-21:
The Support Dashboard screen.

The Support Dashboard screen looks different for every user.

Deleting Your Facebook Account

If you decide to delete your Facebook account, your information becomes irretrievable. Unless you've made a copy of your Facebook data and saved that file somewhere other than Facebook, you'll lose your photos, videos, status updates, comments, friends lists, and private messages.

We give step-by-step instructions for archiving your Facebook data earlier in this chapter, in the "Download a copy of your Facebook data" section. We firmly suggest that you archive your Facebook data before you delete your account so you don't lose anything of value.

When you delete your account, there's no going back. You can't reinstate your account. If you choose to return to Facebook, you have to create a new account and start from scratch.

To delete your account, follow these instructions:

1. **Log in to your Facebook account, and then visit** `www.facebook.com/ help/contact.php?show_form=delete_account`.

   The Delete My Account page appears, with a strict warning that you will not be able to retrieve any data after your Facebook account is deleted.

2. **If you're sure you'd like to delete your Facebook account, click Delete My Account.**

   The Permanently Delete Account dialog box appears.

3. **Provide your Facebook account password and type the CAPTCHA phrase.**

4. **Click Okay.**

   One more warning appears, explaining that your account has been deactivated but not deleted. If you log in to Facebook within 14 days, you have the option to cancel your deletion request.

5. **To confirm you want to delete your account, click Okay again.**

   You still have 14 days to change your mind. If you don't log in to your account within 14 days, your Facebook account is permanently deleted.

Chapter 3: Touring the Interface

In This Chapter

✔ **Understanding how each part of your news feed works**

✔ **Managing your ticker**

✔ **Curating your timeline**

*F*acebook has many features, including the news feed, your personal timeline, and business pages. Each offers a different way to view or access content. This chapter explains how the two most prominent pages — your news feed and personal timeline — work.

In this chapter, we share some screen shots of the news feed and personal timeline and explain the main elements of each. Both the news feed and timeline have a lot of functionality. There's a lot to cover, so let's get started!

Navigating Your News Feed Page

Your Facebook news feed is your main Facebook page. (We sometimes refer to the main Facebook page as your Facebook home page.) You see it every time you log in, and it's where you find the most functionality for interacting on Facebook. Your timeline is important too because it's where you archive your content, but your news feed is where you'll spend most of your time.

We explain the news feed page in terms of five main parts: top navigation, left navigation, your main news feed, right navigation, and the ticker and chat panes (see Figure 3-1). Each of these parts has important functionality. The following sections explain how you can use them to get the most out of your Facebook experience.

Top navigation

The top navigation on your news feed page consists of a blue toolbar. The elements on the toolbar, from left to right, are as follows:

✦ **Facebook link:** This link is the Facebook logo. When you click it — anywhere on Facebook — you return to your news feed page.

✦ **Search text box:** Use this text box to search for friends, business pages, or general information. Facebook refers to the search box as Graph Search.

✦ **Friend requests icon:** Any time you receive a friend request, you see this icon highlighted with a number telling you how many requests you have. You can click the icon, whether it's highlighted or not, to see if you have any pending friend requests. From there, you can confirm the request or click Not Now to ignore the request. If you click Not Now, Facebook will ask if you know the person outside Facebook. If you click Yes, nothing happens. If you click No, Facebook will not allow that person to send you any more friend requests. Remember, if you ignore the request, that person can still see your public updates and become a follower.

✦ **Messages icon:** When someone sends you a private message, this icon is highlighted, with a number telling you how many messages are new and waiting to be read. You can click this icon to see recent messages, send a new message, or see all your messages.

✦ **Notifications icon:** When someone interacts with your content, tags you in an update, responds to a comment thread you posted on, or posts to a group to which you belong, this icon (the globe) is highlighted, with a number indicating how many new updates your friends have added.

✦ **Home link:** This link brings you back to the news feed page, just like the Facebook link on the far-left side of the toolbar.

✦ **Link to your timeline:** This link appears with your name. When you click it, you go to your timeline.

✦ **Privacy shortcuts:** This icon (the lock) opens a drop-down menu that enables you to quickly and easily access and change your privacy settings.

✦ **Account menu:** This icon is either a down arrow or a gear. Click it to display a menu that gives you access to such things as Facebook ads, settings, and the activity log.

The top navigation toolbar is static and appears on every page. It's a handy way to quickly navigate Facebook.

Left navigation

The left sidebar of your news feed page houses links to your timeline, favorites, groups, friend lists, apps, pages, and interest lists. Because you use this navigation quite a bit, Facebook allows you to customize it to make it fit your habits. For instance, if you find that you visit a particular Facebook group quite a bit, you can move that group to your Favorites list so it's readily available at the top of your navigation list. In the next few sections, we explain each of the main navigation choices and provide instructions on moving an item to your favorites list.

If you move your mouse over any of the main categories in the left navigation sidebar, you see the More option. When you click More, the main news feed area displays a list of your groups, lists, business pages, and apps. The list gives you the option to edit individual items and tells you how often you've used the item.

Timeline

At the top of the left navigation, you see your profile picture and your name. When you click either item, you go directly to your timeline. Later in this chapter, we explain the features of your timeline and how to use them to interact with your friends and colleagues.

Favorites

By default, the Favorites list contains links to your news feed, messages, photos, and events. You may or may not see a link labeled Find Friends (if you're new to Facebook, you'll probably see this option). The Favorites list is handy because you can keep all the groups and lists you use the most in one place for easy access. (See Book II, Chapter 5 for information on using Facebook groups and Chapter 4 of this minibook for help creating lists.)

To move an item to your Favorites list, follow these steps:

1. **Move your cursor over the item (group or list name) you want to move to the Favorites area.**

2. **Click the pencil icon.**

3. **Choose Add to Favorites from the menu.**

   The item appears in the Favorites list.

You can rearrange the order of your Favorites list by moving your cursor over one of the items in the list, clicking the pencil icon, and choosing Rearrange from the menu. Then you can click and drag items to change their position. The only item that cannot be moved is your news feed; it stays static at the top of your Favorites list.

To remove an item from your Favorites list, move your cursor over the item you want to remove, click the pencil icon, and choose Remove from the menu. The item moves back to its original place in the navigation. For instance, if you remove a group from your Favorites list, you can still find it under the Groups heading.

Groups

The Groups option won't appear in your left navigation unless you're part of one or more Facebook groups. We explain how you can connect with others through groups in Book II, Chapter 5. When you start participating in a Facebook group, the title of that group appears in the Groups section of the left navigation. You can click the title of a group to find its latest updates.

Lists

In Chapter 4 of this minibook, we explain why lists are useful and how to create one (or several). Because the news feed is ever changing, it's easy to miss updates from people who interest you. Facebook tries to guess what you're most interested in (by using an algorithm — see Book V, Chapter 3), but it doesn't always get it right. Creating lists to organize your friends as well as pages and people you follow helps you quickly see recent updates by specific people. For example, we have lists for local friends, high school friends, blogs, Facebook marketing pages, blogging buddies, and family. When you click the title of each list, your news feed switches from displaying the most recent updates or top stories updates of everyone with whom you're connected to showing updates from the people you included in a particular list. We find we don't miss as many updates from important people when we use lists.

Apps and Pages

The Apps and Pages headers list the applications you have associated with your Facebook account and the business pages you administer, respectively. Both seem to list apps or business pages based on how often you use an app or visit a business page. In addition, the order of a list may change depending on what page you are viewing (for example, the news feed versus a group page).

News feed

You can update your status right from your news feed. At the top of the middle section of the page, you see options for Update Status and Add Photos/Video. Just click the one you want to use, and share what's on your mind.

The main part of your news feed page is in the center of the page. This is where you see updates from your Facebook friends, groups, people you follow, and business pages you've Liked.

Your news feed is made up of the following:

✦ **Top stories:** Displays updates from people or business pages that have gained lots of interaction and engagement. Top stories are based on factors such as how many friends are commenting on a post. Stories are listed according to relevance rather than chronological order.

✦ **Most recent:** Displays a chronological list of the most recent updates from people and business pages to which you are connected.

As you can see in Figure 3-2, you can sort your news feed between top stories and most recent. Facebook uses an algorithm to try to determine your affinity for each person and page with which you're associated on Facebook — sometimes the algorithm is right, sometimes it's wrong. (Read more about the news feed algorithm and other Facebook analytics in Book V, Chapter 3.

Figure 3-2: Click the Sort link to switch between Top Stories and Most Recent.

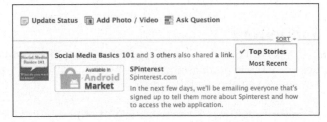

Both top stories and most recent stories can include updates from friends, people you follow, groups, apps, and business pages. Updates from people you haven't interacted with regularly are shown in the ticker in the right sidebar. (We get to the ticker later in this chapter.)

If you want to remove a story from your news feed, hover your cursor over the story until you see an arrow at the top right. Click the arrow to display the menu shown in Figure 3-3, and then choose I Don't Want to See This.

Figure 3-3: It's easy to hide a story from your news feed.

CNN

BREAKING NEWS: The Nevada Parole Board has gra[nted] parole on some charges stemming from 2008 arme[d] convictions, but he won't immediately get out of prison. http://on.cnn.com/1ebuBPu

Follow Post

I don't want to see this

Like · Comment · Share · 👍 1,709 💬 789 🔄 882 · 48 minutes ago · 🌐

After choosing this option you see some or all of the following choices:

✦ **Hide All From:** This option hides that person or business page from your news feed forever so you won't see updates again. Facebook will then ask you the question *Why don't you want to see this?* and provide several responses from which you can choose. Note that some responses lead to additional questions and selections.

✦ **Hide All by *Name of Application:*** You see this option only if the story was posted by a third-party application (such as Post Planner, HootSuite, FarmVille, Twitter, or Instagram). When you select this option, you can hide all updates from that application.

When you post your own status updates, or share photos, videos, or links, they appear in the news feeds of your followers and friends (unless you've applied a privacy setting to those updates; we explain how to do that in Book II, Chapter 2). As you can imagine, you should be careful about what you post because it's likely that many others will see it. (If you have questions about your Facebook privacy, see Chapter 4 of this minibook.)

Right navigation

Facebook tends to roll out changes here and there, and the right sidebar is where things sometimes jump around a bit. By the time you read this, the right sidebar may have changed yet again.

If your chat feature is off, you'll see your ticker in the top of the right sidebar. (We describe the ticker in the next section.) Below the ticker, you have application alerts — usually about upcoming birthdays and events (see Book II, Chapter 7 for more about Facebook events). When you click the birthday person's name, the Today's Birthdays window pops up and provides a place for you to write a quick note to your friend, which is automatically posted to his or her timeline, and buy your friend a gift. Similarly, if you click the name of an upcoming event, the Event pop-up appears and gives an overview of the event, complete with a link to the event page and the option to RSVP to the event.

Under application alerts, you can see sponsored stories. *Sponsored stories* are a type of advertisement that relies on showing you which of your friends have interacted with a company or its business page recently. Sometimes Facebook swaps the sponsored stories area and the ticker, so what you see may be different from what others see.

The right sidebar changes depending on the type of Facebook page you're viewing. Following is a discussion of the basic options you're likely to see on specific types of pages:

+ **Facebook group page:** The right navigation area is an overview of how many members are in the group. Next is a text box so you can add someone to the group. (Just start typing the person's name, and then choose him or her from the list that appears. Remember that you have to be friends with someone to add him or her to a group.) Then you see suggested groups, sometimes you see recommended pages followed by sponsored stories.

+ **Facebook list feed:** If you're viewing a list you created, the right navigation of any specific list displays the Manage List button. Click it to rename your list, edit the people in the list, choose which update types appear in the list, or archive the list. Next, you see the On This List section, which allows you to see a snapshot of the Facebook friends you've included in the list, as well as a See All link to display all the people in the list. Below that is a text box so you can add someone to the list (just start typing the person's name, and then select him or her from the list that appears). The List Suggestions heading is next and provides a list of people Facebook thinks may fit with your list. Click the Add button to add a person to the list, or click x to remove the person from the list.

+ **Facebook messages:** The main Messages page doesn't have a right-side navigation. However, when you click to individual messages, sponsored ads appear on the right side.

Ticker and Chat panes

The ticker and chat panes appear at the far right of your Facebook page. The *ticker* displays updates in real time from your friends, groups, and business pages you follow. Whereas your news feed focuses on displaying content from the people and business pages with which you interact most, the ticker is a running stream of what everyone is doing, whether you regularly interact with them or not.

Chat is texting in real time with someone in Facebook. Chats aren't broadcast through your news feed, ticker, or timeline; they are private. We explain chat in more detail in Book II, Chapter 8.

No matter what page you're looking at — news feed, timeline, messages, groups, and so on — you'll see the ticker and chat panes. However, you can make the panes smaller or larger by clicking and dragging the bar between them.

To hide the ticker and chat panes, click the Hide sidebar icon, as shown in Figure 3-4. The chat panel collapses. If you're on the home page, the ticker moves to the right sidebar; otherwise, you don't see the ticker.

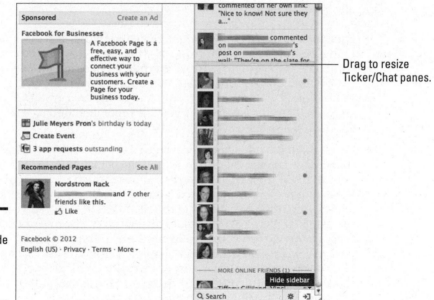

Figure 3-4:
You can hide the chat and ticker column.

Drag to resize Ticker/Chat panes.

As Facebook rolls out more activity applications, you'll see those updates in your ticker. *Activity applications* are the way Facebook wants you to interact with others. Facebook's take is that you're out there living life, and you want a more robust way to share what you're doing. Instead of just Liking a book, you can share that you've read the book. Or you can share that you hiked a trail, watched a movie, or played a game.

If you notice something come through your ticker and want to see more about it, move your cursor over the update, and an expanded view appears. You see the status update and any comments to the status, and you can Like or comment on the status yourself.

When you notice that someone in your ticker has commented on your business page, you can respond right from the ticker as your business! Hover your cursor over the comment, and a pop-up window appears with the option to comment, as shown in Figure 3-5.

Figure 3-5:
Comment as your business page directly from your ticker.

Navigating Your Timeline

Your personal timeline is a record of all the content you've shared throughout your time on Facebook. It's been referred to as a digital scrapbook, and that's fairly accurate. But if you're not the crafty type or not into scrapbooking, don't let that moniker deter you. Your timeline is simply a way to organize your Facebook interactions.

You can highlight important events in your life (Facebook calls these *milestones*), hide updates, or add events after the fact. For instance, maybe you took your first trip to Europe years before you joined Facebook. With timeline, you can create a new update that appears in the correct chronological spot in your timeline. The update can include pictures, music you listened to while traveling, your own travel notes, a map of your travels, and more. When you've created the new event (or *story*), you can feature it so others can have a complete picture of your experience — or you can relive the experience yourself.

Watch Facebook's video about how the timeline works at www.facebook.com/about/timeline.

Familiarizing yourself with the timeline

The timeline has many features you can use to control how you share your content with others — even after you've already shared via the news feed. First, though, you need to know how to find your timeline. After you log in to Facebook, click anywhere you see your name (in the left sidebar navigation, or the top blue navigation toolbar, or in comments you leave). Your timeline appears, similar to the one shown in Figure 3-6.

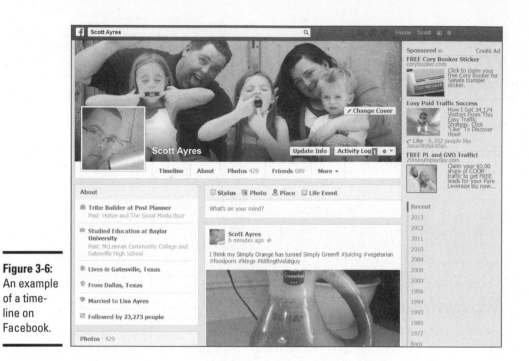

As you can see from Figure 3-6, the timeline is all about the visual splash! Following is a rundown of each item on your timeline:

✦ **Cover photo:** The focus of your timeline, your cover photo can have a big effect when people visit your page. You can choose any of your previously uploaded pictures to use as your cover image, or you can upload a new image.

It's handy to know that the cover image is 851 pixels wide by 315 pixels high, so you can edit the photo before you upload it. You can use a picture that's smaller than 851 x 315, but Facebook stretches the photo to fit, so it may be distorted.

✦ **Profile photo:** The photo you choose as your profile photo becomes your Facebook *avatar* — it's the picture people see next to your status updates, comments, and stories. You can use a photo you've already uploaded to Facebook, or you can upload a new picture. Some people like to change profile pictures regularly, while others like to keep theirs the same. We suggest changing your profile photo only as necessary. Your friends will come to recognize your image, and they will find you easily as they skim the news feed.

✦ **Update Info button:** Click this button to see your About page, where you can update where you work; your education, relationships, and quotes; where you live; contact information; and your short Basic Info and About Me blurbs.

✦ **Activity Log button:** Click this button, which appears only to you (and not to visitors to your page), to view and edit your activity on Facebook, as shown in Figure 3-7. You'll see comments on other's posts and your posts; songs you've listened to; pages, photos, and status updates you've liked; people you've followed; and more. You can see how a post was originally shared and hide a story from your timeline (by clicking the pencil to the far right of the story). To change the share setting for an update you made to your timeline, click the share drop-down list (which sports two silhouettes, a globe, a lock, or a gear, depending on your current setting) and choose a new setting from the menu.

In the default activity log view, you see all your activity. For other views, choose from one of the options in the left sidebar. For example, you can view activity related only to photos, Likes, or games.

Because the timeline makes it easy to find current and past status updates, it's a good idea to review your activity log and check the permissions on previous stories. You may want to hide some of those party pictures from your colleagues.

✦ **Gear Icon:** Clicking the gear icon displays a drop-down list that enables you to view your timeline as others see it — either the public at large or a specific Facebook friend. (You can read more about this setting in Chapter 4 of this minibook.) You can control who can add items to your timeline and who can see things on your timeline as well. In addition, you can manage tags and add a Facebook badge to your site.

Figure 3-7:
See all your activity on Facebook.

✦ **Change Cover button:** This button appears only when you hover your cursor over your cover photo. Clicking it gives you the opportunity to change the cover photo for your timeline. You can use a photo you've already uploaded to your profile or you can upload a new photo.

✦ **Sections:** On the left side of your timeline, just below your cover photo, you see the three content categories: About, Photos, and Friends. You can't change the order of these or remove them.

To display or hide any section, click the pencil icon in that particular section and choose Manage Sections. A lightbox appears. To remove activity or change settings, click the section name (such as Instagram). For sections such as TV Shows, you can click the plus sign to see recommended shows to add to the section or type the names of TV shows in the search box that you'd like to add.

- **About:** You see links to your current employer, education, current city of residence, and relationship status if you've shared that information. You can click the About link or the pencil icon in the About box to edit these items.

- **Photos:** Click Photos to display a page displaying photos you've uploaded, albums you've created, and photos in which you've been tagged. You can also click individual photos and scroll through them. Click the pencil icon to edit all sections or see the photos hidden from the timeline.

- **Friends:** In this section, you see how many Facebook friends you have and profile images of nine of your friends. Click the pencil icon to edit all sections and change your privacy settings, such as who can see your friends list, who you're following, and who can see your followers.

✦ **More:** Hover your cursor over the More link to display a drop-down menu that enables you to manage a particular section such as TV shows, books, Likes, music, movies, events, and groups. After you make a selection, you can edit the content shown to others. If you choose an app such as Instagram, you can remove an image, change the app's settings, or hide the section. If you choose TV Shows, you can see a list of the shows you've watched and want to watch and pages you've Liked related to TV shows. We discuss where these sections appear on your timeline next.

From here, everyone's timeline will look different. You might see sections with apps you've used, pages you've Liked, games you've played, or TV shows and movies you've added.

The right side of your timeline contains all your posts, most recent first, as well as items in which you've been tagged. To see past updates, scroll down or click the date to jump to a specific year.

As you scroll, your cover photo is replaced with drop-down menus that take you to your timeline or certain years. You can post a status update, a photo, a place, or a life event. Continue scrolling and you'll see that the updates continue to load until you get a few weeks or months into the past.

Facebook then shows you *Earlier in* that year and gives you the option to choose between seeing Highlights or All Stories. The left side now displays what was added to your timeline during this period. For instance, Scott can see that in 2013 he added 113 friends and Liked a total of 658 pages. On the right he can continue to see stories posted to his timeline as he scrolls.

If you choose Highlights, Facebook displays any stories you've chosen to highlight as well as stories you posted that were popular. You'll see a range of post dates and an option to see more posts from that date range. If you choose All Stories, every story posted on your timeline will appear.

Each status update has a pencil icon in the upper right. Click that icon to change the date, add a location, highlight the post, or hide that update from the timeline. If the update is from an app such as Instagram, you see additional options, such as Show on Timeline, Allow on Timeline, and Hide from Timeline. You can delete the update or mark it as spam. For photos you upload to your timeline, you see options to edit the album containing the photo and to reposition the photo.

These tools allow you to have complete control over how you share previous updates and content with others.

Hiding a story from your timeline

To hide a story from your timeline, you can visit your activity log or your main timeline.

In your activity log, search for the story by clicking the correct month or year. When you find the story you want to edit, click the pencil on the far right to display the menu shown in Figure 3-8, and choose Hidden from Timeline.

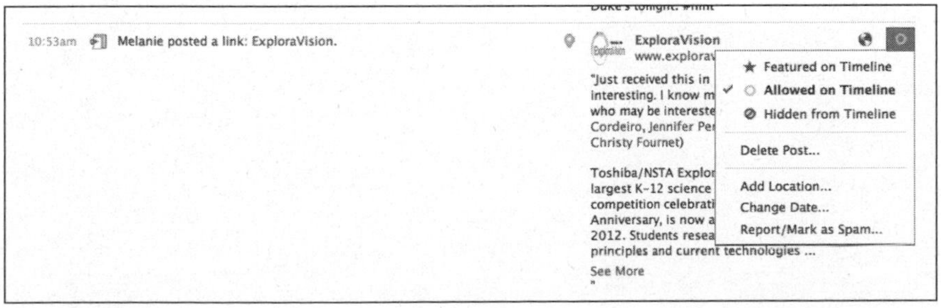

Figure 3-8:
Use the activity log menu to edit stories in your timeline.

To hide a story from your main timeline, move your cursor over the story. When the pencil icon appears, click it to display a menu and then choose Hide from Timeline.

You can reinstate any story by returning to the activity log and choosing Allowed on Timeline.

Your timeline can be an amazing tool for keeping track of your major life moments and sharing them with others. Keep in mind, though, that you don't own your space on Facebook. Although it's unlikely that you'll lose your timeline, there are no guarantees. We recommend that you keep backups of photos and important updates on your own computer (and create a backup of that as well). Facebook shouldn't be your only means of recording photos, video, and any other special content.

Adding a past event to your timeline

You add updates, photos, and events to a past date in the Status box. Facebook lets you choose the year, month, day, and even the time of day for the update.

The timeline is a chronological representation of the content you've shared with others, but it can be more than that. You can create a multimedia profile of your major life events to share with friends, family, and others. You can add photos, videos, and comments by year — even for the years before Facebook was around. You can start with the year you were born and go from there, or you can start at any point you like — you have that control.

Chapter 4: Customizing Your Privacy Settings

In This Chapter

✔ **Knowing how to protect your privacy online**

✔ **Managing your privacy settings**

✔ **Understanding how privacy options change what others see**

✔ **Using Facebook lists**

✔ **Discovering interest lists**

*O*nline privacy is a topic we're passionate about. The way you interact online is trackable and findable (and yes, Google, Facebook, Amazon, and others are tracking your interactions and behavior). You're constantly creating your digital footprint by purchasing items online, using Google to find something, creating a Facebook account, interacting with blogs and websites, and so on. Nothing is wrong with that — in fact, it's almost impossible to *not* have a digital footprint these days.

The important thing to understand is that you, and you alone, are responsible for your privacy. Don't rely on the sites you visit to protect your information. Although it's reasonable to expect a site not to compromise your credit card information, it's up to you to decide what information to share, who to share it with, and how you'll share other information you find. Take the time to review your privacy options and understand how they work. This chapter helps you navigate Facebook's privacy options and explains how you can take control of how you share your information on the Facebook platform.

Understanding Online Privacy

You're always in charge of your privacy — online and offline. The platform isn't responsible for protecting you; protecting yourself is your responsibility. Would it be easier if the tool, in this case Facebook, started out with your privacy set to the highest level instead of the most open level? Perhaps. But consider two things:

✦ Facebook's mission isn't to provide a personal space for you. Facebook wants to create an open community whose members constantly share their lives and milestones with others. It makes sense that Facebook encourages that by setting the default privacy to be more open rather than closed.

✦ Regardless of the default privacy settings, you'll most likely want to tweak them to your satisfaction.

Facebook also engages in *frictionless sharing,* in which the default setting in applications you install is to allow the application to automatically share updates. For example, when you play a game such as Bejeweled on your smartphone, each time you make a high score, a window pops up and asks if you'd like to share with your Facebook friends. Facebook calls that interruption in play *friction* and believes that eliminating that step allows for a smoother interaction between you and the application and allows for more opportunities for sharing on Facebook. Many applications default to frictionless sharing (that is, they automatically share your actions with the news feed), but you can change that setting by visiting your application's dashboard.

You still have full control over what you share. If you don't want to share your actions with people, you don't have to install the application (or if you want the application, at least check to be sure the application offers the option to customize how you share). If you don't want everyone to see your timeline updates, change your share setting to Friends Only. If you want to share your updates with select people, you can customize your updates by clicking the Public button below your Status Update text box and choosing who can and can't see your update.

Consider this: Do you use the free Wi-Fi at your local coffee shop or library or *anywhere?* Are you concerned that whoever is supplying the Wi-Fi isn't covering your privacy? Why not? When you're on public Wi-Fi, someone could easily hijack your passwords and make purchases on sites that you've logged in to, so it's best to change your working and browsing habits when you aren't using a secure Wi-Fi connection. That's your responsibility.

Taking Responsibility for Your Own Privacy

The way Facebook works is that you share information with friends. Some of that information is considered public (your name, user ID, and profile picture), and some of it is considered private, and you can elect not to share it with others (via the privacy settings we discuss throughout this chapter). As we mention previously, Facebook relies on you to customize your settings and actively participate in protecting your privacy.

Check your privacy settings regularly, and adjust them as necessary. Facebook doesn't always alert you to changes.

An important first step in protecting your online privacy, whether with Facebook or another website, is to ensure that you have a strong password in place so your account is less likely to be compromised. Here are a few tips for taking charge of your privacy on Facebook (also see Chapter 2 of this minibook):

✦ **Turn on Facebook's secure browsing option.** Facebook has an option that allows you to browse the site using a secure connection. You'll know you're using the secure connection because the address bar will show https:// instead of http://. This option is on by default. If you turned it off and want to turn it back on, click the down arrow or gear at the top right of any Facebook page and choose Settings. Click the Security link in the left sidebar, and click the Edit link in the Secure Browsing row. Select the Browse Facebook on a Secure Connection (https) When Possible check box, and then click the Save Changes button.

✦ **Enable Facebook login notifications.** If you're concerned that someone may try to access your Facebook account, login notifications will send you an alert when your account is accessed from a device (for example, a computer or phone) that you haven't used before. To turn on login noti-fications, click the down arrow or gear at the top right of any Facebook page and choose Settings. Click the Security link in the left sidebar, and then click the Edit link in the Login Notifications row. Select the Email check box or the Text Message/Push Notification check box (or both, if you want) to receive alerts, and then click the Save Changes button.

✦ **Assign more than one admin to your business page.** If you should ever find your Facebook account compromised or locked, it would be a shame to lose your business page access as well. Choose a person you trust to act as admin for you. (Similar to giving a neighbor a house key in case you lock yourself out.) Doing so will provide you access to the business page if necessary.

Managing and Customizing Your Privacy Settings

We explain how you can control the privacy of individual status updates in Book II, Chapter 2. This chapter explains how you can control your account privacy in general. To access your general Facebook privacy options, click the down arrow or gear icon in the top-right corner, and choose Settings from the menu. Then click the Privacy link in the left sidebar. The Privacy Settings page appears and explains how you can manage your privacy settings.

When you land on the Privacy Settings page, you see the Privacy Settings and Tools heading and the following three questions:

✦ **Who can see my stuff?** Choose who can see your future posts. If you choose Public, everyone on Facebook (whether you've friended them or not) can see what you post, who you tag, and any photos or videos you post. You essentially turn off any privacy settings. You can also choose to show your posts to friends or to yourself, or you can choose the Custom option.

If you choose the Custom option, the Custom Privacy dialog box appears. You can make your account (all your updates and uploads) visible to the following:

- *Friends:* People you are personally connected to on Facebook

- *Friends of Friends:* People connected to your connections; you may or may not know those people

- *Specific People or Lists:* People you have chosen from your list of friends or lists you created

- *Only Me:* No one but yourself

You can also hide status updates from specific people or lists by typing a name or list name in the Don't Share This With text box.

The second option enables you to review anything in which you've been tagged. Click this option to see an activity log for your account. You can delete activity or change an activity's setting.

The third option enables you to limit all past posts to friends only. This feature is handy when you have mistakenly made posts public or you decide to make your postings more private. The Limit the Audience for Past Posts tool allows you to change the share setting from public to friends. Any previous posts you shared as public will be changed as well. Simply click the Limit Old Posts button.

✦ **Who can contact me?** Determine who can send you friend requests. You can choose from everyone, friends of friends, or no one.

The second option lets you filter your Facebook messages. If you choose the strict setting, messages from people you aren't friends with will likely end up in your Other inbox.

✦ **Who can look me up?** The options here are simple. In the first option, you determine who can look you up using the e-mail address or phone number you provided. Like most settings on Facebook, you can choose everyone, friends of friends, or friends.

Next, you decide if you want to allow other search engines to link to your timeline. When the setting is on, it's easier for other search engines to link to your timeline in search results. If you turn off the setting, people will not be able to find your timeline by using a simple Google or Bing search.

For more information on privacy and security, visit `www.facebook.com/security` and `www.facebook.com/help/privacy`.

Blocked People and Apps settings

Facebook provides several ways for you to control how you interact with others (and how they interact with you). On the General Account Settings page, click the Blocking link in the left sidebar. The Manage Blocking page appears and provides options for the following:

+ **Add Friends to Your Restricted List:** We explain lists a little later in this chapter. One of the lists Facebook provides for you is the restricted list. When you add someone to this list, he or she can't see any of your updates unless those updates are public. Luckily, Facebook doesn't notify people when you add them to your restricted list. To add people to your restricted list, click the Edit List link.

+ **Block Users:** If you don't want to interact with someone on Facebook, you can block him from connecting with you. He can't see your updates, and you can't see his. The exception is groups you both belong to and apps or games you both use. To block someone, type his name or e-mail address into the appropriate text box, and click the Block button. A list of people you have blocked appears under the text boxes. You can unblock someone by clicking the Unblock link next to his name.

+ **Block App Invites:** Sometimes, you may have a friend who *really* likes Facebook apps and games and constantly invites you to join them by installing those apps and games. Those invites can clutter up your stream and get annoying. Facebook allows you to block app invites from specific people so your account will ignore future invites. In the text box, start typing the name of the friend whose app requests you want to ignore, and Facebook provides a list of matching names. Choose the correct name from the list, and future requests are ignored. To unblock the requests, just click the Unblock link next to the person's name.

+ **Block Event Invites:** This option is similar to Block App Invites. If you're receiving too many event invitations from someone, you can set your account to ignore future invites from her. In the text box, start typing the name of the friend whose event invites you want to ignore, and Facebook provides a list of matching names. Choose the correct name from the list, and future requests are ignored. To unblock the requests, just click the Unblock link next to the person's name.

+ **List Blocked Apps:** This section lists all Facebook applications you've blocked. To block an application, you can visit its business page (use the Search text box to find the app's business page) and then click the gear icon below your cover photo and choose the Block App link. You're asked to confirm that you want to block the app. To unblock an app, just click the Unblock link next to the name of the application.

Understanding How Privacy Settings Affect What Others See

When you customize your privacy settings, it's helpful to know how those settings affect how you and others see things on Facebook. Want to see how your personal timeline looks to others? Just follow these steps:

1. **Go to your timeline and click the gear icon (next to the Update Info and Activity Log links), and then choose View As.**

   An alert appears at the top of the page that says *This is what your timeline looks like to: Public.*

2. **Click View as a Specific Person, and then type the person's name in the text box to see how your timeline looks to that person.**

3. **Click X when you're finished.**

The next few sections explain how people can find you on Facebook, how friend requests work, and how you can control how you share your status updates.

How people can find you

We've said before that the crux of Facebook is social sharing. Generally, Facebook would love to have everyone's information accessible to all others because it believes that an open exchange is the wave of the future. Facebook may be right. However, many haven't caught up to that vision and demand more privacy.

If you'd like to exert some control over how you're contacted by others on Facebook, the first thing you need to consider is whether you want people to be able to find you on Facebook. To control your privacy settings, click the down arrow or gear icon in the upper-right corner and choose Settings. Then click the Privacy link in the left sidebar. Your choices in the Who Can Look Me Up section determine how visible you are to others via Facebook search. Your choices are as follows:

✦ **Everyone:** If you want anyone to find you on Facebook, choose this option. If you really want an open experience on Facebook, this is the way to go.

✦ **Friends of Friends:** If you know you're not quite ready to friend everyone out there, consider choosing the Friends of Friends option.

✦ **Friends:** Don't want anyone finding you that you haven't already found and connected with first? This is your option. It's the most closed and private option available for personal timeline searches.

Your personal timeline is searchable only within Facebook, but business pages are searchable outside Facebook via Google, Bing, Yahoo!, and so on. The settings you choose in Privacy Settings apply only to your personal timeline. For more information about business pages, see Book IV.

How friend requests work

When you want to connect with someone on Facebook, you send a friend request. Sometimes, you receive a friend request you don't want to approve for one reason or another. Maybe the request is from someone you don't know. Or maybe you know her, but you don't want to connect with her on Facebook for whatever reason. (See Chapter 2 of this minibook for more information and advice about choosing Facebook friends.) You have a few options:

✦ You can choose to accept the friend request and share your timeline freely. If that's the case, remember that you can exclude individuals from specific content by clicking the share drop-down list under your status updates. (The share list sports two silhouettes, a globe, a lock, or a gear, depending on your current settings.)

✦ You can choose to ignore the request (click the Not Now button next to the request) — essentially putting the friendship on hold in the ether by neither accepting nor declining the invitation. Anyone you ignore can still see any status updates that are shared with the public rather than specific people or lists, but he or she can't comment.

✦ You can always accept the friend request and assign the person to a specific list. We love lists because they allow you to control how you share things across the board. We explain lists later in this chapter.

How your updates are shared

Earlier in this chapter, we show you how to set your default privacy for status updates and photos, and we mention that you can set the privacy individually for each status update you share. When you set your privacy to public, you're essentially allowing anyone on Facebook to see your update — but only friends can comment on those updates, with the following exceptions:

✦ If you post a status update that tags someone, anyone who is friends with the person you tagged can comment on your status update — even if you're not friends with them.

✦ If you turn on the Follow option for your Facebook account (see Book II, Chapter 2), anyone who follows your updates can see and comment on any public updates.

On a related note, when Facebook released the timeline version of personal profiles, your updates from previous months and years became more readily available. This may or may not be a problem for you, depending on what you've shared over the years. Luckily, Facebook recognized the issue and included a way for you to change the share setting for individual pieces of content. As you set up your timeline (see Chapter 3 of this minibook), you may choose to customize how you share certain things. To change the share setting for previously shared content, follow these instructions:

1. **Visit your personal timeline and click the Activity Log button directly below your cover photo.**

   Your Activity Log page appears.

2. **Find the status update for which you want to change the sharing preference.**

   If you hover your cursor over the share icon (two silhouettes, a globe, a lock, or a gear, depending on your current settings), you can see the original share setting for a status update, as shown in Figure 4-1.

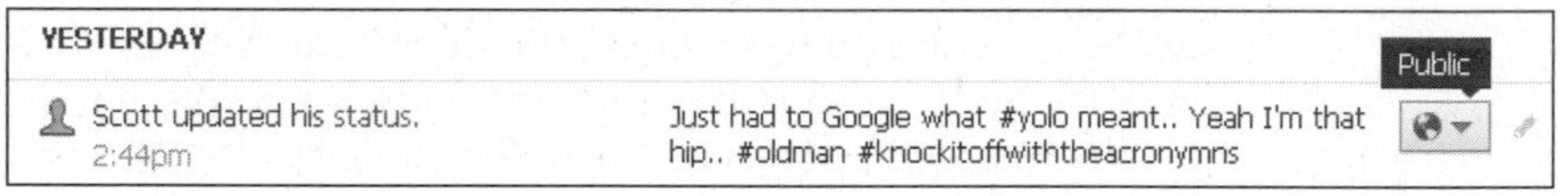

Figure 4-1:
The original share setting for any status update.

3. **Click the share icon and choose a sharing option from the list, as shown in Figure 4-2.**

Figure 4-2:
Change who can see previous status updates.

Utilizing Lists So You Don't Miss a Thing

One of the biggest complaints about Facebook is that the news feed doesn't always show what users want to see. Facebook uses the News Feed algorithm (see Book V, Chapter 3) to track what content you interact with most, and then it tries to determine what updates you want to see. The problem is that it's not a perfect system, and sometimes you can miss updates from people you're interested in keeping up with, but you may not comment on or Like their updates regularly.

To keep track of people easily, we suggest using the Lists feature. You can create multiple lists for various groups of people. For instance, Scott created lists for family, high school friends, local friends, blogging friends, and so on. Each list includes specific people (and yes, there's some overlap because some friends are included in more than one list). When you click a list name, your news feed shows only the recent updates from the people included in the list, so you're less likely to miss an update you're interested in.

You can see a catalog of your current Facebook friend lists in the left sidebar on your news feed page. Click Friends to see a complete list of your lists, as shown in Figure 4-3).

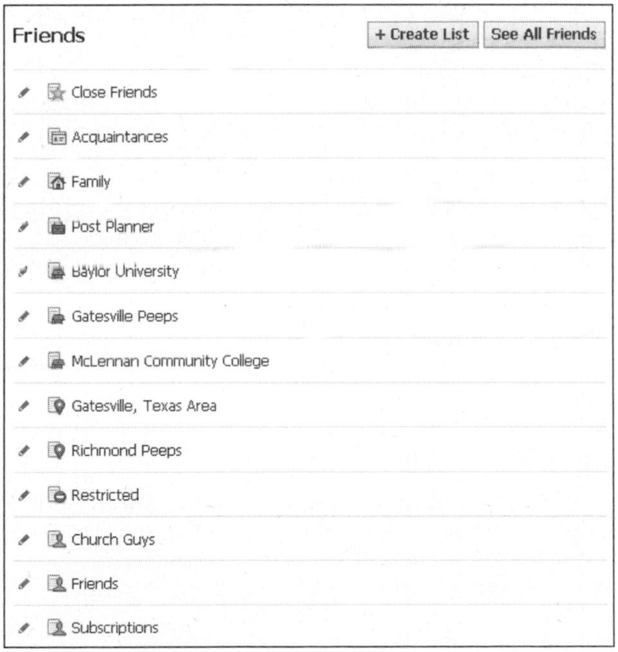

Figure 4-3:
Find your lists in the sidebar under Friends.

You can also use lists to conceal your chat availability. To do that, just click the gear icon at the bottom of your Facebook chat window (it's on the right side of your page). From the menu, choose Advanced Settings. In the dialog box that appears, you can customize who can and can't see you on chat. Click to select one of these options:

✦ **Turn on Chat for All Friends Except:** This option allows you to type specific Facebook friend names or list names in the text box. Those individuals (or those on a list) won't see you as available to chat.

✦ **Turn on Chat for Only Some Friends:** Type the names of Facebook friends or lists you want to be able to see you. This option is handy if you want only a few people to know you're available to chat.

✦ **Turn Off Chat (Go Offline):** If you don't want to be available to chat, select this option. None of your Facebook friends or lists will see you as available.

Facebook creates several smart lists to help you organize your friends, family, and colleagues so you can better track their status updates. These lists compare your shared information about work, education, family, and city with the shared information of your Facebook connections. When there's a match, Facebook adds that person to your smart list. Facebook continues to update these lists as you add or remove friends from your contacts or as your friends update their information. The smart lists Facebook creates are as follows:

✦ **Family:** Facebook populates this list with people you have said you're related to or vice versa. You can add or remove people as appropriate.

✦ **School:** Facebook creates a list for both high school and college/university (if you share that information), and then autopopulates those lists with people from your friends list who have indicated they went to the same high school or college as you. You can edit this list, so feel free to add or remove people as necessary.

✦ **Work:** Similar to school lists, Facebook creates a list (or lists) based on your shared work history. Facebook tries to populate this list with others from your friends list who indicate that they've also worked at a company you shared. If you manually add someone to a work list, Facebook notifies that person.

✦ **Your city:** This is another autopopulated and autoupdated list. Facebook places friends you're connected to in this list, and if anyone updates his or her information to include this city, that person is added to this list automatically. Again, you can edit this list accordingly.

In addition to these smart lists, Facebook creates the Acquaintances and Close Friends lists. Technically, these aren't smart lists because Facebook doesn't automatically populate them or update them, but the lists are there for you to use. You can add people to and remove people from the lists as you like.

Although you can't delete a list made by Facebook, you can add or remove people from those lists or hide the list.

Creating a list

You don't have to use any of Facebook's premade lists, and you can definitely create your own. To create your own list, follow these steps:

1. **Click the Friends link in the left sidebar.**

2. **Click the Create List button at the top of the page.**

3. **In the dialog box that appears, type the name of the new list.**

4. **Type the name of any friends you want to add as members of this list.**

5. **Click the Create button.**

6. **Click the Add Friends link box to add more friends to the list.**

   Use the drop-down list on the dialog box to choose the type of information to use for population. You can choose Friends, Pages, or Following. You can even choose items from each of those options for inclusion in a single list.

If you click the title of a list, you can type an update on that page that is visible only to the people included on that list.

Making a list a favorite

The order of your lists in the left sidebar changes to show the one you most recently edited at the top. If you find you have specific lists you want to check often, we suggest you add them to your favorites (so that the lists are easily accessible). The Favorites list appears at the top of the left sidebar on the news feed page, as shown in Figure 4-4.

Figure 4-4: Your favorites are shown at the top of the left sidebar.

Add a list to your favorites by following these instructions:

1. **Move your cursor over the list you want to move to your favorites.**

   A pencil icon appears to the left of the list title.

2. **Click the pencil icon and choose Add to Favorites from the menu.**

   The list title moves from the Lists menu to the Favorites menu in the left sidebar.

You can change the order of the Favorites menu by moving your mouse over any item in the Favorites list, clicking the pencil icon that appears, and choosing Rearrange from the menu. At that point, you can click and drag any item to a new position in the list. When you're happy with the new order, click the Done link.

Managing your lists

Lists are most useful when they work in a way that fits your workflow. You may find that you need to rename a list; add or remove friends, business pages, or followers from a list; customize what information is shared via a list; or delete a list that is no longer relevant. The editing options you have depend on the list you want to edit. We explain each option in the following sections.

Rename List option

To rename a list, simply click the name of the list, click the Manage List button, and choose Rename List from the menu. A text box appears at the top of the page, as shown in Figure 4-5. Just type the new name there and click Save. *Note:* Not all lists have the option to rename them (for example, you can't rename Close Friends).

Figure 4-5:
Use the text box at the top of the page to rename your list.

Add/Remove Friends option

The Add/Remove Friends option doesn't just apply to friends — you can also add or remove business pages or subscriptions to some lists. To add and remove friends from any list, regardless of whether you or Facebook created it, click the name of the list, and click the Manage List button. Choose Edit List from the menu, and a dialog box appears, showing pictures of the people on this list. In the top-left corner, click the Friends drop-down list to see whether business pages and followers are available to edit. You can also choose On This List to see people, business pages, or followers already included in a specific list. To add or remove a friend, business page, or follower, simply click the picture (a check mark appears by the picture to show it's selected), and then click Finish.

When you accept a new friend or send a friend request, be sure to put that person in a list right then. This way, you don't forget, and the settings apply to your new friend immediately.

Choose Update Types option

Rather than see every update from the people on a given list, you can customize the information you see by following these steps:

1. **Click the name of the list you want to edit.**

The news feed switches to show the updates from people included in that list, and a Manage List button appears in the top-right corner.

2. **Click the Manage List button and choose the Choose Update Types option.**

The menu now includes a list of the types of updates you'll see. The default is to show all types of updates. To not see a particular type of update, click to deselect it.

3. **Click the type(s) of updates you don't want to see in your news feed (for example, Games).**

4. **When you're finished, click anywhere on the page to close the list, and your settings are saved.**

Delete List option

You can delete some lists if you find they aren't useful to you (again, not all lists have this option). Deletion can't be undone, but any content you shared with people in a list is still visible to those people even when the list is gone. To delete a list, click the name of the list you want to get rid of, click the Manage List button, and choose Delete List from the menu. A warning message appears to remind you that your actions are permanent and content is still visible to people in the list. Click Delete List to finish.

Discovering Interest Lists

Like regular lists, interest lists allow you to follow your favorite people, friends, and business pages in one place. The difference between a regular list and an interest list is that when you set up your interest list, others can follow it — and you can follow the interest lists others create. It's another great way to control what you see in your news feed.

It's becoming harder to have your business page updates show up in people's news feeds unless they regularly interact with your page. If your brand is on Facebook, interest lists have the potential to increase your reach each time your business page is included in a list. Why? The people subscribing to a list are particularly interested in those people and business pages sharing relevant information — they are a targeted audience that is more likely to interact with your content.

To find your interest list, navigate to your news feed and scroll down until you see the Interests category at the bottom of the left sidebar. If you don't see the Interests category, click the More link at the bottom of the sidebar.

Below the Interests category title, you see the interest lists you've created or followed. Don't worry if you haven't created or followed any lists; we explain how to do those things in the next section.

Creating or following an interest list

If you'd like to keep tabs on groups of people and business pages, you can create an interest list to do that. As we explain earlier, interest lists are handy because they aren't private to you (unless you set the list privacy settings to Only Me), and you can share your list(s) with others. This is an excellent way to promote topics, brands, or people you support. You can also follow lists that others create.

In the preceding section, we explain how to find your interest list in the left sidebar. From there, you can create a new interest list either by clicking the Add Interests link in the left sidebar or by clicking the Add Interests button at the top of the main column. The main column shows a list of interest lists created by others that you may like. At this point, you can do three things:

✦ **Follow a list.** To follow a suggested list, click the Follow button next to any list you want to follow.

✦ **Search for lists that may be of interest to you.** Type a topic or keyword in the search text box, and Facebook autopopulates the list with relevant interest lists that you may want to follow. Click the Follow button next to the lists you want to keep up with.

✦ **Create an interest list.** We explain how to do this next.

To create a list, follow these steps:

1. At the top of the main column, click the Create List button.

The Create New List dialog box appears, as shown in Figure 4-6.

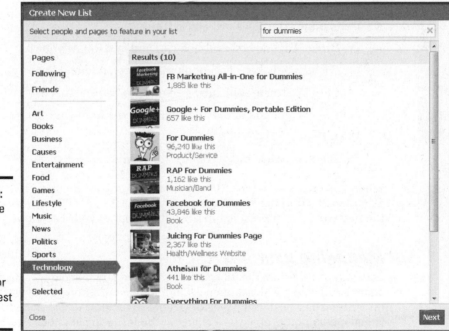

Figure 4-6:
The Create New List dialog box offers several choices for new interest lists.

2. (Optional) Click one of the category choices in the left sidebar.

If you choose Pages, Following, or Friends, you need to type a name in the search text box at the top of the dialog box or scroll through the images shown. Facebook autopopulates results based on what you type.

If you choose one of the other categories (such as Art, Games, or Technology), Facebook finds and shows results related to that category (you may or may not already Like these business pages).

3. **Click the picture of all the items you want to include in your interest list.**

You can also use the search text box at the top of the dialog box to find friends, people, or business pages you follow, and add them to the list as well. Remember that you don't have to click the Follow button on a business page to be able to add the business to your interest list.

4. **Click Next when you're finished. (You can add to the list later.)**

The settings page for your list appears.

5. **In the List Name box, type the name of your list.**

The list name can be whatever you like, but we suggest using common, descriptive words so that others can easily find your list.

6. **Determine your list's privacy settings:**

- *Public:* Anyone on Facebook can find and follow your list.

- *Friends:* Only your Facebook friends can find and follow your list.

- *Only Me:* You are the only person who can see this list.

Followers can't add items to or delete items from your list.

7. **Click Done.**

Facebook displays the news feed for your interest list.

When you create an interest list, it shows up in your regular news feed. You also have the option of reading that interest list's specific feed by clicking the name of your interest list in the left sidebar of your Facebook home page.

Managing your interest list

Your interest lists are meant to evolve. Maybe you'll decide to change your share setting so a wider audience can follow your interest list. Or you may find interesting business pages or people to include — on Facebook, another social media platform, or in real life. In the following sections, we explain how you can manage your interest list.

Changing your interest list's share setting

While looking at the news feed for the list you want to manage, at the top of the middle column, you see the title of your interest list, who created the list (in this case, you), and how many people currently follow your list. You also see an icon indicating the share setting for this list. You can click that icon and change the share setting for your list, as shown in Figure 4-7. Choose the setting that you want, and it takes effect immediately.

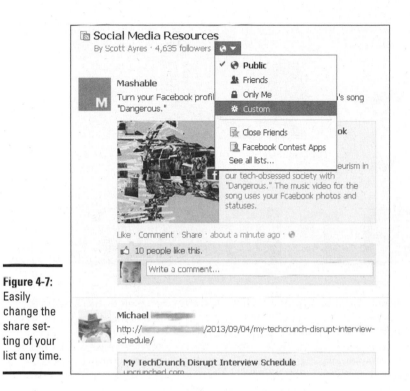

Figure 4-7:
Easily
change the
share set-
ting of your
list any time.

Managing other aspects of your interest list

While looking at the news feed for the list you want to manage, click the Manage List button at the top of the right column. The following options are available:

✦ **Rename List:** Choose this option if you want to rename your list. In the text box that appears at the top of the middle column, type the new list name. Click the Save button to save and implement your changes.

✦ **Edit List:** Choose this option if you want to add or delete people you follow, business pages, or friends from your list. In the dialog box that appears, click the items you want to remove (you can add them back later, if you like). Use the drop-down list in the top-left corner of the dialog box to filter your options by Friends, Pages, or Following, and then type a name in the text box in the top-right corner. Facebook auto-populates a list of items you can add to or delete from your interest list. Click the Finish button to save your changes.

You can navigate directly to a business page or personal timeline to add it to your interest list. For example, Scott visited the For Dummies Facebook Page (www.facebook.com/fordummies) so he could add it to his interest list for social media resources (www.facebook.com/lists/3064736890271). Figure 4-8 shows how he used the gear icon and its menu to add the business page to his interest list.

Figure 4-8:
Visit business pages or personal timelines to add them to your interest list.

✦ **Choose Update Types:** Just like with friends and followers, you can choose which status updates appear in your interest list's news feed. Click Choose Update Types to see the list of options. By default, all options are chosen. To remove an option from the news feed, click it. (Its check mark disappears.) This option is another way to exert more control over the information you see in your news feed so it's not cluttered with stuff you're not interested in.

✦ **Notification Settings:** This option lets you decide if you want to receive a notification when others choose to follow your list. Click Save to save and implement your changes.

Any changes you make to your notification settings apply to all your interest lists, not just the one you're currently editing.

✦ **Delete List:** You can delete an interest list at any time. Choose Delete List, and the Delete *(Interest List Title)* dialog box appears. If you choose to delete a list, it's permanent. You can't reinstate the list later. However, you can create a new interest list (with the same name, even) and add the same friends, followers, and business pages to it. Keep in mind, though, that anyone who followed your list will have to refollow your new list. Click Delete List if you want to continue to delete your list.

Sharing your interest list with others

We mention earlier that one of the features that sets interest lists apart from regular lists is that others can follow your interest lists. To gain followers, you need to share your list to get the ball rolling.

To share a list with others, go to the main news feed for that interest list, and click the Share button at the top of the right column. The Share dialog box appears, and now you can share your list through your own timeline, a friend's timeline, a group, your own business page, or a private message. Use the drop-down list to choose the share option you want to use. Write a quick update inviting others to follow your list (be sure to explain what your list contains and why people would want to follow), and then click the Share button.

You can't share interest lists that are set to appear only to you. To change the share setting for a list, see the "Changing your interest list's share setting" section, earlier in this chapter.

If you share your interest list via a status update, several cool things happen. The status update shows a block of the people or business pages included in your list. When users or fans move their cursor over that block of images, it expands as shown in Figure 4-9. Now the user can click each link to go to that business page or timeline.

Figure 4-9:
See a limited list of the timelines and business pages in your interest list.

The user can also click the See Full List link to see all the personal timelines and business pages in your interest list in a dialog box similar to the one in Figure 4-10.

Figure 4-10:
See a full list of the personal timelines and business pages in your interest list.

The dialog box includes a link to each timeline or business page, as well as the option to Like individual business pages or follow timeline updates.

Chapter 5: Finding Help

In This Chapter

✔ **Finding answers to your Facebook questions**

✔ **Getting help from others in forums**

✔ **Protecting yourself online**

✔ **Finding helpful resources outside Facebook**

As you use Facebook, you'll invariably have questions about how to do something, where to find information, or whether an action is against the Facebook terms of service. In this chapter, we explain how to find Facebook Help Center so you can find answers to your questions. We also show you where you can find information about online safety and privacy for both children and adults.

The Facebook help files cover many topics, and most answers are concise. If you're looking for more complete information, this book and a few resources we point you to later in this chapter will help.

Using Help Center

You can find Help Center at `http://facebook.com/help.php` or by clicking the down arrow or gear icon at the top of the page and choosing Help. The screen shown in Figure 5-1 appears.

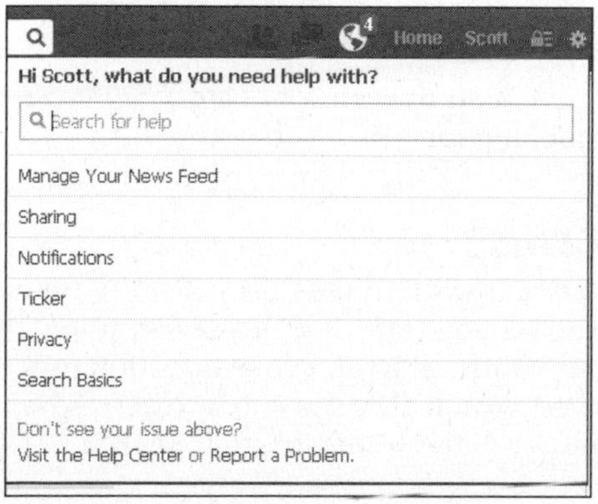

Figure 5-1:
Search for
an answer.

Click the Visit the Help Center link at the bottom of the screen. The Facebook Help Center page, shown in Figure 5-2, appears. On this page, you see

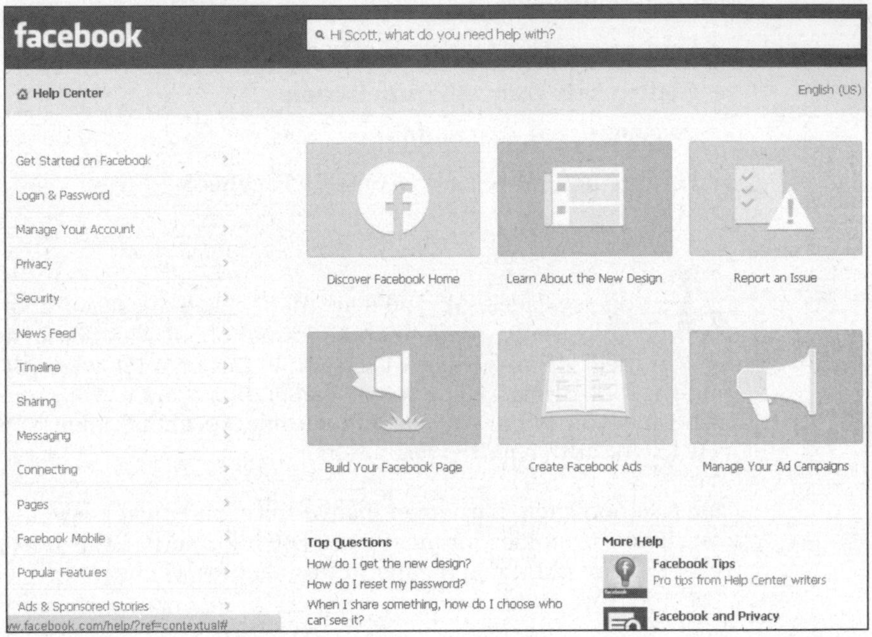

Figure 5-2:
The main Help Center page offers several options.

* ✦ Links to overall help topics

* ✦ A search text box so that you can search for help on a specific topic

* ✦ The Facebook Help Feed, where you can find tips from Facebook about recent updates

* ✦ Community Forum and Feedback links

The following sections provide an overview of each help topic to help you find exactly what you're looking for.

Searching Help Center

If you know what you need help with, it may be easiest to type a keyword or question in the text box. As you type, Facebook autopopulates a list of related questions. You can continue typing your question or term, or you can choose one from the list. You'll also see a link to see more results, which will take you to Help Center–related items for your search.

Facebook returns related questions and answers (even if they aren't exact matches). You can click a question to expand it to show the full answer. If you want to share the question and answer with others, you can click the permalink option under the question to see a single page with the question and answer. Now you can copy/paste the URL (or permalink) for this article and share it on your blog, in an e-mail, on Twitter, or anywhere else you may want to. Or you can click the Share link below the question to share a link to the question and answer on your timeline, a friend's timeline, a group, a business page, or by private message. Use the drop-down list to choose which one to use. Type an explanation in the text box to give some context, and then click the Share Help Content button to share the question and answer.

You can also click the share drop-down list (which sports two silhouettes, a globe, a lock, or a gear, depending on your current settings) to share a link to the question and answer on your timeline, a friend's timeline, a group, a business page, or by private message.

Searching specific help topics

In the left sidebar of the Help Center page, Facebook provides a list of common help topics. When you click a main category, you're shown more specific categories and related questions. You can click each question to expand it and see a detailed answer. In addition, each question and answer has its own permalink or the option to share the question and answer with others.

In addition, the center of the Help Center screen displays six topics that provide answers to the most common questions:

+ **Learn about Graph Search:** Read a description of Graph Search, which is the search box you see everywhere you go on Facebook.

+ **See What's New on Facebook:** Learn about all the changes on Facebook and give Facebook feedback about the changes.

+ **Report an Issue:** If you see something that you feel violates the Facebook guidelines, you can report the user or status update here. Facebook has strict policies and terms of service to protect its users from inappropriate content, bullying, spamming, and other undesirable nuisances.

Facebook has provisions to remove content that violates its terms of service. If you think that a person or business is violating those terms, you can report them, and Facebook will take action if necessary. Any reports you make to Facebook are confidential. The person or business you report will not know who alerted Facebook.

+ **Build Your Facebook Page:** Find in-depth resources that will answer your questions about setting up and running a business page.

✦ **Create Facebook Ads:** Visit this section to understand the Facebook ad guidelines, find answers to questions about scheduling and payment of ads, and much more. This section is geared less toward individual users and more toward businesses and brands, because those are the audiences who generally use Facebook ads and featured stories.

✦ **Manage Your Ad Campaigns:** Find answers to questions about managing your budget, deleting a campaign, editing ads, and more.

Just below these six topics is a Top Questions area that lists the top five questions asked in Help Center. Click any one to go directly to the answer.

Using the community forum

When you click the Community Forum link (at the bottom of the left sidebar on the main Help Center page), you're presented with the Browse Questions page, as shown in Figure 5-3.

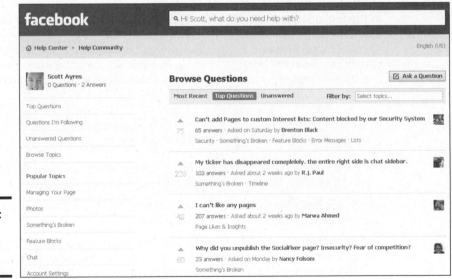

Figure 5-3: See what others are asking.

In the left sidebar, under your profile image, are links to questions you're following and questions you've asked or answered. This is a great reference point to find out if your answer was accurate or not. Next in the sidebar are links to popular discussion topics.

The Browse Questions area in the center of the page has the following three tabs:

✦ **Most Recent:** A list of the questions asked by Facebook users most recently.

✦ **Top Questions:** A list of questions with the most answers and the most votes.

✦ **Unanswered:** Answer a question in the forum before anyone else does.

Click a tab and then click a topic link to see a list of questions from others in the Facebook community.

To ask a question in a forum, click the Ask a Question button in the upper right. The form shown in Figure 5-4 appears. Fill out the form as completely as possible. Include a screenshot if possible. Then click the Post button to post your question to the forum. When asked, decide whether to post your question or change it.

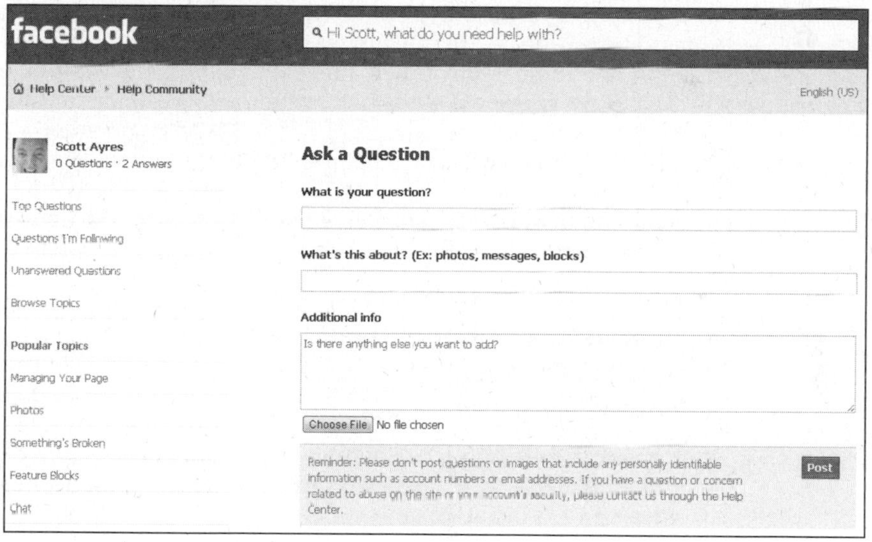

Figure 5-4:
The simplified Ask a Question form.

> **facebook**
> 🔍 Hi Scott, what do you need help with?
>
> ⌂ Help Center › Help Community English (US)
>
> **Scott Ayres**
> 0 Questions · 2 Answers
>
> Top Questions
> Questions I'm Following
> Unanswered Questions
> Browse Topics
>
> Popular Topics
> Managing Your Page
> Photos
> Something's Broken
> Feature Blocks
> Chat
>
> **Ask a Question**
>
> **What is your question?**
>
> **What's this about?** (Ex: photos, messages, blocks)
>
> **Additional info**
> Is there anything else you want to add?
>
> Choose File | No file chosen
>
> Reminder: Please don't post questions or images that include any personally identifiable information such as account numbers or email addresses. If you have a question or concern related to abuse on the site or your account's security, please contact us through the Help Center.
> | Post |

Remember that anything you type here is public and can be seen by anyone using Facebook. Your privacy settings do not apply here.

Getting additional tips

The Facebook Tips business page (www.facebook.com/facebooktips) is a great place to find tips on using Facebook. This page is updated at least a few times a month. If you don't want to check Help Center for updates, you can Like the Facebook Tips page to see its updates in your news feed.

Expecting a response from Facebook

Facebook has over 1.19 billion active users but just under 6,000 employees (see http://facebook.com/press for more Facebook stats). As you can imagine, it's hard for Facebook to address individual inquiries. Unless your issue is legal in nature, Facebook doesn't usually respond to individual questions or issues. Instead, it's best to go through the proper channels and submit the Facebook form associated with the problem you want to solve.

For instance, if you want to report a spam comment left on a status update you made, you can move your cursor over the comment, click the X that appears in the right corner of the comment, and choose whether to delete the comment or report it as spam or abuse. If you need to report a business page, click the gear icon below the cover photo and then click the Report Page link.

Finding Important Facebook Documents

Facebook has specific guideline documents and forms to address particular issues. The problem is that users may not know that the documents exist or where to find them. Many times, these documents provide the most efficient way to answer your own questions or contact Facebook for help.

You may find the following web pages helpful as you navigate Facebook:

✦ **Statements of Rights and Responsibilities:** `www.facebook.com/terms.php`

✦ **Facebook pages terms:** `www.facebook.com/terms_pages.php`

✦ **Promotions guidelines:** `www.facebook.com/promotions_guidelines.php`

✦ **Advertising guidelines:** `www.facebook.com/ad_guidelines.php`

✦ **Report an infringing username:** `www.facebook.com/help/contact.php?show_form=username_infringement` (useful when you need to enforce a trademark)

✦ **Report claims of copyright or intellectual property infringement:** `www.facebook.com/legal/copyright.php`

✦ **If your business page is disabled:** `www.facebook.com/help/contact/357161520978587`

✦ **If your personal timeline is disabled:** `www.facebook.com/help/contact.php?show_form=disabled`

✦ **Facebook site governance page:** `www.facebook.com/fbsitegovernance`

Mari Smith's website has an excellent resource listing 120 Facebook forms you may find useful. The list is updated regularly. You can find it at `www.marismith.com/how-to-contact-facebook-a-directory-of-120-forms`.

Finding Additional Facebook Resources

If you're interested in staying up-to-date on Facebook updates, we suggest checking out a few blogs that make it their business to share Facebook's newest features and how they may affect your personal timeline or your business page. Here are a few of our favorites:

✦ **AllFacebook** (www.allfacebook.com or www.facebook.com/allfacebook) is an unofficial Facebook resource updated several times a day. Articles discuss everything from breaking Facebook news to weekly top pages at Facebook. You can also find tutorials and case studies.

✦ **Inside Facebook** (www.insidefacebook.com or www.facebook.com/insidefacebook) has been dedicated to Facebook since 2006 and is one of our go-to sources for Facebook updates, Facebook marketing, and ideas for using applications on Facebook in new ways. Inside Facebook is home to the *Facebook Marketing Bible,* an extensive how-to for getting the most out of your Facebook business efforts. The book isn't free, but this site regularly shares some of its content in abbreviated form for free.

✦ **The Facebook Newsroom** (https://newsroom.fb.com/) is the official Facebook blog. It's not updated regularly, but it will keep you abreast of major updates or changes to functionality across the platform.

Book II
Connecting with Others

Contents at a Glance

Chapter 1: Creating Your Social Media Persona 93

Chapter 2: Posting and Interacting 105

Chapter 3: Sharing Photos 117

Chapter 4: Sharing Videos 133

Chapter 5: Participating in Groups 145

Chapter 6: Going Mobile 157

Chapter 7: Keeping Up with Events 171

Chapter 8: Having Private Conversations 187

Chapter 9: Games and Gifts 197

Chapter 10: Professional Networking 209

Chapter 11: Managing Connections Gone Awry 221

Chapter 1: Creating Your Social Media Persona

In This Chapter

✔ Understanding the Facebook news feed

✔ Finding your voice on Facebook

✔ Expanding your world by using Graph Search

✔ Developing your business and personal branding

✔ Deciding what to put on a page

✔ Becoming a resource for your friends

✔ Watching your words and behavior

Facebook is a place where you can connect with friends, build a brand, and share your thoughts and experiences with an audience. The Update Status text box at the top of the screen asks "What's on your mind?" to help prompt you to share.

Digging into Facebook is simple enough, but many people find themselves sitting in front of their screen wondering what to say. Sometimes "What's on your mind?" is the hardest question to answer.

In this chapter, we help you answer that question. You also discover how to best feature your personality through Facebook from the point of view of *lifecasting*. You also find out how to add value and enjoyment not only for yourself but also for others.

Understanding News Feed

When you log in to Facebook, the default view is your home page, where you will see the Update Status text box and, just below it, the news feed. See Figure 1-1.

The news feed has two views: top stories and most recent. The most recent view displays all posts and activity from your friends, starting with the most recently posted. The top stories view, which is the default, displays the current top news based on Facebook's understanding of your interests and how you've interacted with other people and pages. In this view, the news feed doesn't show everything your friends have shared.

Update status box

Views

News feed

Figure 1-1:
Facebook
displays
your news
feed on your
home page.

Facebook's news feed is managed by an algorithm called News Feed algorithm, which helps decipher what is most interesting and relevant to you based on your activity. (To find out how this algorithm works and what it means to you, take a look at Book V, Chapter 3.)

Here's an example of how the News Feed algorithm determines what appears in your news feed's top stories. If your mother posts Facebook updates every day about how much she loves her children, and you comment on each one, saying thank you, you'll see all updates from her in your news feed. If your friend Bob posts every day but you never Like or comment on his posts, you'll seldom see his updates in your news feed's latest news. Facebook highlights the people you're most interested in and shows less of those you're not interested in.

Knowing about Facebook's top stories view and News Feed algorithm is important because you can begin to filter your news feed as you want. On the flip side, you'll naturally develop an audience for your updates among those who are most interested in what you have to say. If your primary audience consists of your social friends, you may do better to talk about interesting experiences in your social life. If your audience consists of professional connections, you may find that they're more interested in what you're doing in your work or business life.

The news feed plays a big role in your Facebook success, and you're the star of the show! If you want to get the most out of Facebook, knowing your audience is critical, whether you're using Facebook for personal interests, professional interests, or a mix of both.

If you like to post irrelevant or annoying content, you should be aware of the power of the news feed. Users can choose to hide some or all updates from particular users. Be careful not to be a nuisance on Facebook, or you may be subject to the hide option!

The beauty of Facebook is the power of permission. You connect with people to whom you give permission. They see your updates only if they show an interest, and they can remove your updates if they want. If you embrace these factors, you'll get exactly what you want out of Facebook!

Finding Your Voice on Facebook

People are dynamic. We can be passionate, emotional, funny, or relaxed. If you're like most people, you reserve parts of your character for only a few. Consider doing the same on Facebook.

To further illustrate this point, we'll use an extreme but real example. A person has a bad day at work and needs to vent. She posts on Facebook that she hates her job, forgetting that she added her boss as a friend on Facebook. He sees the update and adds a comment inviting her to not come to work anymore. Although you can express your feelings, think before you click the Post button.

That said, Facebook is also about being authentic. But determining your voice depends not only on being yourself but also on determining your goals with Facebook. For example, you might have one or more of the following goals:

+ Share photos with family and friends.

+ Connect with friends and keep up-to-date on happenings.

+ Network and build professional relationships.

+ Find a significant other.

+ Build a personal brand and establish who you are professionally.

These different purposes each call for a different message. Deciding on a goal will help you envision what you want to accomplish on Facebook and help you to find your true voice.

Lifecasting

People are naturally inclined to share their life stories with others, and sharing has reached a new level with the rise in popularity of social networks. Sharing life moments on the Internet is the most common use of social networks. This act of broadcasting your life (or portions of it) in any medium is called *lifecasting*. On Facebook, lifecasting might entail writing status updates about what you're doing and posting photos or videos that highlight moments in your life. Sharing life moments on Facebook is a great way of creating meaningful connections with friends and family.

For a simple example of lifecasting, see Figure 1-2. This user is proud of her creation and wants to share it with others! What easier way to do that than to simply snap a photo on her smartphone and post it on Facebook?

Avoid putting sensitive information on Facebook. Suppose you snap a shot of your friends in front of your open garage. People can now see all valuables within view of the camera. And if your phone stores GPS coordinates with the photo, someone could use this information to find out where you live. (For information about the potential dangers of photos taken from smartphones, visit `http://technorati.com/technology/gadgets/article/why-iphone-photos-are-dangerous/`.) If your timeline set to be visible to the public, anyone can see that photo. Consider your Facebook privacy settings as well. (For the lowdown on privacy, see Chapter 3 of this minibook.)

Figure 1-2:
Sharing
a baby
shower
creation.

Chrissy
September 12 via iOS

Candy baby shower cake

Like · Comment · Share

16 people like this.

People can see only what you allow them to see. You control the level of privacy of different portions of your timeline, as well as the privacy of specific posts.

Embracing differences

Facebook is a great private network or a great open network. Decide what approach works best for your goals. For example, suppose your friend Joe likes to use Facebook to connect with new people and develop new relationships. One of his Facebook goals is to build his personal brand. His Facebook privacy settings are completely open, and he welcomes new connections. By contrast, maybe your cousin Annie uses Facebook to connect mostly with family and close friends. She allows people to subscribe to her public updates, but she limits her personal connections on Facebook to people she's met and talks to regularly. Her privacy settings are stricter.

Neither approach is wrong because people have different goals. Don't feel apologetic if you want to be more open or more private — but don't take it personally if someone else chooses to be more private.

Knowing what people read

If you want to use Facebook as an effective tool for getting the word out about an event, promoting a blog, or simply increasing the level of connection you have with people, you must understand what people read and respond to.

People share on Facebook in different ways. Whereas one person might post on Facebook because they want other people to comment or Like their posts, others post with no desire or expectation for a response. However, most people read and respond to things that they find interesting. Here are some types of updates that tend to get a lot of views and clicks because they catch people's interest:

✦ Interesting pictures or videos

✦ Simple and concise updates

✦ Updates in which a person is tagged

✦ Funny updates

✦ Controversial statements

✦ Questions that require short answers

✦ Links to interesting posts

Photo or video posts and simple, concise updates are the most popular. Remember that Facebook users first skim their news feed, reading headlines. Then they decide what conversations they want to dive into.

How can you use the knowledge of what your friends are likely to click, comment on, or read? Suppose you're trying to promote a yard sale. Instead of posting a text update, you might post a picture of the yard sale sign and, in the comment, list some of the items you're selling. People are more likely to engage with photos, so you'll be more likely to have greater success.

Status updates should be like headlines — short and simple. If you want to share more than a few sentences, use notes to get into more detail. Those who want the rest of the story will read your notes, and those who aren't interested will be spared a long story in their news feed. You can access notes in the Apps section in the left sidebar. For details, see Book VI, Chapter 1.

Using humor and provoking controversy

Using humor is a great way to engage people. Being lighthearted is inviting. Who couldn't use a laugh now and then? One of Jamie's favorite things to post is something funny that happened to him or that he sees online. Facebook provides an opportunity to share things that you find funny and invite others to share their witty retorts.

Controversy is a great way to start a proverbial fire! People are passionate about ethics, religion, politics, and many other topics. Be careful when you post your opinions on these topics. Debate can be fun — and dangerous. Others can be easily upset about what you post or offended by other commenters. If you're okay with starting a spirited debate, go for it! However, if you take people's differences of opinions personally, maybe you should stick to the humorous side of things.

Speaking to your audience

Who are you trying to reach? In this chapter, we assume that you have a goal on Facebook, such as building a brand for your business or strengthening your connections with friends. Whatever your goal, it should help you determine how to connect with your audience and how to be relevant when you communicate with them.

How do you know what is relevant to your audience? People have a tendency to attract those to whom they speak. If you talk about sports, you'll have better connections with sports fans. If you're an enthusiastic business networker, your Facebook friends list will show a slant toward other avid networkers.

On a regular basis, think about your goals and reassess what you want to gain from Facebook. Doing so will help you determine what you should share on Facebook.

Using Graph Search

Graph Search, shown in Figure 1-3, is a Facebook feature that lets you dive deeper into your Facebook community by searching for specific information across people, pages, friends, photos, and other content shared with you.

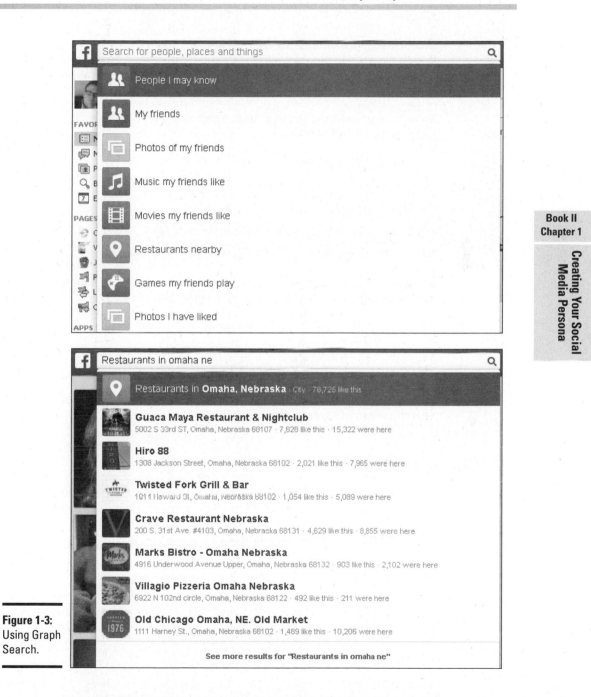

Figure 1-3:
Using Graph
Search.

To use Graph Search, first click in the search box at the top of the Facebook page. (You'll be typing right over the text in the box.) Then type your search phrase. For example, you might type *Friends who live in Philadelphia and like punk music*. As you type, a list of search suggestions appears. Choose one of the suggestions, or finish typing and press Enter.

You can search for different types of information, including your friends' hometowns, educational backgrounds, and interests. You can also search for details about what they like, such as favorite places, restaurants, books, movies, music, and games.

If you're not sure how to begin exploring in Graph Search, try some of the following keyword suggestions:

✦ Photos of fall foliage

✦ Friends who live in my state

✦ Beaches my friends have been to

✦ Italian restaurants nearby that my friends like

✦ Photos of my friends from high school

You can combine phrases, or add things such as locations, timeframes, likes, and interests, to narrow your focus. For example:

✦ Friends who live in Raleigh and work at JumboCorp

✦ Books liked by people who like my favorite books

✦ Photos of my friends in July 2013

Facebook's Graph Search continues to evolve. In the future, you'll be able to search posts, comments, and events.

Building a Brand

Facebook is a great place to build a brand. One of Jamie's Facebook goals was to build a personal brand. (You can say hello to him right now at www. facebook.com/jamiecrager.) Building a personal brand is a little different than building a brand for your business, as you discover in this section.

Building your personal brand

Your personal brand is simply an expression of who you are. In many cases, this is the real you but in a professional context. For example, Jamie has created his professional persona on his personal timeline. His personal brand reflects his active lifestyle, his love of family and friends, and his frequent travels.

Jamie develops his personal brand also through his business page and tends to keep his personal timeline limited to family as well as friends he's met in person. He has also enabled the subscription feature and encourages subscribers. In this way, he can publish some things publicly and keep other things more private.

You may want to express and establish your personal brand through your personal timeline with

✦ Your profile picture

✦ Personal experiences you share through photos and videos

✦ The type of posts that you respond to

✦ The unique and valuable content you share

Because Jamie likes to connect with new people, he relates to his audience by sharing his passions, which include family, friends, and marketing.

To strengthen the professional side of his brand, Jamie had a professional-looking photo taken that he uses across all *his* social platforms to create a seamless and recognizable profile. You don't have to spend big bucks on a photographer; have a friend or family member snap a photo while you are in front of a solid background. And because Jamie values his connections, he respects differences of opinion when he weighs in on a debate.

Building a business brand

When building a brand for your business, you are representing a group of people (your company) rather than a single person. The personality of your business brand on Facebook can be just as lively as your personal brand, but with different considerations:

✦ Create a Facebook page rather than a personal timeline for your business. This is a must. The Facebook terms of service do not allow businesses to create personal timelines; if you do, you could lose your page and your community. We think you'll prefer creating a page anyway because pages have so many more features than timelines, such as custom applications. For the details on pages, see Book IV.

✦ Clearly communicate what your company does.

✦ Create or install customized applications (for example, a newsletter sign-up, an RSS feed for your blog, Google Maps, or even a shopping cart).

✦ Strengthen connections by talking to your customers and responding when they engage.

The ways to build your brand are as vast as the number of business types. Remember that businesses are made up of people. While you're typically speaking to a broader audience with a business page than with a personal timeline, being authentic is still important. If you want to increase customer connections through Facebook, talking about sales won't create the brand perception you want. Merely broadcasting special offers is not inviting and doesn't attract interaction from your customers on Facebook.

A better approach might be to ask questions of customers and start conversations. Establish yourself as the go-to source in your niche by solving a problem, entertaining your audience, or educating them. By giving your customers a reason to come back and inviting them to engage with you, you strengthen connections.

Planning Content for a Page

Oftentimes, companies want to plan the content for their page rather than simply post at will. We say that's a good thing! Here are some of the examples of items you might include on a page:

✦ Links to new blog posts on your website

✦ Promotions for coming events and special offers

✦ Behind-the-scene pictures and videos of your team

✦ Engaging questions for fans

Offer valuable content. Provide information that encourages your customers to interact. If they don't connect with you or interact in any way, your updates will stop showing up in their news feed.

Focus on getting to know your audience, what they respond to, and what time of day they are most active on your page. Then use that information to determine your posting strategy. For details on the performance of your posts, check out Facebook Insights, described in Book V, Chapter 3.

We cover several ideas and best practices for creating a strong business page in Book IV. We also suggest that you check out *Facebook Marketing All-in-One For Dummies*, 2nd edition, by Amy Porterfield, Phyllis Khare, and Andrea Vahl (John Wiley & Sons, Inc.).

Be proper

People often approach the social media world with a more casual and genuine attitude. However, some people let this informal approach go too far and write posts with poor spelling, a bare nod at grammar, little or no punctuation, and text-message abbreviations. Proper grammar, spelling, and punctuation are important because everything you write is a reflection of you or your company

Being a Resource

A friend of ours once spoke of his addiction to news and described Facebook as "hyperlocal news." That description shows how Facebook serves as a resource for some people. Make sure that you're a resource to your readers.

One great way to be a resource is to share online content that you think your friends and fans will find interesting as well. Simply copy the link in the Update Status text box after typing any thoughts that you want to add. Facebook detects any pictures on the web page you're sharing and offers you the opportunity to select a different picture (known as a thumbnail) if the page contains several.

For example, on Jamie's page, he shares news and important information relevant to his community as well as to his niche (social media). Sharing useful information with your audience helps build your brand and adds value to your interactions. If you're using Facebook for your company, consider how you can be a content authority and provide valuable resources that genuinely help your audience. In return, they will look to you for continued guidance and be a core part of your community.

If you still don't know what to say, don't sweat it! Be yourself, but know who you're talking to. The more value you give others, the more you'll get out of Facebook. The Facebook experience is about not just you but also those with whom you connect and share.

**Book II
Chapter 1**

Creating Your Social
Media Persona

Respecting others' privacy

One of the biggest factors of Facebook's success has been the user's ability to choose his or her level of privacy. Some choose to limit their timeline visibility to only friends. Others even have varying levels of privacy for friends. Understanding that others want to protect their privacy is important.

Consider the following tips regarding the privacy of others:

- Don't post information on someone's timeline unless you think the person's other friends will find the knowledge welcome.

- Don't post on the timeline of someone you don't know well.

- If you send a private message to someone who may not be sure who you are, disclose how you know each other.

- Recognize that your comments on a friend's post are public. For example, if a friend posts about having a bad day, she may not be willing to share details in comments.

- When you tag someone in a post, all your friends can see your post, regardless of the tagged friend's privacy settings. Make sure you don't post something that your friend would not like to be made public!

Avoiding Inflammatory or Spammy Behavior

Sure, you don't mean to be a spammer, but if you (accidentally) do the same things that spammers do, how will people know the difference? This advice applies especially to those using Facebook for business networking because some of the fans or followers connected to your business may not know you personally.

Here are some simple tips to help you avoid being mistaken for a Facebook spammer:

✦ **Don't write updates with ALL CAPS.** Some people who write in all caps lack the skill or discipline to capitalize properly. Others are trying to get attention from people who are not interested in their updates. Typing in all caps is the same as yelling, and you definitely don't want to yell at your customers and friends.

✦ **Don't mass-add friends.** When you make a friend request without any context of why you should be connected, many will be deterred and will reject your friend request.

If you want to add someone who you think may not remember you, send the person a private Facebook message, explaining why you would like to be connected. However, some users may have their privacy settings set so that "outsiders" can't send them private messages.

✦ **Do use your own photo as your profile picture.** Remember, this is *Face*book. People appreciate seeing the real you (on your personal time-line) or even your logo (on your business page).

✦ **Don't send private messages with questionable links.** If you share links in a private message, be sure to explain to the recipient what the link is and where it will take them. Sometimes, people won't click a link because it looks too much like phishing. (*Phishing* sites are designed to make people's private information vulnerable to hackers.)

Chapter 2: Posting and Interacting

In This Chapter

✔ **Creating status updates**

✔ **Using replies in business pages**

✔ **Editing updates and comments**

✔ **Interacting with others on Facebook**

✔ **Understanding the follow feature**

The crux of Facebook is sharing real-time information with family, friends, and colleagues. Facebook offers several ways for you to share content with others and to respond to content from others. This chapter explains how you can create and interact with status updates using your personal Facebook account. We also show you how you can use the follow feature to share updates with people who aren't your friends.

If you're looking for info on interacting on your business page, flip over to Book IV, Chapter 3.

Creating a Status Update

A *status update,* also called a *story,* is a short explanation of something you want to share with your Facebook friends. A status update can include just about anything, such as text, pictures, video, and links to a website. Status updates are the main way you share information with others. (You can also use private messages, chat, and comments, but this section focuses on basic status updates.)

To create a status update, you type in the status update text box. You find that box in your news feed and your personal timeline. In your news feed, click the Update Status link at the top of the page. In the text box that appears, you can type your status update, tag people, include your location, attach a file (photo or video), choose a "what are you doing" emoticon, and customize who can see your update.

The status update text box in your timeline, shown in Figure 2-1, offers a little more customization. In addition to tagging, adding a location, attaching files, adding emoticons, and customized sharing, you can add a year or signify that this update is a life event.

Figure 2-1:
Use the status update text box to share content with friends.

As Figure 2-1 shows, you can post a status update as any of the following:

✦ **Status:** This option allows you to post a regular text status update. You can include a link to a blog or website in the update; a preview of the web page will appear with the status update. As we explain in Table 2-1, you also have the option here to tag others, add a year, assign a geographic place, and set the share settings.

✦ **Photo:** If you want to add photos or video, click the Photo icon at the top of the text status update box or the icon below it. We explain how to share photos and video in Book II, Chapters 3 and 4, respectively.

✦ **Place:** You can choose to relate your update to a specific address or general location when you click the Place icon. You can achieve the same thing by creating a regular status update and changing your Place option (see Table 2-1).

✦ **Life Event:** When you click the Life Event icon, you see a menu with the following options:

  • Work & Education

  • Family & Relationships

  • Home & Living

  • Health & Wellness

  • Travel & Experiences

Because life events are usually more important than an average text status update, each of these options has its own submenu that leads to a form to fill out with additional information. You can include pictures, dates, location, and a complete story with each life event update. The life event option is particularly useful as you update and complete your timeline. Book I, Chapter 3 explains how the timeline works in general and why you may want to add events to your timeline.

When you click in the status update text box, icons appear at the bottom of the box, as shown in Figure 2-1 and listed in Table 2-1.

Table 2-1	Status Update Icons
Icon	*What You Can Do*
	Tag people. Click this icon and start typing the names of people you want to tag in your update.
	Add the year. Click this icon to include the year in your status update. If the year is different than the current year, the status update will appear in the correct chronological place on your timeline rather than being posted as a current update. You can also choose the month, hour, and minute if you want to be exact.
	Add a location. Click this icon and make a selection from the list of locations that appears. If you don't see your location, you can type it. You can type the name of a business (say, a restaurant), a city, a state, or even a specific address.
	Share what you're feeling or doing. Click this icon and select from a list of emotions or activities (and accompanying icons) to represent what you are feeling or doing at the moment.
🌐 Public ▼	Customize your share settings. Click this icon to customize how you share an update, before or after you've posted your update. You can share or restrict access to yourself, any person, or any list.

Adjusting how you share content

If you want to change the privacy of a piece of content, you can do that before and after an item is published. When you initially publish something (for example, a text update or link), you can click the share drop-down list to adjust who sees your content. The share list sports two silhouettes (Friends), a globe (Public), a lock (Only Me), or a gear (Custom), depending on your current settings. From the menu, choose to share your update, choose a specific list or specific people, or otherwise customize how you share the item. If you want to change the shares setting for an item you previously published, just click the share icon and change the share setting. Yes, it's that easy!

Everything you share ends up in your friends' news feeds. If you post too much or post uninteresting things, your friends may choose to hide you from their stream or unfriend you.

You can change your notification options right from your news feed. When you see an update from that person, move your cursor over the story, and then click the arrow in the top-right corner. When the menu appears, choose whether you want to get notifications from this specific post. If you want to hide the post, you can choose the I Don't Want to See This option. If you want to be friends but unfollow the person so that you don't see his or her updates in your timeline, click Unfollow. The person will still be able to see your updates, but you won't see his or hers. (And no, Facebook doesn't tell people when they have been unfollowed.)

Adjusting individual privacy settings

When you post a status update, you may want to choose a privacy setting that is different than your default setting. For example, perhaps you want to share a picture with only the people who appear in that picture.

To adjust your privacy settings for an individual post, click the share drop-down list and select Custom. The dialog box show in Figure 2-2 appears. Select the people or groups with whom you want to share that specific content.

Figure 2-2:
Custom
privacy
settings.

> Custom Privacy
>
> ✓ **Share this with**
>
> These people or lists | Specific People or Lists... ▾ |
>
> | Jen McCabe Crager ✕ | Jason Crager ✕ |
>
> Note: Anyone tagged can also see this post.
>
> ✕ **Don't share this with**
>
> These people or lists | |
>
> **Save Changes**   **Cancel**

The new privacy setting becomes the default for your next status update and will appear beside each update. You can change the setting at anytime.

Using hashtags to make content discoverable

A *hashtag* uses the # (number sign) in front of a word, phrase, or topic to change it into a clickable link. If you post something with a hashtag, you or your friends and followers can click that link and see posts on Facebook that include that hashtag. For example, if I click #Houston or #blazefly:

```
Flying to #Houston for #blazefly meetings.
```

I see a feed that contains all the posts and status updates from friends and people I follow that contain those words. You can also search for a hashtag using the search bar at the top of any page.

Note: Not all users have the hashtag feature.

Tagging friends and business pages

Tagging is when you write a status update and provide a link to someone's personal timeline or business page. When you tag a person or page, that person or business is alerted that you've shared something. Figure 2-3 shows a status update in which I tagged my wife Jen. When people see the update, they can click Jen's name to visit her personal timeline. (If I had tagged a business, you could click the business name to visit the business page.) Facebook will alert Jen that I tagged her in a status update.

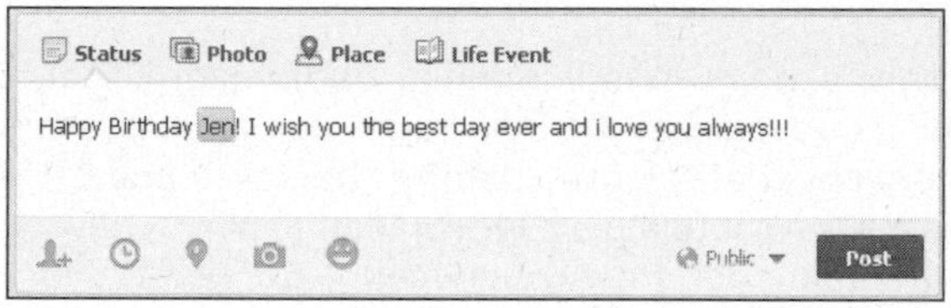

Figure 2-3:
An example of how tags look in a status update.

Status	Photo	Place	Life Event

Happy Birthday Jen! I wish you the best day ever and i love you always!!!

Public ▾   Post

If you tag a friend in a status update, that doesn't mean everyone has access to his or her information. What people see when they click to your friend's timeline will depend on your friend's current privacy settings. (See Book I, Chapter 4 for advice on your privacy settings.)

Tagging a person or page in an update is easy. Type @ and then start typing the name of the person or page you want to tag. For example, if you want to tag Wright's Media in an update, start typing **@Wright's**, and Facebook displays a list of related people and business pages for you to choose from, as shown in Figure 2-4.

Update Status   **Add Photos/Video**

Check out @Wright's Media

Wright's Media
697 like this · 20 were here · 2407 Timberloch Place, Suite B, The Woodlands, Texas 77380

Wright's Media

Wright Tech Media
768 like this · Media/News/Publishing

Wright State University Libraries
570 like this · 418 were here · 3640 Colonel Glenn Hwy (Loop Road off of Center Park Blvd), ...

Gene Wright Composer
1,278 like this · Musician/Band

Figure 2-4:
Use the list Facebook creates to choose whom to tag.

Here are a few tips about tagging:

✦ You can tag up to fifty people or pages in a single status update.

✦ When using your timeline, you can tag people when writing a status update or when commenting on a status update.

✦ You can tag business pages even if you haven't Liked them.

✦ Business pages can't tag individuals in a status update.

✦ Business pages can tag other pages even if the page hasn't been Liked. (See Book IV, Chapter 3 to find out more about how pages can interact with other pages and individual fans.)

✦ Business pages can tag an individual in a comment if that individual left a previous comment in the thread. For instance, suppose someone comments on a post at the Crowdshifter business page. If you aren't Facebook friends with this person, you can't write a new status update and tag that commenter. However, because the person commented on a status update, you can now respond to him or her in the comments section of that same thread and tag that person. Facebook lets the person know that he or she was tagged and can read the response.

It's best to tag people only if you know they won't mind. It's especially important to ask people if you can tag them when you're using Facebook's check-in feature (see Chapter 6 of this minibook for an explanation of Facebook places and check-ins).

If you'd like to control whether people can tag you, adjust your privacy settings. Click the gear icon, click Settings, and then click Timeline and Tagging. You can adjust a variety of settings that help keep Facebook in line with your preferences. (Check out Book I, Chapter 4 for a discussion of your Facebook privacy.)

Allowing Replies to Business Pages

You can give people permission to reply directly to comments left on your business page and start conversation threads, as shown in Figure 2-5. This feature makes it easy to start a discussion or build a community.

When a friend, follower, or fan visits your page, the most active conversations will be featured at the top of your posts. Note that conversation threads are shown in relevance to each viewer and may appear differently based on their connections.

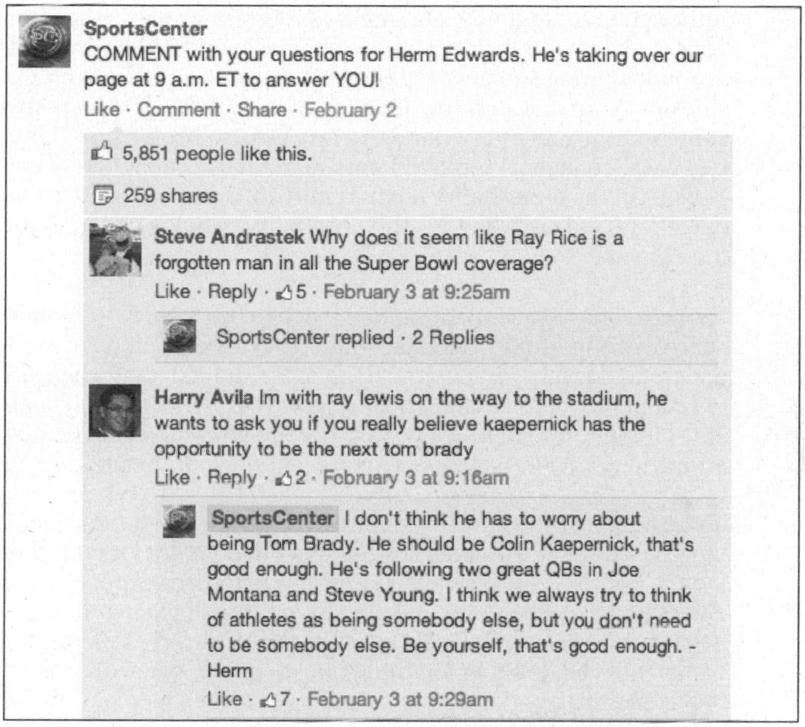

SportsCenter
COMMENT with your questions for Herm Edwards. He's taking over our page at 9 a.m. ET to answer YOU!
Like · Comment · Share · February 2

👍 5,851 people like this.

↪ 259 shares

Steve Andrastek Why does it seem like Ray Rice is a forgotten man in all the Super Bowl coverage?
Like · Reply · 👍5 · February 3 at 9:25am

SportsCenter replied · 2 Replies

Harry Avila Im with ray lewis on the way to the stadium, he wants to ask you if you really believe kaepernick has the opportunity to be the next tom brady
Like · Reply · 👍2 · February 3 at 9:16am

SportsCenter I don't think he has to worry about being Tom Brady. He should be Colin Kaepernick, that's good enough. He's following two great QBs in Joe Montana and Steve Young. I think we always try to think of athletes as being somebody else, but you don't need to be somebody else. Be yourself, that's good enough. - Herm
Like · 👍7 · February 3 at 9:29am

Figure 2-5:
Using replies on your business page.

**Book II
Chapter 2**

**Posting and
Interacting**

To turn on comment replies, follow these steps:

1. **At the top of your business page, click Edit Page and choose Edit Settings from the menu that appears.**

The Settings page appears.

2. **Click Replies.**

3. **Select the Allow Replies to Comments on My Page check box.**

4. **Click Save Changes.**

Removing and Editing Updates and Comments

You may find yourself rethinking something you shared and wanting to remove it. Perhaps, as you update your timeline, you want to remove some past updates as your circle of friends grows or your life changes. Or maybe you commented on someone's status update and you wish you'd been a little more eloquent.

Although you can delete comments (yours as well as those from others on your updates), think first about your reasons for doing so. Social media is about sharing and accessibility. It's about discourse and presenting all sides of a story or an issue. Ideally, that discourse will be respectful, but sometimes it gets out of hand. No one likes to have his or her voice (or, in this case, comment) removed, but sometimes that action is best to keep the peace. On the other hand, if you remove a comment (either yours or someone else's), be prepared for the possibility of being called out for censoring the conversation.

Your timeline is your space, and you decide what is or isn't appropriate for that space. It's important to explain your stance to your circle of friends so they understand your point of view. Remember, though, that when you post content to Facebook, you're inviting people to interact with you and share their opinions on that content. If you choose to remove comments you disagree with, others may not feel welcome to comment on your updates.

If you administrate a business page, removing comments becomes an even bigger issue. Some businesses remove inflammatory or unflattering comments, but that can be a mistake. Your customers expect your business page to be a place where they can interact with you — both positively and negatively. If you whitewash your Facebook business page, allowing good comments and deleting anything questionable, your followers and fans will rebel. (We explain the etiquette and overall management of business pages in further detail in Book IV.)

If you find that you really do need to edit a status update or remove a status update or comment, follow these instructions:

1. **Find the status update or comment on your timeline (or go to your timeline and click the Activity Log button).**

2. **Click the arrow in the top-left corner and select edit or delete.**

3. **Edit or delete a comment as follows:**

   - *To remove your own comment:* Click the pencil icon and choose Edit or Delete.

   - *To remove a comment from someone else:* Click the X.

When you delete a post or comment, it's permanently deleted. You can't get it back. If you don't want to permanently delete a post, you can always change its share settings or hide it from your timeline instead.

Interacting with Other People's Updates

When you share content on Facebook, you're probably doing it so others will interact with it. Let's face it, if everyone just broadcast updates, pictures, and video without receiving feedback, the experience would be boring — and not fulfilling. When we share something, our intent is to have friends comment or Like the content. That interaction is validation that others agree or disagree with us — or an acknowledgment that someone else noticed that we're around and sharing stuff. Either way, we get a sense of satisfaction from those interactions.

Depending on how interesting you found an update, you can interact in the following ways:

✦ **Like:** Clicking the Like button is the easiest way to interact with content on Facebook. When you click Like, you're basically acknowledging that you agree with the status update or like the content of it (whether it's text, a link, a picture, or a video). And if you can't respond right away, clicking Like in a comment is a way to let commenters know you've seen their input.

✦ **Comment:** Responding with a typed message takes a bit longer, but trust us when we say that everyone loves a comment. It's especially nice when those comments lead to a civil discourse on interesting subjects — or build on each other for humorous observations.

✦ **Share:** The ultimate in validation is when you like something enough to share it with your own circle. The person or business page that originally shared an item can see how many times it's been shared.

You can do most of your content interaction via your news feed or the feed for a specific list (see Book I, Chapter 4 for information on lists); you don't have to click to someone's personal timeline or business page to interact with their updates. As you see something in your news feed, you can Like, comment, or share at will.

To share an item, follow these instructions:

1. **Click the Share link below the content.**

The Share This window appears.

2. **Use the drop-down list to choose where to share the content.**

You can share it on your own timeline, on a friend's timeline, in a Facebook Group you belong to, on a business page you administer, or via a private message.

3. **Set the share settings for your update.**

4. **Write a status update introducing the content.**

5. **Click the Share Link button.**

When you share something, it appears on your timeline and in your friends' news feeds (depending on who you shared the update with, of course), and others can see where you found the shared content, as shown in Figure 2-6.

Jeff shared a link.
September 30

Come join the @SiliconPrairie Team: We're hiring an Operations Manager in Kansas City. Get it.

We're hiring an operations manager
www.siliconprairienews.com

Silicon Prairie News has spent almost five years growing its team as a digital media startup, as part of a robust region, to make an impact that resonates around the country. We're preparing to accelerate that

Like · Comment · Share

Figure 2-6:
Sharing
a link.

Understanding How the Follow Feature Works

The follow feature allows a person to follow your public updates without being your Facebook friend. Likewise, you can follow others' public updates if they've enabled the public follow feature. Your account is already set up for following, in fact your Facebook friends already follow you, but you can enable it so anyone can follow you.

The follow feature is handy if you're a celebrity or public figure who may have quite a following but who likes to keep your Facebook friends private or at least confined to those people you've met in person. Or maybe you like to be available to network but still want to keep some things private.

If you have the public follow feature enabled for your account, any time you post content and set the share settings to Public, your followers will see your updates. Those followers will not see any updates that have customized share settings (such as Friends Only).

Adjusting the follow feature settings for your account

To adjust the follow feature settings on your account, just do this:

1. **Click the gear icon on the blue Facebook toolbar and choose Settings from the menu.**

   The General Account Settings page appears.

2. **Click the Followers link in the left sidebar.**

   The Follower Settings page appears.

3. **In the Who Can Follow Me section, select Friends or Everybody.**

   You can select who can comment on your updates, adjust notifications, and add a Follow plugin to your website to attract more followers.

Anyone who clicks the Follow button, whether they are connected to you on Facebook or not, will see your public updates. However, followers will not see your personal data (such as your birthday).

Following other people's updates

You can follow someone's updates as long as that person has selected the Everybody follow option. Just go to the person's timeline and click the Follow button, located in the lower-right of the cover photo. You'll start receiving the person's public updates immediately.

Chapter 3: Sharing Photos

In This Chapter

- ✔ Uploading pictures to Facebook from your computer
- ✔ Using Instagram with Facebook
- ✔ Attaching photos to your comments
- ✔ Making albums to hold your photos
- ✔ Knowing when and how to tag friends in your photos
- ✔ Using applications to share photos on Facebook

*I*t doesn't take long to realize that photos and videos catch attention in your news feed more than simple text updates do. Because pictures stand out, they have a better chance of encouraging interaction (such as a Like, comment, or share). The more an individual interacts with your content, the more Facebook thinks that person wants to see your updates, and the more your updates appear in his or her news feed. (For more discussion on how Facebook determines what shows up in the news feed, see Book V, Chapter 3.)

In this chapter, we explain how to upload images to your personal timeline and your business page, how to create and edit photo albums, and how to tag people in the images you upload. We also introduce you to some third-party applications you can use on your smartphone to upload images to your timeline or business page.

Uploading Images from Your Computer

Facebook displays uploaded photos as a large photo if you upload a single image or a series of smaller photos if you upload several images at a time, as shown in Figure 3-1.

The instructions for uploading images to your personal timeline, a business page, or a photo album are essentially the same, with minor differences in the way the menu is labeled and the ability to tag people when uploading the image.

Photos appear in your news feed unless you customize your sharing options. When you post individual photos to your timeline or news feed without creating an album for them, an album called Timeline Photos is created for you.

Figure 3-1:
Facebook
displays
your photos
in the news
feed.

If you want to upload photos to your business page, you need to navigate directly to your page and start from there. If you want to upload an image and have it associated with your personal timeline, you have a few options. You can

✦ Click the Add Photos/Video link at the top of your news feed page.

✦ Navigate to your timeline and click the Photo link above the status update text box.

✦ Navigate to your timeline and click the Photos link to the right of your personal information under your cover photo.

To upload your image via a regular status update (either on your personal timeline or a business page), follow these instructions:

1. **Click the Add Photos/Video link above the status update text box.**

   Two choices appear. You can upload a photo from your computer or create a photo album.

2. **Click the Upload Photos/Video link.**

3. **Click the Browse button and choose the file you want to upload to Facebook.**

4. **Type a status update related to your photo.**

5. **(Optional) Tag people, add a date and time, link a place, include what you are doing, and customize who will see your image by using the icons in the gray strip below your status update text box.**

6. **Click the Post button to publish your picture and status update in your news feed.**

   Your image is immediately shown in your news feed and placed in the Timeline Photos album. The people who can see your image are determined by your customizations in Step 5. Anyone you tag in the image will be able to see the image.

You may want to use photo-editing software to manipulate your image before you upload it to Facebook. Some photo-editing software allows you to save your image for the web by pulling out extraneous digital information so that your image loads faster on a web page. Unfortunately, saving your images for the web may also cause them to appear grainy when you upload them to Facebook. Photos look their best on Facebook when you save them as .jpg files; other images, such as line art or cartoons, look best when saved as .png files.

Adding Photos with Instagram

Instagram is a free, popular photo-sharing application that can transform photos taken with a mobile device by adding a digital filter, creating unique looks as shown in Figure 3-2.

Figure 3-2:
Instagram integrated with your Facebook profile.

You can integrate Instagram with Facebook in the following three ways:

✦ **Add an Instagram Feed tab on your Facebook page.** Statigram, which is available at `http://statigr.am/instagram-promote`, makes this process easy. You can display your Instagram feed, add a #hashtag feed, and do a whole lot more. Their Photo Gallery widget displays your Instagram photos on your blog or website.

✦ **Add InstaTab to your page:** InstaTab, which is available at `www.facebook.com/instatabapp`, is easy to set up. It enables users to click individual photos and engage with each one.

✦ **Post directly to Facebook through the Instagram app.** The Instagram app is available in the App Store and through Google Play. Simply take a picture on your mobile device or select one in your phone's gallery. Then choose the Share option and select Facebook. To allow Instagram access to your photos, you must connect it to your Facebook account.

Adding a Photo to Your Comments

You can add a photo to your comments, as shown in Figure 3-3. This feature enables you to respond to others not only with words but also with pictures. Include a photo to add humor or to tell a story without a lot of words.

Figure 3-3:
Add a photo to your comments.

To add a photo, simply click the camera icon to the right in the comment section. A pop-up box appears, displaying the contents of your computer. Select the photo from the desired location and click Open.

Creating and Editing Albums

A friend's Great-Grandma Anna used to keep a scrapbook of all the photos she took around her farm. She had formal photos as well as impromptu and illusion photos where she had tried her hand at playing with depth of field to make it look like Grandpa Wayne was holding a pumpkin bigger than he was. All the photos went into an album — and those albums are in a box in a closet. Likewise, Jen has ten or so albums filled with her kids' baby pictures in her closet. Sometimes those albums get pulled out of the closet, but not often. Let's face it, printed photos and albums are passé: Just about everyone is taking photos with their digital cameras or smartphones, storing those photos on their computers, and sharing them with friends via sites like Facebook and Flickr (www.flickr.com) or personal blogs.

Digital albums are handy because you can access your photos any time and share them with friends and family (or the public at large), and they don't take up valuable closet space. Facebook makes it fairly easy to create your own digital photo albums and share your memories (or the latest in your string of shenanigans) with whoever you like. What hasn't changed is the need for organization; storing photos in specific albums on Facebook makes them easier to find later. In this section, we explain how Facebook sorts your photos into albums, and how you can create new albums and control the privacy of those albums.

Any time you upload a photo, Facebook places that photo into an album. Which album your photo ends up in depends on how you uploaded and used the image:

✦ When you upload an image directly to your timeline via a status update, Facebook puts the photo in the Timeline Photos album.

✦ When you want a picture to be part of a specific album, you can upload the photo directly to that album or, if the album doesn't already exist, create an album.

✦ When you share a picture from your phone or other mobile device, Facebook puts the photo in the Mobile Uploads album. See Chapter 6 of this minibook for information on making regular updates with your mobile device.

You can create as many Facebook albums as you want, and you can upload about 1000 images into an album before Facebook considers it full and automatically creates a new album for you (you can edit the new album's name and privacy).

To create an album, you can start from one of two places:

✦ Click the Photo link above your status update text box and choose Create Photo Album, as shown in Figure 3-4. This option works for both personal timelines and business pages.

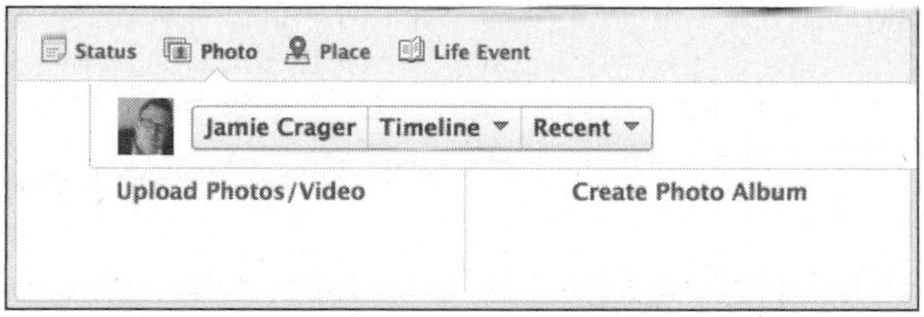

Figure 3-4:
Click the
Photo link
above
your status
update box.

| Status | Photo | Place | Life Event |

Jamie Crager | Timeline ▼ | Recent ▼

Upload Photos/Video   Create Photo Album

✦ Click the Photos link under your cover photo, as shown in Figure 3-5, and then click the +Create Album button in the top-right corner of the page. This option is available only for your personal timeline.

Regardless of your starting point, after you select your first photo from your desktop, the photo album window appears, as shown in Figure 3-6.

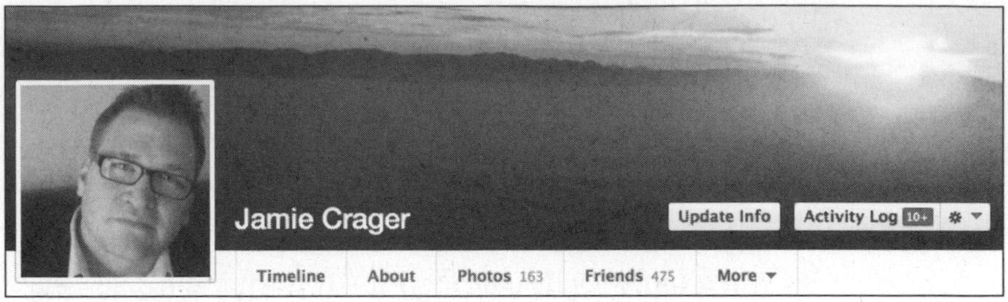

Figure 3-5:
Click the
Photos link
under your
cover photo.

Jamie Crager

Update Info | Activity Log **10+** ⚙ ▾

Timeline | About | Photos 163 | Friends 475 | More ▾

Untitled Album

Say something about this album...

📍 Where were these taken? | Add Date

⇅ Order by Date Taken

Add Photos

Trouble uploading photos? Try the basic uploader.

Figure 3-6:
The photo
album
creation
window.

\+ Add More Photos | ☑ High Quality | Cancel | 🔒 Only Me ▾ | Post Photos

When the photos start uploading, you see the status of your upload (the upload status bar disappears when your images are fully loaded). When your images are loaded, they appear similar to Figure 3-7.

Next, follow these steps:

1. **Type the information you want to include in the album.**

Type the name of the album, the description, the location, and the date. You can also customize the information associated with the photo (as opposed to the album). You can include a comment, tag people, set the date and time the photo was taken, and even provide additional location information.

If you type the name of an existing album, your photos are placed in a new album with the same name rather than in the existing album. To place photos in a specific album, see the instructions in the later section "Uploading new photos to an existing album."

Figure 3-7:
After your new images are uploaded, you can tag them, comment on them, or assign a location.

2. **If you want to arrange the photos in the album so they appear in chronological order or reverse chronological order, click Order by Date Taken.**

3. **If you want to upload more photos to this album, click the +Add More Photos button in the lower-left corner.**

4. **If you want to upload the best version of an image, make sure that the High Quality check box is selected.**

   Note that the image may take longer to upload. If you don't select High Quality, your image may appear grainy. (If you have a poor image to begin with, it will likely still look poor when you upload it to Facebook.)

5. **Set the album's privacy by using the share drop-down list in the lower-right corner.**

   You can choose Public, Friends, Only Me, or Custom. Note that this option isn't available for business pages.

6. **Click the Post Photos button.**

   The Album page appears. From here, you can view the photos in your album or edit your album.

To edit an album, go to your personal timeline or your business page and click the Photos link under your cover photo. On the Photos page that appears, click the Albums link at the top. Then click the picture or title of the album you want to edit, and click the Edit button in the upper-right corner.

The Edit Album page offers editing several options:

✦ **Album Name:** You can change the name of the album by deleting the old name and typing a new one. This option is available for both personal timeline and business page albums.

✦ **Where:** Change the location associated with your album or refine it even more. For example, if you assigned a state location to an album (say, New York), you could change it to reflect the city (New York City), a part of the city (Manhattan), or even a specific location (Dylan's Candy Bar). This option is available for both personal timeline and business page albums.

✦ **Date:** Assign a year and month to your album. You can add a specific date by clicking the +Add Day link. This option is available for only personal timeline albums.

✦ **Description:** You can add or change the description of your album here. This option is available for both personal timeline and business page albums.

✦ **Privacy:** Use the drop-down list to customize your privacy settings for this album. Remember that anyone tagged in a photo that resides in the album can see the photo. This option is available for only personal timeline albums.

✦ **Edit Photos:** Move your cursor over the picture, and click the arrow that appears in the upper-right corner. A drop-down menu appears with the following options: Move to Other Album, Make Album Cover, and Delete the Photo. These options are available for both personal timeline and business page albums.

✦ **Album Contributors:** Add people who are allowed to upload photos to the album and edit information.

When you have finished, click Done to save your changes.

Uploading new photos to an existing album

Photo albums are rarely static, and you probably want to add to them over time. No problem! After you create an album, it's easy to add more pictures to it. Just follow these steps:

1. **Navigate to your personal timeline or business page and click the Photos link under your cover photo.**

2. **Click the Albums link, and then click the album to which you want to add pictures.**

   You're taken to a page for that album that shows all the photos included in that album.

3. **Click the Add Photos button in the top-right corner.**

The Upload Photos pop-up window appears.

4. **Choose the photo(s) you want to upload to your album, and then click Open.**

The Upload Photos dialog box reappears and shows the status of your upload. While you're waiting for your photos to upload, you can edit the information as stated earlier in this chapter.

5. **If your pictures have a recognizable face, click anywhere in the picture to tag a friend.**

6. **Click the Post Photos button.**

The album page reappears and shows all the pictures in that album, including the ones you just uploaded.

Note that you won't see the Add Photos button in the following albums:

✦ **Timeline Photos:** Photos appear in this album only when you post them directly to your personal timeline or business page via a status update.

✦ **Mobile Uploads:** Photos appear in this album only when you upload them from your mobile device.

✦ **Cover Photos:** This album holds only photos you've used as cover photos. (See Book I, Chapter 2 for instructions on how to set your cover photo.)

✦ **Profile Pictures:** This album holds only photos you've used as your personal profile picture. (See Book I, Chapter 2 for instructions on how to set your profile picture.)

✦ **Some third-party app albums:** If you're using a mobile app such as Instagram, you won't be able to manually add pictures to those albums.

If you move your cursor over an album, you can see its pictures without clicking into it.

Moving photos from one album to another

To move a photo from one album to another, navigate to your personal timeline or business page. Then click the Photos link under your cover photo to go to your Albums page. From there, just follow these steps to move your photos from one album to another:

1. **Click the album in which the picture currently resides.**

A page appears displaying all the pictures in that album.

2. **Either click the Edit button in the upper-right corner or the pencil icon that appears when you move your cursor over a photo.**

   Note: The Profile Pictures and Cover Photos albums don't offer the Edit button option.

3. **If you clicked the Edit button, mouse over the picture and click the arrow in the upper-right corner.**

4. **Select the Move to Other Album link.**

   A new page appears, similar to the one shown in Figure 3-8. *Note:* You will see a message alerting you only if the picture you are moving is part of a post.

Figure 3-8:
You can move photos from one album to another.

Move Photo and Delete Original Post?

Select another album for this photo: 👥 Mobile Uploads ▾

Note: This photo is part of a post, so moving it to another album will delete your original post.

[Move Photo] [Cancel]

5. **Click the Move To drop-down list under the picture you want to move, and then select the album to which you want to move the picture.**

6. **Click the Move Photo button.**

   The Album page for the original album appears, but the picture you moved is gone. To see the picture, click the Albums link. On the Albums page that appears, click the album to which you moved the picture.

Editing privacy settings for albums

Privacy is a big issue, especially when it comes to pictures and video. (See Book I, Chapter 4 for a further discussion of online privacy and how you can protect yourself and others.) You can customize not only the overall privacy settings for your Facebook account but also the privacy for individual photo albums in your personal timeline (business page albums are automatically public). First navigate to your timeline, and then follow these steps:

1. **Click the Photos link under your cover photo.**

   The Photos page appears.

2. **Select the Albums link.**

3. **Click the sharing icon to display the drop-down list shown in Figure 3-9, and choose who can see your albums.**

You can choose a general category or list, such as Public or Friends. For finer control, choose Custom and make your selections in the Custom Privacy dialog box that appears.

Figure 3-9:
Determine who can or can't see your pictures.

4. **(Optional) Select an option from the Custom drop-down list, type the name of the people or lists you want to hide the album from in the Hide This From text box, and click Save Changes.**

When you're sharing pictures on Facebook, be aware of the following:

✦ Only the album owner can change the privacy settings. You're in charge of your albums, regardless of who you share them with. And if someone shares an album that contains your picture, that person controls who sees it, not you.

✦ Although you can't change the privacy settings for the Mobile Uploads album, you can change the privacy settings for each picture within that album.

To change the privacy for the individual pictures in the Mobile Uploads album, click the album, and then click the picture you want to work with. The photo viewer appears with that picture, as shown in Figure 3-10. From the sharing drop-down list, select a privacy setting.

✦ If you share an album or a picture with others, they can download those pictures to their computers. If you don't want people to save or share a particular photo (say, if you are doing something questionable or embarrassing), you probably shouldn't upload the photo to Facebook (or anywhere online, for that matter).

Figure 3-10:
Control who
sees your
pictures.

Editing Pictures

Facebook doesn't currently offer the options of full-fledged photo-editing software. If you want control over removing red-eye, enhancing color, or cropping an image, you need to do that with photo-editing software on your computer, such as Adobe Photoshop, Photoshop Elements, or GIMP (free at http://gimp.org). However, Facebook does enable you to do basic edits such as tagging people in a photo, adding a location tag or date to your photo, and rotating your photo.

To find the picture you want to edit, navigate to your personal timeline or business page, and click the Photos link to view your album, photo, and video page. The albums you've created are at the top of the page. You can click any of these to work with a specific photo you've uploaded, or if you scroll down a bit more, you'll see photos and video in which you've been tagged (uploaded by others).

Find and click the picture you want to edit. The picture appears in the photo viewer. Mouse over the image to reveal the options shown in Figure 3-11.

The Facebook photo viewer page has the following options along the bottom of the screen:

✦ **Tag Photo:** You can tag people in photos, videos, and status updates. *Tagging* is like labeling your photo with the names of people who appear in the picture. When you tag people, the photo shows up in their news feed, and they are alerted that you've uploaded a picture of them. To tag someone in your picture, click the Tag Photo button, and then click the person's face. A box appears where you clicked, along with a menu. Type the name of the person you want to tag. You can repeat the process for each person in the picture, if you want.

Figure 3-11:
The photo viewer shows pictures full size and allows you to make several edits.

If you posted the picture to a business page, you can't tag individuals unless the two of you are Facebook friends.

It's considered bad form to tag people or business pages that aren't in your photo. Although Facebook is a social platform, not everyone has the same ideas about how to share on Facebook. You may be fine with others tagging you in photos; others may find it to be an invasion of personal privacy.

Jamie has one friend who scanned in high school senior pictures of people and invited them to tag themselves (few did). We're glad the friend who uploaded the photos didn't tag them herself, but we might go one step further and suggest that if the picture doesn't show you, ask permission before posting it. Not everyone likes to share everything.

Finally, there's the issue of spamming. When you tag someone who isn't relevant to your picture (for example, a Facebook friend who isn't pictured or a business page that doesn't relate to your image), you're spamming them — and no one likes to be spammed.

✦ **Options:** You can edit the location, change the date, rotate the picture left or right, download the image, make it a profile picture, make it a cover photo, get the image link, move to another album, and delete the photo.

When you remove a tagged photo from your personal timeline or business page, the photo is not removed from Facebook. The picture is still visible via the person who posted it originally.

✦ **Share:** When you upload a photo, it appears in your news feed. However, you may want to share a picture again later or share it with a wider audience. Click the Share button, and use the drop-down list to choose where you'd like to share the photo. You have the option of sharing this photo on your timeline, on a friend's timeline, in a group, on your business page (if you administer more than one business page, you see a list of all the pages with which you're affiliated), or via private message. When you've chosen where to share the photo, type a short introduction for the image to give your audience context, and click the Share Photo button.

✦ **Send:** You can send the photo as a private Facebook message, so only the people you sent it to can see it.

✦ **Like/Unlike:** If you want to Like or Unlike your photo, click this button or the link under the photo description.

The top of the right column shows who shared the photo, when they shared it, and how it was posted. Below the photo of the person who shared the photo, you see the photo's caption, followed by the names of everyone tagged in the photo.

Next are the following three buttons:

✦ **Tag Photo:** This button, which is the same as the Tag Photo button under the photo, enables you to tag or add your friends to the picture.

✦ **Add Location:** You have the option of associating a location with your photo. Click this option and type the city or country you want associated with your picture in the Where Was This Photo Taken text box. Click Done Editing to save your changes.

✦ **Edit:** This button allows you to change the description of the photo, tag people who were with you, and set the location of where you took the photo. Just click in the text box that appears; start typing a description, someone's name, or the location; and then click the Save button. ***Note:*** You see this button only if you are looking at your photos. If someone has tagged you, you will not see the Edit button or link.

Next in the right column are options to Like, Comment, Unfollow Post, Share, and Edit.

You also have the option to Report/Remove Tag or Send *[Original Poster]* a message. If you think someone has tagged you unnecessarily in a photo just to get your attention (that is, you're not really in the picture), you can click the Options link under the photo, and then select Report/Remove Tag to mark the image as spam and report it to Facebook or to untag yourself. When you click this link, a dialog box appears, as shown in Figure 3-12. Select the radio button next to the issue(s) you want to report, click the Continue button, and follow the directions. If you accidentally click this link, just click Cancel.

Figure 3-12: Report and remove offensive or spammy photos.

When someone else shares a picture of you and tags you in it, you can click it to edit it, but you'll find that you have limited options because the photo doesn't belong to you — it belongs to whoever shared it. Figure 3-13 shows what a shared photo looks like when you click it.

Figure 3-13: You can't fully edit pictures uploaded by someone else.

Using Smartphone Apps to Share Photos

You won't always be sitting at your computer when you want to upload photos to Facebook. Sometimes you're out and about, and you want to share what you're doing or document an event you're attending. Luckily, several applications for your smartphone are available that enable you to take a picture and share it directly on Facebook. A few you may want to consider are

✦ **Instagram** (`http://instagr.am/; free`): This app allows you to take a picture and choose among several filters to apply before you share the photo. Instagram is one of the most popular photo apps for sharing pictures on Facebook.

✦ **GLMPS** (http://glmps.com/; free): This innovative camera app is currently available only for the iPhone. What makes it stand out from the other apps is that it takes a few seconds of video before it snaps the picture, giving you a better idea of the moment you captured in the picture.

✦ **Camera+** (http://camp1.us/; $1.99): This iPhone app provides a lot of bang for just two bucks. You can set the exposure and focus separately, choose among four shooting modes (including stabilizer and timer), and use the onscreen grid to ensure your photos aren't crooked. When you're finished with the shot, share it on Facebook, Twitter, or Flickr.

And, of course, you can download the Facebook app for your smartphone. The Facebook app allows you to take photos, write updates associated with your photos, tag people, and post everything right from your smartphone. (For more information about using mobile Facebook, check out Chapter 6 in this minibook.)

Chapter 4: Sharing Videos

In This Chapter

✔ Using video to encourage sharing

✔ Uploading video to Facebook

✔ Using apps to share your other video channels on Facebook

✔ Making the most of your video efforts

People on Facebook love video links! After all, the primary goals of Facebook are to connect with people and to share. Video is interesting and easily shared. Also, when you deal with people online primarily through text, sharing a bit of yourself through video allows you to connect with your friends or followers in a more personal way.

Facebook makes it easy for friends and followers to view video: They just click the video and watch it in their news feed. They don't have to view a slideshow (as with images), and they don't leave Facebook (as with clicking a link). Video allows you to interact with your friends and followers on their terms, without asking them to leave their Facebook news feed. When you make Facebook interaction easy for your friends and followers, Facebook rewards you by showing your updates in their news feeds more often. (Facebook uses something called the News Feed algorithm to weight your interactions in Facebook; for more about this algorithm, turn to Book V, Chapter 3.) Video is win-win!

This chapter explains how you can integrate video with your personal time-line as well as your business page. We show you how to shoot video right from your Facebook page, upload video from your computer, and integrate videos from other channels (such as YouTube or Vimeo). We also give you some tips on what kinds of video to share and how to produce great videos.

Benefits of Using Video

The goal of creating video and sharing it on Facebook is to have others also view and share your video content. You probably want all your content shared, but you really want video shared because it counts for so much in the News Feed algorithm.

Consider that the average number of friends a Facebook follower has is 229. When someone shares your video, that video has the potential to be seen by all the followers or friends of that person. When you consider the reach of just one person, you can imagine how a video could go viral quickly if it's shared by several people.

Not many people are using video on Facebook to its full potential. Right now is a great time to be the pioneer and draw people into your business page. Be the first in your niche to embrace it! You can shoot video anywhere and upload on-the-fly if you have your laptop or smartphone with you. It's never been easier to be a roving reporter or share your latest event.

What kind of video should you share? That depends on your audience. Book V, Chapter 2 explains the importance of knowing your audience and giving them what they want — whether they want to solve a problem, learn something, be entertained, or more. Sharing video that gives your audience what they want is the best way to encourage sharing. Here are a few ideas for video to create and share:

✦ **Showcase the best.** Every week, you can showcase a specific product or service to your audience. Sometimes a video does a better job of showing off a product's features than a photo.

✦ **Conduct an interview.** Whether you're interviewing customers with testimonials or simply interviewing an expert in your niche, a video is much more interesting than a written transcript.

✦ **Create a tutorial.** Instructional videos are priceless. Many times written instructions are hard to follow, but a short video showing exactly how to do something is news you can use.

✦ **Be funny.** Most videos shared by friends and fans have one thing in common: They make us laugh. Sharing tutorials or interviews may appeal to part of your audience, but if you want to reach past your audience to their friends, you need to make them laugh. Not every video can be humorous, and that's okay. Just don't be afraid to try something new or step out of your comfort zone.

Another use of video is to connect with your friends and followers in a different way from standard text updates or shared links. If you have something to say fairly quickly, you can create a short video update right from your personal timeline or business page. Facebook video can be a little rough, but it is a quick way to share information with your friends and followers. If you're interested in using a video on Facebook but aren't sure what to discuss, here are a few ideas:

✦ **Ask a short question to start a discussion.** We've seen a few social media business pages do this — fans love it and respond with many comments! Start by asking a general question, briefly give your take on it, and open it up to your fans. You can ask multiple-choice questions, ask questions requiring a one-word answer, or ask about an experience. The goal is to cast a broad net to attract the most answers possible. We think you'll find that people are intrigued by video questions.

✦ **Give a concise answer to a frequently asked question.** If you're receiving the same question over and over, you may want to address it quickly on your business page with a video response. Or, on your personal timeline, you can provide updates to family members (because your most frequently asked question is probably what you're up to personally).

✦ **Promote an event or share highlights from past events.** Offline events are a great way to make a personal connection with your fans. You can create a video invitation to your upcoming conference, book signing, workshop, open house — whatever you're planning. If you have access to video-editing software, you can create a video that includes highlights from previous events, and then upload it to your business page to show fans how much fun they'll have at your event. After your event, use your video-editing software to create and share another highlight reel showcasing your fans who attended (or some of your headlining talent).

✦ **Show off your haul.** Over the past few years, bloggers and vloggers (video bloggers) have started sharing their *haul* (deals they find while shopping). Rather than typing out where you found the deals, what you bought, and how you saved, you can create a video and show off your deal-snagging prowess (and your excitement).

Uploading Video to Facebook

More often than not, you want to share video that you didn't take with Facebook's video app. On Facebook, you can share video from just about any source: a video file from your computer, a video from another social media channel (such as YouTube), or even a video from your smartphone.

Loading a video directly into Facebook, especially for a business page, rather than sharing a link to a video that resides on another platform (such as YouTube), has two benefits:

✦ When you upload a video directly to your business page, Facebook places a link in the top-left corner of the video that encourages people to Like your business page. This link appears only when the user hovers the mouse cursor over the video and appears only to people who haven't already Liked your page.

✦ You can tag others in your video if you're uploading via your personal timeline. When someone is tagged, it shows up in the person's news feed and has the potential to be shared among multiple users.

Sharing video from your computer

First things first: To record a video on your computer, you must have a webcam.

Before you share video from your computer, check that the video is less than 1024MB and less than 20 minutes long. In addition, you must own the video (in other words, you or your friends made the video).

Whether you're posting video to your personal timeline or your business page, you can customize the share setting to determine who sees your video in their news feed. To customize your share setting, click the down arrow next to the Post button.

Because business pages are public platforms, they have fewer customized sharing options.

Although you can limit which followers see your video in their news feed, anyone (follower or not) can visit your business page and click the Video link below your cover photo to see all the videos you've uploaded to your business page. If you have multiple applications or tabs, you may have to click the down arrow to find the video link.

Follow these instructions to upload a video file to your personal timeline or business page from your computer:

1. **Navigate to your news feed or personal timeline and click the Photo link above the status update text box.**

   Facebook gives you two choices: Upload Photos/Video and Create Photo Album, as shown in Figure 4-1.

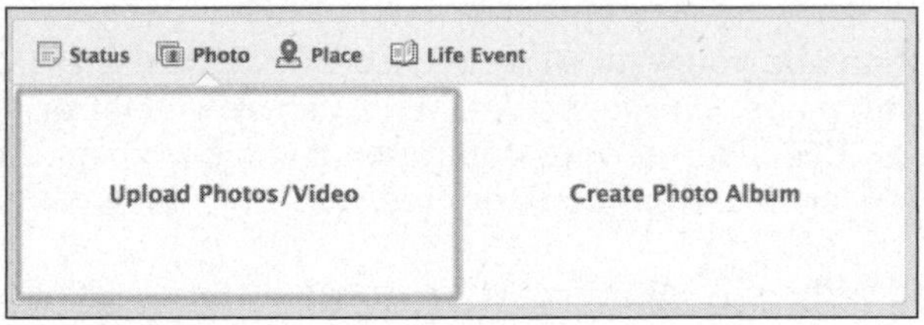

Figure 4-1:
Upload your video.

> 🔲 Status 📷 Photo 📍 Place 🎞 Life Event
>
> **Upload Photos/Video**   **Create Photo Album**

---

2. **Click Upload Photos/Video.**

3. **Type a short status update introducing your video.**

4. **Click the Browse button and find and select the video file you want to share.**

5. **(Optional) Use the toolbar to tag people in your video, assign a location to the video, and set your sharing preferences.**

6. **Click the Post button to publish the video.**

Sharing video from your phone

You can share video from your smartphone in a few ways. We cover using the Facebook smartphone app here, but you can also check out Chapter 6 in this minibook for instructions on using Facebook's mobile upload service.

The Facebook smartphone app doesn't allow you to share video on your Facebook business page. You can share video only on your personal timeline.

An easy way to share video directly from your smartphone is to download the Facebook app from the application store associated with your brand of phone (such as App Store for iPhones or Android Play Store for Android phones).

When you have the Facebook app installed on your smartphone, follow these steps to take video with your phone and share it immediately on Facebook:

Book II
Chapter 4

Sharing Videos

1. **Open the Facebook application on your smartphone.**

2. **Navigate to your personal timeline.**

3. **Tap the Photo button.**

   Your photo gallery appears and you can select one or more photos or videos to upload directly. Facebook allows you to view only the selected photos, not the entire gallery.

4. **To create a video to upload, tap the camera icon in the lower-left corner.**

   Facebook simplifies the interface by letting you choose to take a picture with the center camera icon or the video icon, which is in the lower-left corner. You can choose the front or back camera of your phone and adjust flash options.

5. **Take a video as you normally would with your phone.**

6. **When you've finished recording, tap the Use button.**

   A new page appears with text boxes for Title and Description.

7. **Tap inside the Title text box and type a title for your video.**

   The title appears next to your video in your news feed.

8. **Tap the Description text box and type a description of your video.**

   The description appears as your status update above the video in your news feed.

9. **Tap the Upload button in the top-right corner of the screen.**

   In a few moments, your video will appear in your news feed.

Sharing video from another social media channel

You won't always want to create new video or share video from your computer. Instead, you may find videos to share via websites such as YouTube or Vimeo (two of the most popular video-sharing sites). This section explains how to share videos from those sites on your personal timeline and business page.

Sharing video from YouTube

When you find a video on YouTube that you'd like to share — maybe it's one from your own YouTube channel or one you just found — you can share the video by following these steps:

1. **Click the Share link below the video.**

   An expanded menu appears, as shown in Figure 4-2.

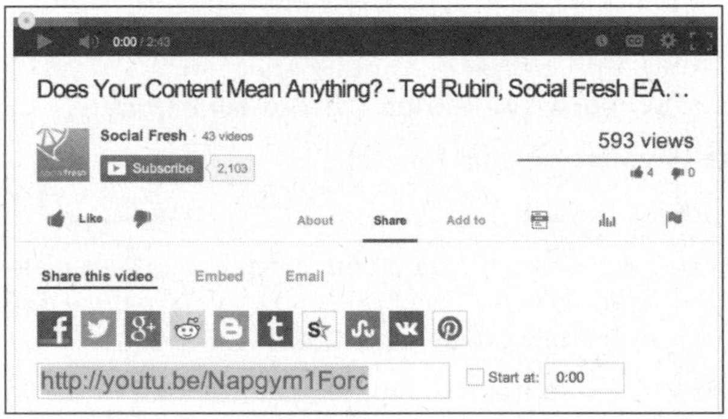

Figure 4-2:
The expanded Share menu on YouTube.

2. **Click the Facebook icon.**

   A new tab opens in your browser, as shown in Figure 4-3.

Figure 4-3:
Sharing content is easy.

3. **In the text box, type a status update to give the video context.**

4. **In the lower-right corner next to Share, use the privacy options to select who should see the video.**

5. **Click the Share button in the lower-right corner.**

Sharing video from Vimeo

When you find a video on Vimeo that you want to share on Facebook, just follow these instructions:

1. **Click the paper airplane (Share) icon to the right of the video, as shown in Figure 4-4.**

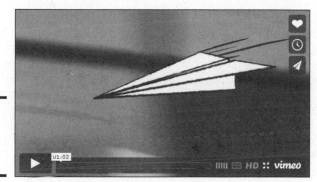

Figure 4-4:
The Vimeo
Share
button.

2. **In the Share this Video dialog box (see Figure 4-5), click the Facebook icon.**

Figure 4-5:
Sharing
a Vimeo
video.

3. **In the text box, type a status update to give the video context.**
4. **Click the Share Link button in the lower-right corner.**

Customizing Your Video

After you've shared a video and it's out in the wild, you can let it run its course or you can customize a few aspects (such as tagging people in the video or editing the title. First, though, you need to find the video you've uploaded to your timeline or business page.

Finding your video on Facebook

To find a video you recently shared on your personal timeline or business page, you can look on your personal timeline or business page to see if it's still visible. If it is, click the title of the video (which is probably something generic like the date and time you recorded the video). If you don't see the video listed on your personal timeline or business page, you can follow these instructions to find it:

1. **Go to your personal timeline or business page and click the Photos link under your cover image.**

    Your Photos page appears.

2. **On the Photos page, click the Albums link, as shown in Figure 4-6.**

    The second album includes all the videos you have created, uploaded, or been tagged in.

Figure 4-6: See all your videos to select one to edit.

3. **Click the video you want to edit.**

    A page appears that lists the video and the editing features. See the next section, "Editing your video," for instructions on customizing specific aspects of your video.

Editing your video

Facebook doesn't currently offer full-fledged video-editing software. If you want control over frame-by-frame content or want to enhance a video with music or text, you need to do that with video-editing software on your computer, such as Final Cut Pro, Adobe Premiere, or iMovie.

When you click a video to edit it, regardless of whether you uploaded the video to your timeline or to your business page, you see a page similar to the one in Figure 4-7.

Figure 4-7:
The video page looks the same for videos shared on your personal timeline or your business page.

The Facebook video page has the following options in the right sidebar:

✦ **Tag Video button:** Click the Tag Video button, and options appear in the top right corner. Click the Who Were with You text box and type the name of the person or people you want to tag in the video. You also have the option of associating a location with your video (perhaps where the video was shot). Click the Where Was This Video Taken text box and type the city or country you want associated with your video.

It's spammy to tag people or pages that aren't in your video or photo. If you posted this video to a business page, you can't tag individual followers unless you're connected with them via your personal timeline (in other words, you need to be Facebook friends with them).

✦ **Add Location button:** Add where the video was taken.

✦ **Edit button:** Click the Edit button to add or change the title of the video, add a description, tag people, add a location, or select a date.

+ **Like link and Comment link:** On the right side of the page, you see a list of comments people have made about the video. You can respond to comments, delete comments, and Like or Unlike the video or comments.

+ **Follow/Unfollow Post link:** When you post a video or comment on a video, the default setting is to receive notification when others comment or Like the video. If you don't want a notification when people interact with your photo, click Unfollow Post. If you change your mind, return to the video and click Follow Post.

+ **Share link:** Click the Share link and use the Share on Your Own Timeline drop-down list to choose where you'd like to share the video. You have the option of sharing this video on your personal timeline, on a friend's personal timeline, in a group, on your business page (if you administer more than one business page, you'll see a list of all the pages you're affiliated with), or via a private message. After you choose where to share the video, type a short introduction of the video to give your audience context, and then click the Share Video button.

+ **Edit link:** Click the Edit link to do the main customization of your video. The Edit Video page has the following options:

  • *In This Video:* You can tag people in your video. Start typing the name of the person you want to tag and then choose them from the menu. You must be connected to the person via your personal timeline to tag them. You can tag other business pages whether you have Liked them or not.

  • *Title:* Give your video a name. The default title is the date and time you recorded the video.

  • *Where:* Type the location where you took the video.

  • *When:* Type the date when you took the video.

  • *Description:* Type an overview of what people can expect to see when they watch your video. Go ahead and use keywords in your paragraph if you can, especially if this video appears on your business page. Keywords will help others find your video.

  • *Privacy:* If you're posting the video to your personal timeline, you can determine who can see the video, using the Privacy drop-down list. If you're posting the video on your business page, anyone can view the video. Your business page is not tied to your personal timeline privacy settings, and the video will be public.

  • *Choose a Thumbnail:* Scroll through the optional thumbnail pictures (if available), and stop on the one you like.

  • *Save, Delete, or Cancel:* If you click Save, your updates (title, description, tags, and so on) are saved. If you click Delete, your video is permanently deleted — no take-backs. If you click Cancel, your updates are not saved, and your video is still published to your timeline.

Below the video itself, you see the following options:

✦ **Options:** This button enables you to edit the location, change the date, rotate the video left or right, edit the video, embed the video, get the video link, and delete the video.

✦ **Send:** You can send the video as a private Facebook message to only selected people.

✦ **Tag Video:** Include your Facebook friends or those who were in the video.

✦ **Share:** Post the video to your timeline, a friend's timeline, a group page, a business page you manage, or a private message.

✦ **Like:** Click to Like the video.

Using Facebook Apps to Share Video on Your Business Page

Business pages have an option not available to personal timelines: You can install Facebook applications. A Facebook application (or *app*) provides additional functionality for a business page. If your business already has a video channel established outside Facebook (for example, on YouTube), you can use a Facebook app to import your video library to your Facebook business page. Flip to Book VI, Chapter 1 for instructions on how to install a third-party Facebook app on your business page.

Facebook video applications are abundant. Here are three you might want to try:

✦ **Hike** (www.facebook.com/HikeSocialApps/app_190754877670914): With Hike, you can easily add YouTube and Vimeo videos to your Facebook page. You can add your entire channel quickly, saving you the work of embedding videos one at a time. Free, pro, and agency versions of the app are available.

✦ **ShortStack's video applet** (www.shortstack.com): ShortStack offers free Facebook applications for up to 2,000 followers. (For the pricing structure when you have more than 2,000 followers, go to www.shortstack.com/pricing.) The ShortStack app allows you to automatically update your Facebook page with your YouTube or Vimeo playlists.

✦ **Vocus** (http://vocus.com): Vocus is a marketing and PR platform that includes social platform integration. The monthly fee ranges from $300 to $2500 per month based on the features you need. (See http://vocus.com/pricing/ for a full explanation of Vocus pricing.) Depending on the plan you choose, Vocus may include marketing campaigns, e-mail templates, landing pages, news releases, publicity alerts, content monitoring, local listings, analytics, and other services.

Producing Great Video Clips

Shooting good video takes practice. It would be great if we all had access to hair and makeup artists and professional videographers at our whim. Even without those people at your disposal, you can still ensure that the video you create is the best it can be. Here are a few tried-and-true tips:

✦ **Have a script.** Depending on what you want to accomplish, it's almost always better to put some thought into what you'd like to say *before* you try to say it. You can write a complete script or just an outline.

✦ **Keep practicing.** As with everything, practice makes perfect. If you're not comfortable in front of the camera, don't give up. Film a few practice runs, and watch them. Make notes about what you want to change, and practice again. It may be uncomfortable in the beginning, but you'll get used to it — and your video will improve.

✦ **Slow your speech.** A common mistake people make when recording video is speaking at their normal rate. Slow down a little. If you're nervous, you'll probably speak even faster than normal, so keep that in mind and consciously slow your speech. Remember, it's okay to pause. That's a normal part of speech.

✦ **Consider your background.** It's possible you've stopped seeing that pile of laundry in the corner that you're going to put away tomorrow, but we promise that your friends and fans will notice. Find a background that won't distract from you and your message.

✦ **Check your lighting.** It's a bummer when you nail the script but can't see yourself because you forgot to do a test run to ensure that your lighting was bright enough.

✦ **Film someplace quiet.** Sometimes you become so used to background noise (kids, pets, the TV, even the heat or air conditioner running), you don't hear it anymore. Unfortunately, your camera picks it up. Background noise is distracting, and in some cases, it can be louder than your own message.

✦ **Use a tripod.** Even if you're a brain surgeon with super-steady hands, don't try to hold the camera while you're filming yourself. When you speak, you move as you gesticulate to enforce your point. Your video will suffer. Using a tripod ensures that your video will be smooth.

Chapter 5: Participating in Groups

In This Chapter

✔ **Creating your own group**

✔ **Customizing your group's image**

✔ **Establishing group settings**

✔ **Sending invites**

✔ **Posting and sharing documents**

✔ **Deleting groups**

*B*esides enabling you to connect with your friends one on one, Facebook allows you to create connections based on similar interests and activities by forming *groups*. A group enables you to create a place (private or public) where members can post pictures, upload videos, post messages, share documents, chat, or schedule events. Pretty much all the features that you experience in Facebook as a whole can be focused specifically to friends in a group. In this chapter, you find out how to create and interact with Facebook groups.

Discovering Groups

Groups can be completely private or totally public. Groups can even be secret, where you can see that the group exists only if you're a member. We discuss these options a little later in the chapter.

Participating in a group is a big reason why people join Facebook. Groups allow you to build a meeting place specific to people with similar interests so you can all connect, share documents, chat, and post updates. Facebook groups are useful because they allow you to

✦ Organize and communicate with a group of coworkers

✦ Share important, yet private, information within a closed group

✦ Plan an event or other collaborative project

✦ Build a community for those with similar interests

Facebook groups are valuable for creating an additional connection with people you are linked to within an organization such as a church, school, or job. They are also a great way to meet people with common interests, such as baseball card collectors. A group provides a place where you can meet these people and develop connections before you extend the invitation for a one-on-one friend relationship.

If you want to see which groups you belong to already, look on the left side of your news feed (click the Facebook logo at the top of the screen to go to your news feed), as shown in Figure 5-1. In the left sidebar you see the Favorites, Groups, Pages, Lists, and Apps categories (among others). (For more about this part of your page, see Book I.)

Figure 5-1:
Click the
Create
Groups link.

GROUPS
- Frankie Does LA
- Marketing Folks
- Create Group...

MORE ▾

The Groups section displays some of the groups you've been made part of, and typically those in which you're most active. By default, when someone invites you into a group, you're automatically included in that group. We tell you how to leave a group later in this chapter.

Creating a Group

Creating your own Facebook group is easy. When you create a group, you are automatically assigned as the administrator (admin) of that group. The group admin can edit the group's description and settings, add other administrators, and remove or ban members.

To create your own group, follow these steps:

1. **In the top-right corner of the Groups list, click the +Create Group button.**

A dialog box appears, as shown in Figure 5-2, asking for a group name, the friends you would like to add to the group, and the privacy settings of that group.

Figure 5-2:
Creating
a group
and adding
members.

2. **In the Group Name text box, type a name for your group.**

    Give your group a descriptive name. That way, the intended topic of the group is clear, and it's easier for interested parties to find it (if it's not a secret group).

3. **Add a member in the Members text box.**

4. **Repeat Step 3 until you've added all the members' names.**

5. **Select the privacy settings of the group:**

    • *Open:* Anyone can see the group, who's in it, and what members post.

    • *Closed:* Anyone can see the group and who's in it, but only members can see posts.

    • *Secret:* Only members see the group, who's in it, and what is posted.

6. **Click the Create button.**

7. **(Optional) Select an icon and click OK.**

As you can see in Figure 5-3, the group page is similar to your home screen, except what you see is all contained within the group. If the group is set to private, only you and other group members will be able to see the posts.

Figure 5-3:
The group
home
screen.

After creating your group, you can invite friends to the group (you must be connected with someone to invite them to your group) and begin posting. Your friends will receive a notification that they have been invited into the group.

You can also grant administrative privileges to other group members. To do that, click the (#) of Members link in the About section below the group cover image on the right side. A list of members appears. Select the gear icon below the member to whom you want to grant admin privileges and choose Make Admin. A dialog box appears, letting you know that if you make that person an admin, the person can edit group settings, add members, and make others admins as well. If you agree, click the Make Admin button.

To take away someone's admin status, click the gear icon below the members name and then click the Remove Admin link. It's important to note that if you make someone an admin, the person can take away your admin status.

Personalizing Your Group's Image

Groups are always more personal with a little customization. When you create a group, the group page shows a row of members' profile pictures (see Figure 5-4). If there are enough members, these photos rotate each time the group page is refreshed. If you click a member photo, the screen displays the person's Facebook page.

Figure 5-4:
Group member profile pictures are the default group header.

If you're an administrator of a group, you can also upload and display a customized graphic like the one in Figure 5-5 (just be sure it's at least 851 pixels by 315 pixels).

Figure 5-5:
A group can have a customized graphic header.

Here are a few ideas for custom graphics:

✦ A logo (if you own the rights to it)

✦ A picture of the people in the group

✦ A picture of a common meeting place

✦ Any image that is descriptive of the group

The image will be seen on the home screen of your group. If you're the admin for a group, you can upload a picture by following these steps:

1. **Navigate to the group page.**

2. **Hover your cursor over the top-right corner, below the group cover image, and click the Change Group Photo icon that appears.**

3. **Click the Upload a Photo option.**

4. **Choose an image file from your computer.**

   The photo appears as the group's new cover image.

5. **(Optional) Click and hold to drag the image; reposition it if necessary.**

6. **Click Save Changes.**

You can change the group cover image again any time you like. Or you can revert to the member profile pictures. To change your group cover image, move your cursor over the group image, and then click the Change Group Photo button that appears. A menu is displayed with the following options:

✦ **Upload a Photo:** You can upload a new photo from your computer for your group cover image.

✦ **Reposition Photo:** You can move around the existing cover image.

✦ **Remove Photo:** You can remove the current cover image, and the group member profile pictures will reappear as the cover image.

✦ **Choose from Group Photos:** Select photos uploaded by the group.

Establishing the Settings for Your Group

The default settings for your group were set when you created it, with the option to make your group open, closed, or secret. If you're the administrator for a group, you can modify a few additional settings in the Edit Group settings area.

Find the Edit Group settings by clicking the gear icon in the top right, under the cover photo, and choosing Edit Group Settings from the menu. You can change the following settings:

✦ **Group Name:** To rename the group, simply click inside this text box, highlight the current name, and then type over the name to change it.

✦ **Group icon:** By default, the group icon is a generic group image. If you didn't choose an icon when you created the group — or you want to change the one you did choose — click the Group Name drop-down list (shown in Figure 5-6). You are presented with around 50 options for icons. Select an icon that is relevant to your group's purpose. This icon will appear in the left sidebar of the group member's Facebook home page next to the group's name, and also on the group's main page at the bottom of the group's cover image. It does not appear in the news feed when members update the group.

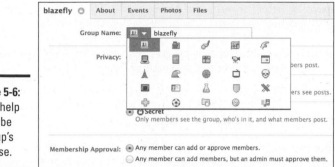

Figure 5-6:
Icons help
describe
a group's
purpose.

+ **Privacy:** Below the name section on the Edit screen are the group visibility options: Open, Closed, and Secret. Select the privacy level you want.

+ **Membership Approval:** Select whether any member can add or approve members or whether an admin has to approve new members.

+ **Email Address:** You have the option of setting up an e-mail address for the entire group. The name you choose can't be less than five characters. Any message sent to this e-mail address will go out to each member of the group. Click the Set Up Group Address button, and type a prefix for the e-mail address. The domain is @groups.facebook.com, as shown in Figure 5-7. Click Set Address to finish.

Figure 5-7:
Creating
an e-mail
address for
your group.

+ **Description:** Type a description of your group in the Description text box. If your settings are not set to secret, nonmembers can see the description.

+ **Tags:** Enter keywords that describe your group.

+ **Posting Permissions:** Select who can post to the group — only members or only administrators. Although there may be some instances where you'd want to limit posting, we think it's best to allow members to post to the group. After all, you created it to share your thoughts and interests, right? Communities thrive on give and take.

✦ **Post Approval:** Select whether all group posts need approval by an admin before others can see them in the group timeline.

Be sure to click the Save button to save your changes, or they'll be lost when you navigate away from the Edit Group settings page.

Inviting People to Join Your Group

Inviting people to join your group is simple. The only requirement is that you be connected to them as a friend on Facebook. You can invite friends into a group in one of three ways:

✦ Add people to the group when you create it.

✦ Add people to the group at any time after it has been created.

✦ Accept requests to join your group.

Adding members when you create a group

When you create a group, the first step after naming it is to select friends to be a part of the group. You do this by entering names in the dialog box (refer to Figure 5-2).

Start by typing the name of the first person you want to add. Facebook automatically displays relevant names (as well as profile pictures) as you type. For example, if you type **chri**, you will see people from your friends list whose names start with *Chri,* such as Christy, Christopher, Christina, and so on. When you find the correct person, simply click the name.

Adding members to a group any time

You can add new members to your group any time you want. Click the +Add People to Group box (under the About section) and start typing a name. (Remember that you need to be Facebook friends with someone to add them.) Facebook displays a list of possible people to add. Simply select the person from the list, and he or she is added to the group. You can also click the gear icon below the cover photo to the right and choose Add People.

Accepting a request to join your group

When someone wants to join your group, he or she issues a request by clicking the Join Group button, shown in Figure 5-8. (People can find your group if it is an open or closed group, but not if it's a secret group.)

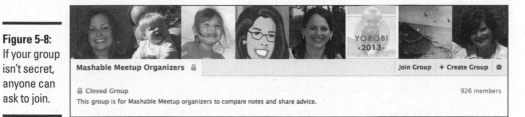

Figure 5-8:
If your group isn't secret, anyone can ask to join.

You as a group member (or as an administrator) will see a notification that someone has requested to join your group, as shown in Figure 5-9.

Figure 5-9:
Group request notification.

The request is displayed also on the right side of the group screen, as shown in Figure 5-10. To add the person to your group, click the checkmark button; to reject the request, click the X button.

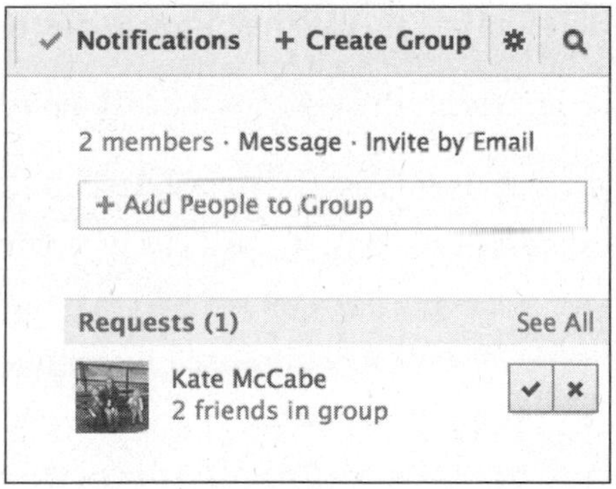

Figure 5-10:
Group request on the group screen.

Posting to a Group

The posting permissions on the Edit Group settings page determine who can post to a group. The admin of a group can choose to allow all group members or only admins to post. As we mentioned, we think it's best if all members of a group are allowed to interact — it just makes for a more interesting community.

To post an update to a group, follow these steps:

1. **Click the group title (on the left side of the news feed).**

   The most common groups you interact with will show up here. If the group you're looking for does not appear, you can select More, which appears above the group list as you hover your cursor over it.

   If you don't find the group here, type the name of the group in the search text box at the top of your screen. As you type, relevant results appear below the search box. Click the group you're looking for to go to the group page.

2. **At the top of the group screen, click in the Write Post text box and type your update.**

3. **(Optional) Enhance your update by adding a location, photo, video, or poll, or an icon indicating what you are doing.**

   Click Add Photo/Video to add a photo or video; click Ask Question to take a poll; or click Add File to add a file. See Chapter 2 of this minibook for details on adding a video, a link, and a picture.

4. **Click Post to post your update.**

Sharing Documents in a Group

Members of a group can create and share documents within the group. Documents can be edited by any member of the group at any time. Group members may find this to be a valuable tool for a number of reasons. You may want to use the documents feature in groups, for example, when you're

✦ Collaborating on a list of items to bring to an event.

✦ Working together to write a plan for your business or organization.

✦ Collecting pictures with a narrative of a recent trip that members of the group took together.

To create a group document, follow these steps:

1. **Click the Files tab below the group cover image.**

   You see two buttons on the top right: Create Doc and Upload File.

2. **Click Create Doc.**

3. **Type a title for your document.**

4. **In the large text box, type your document.**

   Documents have basic formatting options, including bold and italic text, numbered lists, and bulleted lists.

5. **When you've finished typing and formatting your document, click the Save button to save your changes and publish the document to the group.**

Group members will see a preview of the document as they would any update in the group's news feed. Click the Continue Reading link to see the full document. When a member clicks the Files link, a page appears displaying the title of each document. The member can then click a title to view the full document.

To edit the document, a member just clicks the Edit button in the top-right corner. Members can comment below documents as well. Only group admins can delete a document; to do that, just click the Delete link.

Leaving a Group

Sometimes you might lose interest in a group and want to remove yourself. The process of leaving a group is simple.

If you're the sole administrator for the group, we highly recommend that you appoint someone else as the admin for the group before you leave. Otherwise, another member can make himself or herself the admin.

To leave a group, click the gear icon below the group cover image and choose Leave Group from the menu. A warning dialog box appears, as shown in Figure 5-11.

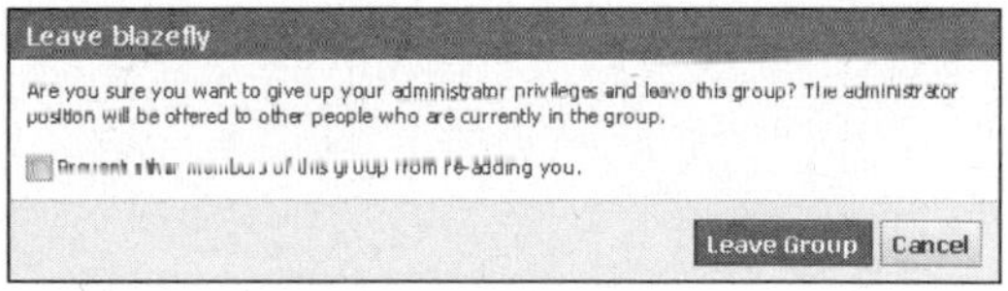

Figure 5-11:
Leaving a
group.

Leave blazefly

Are you sure you want to give up your administrator privileges and leave this group? The administrator position will be offered to other people who are currently in the group.

☐ Prevent other members of this group from re-adding you.

[Leave Group] [Cancel]

You can select a box that prevents other members of the group from adding you again. You can also report the group if it's malicious or inappropriate. You might report a group if it

✦ Harassed you or a friend

✦ Sent spam or is a scam

✦ Promoted hate speech, violence, or harmful behavior

✦ Has been sexually explicit

Report a group only if there is a legitimate reason to do so. When you report the group, Facebook will review the info and determine whether to disable the group.

Deleting a Group

To delete a group, the admin (if it's not you) must remove each member by clicking the gear icon below the person's name in the Members section. Then the admin must remove himself or herself and select the Delete Group option that appears.

Chapter 6: Going Mobile

In This Chapter

- ✔ Using the Facebook smartphone app
- ✔ Using the Facebook mobile website
- ✔ Using Facebook on simple mobile phones
- ✔ Checking in

The capability to go mobile is certainly a big reason why Facebook has experienced such success. Take Facebook with you to capture parts of your life and share it with family and friends. Picture this: You're at a ball game, you catch a fly ball (we've seen it on TV so we know it happens), and you want to share that excitement with your friends. What do you do? You share it on Facebook — not just a status update but also a picture of the ball as visual proof of your story.

Facebook also has implemented Location Services into the mobile experience. That's where Facebook uses GPS and other services to note where you are in an update, if you allow it to. With Location Services on, you can check in to venues and tag that place on your update. In this chapter, we talk about what Facebook is like when you go mobile.

Location Services allows apps on your phone to use cellular, Wi-Fi, and Global Positioning System (GPS) data to identify your approximate location — as long as these settings on your smartphone are turned on and connected to their respective networks. The information is always collected anonymously, and your personal information is not used or identified. Using Location Services with Facebook allows Facebook to associate a location with your update and enables you to search for events or places in your area.

Going Mobile

Many Facebook features that you're accustomed to on your full-screen computer browser can be accessed through the mobile site or a mobile app on your smartphone. The site has been reformatted to fit the phone's screen, and you use touchscreen features in most cases. Facebook is a little different in your mobile browser or smartphone app, but it's still familiar.

You can not only update statuses, share photos, and more but also take advantage of Location Services, present in many smartphones. So although you give up some features in the standard Facebook site, you gain other features. Furthermore, most phones have cameras, so you can easily share a little piece of every experience you have by snapping a shot and sending it directly to Facebook.

Going mobile is a great way to enjoy Facebook. As Facebook continues to improve its mobile site and apps, it enables you to access more features that previously were limited to only the desktop version of the site. As shown in Figure 6-1, Facebook mobile allows you to access the search feature, your personal timeline and business page, your news feed (just as you would see it on your desktop), all your groups, and chat services.

Figure 6-1: Accessing Facebook on a smartphone.

Using the Facebook Smartphone App

Because many different smartphones are available, the Facebook app on your phone may look different from the screenshots you see in this chapter, and it may have some different features as well. (We used the Facebook Android app on the Note 3 to capture the images in this chapter.)

Features of the smartphone app

Here's a rundown of the major features of the smartphone app:

✦ **News feed:** When you first open your Facebook app, the default screen is the news feed, shown in Figure 6-2. The news feed displays the full status updates of your friends, similar to the desktop view.

To view your news feed by top stories or most recent stories, select the navigation menu in the top-left corner, tap the gear icon next to the news feed, and make your choice from the menu that appears.

As you browse your mobile news feed, you see previews of pictures, along with the option to Like or comment on an update. You also see a note of how many comments or Likes a post has received.

Figure 6-2:
The news feed on the smartphone app.

✦ **Likes and comments:** If you want to interact with a post, you have several options:

- To immediately Like the post, tap the Like link.

- To leave a comment, tap the Comment link. The Comment screen appears, as shown in Figure 6-3. Type your comment and then tap the Post button.

- To see the entire thread of comments related to a post, tap the Comments link (or tap the comment bubble at the bottom of the post). You also have the option to type a comment and join the conversation, as shown in the Write a Comment area at the bottom of Figure 6-4.

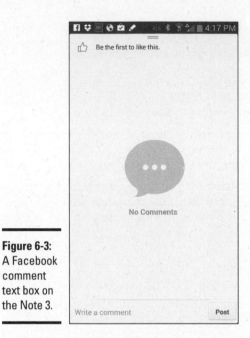

Figure 6-3:
A Facebook comment text box on the Note 3.

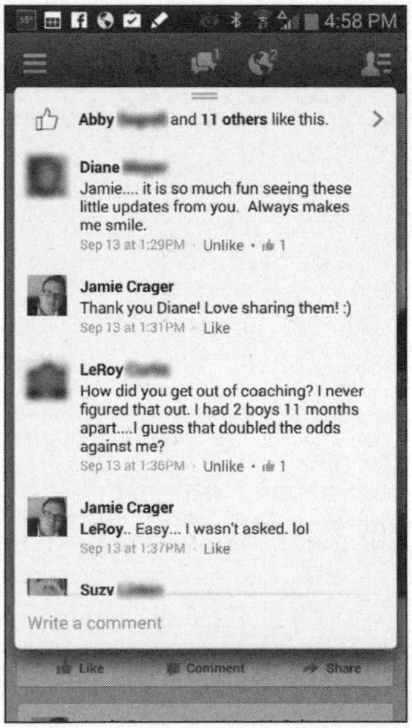

Figure 6-4:
Comment thread on a Note 3.

✦ **Left sidebar:** Tap the navigation icon at the top left of your screen (it looks like three stacked lines) to view the left sidebar. You will then be able to sort the news feed; access messages; view events; visit your friends' pages; find nearby places; see updates from your pages, lists, groups, and those you are following; and see the apps that you have installed. You can also access App Settings, Account Settings, Privacy Settings, and Code Generator; edit your favorites; report a problem; visit Help Center; and log out.

✦ **Notifications:** All your notifications appear at the top of the screen, similar to what you see on the top right of your desktop screen. If you have a notification, a red badge appears on one of the following icons:

- *Friend requests:* The silhouette of two heads indicates you have a pending friend request. Tap the icon to respond to this friend request.

- *Messages:* The chat boxes indicate you have a message in your inbox. Tap this icon to go to your inbox. (You can access your inbox from the left sidebar as well.) Then, to start a private message with a friend, tap the messages icon (the cartoon bubbles) in the upper-right corner and select your friend from the list on the right.

- *General notifications:* The globe tells you that you have general notifications, such as someone Liking a post, commenting on a post, or inviting you to an event. Tap this icon to see a list of your most recent notifications.

✦ **Status updates:** You can create a mobile status update from the news feed screen or your personal timeline. If you're looking at your main news feed, find the Status, Photo, and Check In buttons at the top of the screen. Then:

- *To write a text update,* tap the Status button and begin typing in the text box that appears. You can tag others with you, share where you are, take a picture, add an icon that indicates what you are doing, and customize your sharing options for this update.

- *To share a photo or video,* tap the Photo button. Tap the Take Photo or Video button to begin shooting, or tap the Choose From Library button to select a photo or video you've already captured.

- *To select a place near you,* tap the Check In button. (We cover the Places feature at the end of the chapter.) If you need to add a new place, start typing the name of the place in the Search text box. If the place doesn't appear as you type, you can add it by tapping the Add *Place Name* option, as shown in Figure 6-5.

**Book II
Chapter 6**

Going Mobile

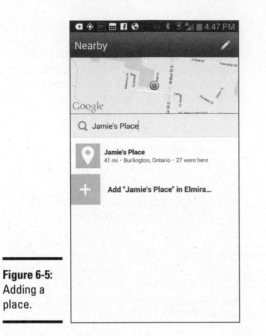

Figure 6-5:
Adding a
place.

Updating your status on the Facebook app

To post a status update using the Facebook app, follow these steps:

1. **Tap Status.**

The Write Post screen appears, as shown in Figure 6-6.

Figure 6-6:
The Update
Status
screen.

2. **Begin typing what you'd like to share.**

3. **If you want to tag a friend in your status update:**

    a. *Tap the friend icon.*

    The friend icon looks like a silhouette with a plus sign. A screen appears with a list of friends in alphabetical order.

    b. *Use the search text box at the top to type a name.*

    Facebook also provides a list of all your friends, with suggested friends near the top.

    c. *Select the name or names from the suggested list.*

    d. *Tap Done to return to your update or post.*

4. **If you want to indicate your location (check in):**

    a. *Tap the pushpin icon.*

    b. *Type your location in the search bar or select it from the recommended locations below the search bar. (If your location doesn't appear, tap the Add Your Location option.)*

5. **If you want to add a photo or video:**

    a. *Tap the camera icon.*

    b. *Select the photo or photos from your gallery by tapping the check mark in the upper-right corner of each photo.*

    You can also tag people in the photos you select.

    c. *Tap the pen icon in the lower-right corner.*

    You see your photo or photos in your status update box.

6. **If you want to add a What Are You Doing icon:**

    a. *Tap the happy face icon to open a list.*

    b. *Select a category and then choose a subcategory.*

    c. *Select the subcategory.*

7. **If you want to select the audience for your update:**

    a. *Tap the privacy icon in the lower-right corner.*

    b. *In the list that appears, select whether to make your update public, to share only with friends, or to be more selective.*

    The icon changes after you update this setting.

8. **Tap the Post button to share your update.**

You can post only as yourself when using the mobile Facebook app; you can't post as your business page (see Book IV, Chapter 2 for a full explanation of how to use Facebook as yourself or as your business page). That means if you post an update to your business page from your mobile device, you're posting as you, not as your business page. As a result, your fans won't see your updates unless they are friends with your personal timeline on Facebook.

Understanding the limitations of the Facebook app

The limitations of mobile apps grow fewer and fewer as the capabilities of mobile devices increase. The main limitation is a smartphone's smaller screen size, which changes the way you use the functions of Facebook. And because touchscreen devices are common, the way you interact with the application is different.

Finally, iOS (the iPhone, iPod touch, and iPad operating systems) and the Android operating system are the most popular smartphone and tablet OSes. If your mobile phone doesn't use one of these operating systems, it might have fewer features because less development attention is paid to less popular mobile operating systems.

Accessing Facebook on a Smartphone or Tablet

Facebook's mobile website is called Facebook Touch Mobile. The look and functionality of the Facebook mobile website (not the smartphone app) differs little from one mobile device to the next because much of the user interface is built into the website, not the device's operating system. With the mobile site, Facebook detects what browser you're using and loads the compatible version of the mobile site.

To access Facebook Touch Mobile, simply open your (touchscreen) mobile device's browser and type `touch.facebook.com`. Your browser is automatically detected and the mobile site loads. Figure 6-7 shows a Facebook business page using the Facebook Touch Mobile site on an Android phone. This site looks similar on iPhone devices as well.

Figure 6-7:
A timeline
on Facebook
Mobile
(shown on
an Android
phone).

When you comment on other people's photos using the Facebook Touch
Mobile site, the appearance is slightly different than on the Facebook app.

Using Facebook on a Cellphone

If you want to go mobile but don't have a smartphone, you can still post
Facebook updates using text messages on a regular cellphone. With
Facebook's text-based services, you can

✦ Update your status

✦ Add a friend by name or phone number

✦ Subscribe to someone's status for mobile updates

✦ Unsubscribe from someone's status updates

✦ Upload photos

All these features are performed by texting the appropriate code to
Facebook's short code 32665 (which spells FBOOK on your alphanumeric
phone keypad).

Unless you have unlimited texts with your cellphone plan, keep in mind that
text messaging rates apply to texts you send to Facebook. Don't end up with
a huge cellphone bill next month because you texted a few hundred status
updates, photos, and such.

Setting up your Facebook account to accept text messages

To be able to use Facebook via SMS (that is, text messages), you first have to set up your mobile phone with your Facebook account. To do so, follow these steps:

1. **Log in to Facebook.**

2. **Click the gear icon and choose Account Settings.**

The General Account Settings page appears.

3. **In the left sidebar, click the Mobile link.**

The Mobile Settings page appears, so you can add your mobile phone to your Facebook account.

4. **Click the button to add a phone to your account.**

If prompted to add your password, do so.

5. **Select your country and carrier, and then click Next.**

6. **When prompted, text the letter F to** 32665 **from your phone.**

The Activate Facebook Texts dialog box appears, as shown in Figure 6-8, asking for the confirmation code. You should receive a text message with that code within a few minutes.

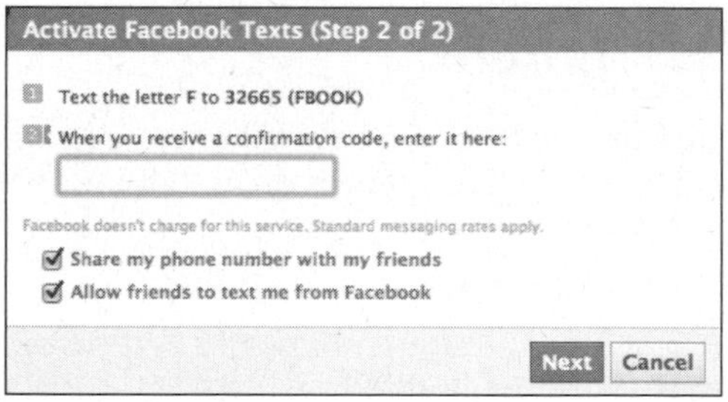

Activate Facebook Texts (Step 2 of 2)

▨ Text the letter F to 32665 (FBOOK)

▨▌ When you receive a confirmation code, enter it here:

Facebook doesn't charge for this service. Standard messaging rates apply.

☑ Share my phone number with my friends
☑ Allow friends to text me from Facebook

Next Cancel

Figure 6-8:
Enter the confirmation code.

7. **Enter the confirmation code, and then click Next.**

You have completed the process of enabling Facebook SMS messages for your phone.

Updating your status via text

After you confirm your cellphone number with Facebook, you can use Facebook SMS features to keep your friends up-do-date and vice versa, no matter what kind of mobile phone you have. Here's how:

✦ **To update your status,** text the status to 32665 from your mobile phone.

✦ **To add a friend,** text the name of your friend (for example, John Smith) or your friend's phone number to 32665.

✦ **To subscribe to a friend's updates** so that they come directly to your phone as text messages, text **Subscribe** and your friend's name (for example, *Subscribe Jane Smith*) to 32665. Text **Unsubscribe** along with the friend's name to cancel the friend's updates.

✦ **To stop SMS updates,** text **Stop** to 32665.

After you've added your mobile phone number to your account, your number appears on the info page of your timeline. This information enables friends to send you text messages via Facebook messages. (Discover more about messages in Chapter 8 of this minibook).

If you don't want your Facebook friends to have access to your mobile number via Facebook, simply disable the setting. As you can see in Figure 6-9, two check boxes allow friends to send you text messages and to share your number with friends. Deselect these check boxes to keep your mobile number private.

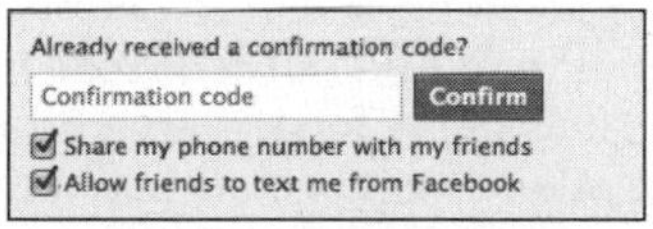

Book II
Chapter 6

Going Mobile

Figure 6-9:
Allow (or restrict) texts from friends via Facebook.

Already received a confirmation code?

| Confirmation code | Confirm |

☑ Share my phone number with my friends
☑ Allow friends to text me from Facebook

Changing your mobile number

If you need to change the mobile number associated with your account, click the gear icon and choose Account Settings. Click Mobile, and then click the Remove link next to your mobile number on the Mobile Settings page. After doing this, you need to go through the setup process to add a new phone number, as described in the earlier section, "Setting up your Facebook account to accept text messages."

Using your cellphone to text pictures and posts to Facebook

If you want to text (send) pictures to Facebook from a simple cellphone, you can do so by sending a text (MMS) message. To do this, text **photos** to 32665, and you will receive a message telling you the e-mail address to send pictures to. If your mobile plan and phone support picture mail, you can send a message to an e-mail address in the same way you would text to another phone number. When you text a picture to the Facebook e-mail address, Facebook updates your status with the photo that you included in your message.

Checking In to Places

When you are out and about, Facebook Places allows you to check in to a physical location (for instance, a restaurant) with your mobile phone. Your check-in becomes a status update in the news feed, with location information telling your friends where you are. Places is a social utility to connect with friends who work, live, or study around you. Because people use Facebook to connect with others, Places is a way to connect with others in real life while also connecting on Facebook.

To use Places, you need to enable Location Services on your smartphone so that Facebook can search for places near you based on your GPS location. Places allows you to see other people who have checked in to that location, as well as tag friends who are with you at that time. Being tagged in Places by a friend is much like being mentioned in a status update.

Using Places to connect

Facebook places are locations listed in Facebook where people can post an update that they are there, or comment and find out who else has checked in to that location. In some cases, a business may have merged their Places listing with their business page, which makes the place and the business page one and the same. In this case, when you check in at that business, your update will link to the business page.

Have you ever gone to a concert or sporting event, only to find out later that your friends were there as well? With Facebook Places, you can connect in real time with friends who choose to check in to Places.

Recently, Jamie went to a football game and checked in via Facebook Places. As he checked in, he discovered a friend had checked in as well! Although thousands of people were at the game, Places allowed Jamie to discover friends who were there.

You can use Places on an iPhone or on Android devices, as well as using the browser of any web-enabled mobile device. The examples in the following sections use the mobile version of Facebook. The iPhone and Android apps may look a little different, but most of the functionality is the same.

Using Location Services

To use Facebook Places, you can access the function from your smartphone (using GPS or Location Services), or you can access it from your computer (such as a laptop while you're at a location). To access Places with a mobile device, you need a smartphone to access the full mobile browser capabilities. You must enable Location Services so that Facebook can access your phone's location and find places near you. The first time you use Places, you see a screen asking you to allow Facebook permission to access Location Services.

Finding your place

When you're at a location where you'd like to check in, pull out your mobile phone and open Facebook. (You can open Facebook through your phone's browser or use the Facebook app.) Tap the Status button at the top of the screen. A box appears, where you can enter your status.

To check in to a location on your smartphone, follow these steps:

1. **Tap the check-in icon (the pushpin) at the top of the Facebook app.**

   Alternatively, you can tap Check In on the opening screen of your mobile app.

2. **A list of nearby places appears, as shown in Figure 6-10; select the appropriate Place.**

   If you don't see the place in the list, search for it by name. If the place isn't already in your Places list, you see the option to add it.

   If you're using one of Facebook's official apps (on an iPhone or an Android device), what you see on the device may look a little different than the screen in Figure 6-10.

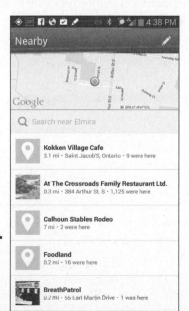

Figure 6-10:
Checking
in to a
location.

3. **Enter your status.**

   After you select the place and add a status update, that place becomes a link in your status update.

4. **(Optional) Tag friends who are with you as follows:**

   a. *Tap the add friends icon (the silhouette with a plus sign) below the Post text box.*

   b. *Type your friends' names or select their names from the list.*

   c. *Tap Done.*

   When you tag friends, Facebook links to their timelines in your update and indicates that they are with you where you checked in. If they're already using Places, it will be as if they checked in without having to do anything. Tagging a friend will appear in your check-in details, as well as on your friends' timelines.

   If you accidentally tag the wrong person, you can remove the tag by deleting the person's name or by tapping the check mark that appears next to his or her name.

5. **Click Post.**

Finding friends on Places

You can find out who else is on Places in two ways:

✦ Check into a place and seeing who is already there and has checked in.

✦ Look at recent check-ins from your friends after clicking Places from your home screen.

You can adjust the privacy settings each time you check into a place to customize who can see your check-in.

Chapter 7: Keeping Up with Events

In This Chapter

✔ **Finding events on Facebook**

✔ **Creating your own events**

✔ **Privacy settings for events**

✔ **Using Facebook to promote events**

*F*acebook is a great tool for connecting with your friends and finding out what they're doing. And with Facebook events, you can plan and promote an occasion, invite friends, and then see who has declined and who is planning to attend.

Planning and keeping track of events in life can be challenging. Facebook makes it simple to set up small events, such as a dinner party for six, or a large event, such as a concert you're promoting beyond your own network. Facebook makes it easy to see what events you're attending and who else is going. You can even coordinate events with popular online calendars such as Google Calendar or Mac's iCal.

What makes Facebook events so great is their integration with other Facebook activities. Users can share with friends and comment on events to which they are invited. Public events appear in your news feed, so you have the opportunity to let your friends know what's going on. Your friends then have a link to find out more, share information, include pictures, and join the event. If you want to get the word out about your event, friends that RSVP to the event can invite their friends on Facebook, too!

In this chapter, we show you how to use Facebook to manage all the events you're attending, RSVP to events, and interact with friends on the events screen. We also show you how you can use Facebook events to create your own events and promote them to friends and beyond.

Introducing Events

Events are an easy way to interact with others. To plan an event in Facebook, you need to understand how people discover events in Facebook. When an event is created and you invite people, they see it in two areas:

✦ In their notifications (see Figure 7-1)

✦ In the Favorites section on the left side of the news feed

Figure 7-1:
Event
notifications.

Notifications for event invitations are mixed in with other notifications, so if you don't pay close attention to notifications, you might miss one. Keep in mind that the situation is the same for your friends.

Events describe the time, place, and details about the gathering, and also list the attendees. The great thing about the virtual world is that the event place can be anywhere. For example, if you're planning a worldwide "hug a puppy" day, a Facebook event is the ideal way to do so. People that respond to the event invitation are shown as attending. They can post links, pictures, and videos, as well as share the event and invite others. When people join an event, they're notified any time someone posts something in the group. A Facebook event can be a way to bring people together, even if they're not actually physically close together.

Understanding Events Basics

The Facebook events feature enables you to do a lot more than just send out invitations. You can

+ Create an event

+ Define the details and location

+ Share the event as a status update

+ Share pictures, links, and videos on the event's home page

+ Make the event private or public

+ See what events are going on now and later

✦ RSVP for events and see who else is attending

✦ Synchronize Facebook events with your online calendar (such as iCal or Google Calendar)

The Events section is below the Favorites category, in the left sidebar of your news feed. Click Events and you'll see the current events to which you've been invited (as well as the birthdays of your friends). You can view events in a list view or a calendar view. You can also join the event (RSVP), decline the event, or send a Maybe response from here. Click any event to go directly to that event's home page, where you can see specific information.

Getting the lay of the land

As shown in Figure 7-2, a Facebook event has a concise layout that enables you to see all the basic details of the event and interact with those invited to the event.

Figure 7-2:
An event's
home page.

An event's home page displays the following details:

✦ **Picture:** When creating an event, you can upload a picture, too.

✦ **Time, location, created by:** Be sure to include basic information such as when the event starts and its location. When you create an event, the page includes a link so people can click directly to your Facebook personal timeline or to a business page.

✦ **More information:** Part of an effectively planned event is explaining what the event is, why you're hosting it, and any other relevant information attendees may find useful.

✦ **The event wall:** This feature is a great way for the invitees to share with each other. You (and attendees) can post links, videos, photos, and any text post that you want, which is shared with all invitees.

✦ **Edit Event and Message Guests buttons:** Visible only to the event creator, the Edit Event and Message Guests buttons enable you to make changes to the event and send a message to everyone that has RSVP'd, respectively.

✦ **+Join, Maybe, and Decline buttons:** If you're not the creator of an event, these buttons appear at the top right of an event's home page. Click Join if you will be attending the event; click Maybe if you're not sure; and click Decline if you will not attend the event. When you click Join or Maybe, you may have the option to invite more friends if the event creator has enabled that option. If you click Decline, you can write a post on the wall with your regrets (remember that the event wall is public). Or you can click Skip if you'd rather not leave a note. If you change your mind about your RSVP, you can click the Going button at the top of the page and change your RSVP status.

Kinds of events

You can plan, promote, and host an unlimited variety of gatherings by using Facebook events. Events fall into two categories:

✦ **Public events:** If your event is at a public venue and anyone is welcome to attend, make it a public event. With public events, anyone can find the event and add themselves to the guest list. Concerts, rallies, festivals, and town meetings are all ideal as public events. You can tell whether an event is public simply by looking at the event's home page. The title of the event at the top of the screen will say that it is a public event (refer to Figure 7-1). You also have the option to invite friends, share the event via your personal timeline, and RSVP to the event.

✦ **Private events:** Private events are for private parties where the attendance is by invitation only. Private events can be seen only by those who are on the invitation list, and they do not appear in search and results. When an event is private, you see Invite Only below the event title, as shown in Figure 7-3. Some great uses of the private events function are private birthday parties, business meetings, and weddings. If you're planning to surprise someone and are organizing the plan on Facebook, make the event private. The administrator (creator) of a private event can allow users to invite others in the Event Settings screen or limit this function to the event administrator only.

Figure 7-3:
A private
event.

Later in the chapter, we explain how to create these sorts of events and establish event permissions as public or private.

Finding and Interacting with Events

If you're looking for something to do this weekend, Facebook events might be the place to go. Maybe you're searching for concerts in your area or something fun for the kids. Perhaps you just want to see how your friends are planning their day or weekend. You can use the Event search function for all these reasons.

Some people may make their event public, but not necessarily because it's truly a public occasion. One reason why people might make an event public is so people they forgot to put on the guest list can still find the event.

Searching events

To find an event you've been invited to, start on your main news feed page. If you've recently been invited to any events, you see these in the Favorites section on the left side of your home page, as shown in Figure 7-4. You can see upcoming events also in the upper-right corner of the news feed page, just below the top navigation, as shown in Figure 7-5.

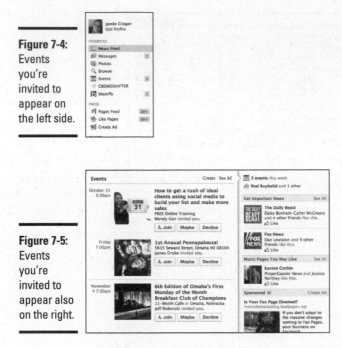

Figure 7-4: Events you're invited to appear on the left side.

Figure 7-5: Events you're invited to appear also on the right.

Below your profile picture on your home page is an Events link. This link takes you to the page where you can view all events that are in your event list, including invitations and events to which you have sent an RSVP.

When you click the Events link, you see an additional option, Friends' Events. This option enables you to see all upcoming public events created by your friends, organized into three groups:

✦ Today

✦ This Week

✦ This Month

These events include events that your friends are going to, even if you are not friends with the event creator. Click the title of any event to find out details and RSVP to the event.

RSVP to an event

When you're invited to an event, you receive a notification indicating that your friend has invited you. That event invitation also appears in your events list.

You can respond to an event in three simple ways. On your home screen, click the Events link below your profile picture to go to the events page. You see any events to which you've been invited. Then do one of the following:

✦ To the right of the event, click Join, Maybe, or Decline to RSVP.

✦ Click the Invites button at the top of the page. The Event Invites page appears, as shown in Figure 7-6. Click Join, Maybe, or Decline. Or if you want to see more information about the event, click the title of the event.

✦ Click the event title to go directly to the event's description. Click Join, Maybe, or Decline to RSVP. When you decline an invitation, you have the option to ignore future invitations from this sender.

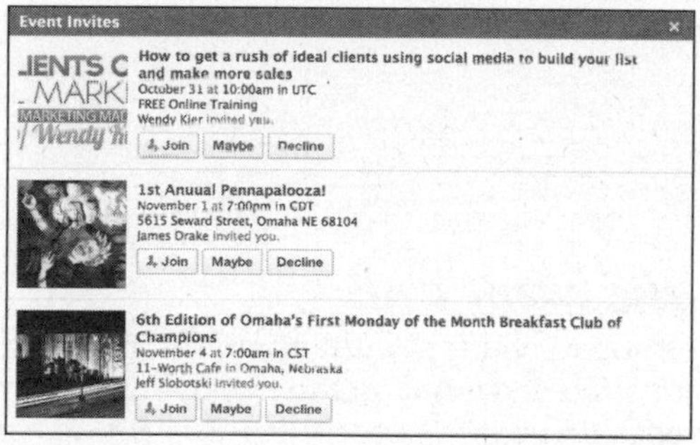

Figure 7-6:
Event
invites.

Event Invites

How to get a rush of ideal clients using social media to build your list and make more sales
October 31 at 10:00am in UTC
FREE Online Training
Wendy Kier invited you.
Join Maybe Decline

1st Annual Pennapalooza!
November 1 at 7:00pm in CDT
5615 Seward Street, Omaha NE 68104
James Drake invited you.
Join Maybe Decline

6th Edition of Omaha's First Monday of the Month Breakfast Club of Champions
November 4 at 7:00am in CST
11-Worth Cafe in Omaha, Nebraska
Jeff Slobotski invited you.
Join Maybe Decline

On the events page, if you move your mouse cursor over the event title in calendar view without clicking, you'll see some details about the event, as well as options to RSVP.

Checking out who is attending the event

Face it, the cool factor is important for most people. Who wants to go to a party if no one awesome is going to be there? To better plan your appearances, you can see who has already stated that they're attending an event. The left sidebar of an event's home page lists the people who have submitted their RSVP to the event, as shown in Figure 7-7.

As long as the guest list has been made public, you can see who responded as Going, Maybe, and Invited. If the administrator has chosen to not show the guest list on the event's home page, you can't see who is attending.

Figure 7-7:
Those
that have
RSVP'd to
an event.

Interacting on the event wall

The event wall enables you to connect with others on the guest list before and even after the event. You can write on the event wall after you accept the invite (join the event). If you don't accept the invite, you can only comment on updates from other people, as shown in Figure 7-8.

Figure 7-8:
Interacting
on an event
wall.

Synchronizing Events and Birthdays with Your Online Calendar

If you're like us, you've grown to depend on the mobile calendar on your smartphone or the iCal, Microsoft Outlook, or Google Calendar that you access on your computer. If you're going to take your Facebook events and birthdays seriously, synchronizing your calendar is a must.

You can synchronize events and birthdays with your calendars in three ways:

✦ Sync a single event by e-mail

✦ Sync a single event by downloading the calendar file

✦ Sync all your Facebook events by subscribing to the calendar feed

You may find it valuable to synchronize all events if you're close with all the people you connect with on Facebook, or if you like to see what's going on at a glance from your online calendar. Some people like to have all their friends' birthdays in their calendar, and this is a great way to do that. You'll never miss a birthday again.

If you prefer to be more selective with what goes on your calendar, you may feel that a single appointment here and there is all you'll need to transfer. You can do this easily, too.

Synchronizing all your events

To synchronize all your events on Facebook with your other calendars, follow these steps:

1. **Click the Events link below your profile picture to go to the events page.**

2. **Click the gear icon in the upper-right corner, next to the Today button, and choose Export, as shown in Figure 7-9.**

Figure 7-9:
Export
events
to other
calendars.

3. **Select the Export Your Friends' Birthdays link or the Upcoming Events link (see Figure 7-10).**

If you're using iCal or Microsoft Outlook, clicking the link opens that calendar tool, displays a URL link, and asks you to confirm that you're subscribing to the calendar. If you're using an online calendar, such as Google Calendar, you need to copy the URL link and enter it in your calendar.

Figure 7-10: The Export Events and Birthdays dialog box.

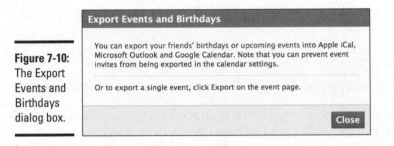

Export Events and Birthdays

You can export your friends' birthdays or upcoming events into Apple iCal, Microsoft Outlook and Google Calendar. Note that you can prevent event invites from being exported in the calendar settings.

Or to export a single event, click Export on the event page.

Close

4. **Click Subscribe to sync your Facebook events and birthdays with your calendar.**

Synchronizing a single event

To synchronize a single event to your calendar, do the following:

1. **Navigate to the events page.**

2. **Click the Export link at the bottom of the left sidebar, or click the gear icon in the upper-right corner and select Export Event.**

The Export Event dialog box appears.

3. **Choose whether to save the event to your calendar or have the event e-mailed to you.**

You can select from any of the e-mail addresses you have associated with your Facebook account.

4. **Do one of the following:**

- **If you chose to save the event to your calendar:** Click Export. The event will be downloaded to your Downloads folder. Select the file to open the event in your Calendar, and then click Save.

- **If you chose to have the event e-mailed to you:** You'll receive a calendar invite by e-mail. Click Add to Calendar in the e-mail message.

You can also choose to Subscribe to all upcoming events on your calendar by clicking the link at the bottom of the Export Event dialog box.

Creating an Event

To create your own event, you need to provide basic information about the event. In just a few minutes, you can tell all your friends the what, where, and when of the event.

To create an event and fill in the details, follow these steps:

1. **Navigate to the events page, and click the +Create an Event button, in the top right.**

   The Create New Event dialog box appears, as shown in Figure 7-11.

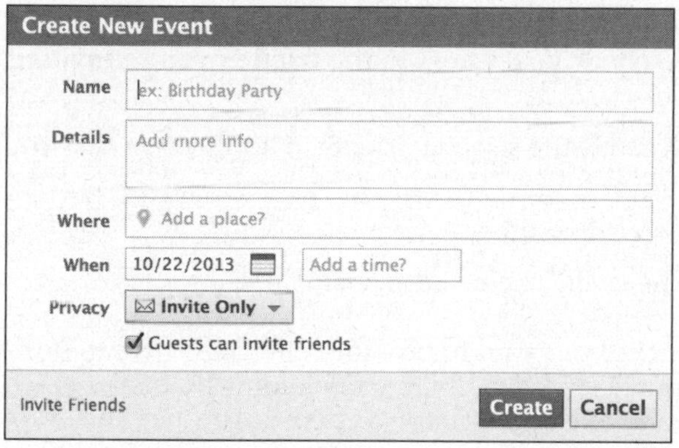

Figure 7-11:
Create your
event and
fill in all the
details.

Create New Event

Name	ex: Birthday Party
Details	Add more info
Where	📍 Add a place?
When	10/22/2013 📅 Add a time?
Privacy	✉ Invite Only ▾
	☑ Guests can invite friends

Invite Friends   **Create** **Cancel**

2. **In the Name text box, type a name for the event.**

3. **In the Details text box, type the details of the event.**

   You might tell your guests what to wear (casual or black tie, for example), what to expect, or what to bring (a dish if you're hosting a potluck, for example). You can type anything you want in the Details text box.

4. **In the Where text box, type the meeting place.**

   Typing in this text box starts a search for places with that name. You can type the name of a place (such as Meadowbrook Country Club), or you can type the address of the venue.

5. **In the When text box, click the calendar icon and choose the date of your event.**

6. **In the Add a Time text box, type the time of your event.**

7. **Make a selection in the Privacy drop-down list:**

   • **Public:** Public events are open for everyone to see and anyone can RSVP. In addition, public events show up in search results. People who visit the public event's home page can leave comments on the event wall, including uploading pictures, links, and videos.

Note: You can comment on other people's updates if you have not accepted the invite. You can leave a status update only if you joined the event.

- **Friends of Guests:** Invited guests can invite other people to whom you may not be connected. The event won't be seen by those who are not on the guest list, but anyone on the guest list can add others to the guest list.

- **Invite Only:** Only people you invite can view and join the event.

8. **If you want to allow guests to invite friends, select the Guests Can Invite Friends check box.**

9. **Click the Invite Friends link at the bottom left.**

    The Invite Friends dialog box appears.

10. **Select the check boxes next to the friends you're inviting, and then click Save.**

    Facebook sends the selected friends a notification that you have invited them to the event.

11. **Click the Create button.**

    You see the event's home page again.

For any event that you want to promote and get others to promote, be sure to make it a public event so that it can be found and shared by others. Doing this may open up the opportunity for people to share the event and help you to promote it.

Adding a picture to your event

An event picture is not required, but it sure helps, especially if you want to get people excited about your event. A good picture can help describe the event (see Figure 7-12).

To upload a picture for your event, navigate to your event's home page and follow these steps:

1. **Click the Add Event Photo button, at the top right.**

    The Add Event Photo dialog box appears.

2. **Choose one of the following:**

    - **From My Photos:** Click the picture you want to add.

    - **Upload a Photo:** Locate the photo and then click Open.

3. **To make changes, move your cursor over the photo (at any time) to display the Change Event Photo button. Select that button and make your changes.**

    You can choose another photo, reposition the photo, and remove it.

Figure 7-12:
Add an
event photo.

Inviting friends

When you invite friends, you can send them a basic invitation or you can send them a personal message explaining what the event is and why you want them to come. You can invite friends when creating the event or after the event is created. Guests can also invite friends if you allow them to do so.

To invite friends to an event, follow these steps:

1. **When you're creating an event, click the Invite Friends link.**

Note: If you're inviting guests to an event after it has been created, whether you're the event creator or just on the guest list, click the Invite Friends button at the top right of the event's home page.

The Invite Friends dialog box appears, as shown in Figure 7-13.

2. **Select the check box that appears next to each profile picture for each friend you want to invite.**

Use the Search by Name drop-down list to search for friends. As you type, the list of friends narrows to match the name you're typing.

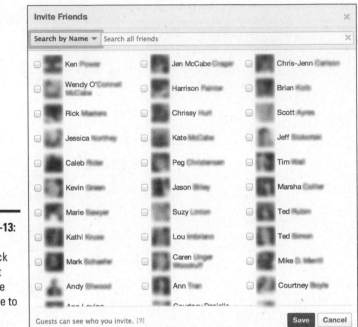

Figure 7-13:
Select
the check
box next
to people
you'd like to
meet.

You can use the list also to invite entire lists, groups, and attendees of other event pages.

3. Click the Save button.

Your invitations have been sent!

Making changes to an event

If you would like to turn off the display of the guest list for a public or a private event, click the Edit button (below the event Photo) and deselect the Show Guest List check box. You might deselect this option when you don't want the guest list to be public information prior to the event. Or you might deselect this option for an event in which you don't want people to decide whether to go based on the guest list.

Click the gear icon in the upper-right corner of the event's home page to display the following settings:

✦ **Edit Hosts:** Add or delete the event's hosts.

✦ **Message Guests:** Send a message to specific guests or all guests.

✦ **Create Repeat Event:** Create a new event with the same details of the current event.

✦ **Stop Notifications:** Turn on or off event notifications.

✦ **Export Event:** Export the event to a calendar or send it to an e-mail address.

✦ **Promote Event:** Promote the event through a Facebook ad.

Promoting Events on Facebook

The features described in this chapter are designed to make it easier to promote events. With as many event invitations that people send out, it can be easy to miss or gloss over events that don't catch your attention. Here are some simple best practices that can help you make a Facebook event more successful:

✦ Make sure your event is public, so it's easy for people to see the event or find it in a search.

✦ Give the event a name that makes it clear why someone would want to come to the event. For example, if the event is a concert, be sure to include the name of the artists. It also helps to include the city name so that people searching for local events can find it.

✦ Share the event in your status update with a link to the event's home page. That gives people an additional place to find out about the event if they didn't see an invitation. You can do this by copying the link from your browser when you're on the event's home page. Better yet, just click Share at the top of the event's home page!

✦ Send out messages to guests with updates about the upcoming event. Getting people more involved before the event makes a big difference. Just be sure you don't send too many updates.

✦ Post pictures and videos on the event wall. These notifications will go to everyone on the guest list. Pictures get a lot of clicks because they're eye-catching and engaging.

✦ Send a personal message to a few people you know and ask them if they can help you share your event.

✦ Only invite people who you know would be interested in your event. For instance, if you're holding a local event, just invite your local friends (unless you know an out-of-towner will be visiting). Many people stop checking their event invitations simply because so many are irrelevant to them.

✦ Use Facebook ads. Click the gear icon in the upper-right corner and select the Promote Event link. Then follow the instructions on the Advertise on Facebook page.

Chapter 8: Having Private Conversations

In This Chapter

✔ Sending a message to friends and nonfriends

✔ Chatting with multiple friends

✔ Making video calls

✔ Using Facebook e-mail addresses

Communicating with your friends goes far beyond the timeline, where everyone can see your conversation. Private conversations on Facebook come in several forms. With Facebook's messaging features, you can connect with friends by text chat (or instant messaging), by video calls, through private e-mail–like messages, and from your message inbox. You can even create chat conversations with groups of friends.

In this chapter, we cover all the aspects of private messaging on Facebook. We describe how to initiate messages or chats with your friends, as well as how to initiate video calls and group chats.

Introducing Facebook Messaging Options

The many options for communicating on Facebook give you a lot to think about. Fear not, for all Facebook messaging features are integrated seamlessly. First, we provide an overview of the types of message options, and then we explain how each works and how you can use them in later sections.

When it comes to private conversations, Facebook has the following messaging functions:

✦ **Messages:** Messages are like e-mail in Facebook. Similar to your typical e-mail, you have an inbox and places where other messages are stored, such as Sent Messages or Archived Messages. You receive notifications of new messages along with your other Facebook notifications in your Facebook toolbar (the blue strip across the top of all Facebook pages). Figure 8-1 shows the messages screen (the inbox).

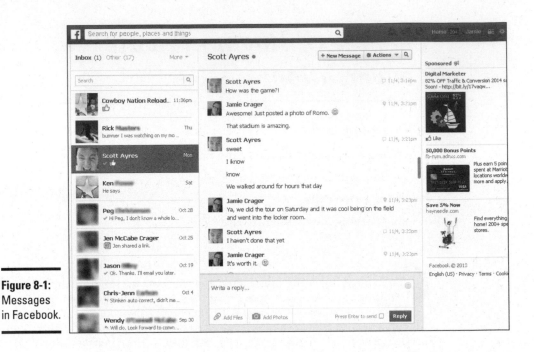

Figure 8-1:
Messages
in Facebook.

✦ **Chats:** Chats are the same as instant messages — real-time text conversations between friends. Chats appear on the bottom of your screen in the browser with the friend's name at the top of the message, as shown in Figure 8-2. You can have several active chats at a time. If you chat with several friends, you would simply have a chat box open for each conversation.

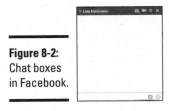

Figure 8-2:
Chat boxes
in Facebook.

✦ **Video calls:** Video calls are just like phone calls between two people, except that you have the benefit of being able to see the person you're talking to on your screen. Video calls use your computer's web camera and microphone. A video call conversation with people far away makes them seem close.

✦ **Pokes:** Pokes are the least significant part of this chapter. The poke feature enables you to send a meaningless notice to a friend. Because pokes are between two people, we include them with private conversations. To poke someone, you navigate to their timeline and click the gear icon under the cover photo. Choose Poke from the menu that appears.

✦ **Group chat:** Chatting with multiple people in the same conversation is the only defining factor of group chats. It works just like regular chat, except you can get all your friends in the same "room" at the same time; we explain how a little later in the chapter.

✦ **Facebook e-mail addresses:** When you set up your timeline, Facebook allows you to set up a Facebook e-mail address, which ends in `@facebook.com`. This address enables people to send messages directly to your Facebook account from any e-mail provider, as shown in Figure 8-3.

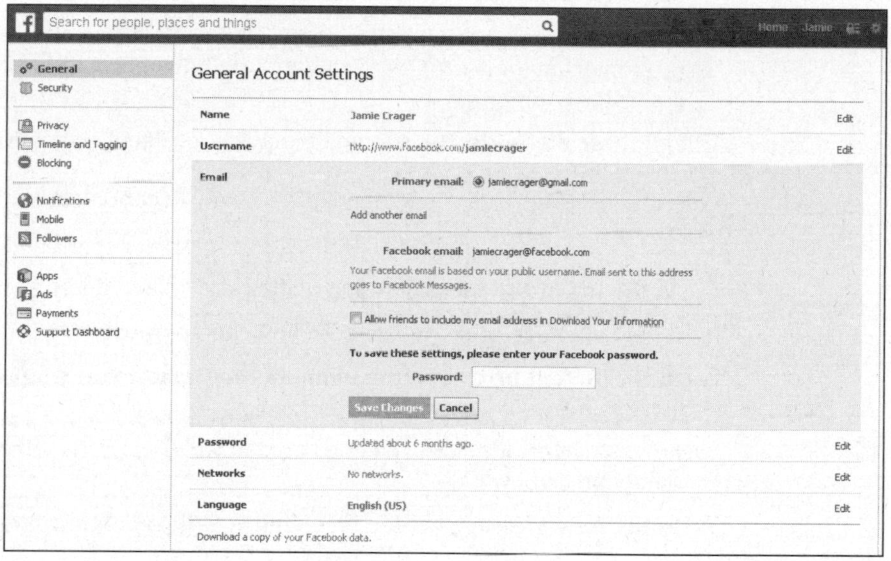

Figure 8-3: An @facebook.com e-mail address.

You can send messages on Facebook several ways. The following sections discuss your options.

Sending Messages

Sending a Facebook message is one of the most popular ways to interact privately with friends, business pages, and others you may not be connected with yet. Messages are closely integrated with Facebook chat — those two features often overlap. This section explains how to use Facebook messaging to contact others (we'll explain chat right after).

Messaging friends

Messages between you and a friend are organized in one continuous stream. Chat and message histories are threaded together. Essentially, all your private communication with a friend is combined in one place, regardless of the format of the conversation. If you turn on text updates, messages exchanged with that friend via text are stored in the message thread as well.

You can send a friend a message from the following places in Facebook:

✦ On your friend's timeline, click the Message button in the lower-right corner of their cover photo.

✦ Click the message icon in the blue toolbar at the top of all Facebook pages (it looks like two speech bubbles), and then click See All.

✦ Click the Messages link below your profile picture on the news feed. (You may have to scroll down a bit if you have lots of items listed in your Favorites category.)

With all these methods, the screen displays your Facebook inbox.

To send a message to a friend, navigate to your Facebook inbox and follow these steps:

1. **At the top of the messages page, click the +New Message button.**

A new message box opens where you can compose your message.

2. **In the To text box, type the name of the person you want to message.**

As you begin typing, relevant names of friends appear. As you type, the results narrow. Click to select a name in the list. Or, to select the top name, press Enter.

3. **In the New Message screen (see Figure 8-4), type your message.**

Figure 8-4: Sending a message.

4. **(Optional) Click the following to send additional content:**

   - *Click the paperclip icon to attach a file to your message.* You can attach just about anything you can attach to a traditional e-mail message.

   - *Click the camera icon to upload photos.*

   - *Click the emoticons symbol to add cartoon faces that express a certain emotion.*

5. **If you want to use the Enter key to send your message, select the Press Enter to Send (Quick Reply Mode) check box.**

   If you select this check box, and want to start a new paragraph in the message, press Shift+Enter.

6. **Click Send (or press Enter if you selected Quick Reply Mode), and your message is off!**

   Your friend receives a notification of the message almost instantly.

After you send your message, you can click the Actions link in the upper-right corner, next to the +New Message button. Doing this will provide you with options to edit that message thread, as shown in Figure 8-5. *Note:* Messages that include more than one person will display additional options such as Create Group, Add People, and Leave Conversation.

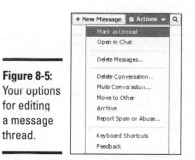

Figure 8-5:
Your options
for editing
a message
thread.

Messaging nonfriends

Sending messages to someone who is not a friend (someone who is not on your Facebook Friends list) works similarly to sending messages to friends. Because the person isn't on your Friends list, when you type her name in the New Message screen, it won't show up. To send her a message, you have to start by visiting her timeline.

To get to her timeline, type her name in the search text box at the top of your home page. Relevant results appear as you type. Click her name to go to her timeline. On her timeline, click the Message button in the lower-right corner of her cover photo. The New Message dialog box appears; type your message as you normally would.

Users have the option to disallow messages from people who are not their friends (or at least friends of friends). If a user chooses that level of privacy, you won't be able to send him or her a message.

When people receive messages from a person they don't know, they may be naturally suspicious. To avoid that, make sure you provide context in the content of your message. You're more likely to receive a response if you explain how you know each other (mutual friends, for example) and why you're contacting the person. In other words, include a message such as "We met at the Indianapolis Volleyball Competition."

Links from strangers are suspicious. If you must share a link, it's best if the link includes a preview of the destination site. Keep in mind that people are less likely to click a link shared by a stranger because of the threats of spam and phishing sites.

Chatting with Friends

When you and a friend are logged in to Facebook at the same time, you can exchange messages instantly and enjoy a real-time conversation. Real-time messaging also comes in the form of video calls in the chat screen — Facebook integrates with Skype to provide this feature (as described later in the chapter).

The Facebook chat features work seamlessly with Facebook messaging features. When you send a chat message to one of your friends, and she goes offline before receiving it, the chat message is automatically sent to her message inbox.

Initiating a chat message

When you are logged in to Facebook, an adjustable box appears in the right sidebar below the Facebook ticker. This box contains a list of friends with green dots by their names. These are your friends who are online (or were recently online). If you previously had your chat sidebar open, it may appear this way by default when you log in again.

Click any one of the names, and a chat box appears at the bottom of your browser screen. Type your message in the text box to chat.

To the right of someone's name in your chat list is a dot indicating availability. A green dot indicates that the person is online and available for chat. When someone remains idle for a period of time or logs off, the dot no longer appears.

At the bottom of the chat window, you can search for contacts. Click the gear icon to turn off chat, enable chat sounds, or chat from the desktop. You can also hide the right-hand sidebar.

Chatting with more than one friend

How about getting all your friends together, no matter what part of the world they're in? You can easily invite several people into a chat conversation. To do so, follow these steps:

1. **After initiating a chat, click the silhouette icon or the gear icon, at the top of your chat box, and select Add Friends to Chat (see Figure 8-6).**

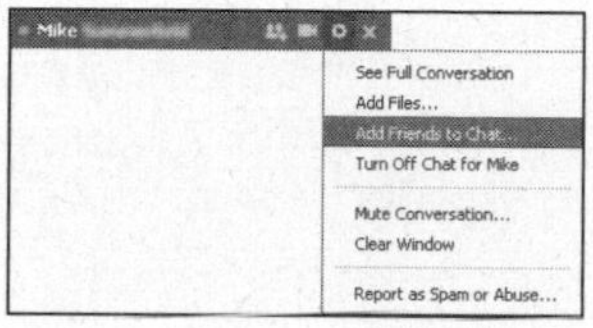

Figure 8-6:
Chatting
with more
than one
friend.

**Book II
Chapter 8**

**Having Private
Conversations**

2. **Begin typing the names of the people you want to add to the chat and then select their names, as shown in Figure 8-7.**

   You are inviting additional friends into your chat conversation.

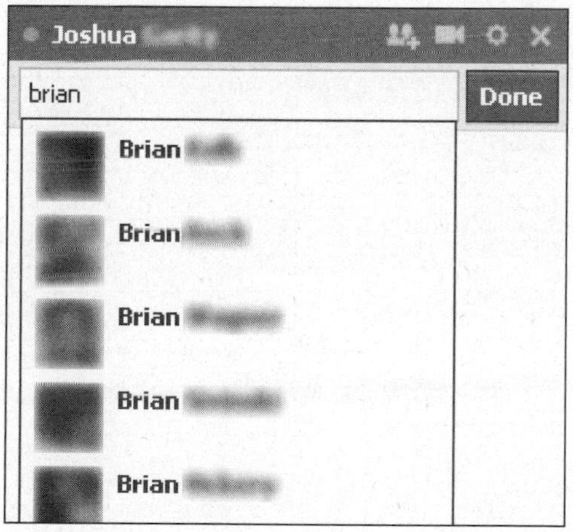

Figure 8-7:
Selecting
friends
to add to
a chat.

Going offline or limiting your availability

You can always turn off chat while you are logged in to Facebook. Simply click the gear icon at the bottom of your chat list and choose Go Offline.

You can also turn on or off sounds. Click the gear icon at the bottom of the right sidebar (chat list) and select or deselect Chat Sounds. When a check mark appears next to Chat Sounds, you hear a little blip sound when someone sends you a chat.

If you want to limit your chat availability to people in certain groups, you can do so. Limiting your availability can be nearly as specific as the privacy settings for your timeline and status updates. With Facebook's group settings (which we talk about in Book II, Chapter 5), you can make yourself available only to specific lists or to anyone except a specific list.

Figure 8-8 shows how you can hide yourself from a friend. Click the friend's name, and then click the gear icon in the dialog box that appears. Choose Turn Off Chat for *[Name]* and that person won't see you as available to chat.

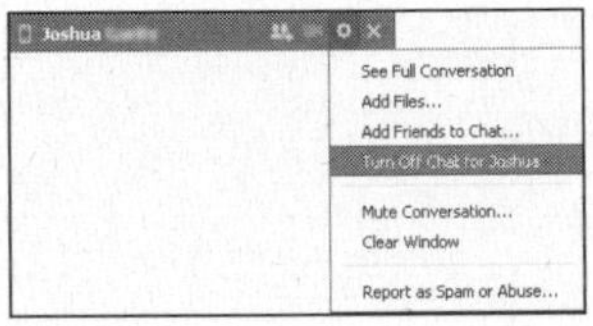

Figure 8-8:
Limiting
your chat
availability.

Figure 8-9 shows how you can use the Advanced Chat settings to limit who sees you on chat. To use the Advanced Chat settings, click the gear icon at the bottom of your chat sidebar and choose Advanced Settings. The dialog box in Figure 8-9 appears. From here, just select the settings you want to implement and then click Save.

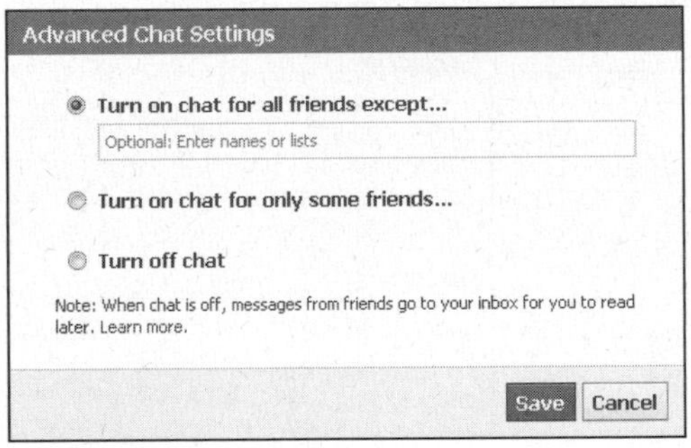

Figure 8-9:
Advanced
chat
settings.

Making a Video Call

Talking with your friends face to face no longer requires that you be in the same room. Facebook has integrated Skype video-calling features that make it possible for you to video chat with any of your friends, so long as you both have a web camera connected to your computers.

When you initiate a video call for the first time, you need to complete a quick one-time setup. Then you see a Call button on your friend's profile page or chat box if he or she has also set up video chat.

To set up video chat, you must first initiate a call with a friend:

1. **Click the Call button in the lower-right corner of your friend's cover photo or the video camera at the top of the chat box.**

   You're asked to set up video calling, as shown in Figure 8-10.

Figure 8-10: Setting up video calling.

2. **Click the Install button.**

3. **If you are asked to download a file:**

   a. *Click Save File.*

   b. *After the file has downloaded, open and run it.*

   The file is a plugin that Facebook needs on your computer for video calling to work.

Facebook initiates the call with your friend. In the top-right portion of the screen is what your friend sees, as shown in Figure 8-11. The big picture is where you see your friend. To end the call, click the Close (X) button in the top-right corner (Windows) or the red button in the top left corner (Mac).

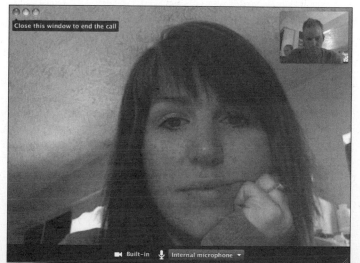

Figure 8-11: You and your friend on a video call.

Your Facebook E-Mail Address

When you sign up for Facebook, you're issued an e-mail account with the address *username*@facebook.com. You have one opportunity to change that address. To do so, you must change your username. Facebook will update the new address and it will be added to your contact info in the About section of your timeline.

Facebook e-mail addresses provide an e-mail platform that is similar to traditional e-mail services (such as Gmail or Yahoo!). Facebook e-mail addresses provide a seamless integration with Facebook messaging, which essentially expands your communications reach.

The biggest limitation to Facebook e-mail is that a message you send to an e-mail address from Facebook is limited in terms of content by Facebook's features. You can attach only what Facebook allows you to attach, and there is no subject line.

Chapter 9: Games and Gifts

In This Chapter

✔ **Finding games on Facebook**

✔ **Inviting friends to play**

✔ **Making in-game purchases**

✔ **Changing privacy settings for games**

✔ **Playing Facebook mobile games**

✔ **Buying gifts and gift cards**

Remember when you were a kid and you had a game system? (Maybe you're even old enough to remember cartridge-based game machines or going to an arcade to play video games.) If you wanted to enjoy playing games with your friends, they had to come over. (You were the cool kid if you had a game machine.) Now you can play games with friends on Facebook.

Facebook is dedicated to connecting people for whatever purpose they choose. Some people make business connections; others make social connections. Facebook's integration with apps and games means that you can also enjoy the fun of a game or two with your friends, even if they're located on the other side of the world.

Facebook Games

In most cases, games are created by third-party application developers. The game apps often use Facebook's core features through Facebook Connect to make playing more social. (See Book III, Chapter 2 to find out more about Facebook Connect.)

Following are some of the features native to Facebook that make playing games more fun and more social:

✦ Inviting your friends to join you in games

✦ Tracking progress with your timeline to earn points or badges

✦ Sharing badges on your Facebook timeline

✦ Seeing which friends are also currently playing a game

✦ Finding new games that your friends are playing

The term *app* refers to any third-party software program designed to be used with and to enhance existing online software. Accessing games through Facebook is an example of using an app whose sole purpose is game play.

The games people play on Facebook are not made by Facebook and are not part of Facebook.com. Because Facebook allows third-party integration of games and other apps, anyone with web software development skills can follow the appropriate procedures to build a game. Some Facebook games are made by larger software development firms that specialize in Facebook games, and others are made by individuals. Thousands of developers make Facebook games and other Facebook apps.

In the old arcade days, you dropped a quarter or token into the machine to play the game. Facebook games work similarly, but you usually can play the game for free in the beginning. To continue through the game or to buy virtual items, you can purchase directly through Facebook.

Some games are sponsored by brands looking to expand visibility of their products. For example, *The Sims Social* struck a deal to "run on Dunkin'," so Dunkin' Donuts brand consumable items appear in the game, as shown in Figure 9-1.

Figure 9-1: Branded items appear in games.

It's also common for advertising to appear to the side of the game you're playing. Advertisers attempt to highlight products that they think will appeal to the game's players. Some advertisements prompt for users to Like the company's Facebook page or to make a purchase right on the spot.

Playing Games

Games are hosted on the App Center page (www.facebook.com/appcenter). The left side of the screen displays some of your latest game notifications, which include invitations to games or a notice that your friend has made a move and it is your turn. (You need to be logged in to Facebook to see the game invitations from friends on the App Center page.) The bottom part of the App Center page (see Figure 9-2) displays the following information about other games:

+ **Suggested:** Personalized game suggestions.

+ **Top Rated:** The games rated the highest and used most frequently.

+ **Trending:** Games whose use is growing rapidly.

+ **Friends':** Games that your friends have used recently.

+ **Top Grossing:** Games with the most in-app purchases.

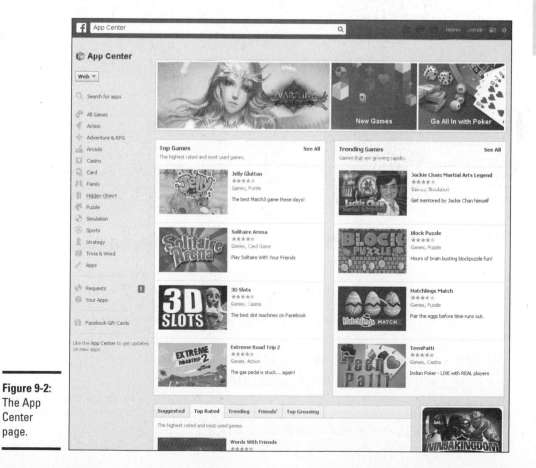

Figure 9-2:
The App
Center
page.

The main part of App Center displays promoted games (at the top), new games, top games, and trending games.

Finding the games your friends are playing

You can find out what other games your friends are playing so you can join in the fun. Check out one of the following:

✦ **App Center:** When you go to www.facebook.com/appcenter, you see which games your friends are playing. Scroll down and click the Friends' tab. You see a list of games and other apps with information indicating which friends are playing these games (or using these apps), as shown in Figure 9-3.

Figure 9-3: Find games being played by friends.

✦ **Invites and news feed updates:** If you're invited to a game by a friend, you can rest assured that your friend has been playing that game. Many of the games have an Invite option. This feature makes Facebook games social! You can access any invites by clicking the Requests link in the left sidebar.

Allowing games to access your information and timeline

Whether you are discovering games on your own or have received an invitation from a friend, games request access to some of your information and your timeline, as shown in Figure 9-4.

Figure 9-4:
Allowing
games per-
mission to
access your
timeline.

The permissions that games need vary, but in most cases they want to know
the following:

✦ **Basic information:** This category includes general information in your
   timeline, such as your name, profile picture, gender, networks, user ID,
   and list of friends. Games might need this information to access your
   friends list to suggest people to invite. Or a game might want to use
   your name or gender to properly address you within the game. Games
   also use this information for marketing, to display relevant ads.

✦ **E-mail address:** The e-mail address associated with your Facebook
   account might be shared so that the game can send you notifications
   related to the game or other e-mail content. The e-mail content will always
   be related to the game in some way, but it might include suggestions
   of other games made by the same developer or notifications that it's your
   turn if you've been engaged in a game with a friend.

✦ **Your birthday:** You are giving the game permission to access the day
   you were born.

✦ **Publish games and app activity:** The activity referenced here includes
   your scores in a game or other accomplishments. This activity might
   be published on your timeline. Your activity is populated automatically
   when you use Facebook. Games and any other apps have to be granted
   permission to do this.

✦ **Publish to Facebook as me:** You are giving the game permission to post
   an update on your timeline as if you posted it. The game will post something related to the game, which may include status updates, notes,
   photos, or videos. You can select a privacy level to determine who can
   see these updates.

It's up to you to allow games to access your timeline. In most cases, the game will only request permissions for the functions required for you to use the game. Some permissions are optional, which means you can still allow it but have to confirm before the game takes the specified action, such as posting on your timeline or sending invitations to your friends. These actions are permitted in advance but don't happen without your knowledge. They are part of the game activity.

To permit access to a game, click the Play Game button or the Send to Mobile button on the right side of the game's page.

Inviting friends to a game

After you enter a game, the next step is to play. Because games are more fun with friends, many games prompt you to invite your friends and share the game with them. Some games are designed to play with others, such as Scrabble. When you enter the game, the game prompts you to invite friends, as shown in Figure 9-5.

Figure 9-5: Inviting a friend to play Scrabble.

Many games give you the option to send an invite to a group of friends by selecting from your entire friends list, as shown in Figure 9-6. In the case of the DoubleDown Casino game, you get more chips for game play when you invite your friends.

Figure 9-6:
Inviting all
friends to
play Double
Down
Casino.

Accepting invitations from friends

When you go to the App Center page, you see your pending game invitations
from friends. These invitations allow you to accept or decline the invitation.
To accept, all you have to do is click the Accept button on the right side of
the invitation, and the game opens. (Remember that the app will ask you for
access permissions at this point.)

Blocking unwanted games

You can always decline invitations to games. In addition, you can go a step
further and block invitations from a game. When you receive an invitation from
a game that you want to block, click the Ignore All link in the text of the game's
invite. (The link is usually in blue and appears below the game title.) By clicking
Ignore All, you will no longer receive invitations from any of these games. If you
change your mind, you can always go directly to the game to gain access.

Making In-Game Purchases

Games aren't produced for free. Game developers make money for their
services through advertising and sponsorships, as well as from players paying
to play the game. To accommodate this, Facebook lets you make in-game
purchases by using Facebook's purchasing methods.

To set up a credit card to keep on file with Facebook so that you can purchase
items, follow these steps:

1. **Click the gear icon in the top-right corner of your page and choose
    Account Settings.**

2. **Click Payments, on the left side of the page.**

   The Payments Settings page appears, as shown in Figure 9-7.

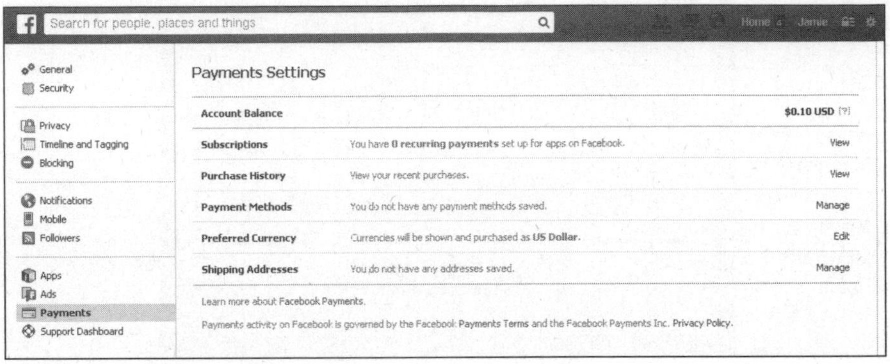

Figure 9-7:
Add payment methods and see activity.

3. **Click the Manage link to the right of Payment Methods.**

   Facebook and its applications allow you to pay in several ways, such as with a standard credit card, your mobile phone provider, a gift card, or your PayPal account, as shown in Figure 9-8.

4. **Fill in your payment information and click Add.**

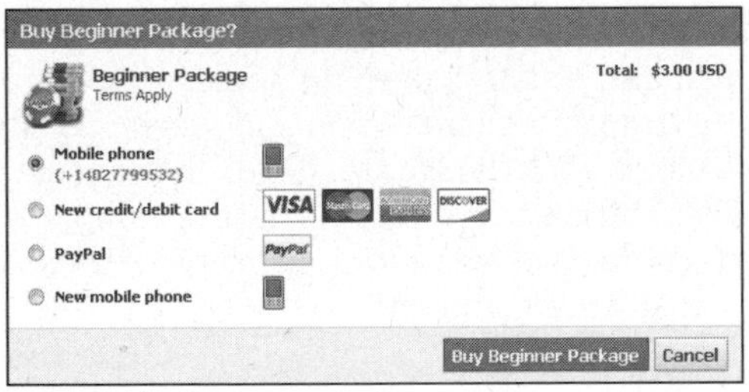

Figure 9-8:
In-game options to purchase items.

Changing a Game's Privacy Settings

You can control what your friends see in the ticker from your games. (The *ticker* is the list of updates in the top-right corner of the screen.) Maybe you want friends to see updates for a favorite competitive game, but for another game you want to be able to relax and ignore the competition.

To control these settings, follow these steps:

1. **Click the gear icon and choose Settings.**

2. **Click Apps in the left sidebar.**

   The Apps Settings page appears, displaying all the apps for which you have granted permission, as shown in Figure 9-9.

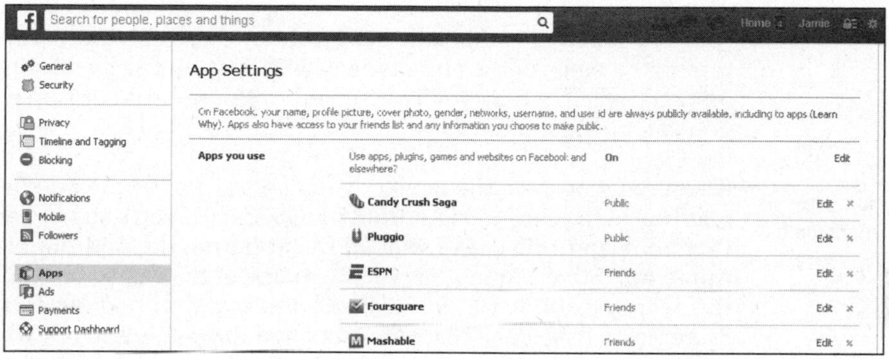

Figure 9-9:
Settings for your apps and games.

**Book II
Chapter 9**

Games and Gifts

3. **Click the Edit link to the right of the app you want to change.**

   The settings and permissions for that app appear.

4. **In the Visibility of App section, at the top, click the Share drop-down list and change the game's privacy setting.**

   This share drop-down list is shown in Figure 9-10.

5. **Click Close.**

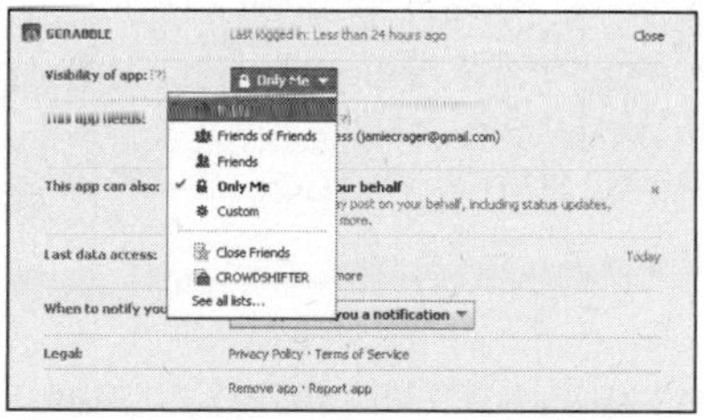

Figure 9-10:
Setting the privacy for specific apps.

Games on Facebook Mobile

Some Facebook games are available on your mobile device. As well, most mobile browsers allow you to view the full desktop version of Facebook, so you can play Facebook games that way. (Playing on a mobile device often isn't as enjoyable as playing on the computer, though.)

To use your mobile device to find the games that you've played on your computer, click the gear icon in the top-right corner of your page and choose Account Settings. Then click Apps in the left sidebar. Select the game you want to play, and you are taken to the Android store or the Apple store, depending on the device you're using.

On the Facebook mobile site (m.facebook.com), you can find games by typing the name of the app in the search text box or by clicking the Games link on the left. Again, you're directed to the Android or Apple store, where you can download the game.

If you're using a mobile device, you can search for the app in the search text box of the Facebook Android or IOS app. (If you don't already have the Facebook app, you can download the app from the Android Play Store or Apple App Store.) After you type the name of the game you want to play into the Search text box within the Facebook app, you're directed to the App Store if you have not already downloaded the game, and it will prompt you to download the game to your device. For example, type **Bejeweled** into the Search text box to find Bejeweled Blitz, download the Bejeweled Blitz app from the App Store, and start making those hypercubes and blowing up gems. After you've downloaded the game, you can go to it directly from Facebook to play.

When you play games on the Facebook app or through the Facebook mobile site, your activity is posted on your personal timeline, in the same way when you're playing on your desktop computer.

Facebook Gifts and Gift Cards

Facebook has made it easy to send your connections a gift or a gift card appropriate for many occasions. Sometimes a gift can mean more than a private message or a status update wishing someone "Happy Birthday."

Gifts

You can use Facebook Gifts to send friends and family members something to let them know you are thinking of them. Share in a celebration or just make someone's day brighter. Simply select and pay for the gift, add your personal note, and your gift is ready to go.

To order a gift, follow these steps:

1. **Go to a friend's timeline.**
2. **Click the gear icon in the lower-right corner of the cover photo, and then click the Give Gift link, shown in Figure 9-11.**

Figure 9-11:
Click the
Give Gift
option.

3. **On the Facebook Gifts page, shown in Figure 9-12, select a category at the top of the page.**

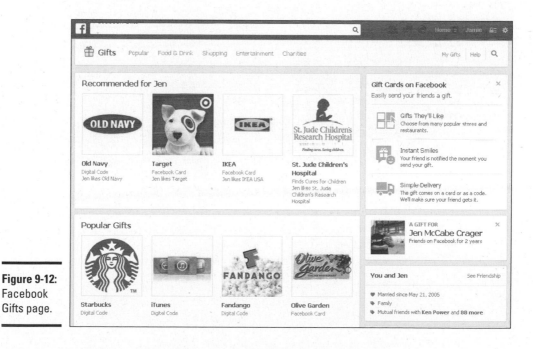

Figure 9-12:
Facebook
Gifts page.

4. **Select your gift by clicking its Choose This Gift button.**

5. **Choose your e-card and add a note.**

6. **Click Save Card & Review Order.**

7. **Review your order details, and then click Buy Gift.**

   You can add payment options, see shipping details, share on the timeline of the person to whom you are sending the gift, and select when you want to notify the person that he or she is receiving a gift from you.

Your friend won't see the price of the gift, but it can be swapped for another similarly priced gift before it ships.

Gift cards

Facebook gift cards are an easy way to buy items in your favorite games and apps on Facebook. Use a gift card yourself or give one to a friend. You can purchase a gift card by clicking the Facebook Gift Cards link on the App Center page. You'll find the link near the bottom of the left sidebar (refer to Figure 9-2).

After you click the link, you will be taken to a page where you can redeem the gift card, find a store that sells Facebook gift cards locally, or buy online at target.com.

Chapter 10: Professional Networking

In This Chapter

✔ **Using Facebook for networking**

✔ **Expanding your network**

✔ **Building stronger engagement**

✔ **Using business pages for networking**

Expanding your reach in business isn't easy — tons of meetings and a lot of effort are required to keep in touch with your contacts. The key is to be remembered by the people with whom you build a network, so that when they need your services — or know someone who does — they will deliver the business to you.

Facebook is not a replacement for face-to-face meetings, but it is a way for those meetings to reach further. In this chapter, we talk about how you can use Facebook as a tool that extends the reach of your networking and enhances business relationships. We also talk about some innovative ideas that can make you a networking power user.

Before You Begin Networking

Everyone is a little different in the way that they use Facebook. Some people are private and others are open. If people prefer not to add professional contacts to their friends list, don't take it personally.

Also be conscious of what you say online. If you feel the need to be inappropriate (or otherwise have private content to share), filter who sees which updates.

Be conscious of the message you're sending. Your message includes your profile photo, your other photos, the content of your Info page, your status updates, and even your friends' responses.

Customizing your profile photo for networking

To put your best foot forward, consider the appearance of your personal timeline. The best place to start is your profile picture, which is perhaps the most important part of your timeline. Your profile photo identifies you and suggests who you are. You want to determine where you want to be between a professional appearance and a friendly personality. Figure 10-1 shows Brian's profile picture. He wanted to present who he really was, straddling the lines of business and personal.

Figure 10-1: A professional yet casual profile photo.

Getting to know the space

After you have a profile picture, you have a little more work to do for a complete timeline. Consider the following areas:

✦ **The cover photo:** The cover photo is the image that covers the top of your timeline. Choose an image that represents you or that you think looks nice.

✦ **The About section:** Tell a bit about yourself. Be genuine, and be sure to share what you do for a living and why you love what you do.

✦ **Work and Education in the About section:** Make sure you fill in your work and education information. This section is one of the first places people look when learning about new connections.

✦ **Contact Info in the About section:** Here people can find out how to connect with you outside social media.

Anything beyond these areas is optional.

Using Facebook for Professional Networking

Several things are important when you're using Facebook to network: being professional and being personal. These may sound contradictory, but they aren't. In fact, they should complement each other. Facebook is all about making personal connections. People appreciate that you're a real person with real things going on in your life. We think the best professionals to connect with are those who are regular people as well. When you let those two areas of your life — personal and professional — blend, you can make some good connections.

Most businesses are based on relationships. People are more likely to buy products and services from people they know, like, and trust, so one of your goals may be to connect with other professionals in your niche via Facebook. When you make connections on Facebook, you can share life experiences and have conversations; you can begin to get to know others and build trusting relationships.

The concern some may have is how to connect with business contacts on Facebook without seeming overzealous. We have some ideas about how you can approach your professional networking on Facebook.

Most networking starts with some sort of meeting. If you're looking to expand your network, have a cup of coffee with someone every now and then. Talking with someone face-to-face almost always helps strengthen a relationship. After you've met with someone you'd like to connect with on Facebook, send the person a personal message, such as "Hey, Tom, great getting together for coffee! Thought I would go ahead and connect on Facebook," and then send them a friend request. Remember, though, that not everyone likes to mix professional and personal lives, so don't be offended if Tom replies, "I enjoyed coffee too, but I like to keep my Facebook for family and friends. Why don't you connect with me on my business page?" Remember that Facebook is a personal space and everyone uses it differently. Tom may need to know you better in person before he feels comfortable connecting with you on Facebook.

One effective old-school way to connect is to combine your Facebook status updates with offline messaging. For example, Andy Ellwood, cofounder of Bond, an application that allows you to send gifts and handwritten notes from your iPhone, invites viewers of his status updates to download the app and send their first notes for free by giving out a promo code, as shown in Figure 10-2.

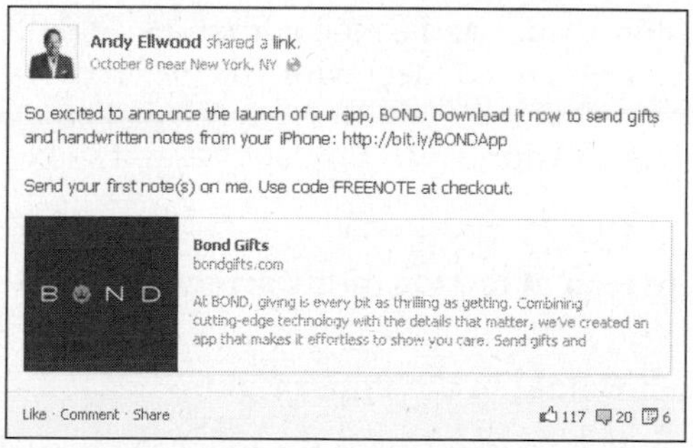

Andy Ellwood shared a link.
October 8 near New York, NY

So excited to announce the launch of our app, BOND. Download it now to send gifts and handwritten notes from your iPhone: http://bit.ly/BONDApp

Send your first note(s) on me. Use code FREENOTE at checkout.

BOND

Bond Gifts
bondgifts.com

At BOND, giving is every bit as thrilling as getting. Combining cutting-edge technology with the details that matter, we've created an app that makes it effortless to show you care. Send gifts and

Like · Comment · Share   117   20   6

Figure 10-2:
Helping your network by offering value.

Offer value and quality to your network even if the offer is free. When you have the best interests of others in mind, you win.

When you connect with professional contacts on Facebook, be sure to continue the relationship by commenting on their Facebook updates. Connecting casually through some simple conversation keeps you at the top of a person's mind. Your conversations don't have to be all about business. Just build the relationship! You can ask your contact if he or she would like to connect in person or on video chat just to catch up on what's new. Or you may simply ask how you can be of service — helping your new friend make additional connections is a great way to build that relationship.

Having personal and professional conversations

It's okay to engage in a conversation about everyday life, as well as more sensitive topics, as long as you have mutual respect and decency. Opportunities to connect with friends of friends can open up in these sorts of conversations. When two people join in a conversation in the post of a mutual friend, you've been virtually introduced, and this might be a great time to send a friend request if you think you might be good connections for one another.

Your professional contacts are regular people like you, and they have lives, families, friends, and experiences to share. It's okay to talk business, and it's okay to talk personal. Just don't put energy into a strict outline. Be yourself and have a little fun.

Building connections with professional contacts

If you'd like to expand your personal timeline network to include professional peers, you can use your e-mail account's Contact list to invite people to friend you on Facebook. You may like this option because it offers you the chance to connect with those people in a more casual environment.

Importing your e-mail Contact list is perhaps one of the easiest ways to quickly increase your network. All you have to do is upload the properly formatted list of your friends' names and e-mail addresses, and they will automatically be sent an invitation to connect with you on Facebook.

Follow these steps to import your e-mail Contact list and send friend requests:

1. **Click the silhouette icon at the top of the screen, as shown in Figure 10-3.**

2. **Click the Find Friends link, in the upper right.**

   The Friends page appears and displays the following:

   • Any outstanding friend requests.

   • The option to manage your friends lists.

   • The option to import contacts from Skype, Gmail, Windows Live Messenger, iCloud, Outlook.com, and other e-mail clients.

- A list of people you may know but are not connected with yet.
- The option to search for friends by name, hometown, city, mutual friend, gender, and age.

Figure 10-3:
Your list
of friend
requests.

3. **In the Add Personal Contacts section (top right), click the source from which you would like to upload.**

   You see several options, as shown in Figure 10-4. When you select an option, you see further options on how to access contacts from that source and upload them to Facebook.

4. **Follow the onscreen instructions to download or access a list of contacts to add as friends.**

5. **Click the Choose File button, select the file you just created, and then click Upload Contacts, as shown in Figure 10-5.**

   This step may vary, depending on your e-mail.

   You're alerted to how many people will be invited to join you on Facebook. Facebook recognizes e-mail addresses that are associated with an account on Facebook. Unrecognized e-mail addresses appear in a second list. You have the opportunity to invite these friends to join Facebook and connect with you.

6. **Click Confirm to send the invitations.**

Add Personal Contacts

Choose how you communicate with friends.
See how it works, manage imported contacts, or give feedback.
🔒 Facebook won't store your password.

jamiecrager

Skype Password

Find Friends

Figure 10-4: Choose where you would like to find friends.

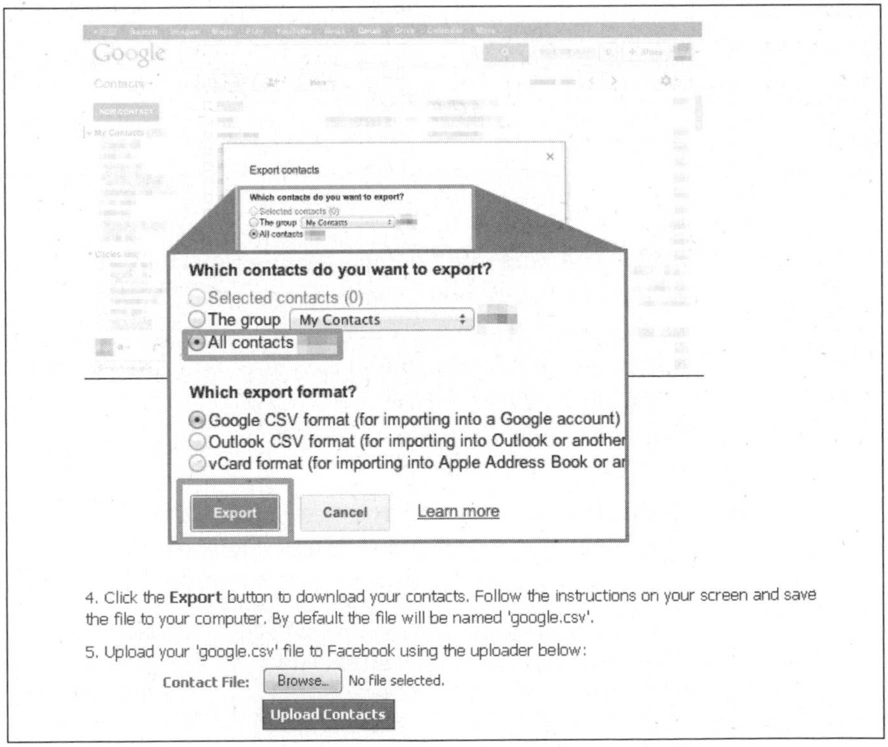

Export contacts

Which contacts do you want to export?

○ Selected contacts (0)
○ The group My Contacts
● All contacts

Which export format?

● Google CSV format (for importing into a Google account)
○ Outlook CSV format (for importing into Outlook or another
○ vCard format (for importing into Apple Address Book or a

Export   Cancel   Learn more

Figure 10-5: Upload the file to send an invitation to connect.

4. Click the **Export** button to download your contacts. Follow the instructions on your screen and save the file to your computer. By default the file will be named 'google.csv'.

5. Upload your 'google.csv' file to Facebook using the uploader below:

Contact File: Browse...   No file selected.

Upload Contacts

Some people set up Facebook with one e-mail address and conduct all their regular e-mail communications through another e-mail address. If someone's e-mail appears in the list of people not found on Facebook, it doesn't mean the person isn't on Facebook. Try searching for that person by name or by another e-mail address. (See Book I, Chapter 2 for more about finding friends.)

Expanding Your Network

It's easier than you think to increase your network on Facebook if you're actively connecting with people. Keep in mind that if you're randomly adding people but aren't connecting with them, you aren't likely to benefit from that network (and neither are they). The same is true if you're collecting Likes but not nurturing your business page community.

Making meaningful connections is important. The following sections describe some ways to expand your network.

Providing exclusive content to friends and followers

One way to get more connected with your network via your business page is to provide exclusive content for your friends and followers. We've seen several businesses offer coupons, free e-books or chapters, and other value-add items to their new friends and followers.

These businesses use a third-party application (such as Heyo, North Social, ShortStack, or Wildfire) to create engaging pages and content and get visitors to Like the page, share the page and its content, or sign up for a newsletter or downloadable content by joining an e-mail list.

Establishing yourself as an authority

When you're expanding your network, the kind of information you share has an effect on whether others want to connect with you (either via your personal timeline or your business page). People that share puddles of annoying updates often lose connections with people who are interested in the latest news, business ideas, or clean humor. Think about the people you're trying to reach so that you can share the right kind of information to expand that audience.

If you provide great content, creating an incentive for people to connect with you on Facebook is easy. For example, a business consultant may provide daily expert advice on increasing the reach of a business. The great advice she offers people is an incentive to be her friend or follower on Facebook.

Rocking the boat

If you know your audience well enough, you may be able to introduce some moderated controversy into your status updates (either on your personal timeline or your business page, depending on your goals and your audience for each). For example, Nathan knew that if he built his social media audience, he could attract new business for his company. One of his core goals was to engage with his followers and friends on Facebook through controversial conversation about politics.

While you may think that this could be a turnoff, he looked at it in a different way. His predominantly professional audience considers politics an important topic of conversation. Mutual respect is shared with those who engage in such conversation, even if they're on opposing sides.

If you decide to try this method, clearly define the rules with your audience. For instance, any comments with derogatory remarks or name-calling will be deleted. Establishing the guidelines for debate is especially important for your business page because it tends to come under closer scrutiny. Friends and followers don't like to be censored, and if you delete their comments without clear reason, the backlash can be intense.

Building Stronger Engagement

Engagement is the key to nurturing any network. The more you can encourage people to talk back to you, share your content, or tell their friends about you, the stronger your Facebook community is — and the more people want to connect with you. Facebook uses an algorithm currently called the News Feed Algorithm that, in simple terms, keeps track of the personal timelines and business page you interact with most. You can read more about this algorithm in Book V, Chapter 3, but we wanted to mention it here because it has an effect on how you create and share content with your audiences.

Here are a few tips to use to build engagement with your fans and friends:

✦ **Post something fun every now and then.** The News Feed Algorithm promotes stories from people you show more interest in. If you Like and comment on someone's stories regularly, you see more from that user in your news feed. If you think you have to be stiff just because you're posting to your business page, we want to encourage you to loosen up! If you lighten the mood and share fun information, people will engage a bit more, which will help your business page updates show up in your friends' and followers' news feeds more often.

✦ **Don't share long status updates.** The news feed is fast paced. Keeping your updates short ensures that you can capture the attention of your readers. Longer updates are commonly overlooked when people are scanning the news feed for the latest interesting news. For this reason, a short update is going to catch more attention than a long one. If you need to share more information, we suggest providing a link to a blog post.

✦ **Share pictures, video, and links.** Statistically, updates with pictures capture the most engagement because Facebook is visual. Couple that with the quickly moving news feed and it's easy to see how a photo or video catches the eye more quickly than a text update. When you share a link, Facebook automatically pulls a picture from the page so viewers can see a preview of the link. This feature helps increase the chance that people will take notice and click through to see more.

✦ **Comment on your friends' posts.** Building community means you have to be part of that community. Unless you're a celebrity (if you are, congratulations and thanks for reading this book), you won't always attract activity to your business page without taking the time to connect with others. If you want to gather more comments on your business page, be sure you're taking the time to comment on other business pages (either as yourself or as your business — we explain how to do that in Book IV, Chapter 2). If you're networking more with your personal timeline, commenting on a friend's status update may prompt her to take a look at the stories you're sharing. The truth is, if you want better engagement, go ahead and engage with people!

Book II
Chapter 10

Professional
Networking

Networking via Your Business Page

If you want to network in a different way, you might want to promote a business page. (See Book IV for information on business pages.) Business pages allow you to promote your business while keeping your personal timeline separate. However, you don't have to stick to business only! You can definitely let your personality shine through on your business page (and your customers will appreciate the effort). In this section, we discuss how you can introduce your business page to new and existing contacts.

Sharing a business page with a friend

It's simple to share your business page with your current Facebook friends. Follow these steps:

1. **Go to your business page's Admin panel at the top of your business page.**

You need to be signed in under your personal account and visit your business page. You can't access this feature using Facebook as a business page.

2. **Click the Build Audience button.**

You must view the business page from your personal account; if you view it as the page administrator, you won't see the necessary options.

3. **Choose Invite Friends.**

The dialog box shown in Figure 10-6 appears, listing all your friends.

Figure 10-6: Select the friends you would like to invite.

4. **Click Invite next to each friend you would like to ask to Like your business page and then click Close.**

The default list shows all your friends. You can search based on certain criteria by clicking the Search All Friends list and choosing friends based on recent interactions with your business page, where your friends live, whether they're in other Facebook groups you've joined, or your lists.

Another way to share your business page is to use the Share Page feature, which is available from your Admin panel (Build Audience⇨Share Page) or your business page (click the gear icon below your cover photo and choose Share from the list). With either method, the Share This Page dialog box appears (see Figure 10-7), and you can share your business page on your personal timeline, on a friend's timeline, in a group, on a business page you manage, or via a private message. Choose where you want to share your business page, type a note in the text box, and then click Share Page.

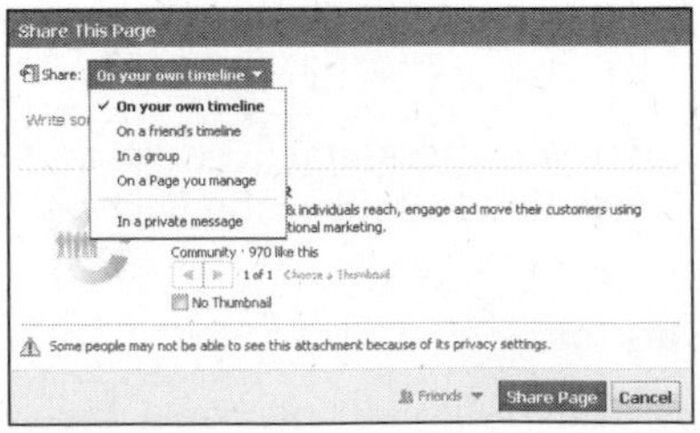

Figure 10-7: Share a business page.

Inviting e-mail contacts to Like your business page

Facebook enables you to invite your e-mail contacts to Like your business page. Simply follow these steps:

1. **Go to your business page's Admin panel.**

   The Admin panel navigation is located in the top-right corner of your business page.

2. **Click Build Audience⇨Invite Email Contacts.**

   The Invite Email Contacts dialog box appears, similar to the one shown in Figure 10-8. Your screen may be different, depending on the e-mail apps you have installed, such as MailChimp or Constant Contact. *Note:* You can invite contacts also from Skype, Windows Live Messenger, iCloud, or a custom e-mail provider, and you can even upload a CSV from your computer.

Book II
Chapter 10

Professional
Networking

Figure 10-8: Invite people via e-mail upload.

3. **Click the Invite Contacts link next to the e-mail provider you want to use.**

4. **Follow the instructions provided.**

   Depending on which app or option you choose, the instructions will require you to log in to your account or upload a file.

   An invitation to Like your business page will be sent to your contacts.

Chapter 11: Managing Connections Gone Awry

In This Chapter

↙ **Unfriending or hiding a friend's updates**

↙ **Blocking a person**

↙ **Leaving groups and Unliking business pages**

↙ **Blocking unwanted apps**

↙ **Removing timeline content**

↙ **Fixing a compromised account**

*W*hile you're building connections and reaching out to new people, your name starts to show up in more places as you share mutual friends or interact by commenting on a friend's post. You should find more people reaching out to you. Maybe some of your newfound friends invite you into their groups, or invite you to strangers' birthday bashes, or ask you to play games with them as they post tons of updates about their latest win in AquaVille. Sometimes, you'll find yourself with Facebook connections that turn bad.

If you need to purge your social connections, hope is available. In this chapter, we help you to navigate through Facebook to remove connections and keep your social sphere in order. We also illustrate how to remove content from your own timeline if you find that you've shared some things that you may want to keep out of the wrong hands.

The last thing we cover is Facebook viruses. In most cases, viruses can be avoided — and we explain how. And if your Facebook account has been infected with a virus, we tell you how to fix your account.

Unfriending or Hiding

When you first sign up for Facebook, it's easy to get excited about adding every friend you've ever had since preschool. This becomes an issue when you find that some of these long-lost friends are overzealous with their sharing, inviting, and gaming. As you accumulate friends, you may find that you need to purge your friends list. Here are a few reasons why you may want to do this:

✦ A friend frequently shares offensive or defamatory updates.

✦ A friend inappropriately comments on your posts.

✦ You want to maintain a higher level of privacy.

✦ You want a more easily managed friends list.

✦ You're entering the witness protection program.

All kidding aside, sometimes you just find that you have to make some changes to your Facebook friends list. In some cases, you may want to unfriend someone; in other cases, you may want to hide someone's updates but keep them as a friend. No problem. The next few sections explain how to do both.

Hiding updates from a friend or business page

If you don't want to see the updates of a particular person or business, whether because the updates are offensive or simply boring, hiding those updates is an alternative to unfriending. You can hide all updates or a single update from any friend or business page right from your news feed by clicking the arrow in the upper-right corner.

The people who show up in your news feed are those to whom you are friends with or follow. To hide updates from someone, follow these steps:

1. **In your news feed, find an update from the person to whom you want to unfollow.**

2. **Move your mouse pointer to the right side of the update and click the arrow icon that appears.**

The drop-down list shown in Figure 11-1 appears. The options are related to what updates you see from this friend or business page in your news feed. Click I Don't Want to See This to hide this single update.

Figure 11-1:
Hide updates from a friend or a business page.

3. **To never see updates from this friend or business page in your news feed, click Unfollow *[Name]*.**

   You still have this person as a connection (or friend), but you will no longer see the person's updates in your news feed. If you unfollow a business page, you will no longer be connected to them.

Unfollowing a friend's updates only removes the person's updates from your news feed. The person can still see your updates and comment on your posts. If you would like to comment on that person's posts, go directly to the person's timeline by typing his or her name in the search text box at the top of your home page.

Removing someone as a friend

When you unfriend someone on Facebook, you prevent the person from commenting on your posts (unless they are shared publicly) or seeing any pictures or updates that you have not made public. And because you're no longer friends, you can't see that person's private content either.

Former friends will not receive any notice that you have unfriended them. They will only be able to see that you aren't connected by going to your timeline and seeing the +1 Add Friend button or looking through their friends list.

Remove someone from your friends list by following these steps:

1. **Go to the friend's timeline.**

   Click the friend's name in your news feed or begin typing the friend's name in the search text box and select the name from the list that appears. Or you can click the Friends link, below your cover photo, and select the name from the list that appears.

2. **From the friend's profile, click the Friends button (on the bottom right of their cover photo). Or from your friend's timeline, click the Friends button to the right of the picture.**

   A drop-down list appears as soon as you move your mouse over it, as shown in Figure 11-2.

Book II
Chapter 11

Managing
Connections
Gone Awry

Figure 11-2:
Unfriending
a friend.

3. **Click Unfriend.**

Currently, Facebook doesn't allow you to unfriend a group of users. If you have multiple people you would like to unfriend, you have to visit each person's timeline and unfriend them one by one.

Blocking Someone

If things have really gone bad, and you want to ensure that a certain person does not have the ability to send friend requests, send messages, or see your information, you can block that person. This feature is helpful if someone is spammy or malicious.

To block someone, follow these steps:

1. **Go to the friend's timeline.**

   Click the friend's name in your news feed, type the friend's name in the search text box, or click the Friends link below your cover photo.

2. **Click the gear or silhouette icon under the cover photo and choose Report/Block from the drop-down list, as shown in Figure 11-3.**

   Or from your friend's timeline, select Friends and then select Report/ Block from the drop-down list.

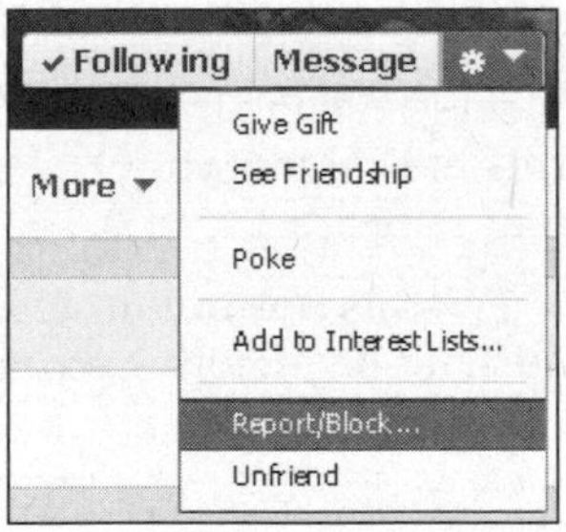

Figure 11-3: Blocking someone.

> ✓ Following   Message   ❖ ▾
>
> More ▾
>
> Give Gift
> See Friendship
>
> Poke
>
> Add to Interest Lists...
>
> Report/Block...
> Unfriend

3. **In the dialog box that appears, select the Block *[Name]* option, as shown in Figure 11-4.**

4. **(Optional) If you believe the person's content is spam or inappropriate, select the appropriate reporting option.**

5. **Click Confirm.**

   After you click Confirm, you have blocked the individual and can no longer communicate with that person on Facebook (and that person can't communicate with you). You also see a confirmation dialog box, with a link to the Family Safety Center, which offers information on how to handle harassment.

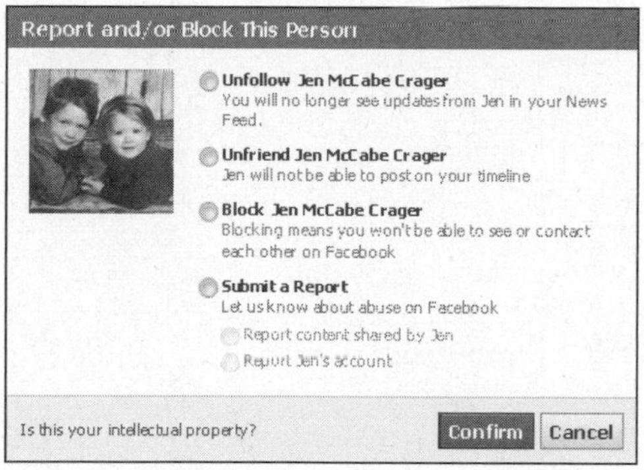

Report and/or Block This Person

○ **Unfollow Jen McCabe Crager**
You will no longer see updates from Jen in your News Feed.

○ **Unfriend Jen McCabe Crager**
Jen will not be able to post on your timeline

○ **Block Jen McCabe Crager**
Blocking means you won't be able to see or contact each other on Facebook

○ **Submit a Report**
Let us know about abuse on Facebook
○ Report content shared by Jen
○ Report Jen's account

Is this your intellectual property?   **Confirm** **Cancel**

Figure 11-4: Additional options to block or report someone.

Book II
Chapter 11

Managing Connections Gone Awry

Only report a person when absolutely necessary. What you believe to be inappropriate may not violate the Facebook terms. If you're offended by something that someone has posted, send the person a message about it directly or unfriend the person. If you're certain that the content violates Facebook terms, select the appropriate option in the Report and/or Block This Person dialog box.

When you block someone, that action is between you and the person you blocked. Blocking doesn't remove the person from Facebook or report the person to the Facebook compliance team. Blocking only prevents you and the individual from being able to communicate on Facebook. If you find that you made a mistake, you can edit your block list in your privacy settings. (See Book I, Chapter 3 for information about finding and choosing your privacy settings.)

Leaving Groups

The creator or administrator of a group can add any Facebook friend to the group — even if the person didn't want to be a member. That person is then included in all updates in that group.

If you've become a part of a group that you would rather remove yourself from, follow these steps:

1. **On the left side of your home screen, click the More link by the Groups section, as shown in Figure 11-5.**

   (To see the More link, hover your cursor over this area.) You see all the groups of which you are a member.

2. **Click the pencil icon to the left of the group name.**

   You have the options to add the group to your favorites, edit settings, or leave the group.

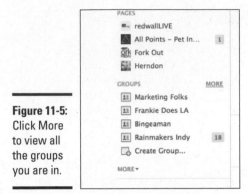

Figure 11-5:
Click More
to view all
the groups
you are in.

3. Click Leave Group.

You are no longer a member of the group and will no longer receive updates from the group.

Unliking Business Pages

Business pages are opt-in, which means you have to Like the business page to see the page's updates in your news feed. Sometimes you lose interest in a business page. Perhaps the business page is posting too much or not posting enough, or maybe you don't find the content interesting. In those cases, you may want to Unlike the business page — and that's an easy task.

To Unlike a business page, go to the business page. Under the cover photo, click the gear icon to see the drop-down list shown in Figure 11-6 and click Unlike. Or click the Liked button next to the gear icon and then click Unlike. You will no longer see updates from the business page in your news feed.

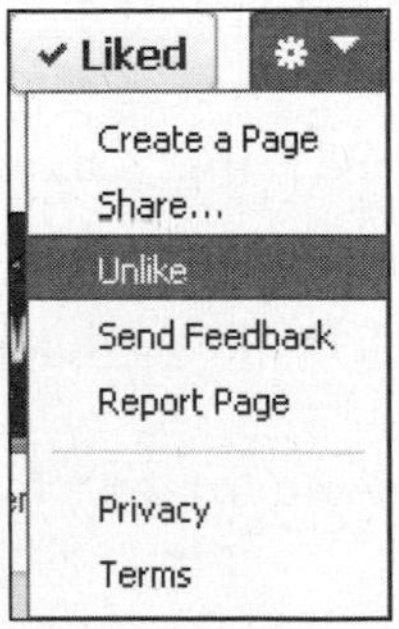

Figure 11-6:
Unliking a
business
page.

Unliking multiple business pages at a time is not possible with Facebook's current design.

Blocking Apps

To use an app, you have to permit it access to your personal timeline. Often, especially with games, the app will prompt you to invite others to participate. Your friends may (without even realizing it) be inviting you to the same game repeatedly, whether or not you've previously declined an app's invitation. To stop receiving invitations or announcements from an app, you can block it.

When you receive an invitation from an app that you'd like to block, click X, to the right of the app, and then click the Block *App Name* link.

If you want to unblock an app or just review which apps you've blocked, follow these steps:

1. **Click the gear icon on the top blue bar and choose Settings from the list.**

2. **In the left sidebar, click Blocking.**

The Manage Blocking page appears, as shown in Figure 11-7. At the bottom of the page you can view which apps you've blocked.

3. **To unblock an app, go to the Block Apps section and click the Unblock link next to the app's title.**

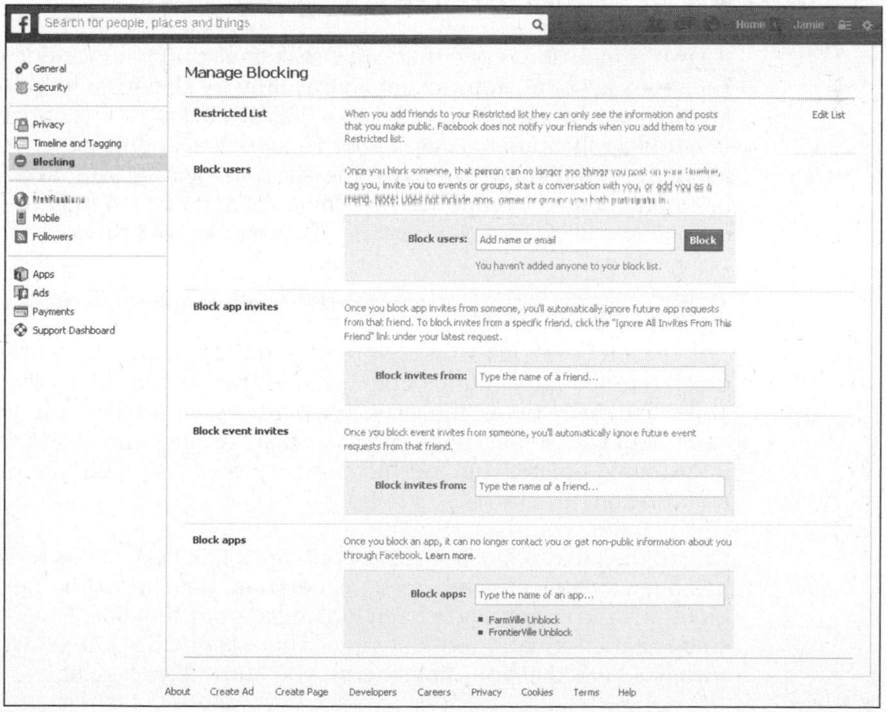

Figure 11-7:
View and manage blocked apps.

Removing Content from Your Timeline

If someone has spammed you or posted inappropriate content on your personal timeline, you will most certainly want to remove those posts. To do this, just move your cursor over the post and click the arrow icon that appears at the top right, as shown in Figure 11-8.

Figure 11-8: Removing content from your timeline.

A menu appears; click Report/Remove Tag or Hide from Timeline to remove the post from your timeline.

When you have posted content that you want to remove, you have the option to delete the entire post as well as hide it from the timeline.

Avoiding Facebook Viruses

A *virus* is malicious code that can wreak havoc on your (and your friends') Facebook account. You can get a virus only by clicking a link and downloading something (usually an .exe file) or clicking a link and allowing an infected application to access your Facebook account. When your Facebook account is infected with a virus, the virus will access your account and post infected updates to your friends' timelines and make it difficult for you to use Facebook. As you can imagine, it's best to avoid them.

Spotting a virus

The reason Facebook viruses spread so quickly is that they are hard to discern from regular status updates, and they appear to be shared by people you trust. Many times, the virus link piques your interest and you almost can't help yourself because you can't believe someone would share that information online. That morbid curiosity is exactly what the hackers are counting on.

One of the most popular viruses contains a link that claims to tell you who has been looking at your Facebook personal timeline. Although you may be interested to see who's been looking at your timeline, Facebook doesn't share that information with anyone. There is no app that allows you to see who has looked at your timeline, so you know it's a fake link.

Another popular trick is to use a link that allows you to watch a video of something "you won't believe!" or even a supposed video of you doing something funny or humiliating. If it's a legitimate video, it will play when you click it. If you're asked to download anything or allow an app to have access to your account, it's probably not a legitimate link and you should cancel immediately.

Facebook apps ask you to allow them to access your personal timeline information. (See Book VI for a full explanation of Facebook apps and how they work.) For instance, after you enter a giveaway or contest on a business page, the application for the promotion may ask if you'd like to share the link with your friends. To share the link, you have to allow the application to have access to your personal timeline. Or if you want to buy something from the Payvment Shopping Mall on Facebook (`www.facebook.com/payvment`), the Payvment app asks permission to access your account. In both instances, you must allow the application access to your account to complete your task, and the app is from a legitimate company.

**Book II
Chapter 11**

Managing Connections Gone Awry

If you click a video, photo, or sales link and are asked to allow an app to complete a transaction, you may want to research the company further or click away from that page. Knowing which Facebook applications to allow and which to click away from can be tricky.

One way to avoid getting a dreaded virus is to pay attention to what's showing up in your news feed. Many times, a virus will become so prolific that all your friends seem to be sharing the same link.

To avoid Facebook viruses, consider the following questions:

✦ **Does the link have a questionable image?** If you see an inappropriate picture with the status update, the link is probably a virus. Facebook is strict about pornography and shuts down pages that are considered adult.

✦ **Is this the type of link my friend usually shares?** If not, don't click. If you're tempted to click, first hover your cursor over the link and look in the lower-left corner of your browser. You see the URL attached to that link. If it's not a URL you're familiar with, don't click the link. Many virus links use `.info` in the URL.

✦ **Is this link related to a hot topic or current event?** You can expect a new rash of viruses when important current events occur.

✦ **Do I know the person who claims to have tagged me in a photo or video?** Beware of any message, link, or video claiming that someone has tagged or commented on a photo of you. Look to see if you know the person who supposedly tagged you. If you don't know the person, don't click the link. If you do click the link and you see a blank page, change your password immediately. If you're asked to allow an app to do something, do not click the Allow button — just click away from the page.

✦ **Am I on a legitimate Facebook page?** Occasionally, you may mistype the main Facebook URL and end up on a fake Facebook login page. If you type in your login information and click Submit, that page takes your information and accesses your Facebook account (technically this isn't a virus; it's called *phishing*). Always double-check that your browser is pointed to `www.facebook.com/index.php` before you type your login information.

If you ever end up on a page that says your Facebook session has timed out, do not type in your login information. Facebook sessions don't time out. Instead, point your browser to `www.facebook.com/index.php` and log in as necessary.

Fixing your account

The first thing to do when you discover that you have a Facebook virus is to change your Facebook password. To do that, follow these instructions:

1. **Log in to your Facebook account.**

2. **Click the gear icon on the blue bar and choose Settings.**

   The General Settings page appears.

3. **Click the Edit link on the Password row.**

   Three text boxes appear, labeled Current, New, and Re-type New.

4. **In the Current text box, type your current password.**

5. **In the New text box, type a new password.**

6. **In the Re-type New text box, type the new password again.**

7. **Click the Save Changes button.**

Now that you've changed your password, write a status update alerting your friends that you clicked a bad link and had a Facebook virus. Tell your friends not to click any links that appear to be from you — and refrain from posting links for a while so people don't worry about which links are good or bad.

If you know specific people who received a viral link from you, hcad over to their Facebook timelines and delete the message if you can. Also tell them not to click the link.

Finally, check to be sure that the application carrying the virus isn't lurking on your account. It's probably not, but it's best to be sure. Plus, now is a good time to clean out the apps you're not using anymore.

To check the apps connected to your account, follow these steps:

1. **Log in to your Facebook account.**

2. **Click the gear icon on the blue bar and choose Settings.**

   The General Settings page appears.

3. **In the left sidebar, click the Apps link.**

   The Apps Settings page appears.

4. **Click the Edit link next to any apps you don't remember installing or that you don't use regularly.**

   The app information expands to give a full overview of the app.

5. **Click the Remove App link.**

   A confirmation dialog box appears.

6. **Click the Remove button.**

   The app is now removed from your account.

If you don't see an app that looks like it's related to the virus, that's okay. It may not be there. Changing your password is what really matters; checking for the app and removing it are just insurance.

Book III
Connecting to Other Social Media

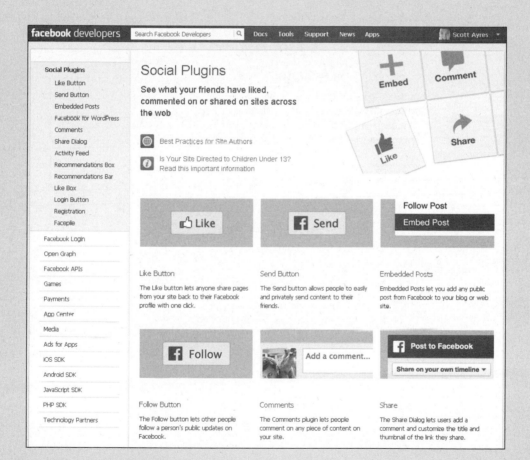

Contents at a Glance

Chapter 1: What Is Social Media?............................235

Defining Social Media...235
Making the Internet Friendly...237
Getting to Know Other Social Media Platforms..........................238
Understanding What Social Media Means to Marketers..............242

Chapter 2: Connecting Facebook to Everything Else.............245

Understanding the Basics of Facebook Platform........................245
Finding Common Uses for Facebook Platform............................247
Connecting to Facebook...249
Using Facebook Social Plugins...252
Using Facebook Badges for Social Proof...................................255
Integrating Facebook with Marketing Efforts for Your Business............256

Chapter 3: Flying on Autopilot 259

Automating Facebook to Achieve Marketing Goals....................259
Scheduling Updates with Post Planner or HootSuite..................260
Setting Up Notifications for Business Pages..............................263
Connecting Your WordPress Blog to Facebook...........................264

Chapter 1: What Is Social Media?

In This Chapter

✔ **Defining social media**

✔ **Delving into what makes up social media**

✔ **Understanding how Facebook compares and competes**

✔ **Garnering what social media means to you and to marketers**

*I*n this chapter, we explain more about what social media is and how you can use it. We also introduce you to some other social media platforms — Twitter, LinkedIn, Google+, Pinterest, and Instagram — and tell you how they're different from Facebook and why you may want to check them out. Throughout the chapter, we primarily focus on what social media means to marketers, but much of what we share can be applied to your daily personal life as well. Even though you may not be selling a product, you're still building your online reputation.

Defining Social Media

Social media is connecting with people using digital tools, such as Facebook. Facebook has taken the fundamental elements of how people connect, and made it possible to do much more with those connections. You can meet new friends in parts of the country (or world) you've never visited, network with business peers and share ideas, create interactive marketing campaigns that bring more sales, and bring a new level of customer service to your clients. Or, if you prefer to use social media just to keep up with friends and family, you can do that. Sharing photos, videos, and day-to-day updates about your life has never been easier. The personal aspect of social media brings endless options.

As the number of users of online social communities grows, businesses have found opportunities to join the conversation, too. *Social media evangelists* (people who make it their mission to promote and teach social media) insist that if you're in business, you must use social media because that is where your customers are connecting. Those customers are seeking new interactions, rating products, and making buying decisions based on the feedback of their peers.

In the past, media had been mostly broadcast and reserved for people who had the money to spend on it. Advertising is a good example. When a company wants to promote a product or service, they may buy television or radio ad space and broadcast their message to you. You don't have the option of interacting with that ad; you just absorb the information or ignore it. The communication in those instances is one-way. In the mid-1990s, Marc Andreessen developed a friendly face for the world wide web (the web browser), and the Internet as we know it started becoming mainstream. Companies started building websites (static at first, then more fluid) to broadcast their messages. Customers started using the Internet to find information, comparison shop, and, yes, kill time.

Over the past 20 years, the Internet has evolved. Companies can no longer get by with just an online brochure. Well-written and well-placed reviews can help or hurt a company, so customers have a certain amount of say in the conversation that they haven't had before. The growth of social media — the open conversations between friends or companies via digital platforms — has changed the way we live and do business.

Media is no longer top-down; it starts with the individual, not the company. Consider our earlier example of television and radio advertising. In those situations, you have the option of turning off the device or changing the channel. Social media platforms (such as Facebook) allow users to have more control over who they interact with. They decide who they want to hear from and what they want to hear from them — they can finely filter the messages they see. More importantly, they also have the option to weigh in and voice an opinion, and these actions may influence their friends to do the same.

Connecting — either with friends via their personal timeline or with businesses via their business page — is the centerpiece of social media. Facebook didn't invent the friending feature of social networking sites, but it sure has made a good use of it with the capability to adjust the levels of connection you have with people and businesses. You can share or consume more information with certain groups and less with others. (If you want to take your social media connections up a notch, flip to Book II, Chapter 10, where we discuss advice for social networking.)

The capability to filter content in a way that makes sense to you is important when you're choosing who to interact with. Most social media platforms have a list feature that allows you to group your connections and friends into categories that make sense so you can filter their shared information in your social media feeds. You can learn more about Facebook lists in Book I, Chapter 4.

 People accumulate friends via social media for a number of reasons, such as professional networking or keeping in touch with family. If you're trying to build your network, start by friending people you know personally, and then create new relationships through the mutual connections of those friends by engaging in conversations.

Blogging and microblogging

The term *blog* (a combination of web and log) was coined in the 90s to describe the phenomenon of online journals. It all started in 1980 with Usenet, a digital bulletin board where anyone could post a message for all to see. People would be alerted to the latest updates (called posts or articles) through an alert system called a news feed. The first blogs required that the user know some basic HTML to insert the content. Later, the arrival of content management software made creating and maintaining a blog easy.

Blogs allow people to have their own websites where they can post entries, writing about whatever they want, and visitors can respond to posts by leaving comments. Some blogging platforms allow for communities in which users can post stories or questions to other users in the community. Although some bloggers use their blogs as an online diary, many bloggers write articles and reviews, host giveaways, and much more. Blogging can even be a source of income from ads and sponsorships.

Similar to blogging, *microblogging* is an update on your personal page on the web, except (yep, you guessed it) with short posts, typically a sentence or two at the most. Posting status updates on Facebook is a form of microblogging. Twitter and Tumblr are two other common microblogging hosts.

Making the Internet Friendly

Years ago, Scott was looking for something on the Internet and didn't know how to find it. Someone at work advised him to go to a website called Ask Jeeves, where you could type a question and Jeeves would return an answer. But every time Scott asked a question, Jeeves would just return a list of websites that may or may not have been what he was looking for. Scott didn't find this very useful.

Social media sites such as Facebook have changed the terrain of the web in a big way. Now you can ask all your friends the questions you would previously ask that imaginary butler. The ability to ask online (or *crowdsource*) and share your experiences (providing social proof) has a major effect on your decisions. For example, if you're searching for a contractor to put a new roof on your house, you might give preference to the company that a friend recommends.

The Internet is about not just reading information but also connecting with friends and building relationships. People make purchasing decisions, plan activities, and build friendships all with the use of the Internet. The Internet in its infancy was used more for its utilitarian purposes, but human nature has put an emphasis on what matters most to us — relationships.

Getting to Know Other Social Media Platforms

Although you bought this book to find out all about Facebook, we want to introduce you to some other social media platforms as well. Facebook is one of many options for connecting with others online. And, although Facebook is the largest social network, each of the others has important features and uses.

Introducing Twitter

Twitter is a microblogging site that enables you to post short updates of 140 characters. Twitter feeds real-time *tweets* (posts) from all the people you follow, and also feeds all your real-time tweets to those who follow you. Twitter is opt-in based, which means you simply subscribe to the feed of an individual you want to follow. Others can choose to subscribe to your tweets in the same way.

Many like the simplicity of Twitter. Because posts are limited to 140 characters, Twitter provides a concise sharing and communicating experience, as shown in Figure 1-1.

Figure 1-1: Sharing in 140 characters or less.

Twitter is a simple platform, and the original interface (at `http://twitter.com`) offers few features. You can post statuses and share links to photos, videos, and articles. Like Facebook, Twitter allows you to create lists of people based on any criteria and therefore filter what you see in your Twitter stream so you can focus on what you want and ignore what you don't. Unlike Facebook, Twitter does not have business pages, groups, events, and so forth.

Twitter relies on third-party apps (such as HootSuite or TweetDeck) to provide additional features, and those features are delivered outside Twitter. That means you have to visit the third-party's website or install an application on your computer or phone. This process isn't a big deal, and most people find that using these applications enhances and streamlines their Twitter experience.

Introducing LinkedIn

LinkedIn is designed for professional networking (see Figure 1-2). By design, LinkedIn tries to limit your connections to people you know or with which you've done business. When you add a person as a connection, LinkedIn asks for verification of how you're connected to the person in real life. LinkedIn prefers that you know your connections because recommendations and introductions on the site are key. If you're connecting to everyone willy-nilly, you can't vouch for their professional integrity.

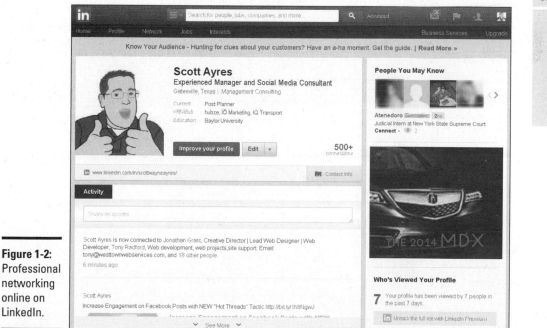

Figure 1-2:
Professional networking online on LinkedIn.

On LinkedIn, when you see that someone is connected to someone else, that connection is a type of social proof. If Jay is connected to someone Scott wants to meet, he can ask him for an introduction. Likewise, if Jay is looking for someone to hire and finds someone connected to Scott, he could ask him for more information about that person's abilities and how he handles changing deadlines. In both cases, we rely on the other's connections to be based on interaction and experience.

Your LinkedIn profile is your online resume and highlights your skills, experience, and recommendations. When you've provided a service to someone or worked with someone, you might ask the person to write a letter of recommendation for you on LinkedIn. You can put these recommendations on your profile, alongside a list of your experience.

People you're connected to can also endorse you based on different skills. And you can endorse them. These endorsements are helpful when a prospective employer is searching LinkedIn for someone with a certain skill set.

Although LinkedIn doesn't provide the same kind of socializing you find on Facebook, it's still a great way to connect with your professional peers. LinkedIn offers groups based on interests, career niches, and many general topics. Similar to online professional organizations, these groups are places where you can bounce ideas off others or ask (and answer) questions. Groups are an excellent way to network with other professionals and establish yourself as the go-to person for answers in your niche.

Like Facebook, on LinkedIn you can post updates, as shown in Figure 1-3. Users can Like and comment on someone's post, as well as share it with friends.

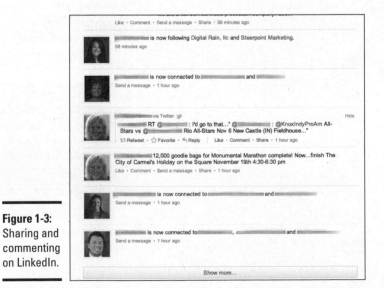

Figure 1-3:
Sharing and commenting on LinkedIn.

Introducing Google+

If you have a Gmail address, you can sign up for Google+ in a matter of seconds. Google+ (pronounced "Google plus") is Google's answer to social networking. Many say Google+ is designed as a Facebook competitor, and Figure 1-4 shows how Google+ looks similar to Facebook. Google clearly studied the market to see what was working and what was not, and built its social network accordingly.

Figure 1-4: Google+ uses status updates and comments.

Google+ is integrated with Google's suite of online tools (such as its search engine, Gmail, and its photo-sharing and -editing tool, Picasa) via the black toolbar across the top of the screen (refer to Figure 1-4). In this way, you have all your Google tools at your fingertips.

Google+ also makes it easy to add friends, especially for Gmail users. When you create your account, Google+ uses the names in your Gmail address book to suggest people with whom you might want to connect. If you want to add someone later, just type the person's name in the search bar at the top of the page and Google+ returns a list of possible matches. Click the name and you can quickly add the person to your circles (which we explain next).

Like Facebook and Twitter, Google+ allows you flexible privacy and custom sharing. In Google+, these features are built into *circles,* which are a way of organizing users into categories so you can filter the information you share and with which you interact. Like the Facebook list feature, circles let you limit who sees what updates and what updates you see.

Much like Facebook, Google+ enables you to share photos, videos, links, and more in a news feed–like environment. Although you can view both pictures and videos in the news feed, Google+ presents them in a bigger, more visually catchy way.

Introducing Pinterest

Pinterest is a scrapbook-style photo-sharing site that enables users to create theme-based image collections. These collections center on events, hobbies, businesses, sports, and more. Pinterest users can upload *pins* (images) and organize them into *pinboards* (image collections).

Users can browse the site and repin someone else's image to their own board, which can result in some great viral sharing if they've uploaded an image that is highly sharable. Many websites have installed a Pin-it plug-in to enable you to click images on their site and pin them to your own board. Businesses do this because the image links back to the original article from which it was pinned.

Pinterest has become hot among businesses as well as individuals. Brands can build their own page and pin images to create a virtual storefront. These images contain links so that users can buy these products from the business.

When you sign up for Pinterest, you can choose to use your e-mail address or connect using Facebook.

Introducing Instagram

Instagram is a photo- and video-sharing app that allows users to take pictures and videos with their mobile devices and share them with others. Users can quickly share the images or videos directly on sites such as Facebook, Twitter, Tumblr, Flickr, and Foursquare.

Unlike the social site mentioned previously in this chapter, you can share pictures and videos from only your mobile device, not your desktop. However, you can log in to the site and comment, or you can comment on posts from your desktop. With the many filters available in Instagram, you can create stunning images.

In April 2012, Facebook purchased Instagram for approximately $1 billion in cash and stock.

Understanding What Social Media Means to Marketers

Marketing always follows people. People watch TV, so companies spend big money to be in front of those viewers through commercials. The same is true for billboards on busy streets, the pages of popular magazines, and almost any other media source you can imagine. Social networks provide a unique form of visibility for brands. On social networks, people don't just passively watch — they interact. In this way, businesses can reach consumers through both interaction and standard advertising.

Facebook and advertising

Advertising on Facebook is one of the best ways to target a specific demographic. Every day, marketers try to discover where their customers are and what message to send to them through advertisements. Facebook has the potential to remove some of this mystery. Facebook advertising can be based on the fine details that someone shares on his timeline, including age, location, likes, interests, and other demographic info. Because Facebook ads are based on a pay-per-click model, any small or large business can run a Facebook ad and still work within their marketing budget. To find out more about Facebook advertising, see Book V, Chapter 4.

Interaction is a unique yet important way for a company to connect with its customers. Facebook allows this interaction through business pages, where a brand or business can create a conversation instead of a canned ad. This conversation-based mentality has been linked to higher brand loyalty. Determine for yourself whether your company should be on Facebook. For many brands and companies, being on Facebook is a critical piece of doing business.

**Book III
Chapter 1**

What Is Social
Media?

Chapter 2: Connecting Facebook to Everything Else

In This Chapter

✔ Understanding the basics of Facebook Platform

✔ Connecting your Twitter account to Facebook

✔ Using Facebook badges

✔ Integrating Facebook into all your marketing efforts

*F*acebook is a lot more than a place for status updates. It offers fantastic ways for people to connect with friends and for businesses to connect with customers while they enjoy all the features of Facebook across the web. This chapter introduces the ways that you can connect your personal timeline and business page in the areas of your choosing. We explain how to integrate Facebook with Twitter, add social-sharing tools to your website and blog, and add a social networking element to your offline marketing activities.

Understanding the Basics of Facebook Platform

Developers are provided with a set of tools globally called *Facebook Platform*. Facebook Platform refers to the API (Application Programming Interface) that developers use to connect a website or app to Facebook. Any time you use Facebook to log in to a site or you click the Like button on a website, the website owner has used Facebook Platform to provide these features in the website.

Facebook Platform is used in many ways; in the context of websites, it is often called Facebook for Websites. Facebook for Websites allows you to enjoy all the social features of Facebook while maintaining the safety features that prevent your data from being accessed maliciously. Facebook offers several options to website and app developers to make your experience on the web more social.

Facebook for Websites enables you to sign in to other sites or online services using your Facebook e-mail login and password and automatically take your Facebook profile information to your favorite sites. Because of Facebook's tremendous popularity, it's common to find sites and applications that have utilized Facebook for Websites, simplifying your online activity. For example, if you use Pinterest, you can log in using Facebook — you don't have to make another user profile to create a Pinterest account.

Many of the sites using Facebook for Websites require you to give them permission to access certain information in your timeline or business page, as shown in Figure 2-1. Facebook describes this function as an application (or app) and requires you to give the app specific permission to access your timeline or page.

Figure 2-1:
Apps request permission to access your timeline or page.

The information that the app accesses is normally just what it needs for the function and purpose of the app. For example, if you're using the social check-in site Foursquare, you might receive badges posted on your timeline as a trophy or an award when completing certain check-ins. For this reason, Foursquare needs to access your timeline feed.

Some websites or applications are designed to enhance Facebook business pages. If you're managing a business page and attach an app to it, the app's access will be to that business page you administer (you can determine which ones; when you install an app, it doesn't have to apply to all your business pages).

When the app requests access, the request shows the specific things that the app needs to access. For instance, in Figure 2-1, Scott is installing the Twitter app on his personal timeline. The app needs to post to Facebook as him. Why does the app need to post on Facebook as him? Well, Scott is installing the Twitter app so that when he posts to Twitter, the same update is broadcast to both Twitter and Facebook.

Facebook's OAuth service allows applications to follow a standardized way of ensuring privacy and security while letting apps you choose connect with Facebook and engage with the features and functions of the platform. *OAuth* is the permission tool that verifies that your information is safe and accessible only as authorized. For you as a user, authorizing other applications is simple. Most applications have an easy process by which you give them permission to access Facebook.

The OAuth process allows you to have peace of mind when using certain services or applications. Some sites eliminate their own form of sign in and use Facebook Platform. For example, popular sites such as Pinterest, Etsy, and ShortStack enable you to sign up or log in with your Facebook account rather than with an e-mail and a password. In this way, you can manage your online connections without having to create accounts.

Finding Common Uses for Facebook Platform

Facebook Platform allows developers and site owners to use various Facebook features outside Facebook. The following list describes ways you might use Facebook Platform:

✦ **Login information:** Facebook for Websites eliminates the need for you to create a user account on a site. Instead, you sign into Facebook, and Facebook signs you into the site. Figure 2-2 shows the Connect with Facebook button on the Klout site.

Facebook Platform is handy for people who would like to use the features and benefits of Facebook in other websites or applications. When you log in to another site using Facebook, you gain access to tools for sharing, commenting, and connecting in the same way as in Facebook.

Figure 2-2:
Click
Connect
with
Facebook to
log in.

✦ **Facebook games and apps:** Games such as Angry Birds (see Figure 2-3) are a kind of app used in Facebook. This type of app has a specific functionality that allows you to access certain functions, such as playing games against your friends.

facebook
Search
ANGRY BIRDS
BETA
PLAY

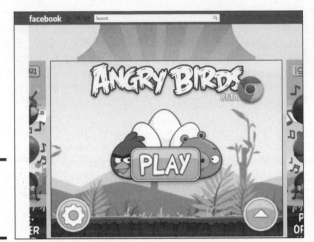

Figure 2-3: Playing games in Facebook.

- **Facebook comments on other sites:** You can leave comments on blogs or other sites that use the Facebook comment feature just as in Facebook. When a blog or article includes Facebook comments, the comments section shows your Facebook profile picture, as shown in Figure 2-4. Comments posted on a website are visible in the website, regardless of the user's privacy settings. If you want to post the comment to your personal timeline, click Post to Facebook. The comment will be visible to only those who are permitted to see your timeline.

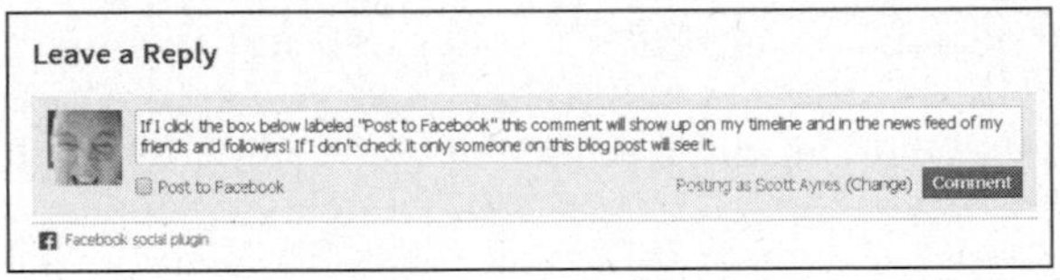
Leave a Reply
If I click the box below labeled "Post to Facebook" this comment will show up on my timeline and in the news feed of my friends and followers! If I don't check it only someone on this blog post will see it.
Post to Facebook
Posting as Scott Ayres (Change)
Comment
Facebook social plugin

Figure 2-4: Comments on other sites.

- **Social bookmarking:** Sites such as Pinterest, a social media site for pinning photos that you find on the Internet and want to reference later (for say, home decorating ideas), also enable you to use Facebook to log in (see Figure 2-5). If you log in to Pinterest using your Facebook account, you can easily find out which of your Facebook friends are also using Pinterest. This saves you the work of manually searching for friends you want to follow on Pinterest.

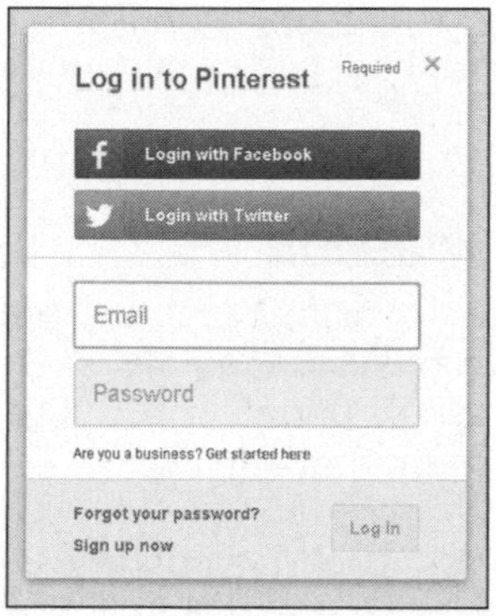

Figure 2-5:
Use
Facebook
to log in to
social book-
marking
sites.

+ **Like, Share, and Recommend buttons:** The site owner can embed these buttons into his or her site. With the click of a button (see Figure 2-6), you can share interesting content from sites with your friends. When you click the Like, Share, or Recommend button, a post appears in your friends' news feeds with a link back to the site. In some cases, you can write a short note about the link to give it context.

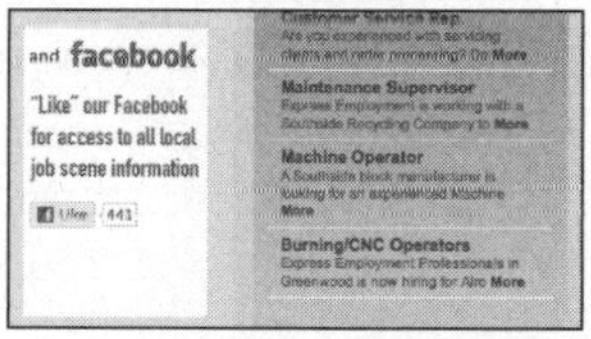

Figure 2-6:
A Like
button on a
website.

+ **Posting tweets to Facebook with the Facebook app for Twitter:** As you create tweets in Twitter, the Facebook Twitter app allows you to post your tweets directly to your Facebook stream automatically. This feature is helpful if you want to seamlessly syndicate each tweet as a Facebook status as well. Similarly, many social media sites such as Foursquare and Instagram offer you the ability to automatically include your activity in your Facebook activity.

+ **Sharing your blog posts on Facebook:** Bloggers may find it useful to share blog posts on Facebook as a way of alerting their readers that they have added a new post. Some third-party tools allow a blogger to post a status update previewing the post along with a link directing readers right to the blog post.

Connecting to Facebook

Many people and businesses don't have time to manually post updates to all the various social media platforms. Instead, they cross-post from one site to another automatically — when one account is updated, it sends a post to the others. In this section, we briefly discuss how you can connect Facebook to your blog, Twitter, and Google+.

Connecting your blog to Facebook

If you want to drive traffic to your blog site using Facebook, you can use a third-party app to connect your blog to Facebook. An app such as HootSuite or Post Planner enables you to post a status update with a link to the blog post. This method differs based on the app that you use.

HootSuite and Post Planner are typically used for posting status updates to several accounts from one screen. Both apps enable you to schedule the updates so you can control when they're posted. (See Chapter 3 of this minibook for more about scheduling updates with third-party apps.)

To connect your blog and Facebook in HootSuite, follow these steps:

1. **Log in to HootSuite at** `http://hootsuite.com`.

2. **Click the gear icon in the left panel.**

3. **Click RSS/Atom.**

4. **Click the plus sign to add a new feed.**

5. **Add the URL of the feed, and then select the social account to which you want to send the feed.**

6. **Click Save Feed.**

Connecting your Twitter account to Facebook

Some Twitter users connect with people in a different way than they do on Facebook, while others prefer to syndicate their Twitter updates to the status updates on their Facebook personal timeline (this feature doesn't work with a business page).

Think carefully before integrating Twitter and Facebook. You don't always have the same audience in both places, so the information you share on each platform may not be relevant in both places. Or, if you do have the same audience, you want to be sure you're not inundating them with the same information at the same time in several places.

Connecting your personal timeline to Twitter is easy:

1. **Go to your personal timeline, and type** Twitter **in the search box at the top of the screen.**

   The first result in the list is most likely the original application. The app you're looking for is simply named Twitter and displays the Twitter name and bird logo.

2. **Click Twitter in the list.**

   The page shown in Figure 2-7 appears.

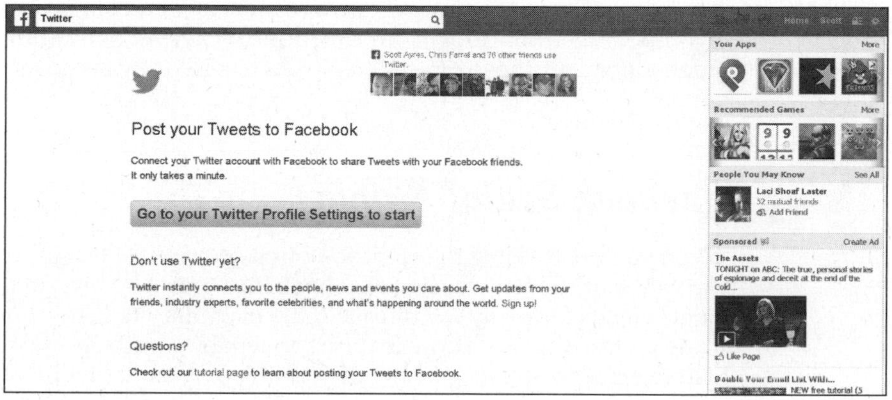

Figure 2-7:
Post your
tweets to
Facebook.

3. **Click the yellow button to go to your Twitter settings.**

   The Twitter login screen appears.

4. **Type your Twitter username or e-mail and your password in the appropriate text boxes, and then click Sign In.**

   Your Twitter Profile page appears.

5. **Click the Connect to Facebook button.**

   A screen appears, asking for permission (refer to Figure 2-1).

6. **Click Okay.**

7. **Change the privacy settings, if desired, and then click Okay.**

   Now all of your updates on Twitter will also post as a Facebook status update. Keep in mind that @replies and direct messages will not post to your Facebook status.

Book III
Chapter 2

Connecting
Facebook to
Everything Else

People update frequently on Twitter. Facebook is a different environment. If you're a busy tweeter, consider whether or not it makes sense for you to syndicate your Twitter feed to Facebook.

Connecting Google+ to Facebook

You can connect Google+ so that posts there also go to Facebook. However, you can't post from Facebook to Google+.

To connect Google+ to Facebook, you need to install an extension on Google Chrome (the web browser), such as `http://socialba.com`, or use a site such as `http://friendsplus.me/` or `https://ifttt.com/`.

A quick search in the Google Chrome store provides many extensions for cross-posting from Google+ to Facebook. However, we caution you to take a deep look into these extensions to make sure they are from a trustworthy source.

Using Facebook Social Plugins

When you're browsing the web, you often see several features that make the web more social by using Facebook Platform. The biggest benefits are a single sign-in for many websites and the capability to Like a business page while on the website. These features are enabled with *Facebook plugins,* also referred to as *social plugins.* Facebook plugins are found at `http://developers.facebook.com/docs/plugins/`, as shown in Figure 2-8.

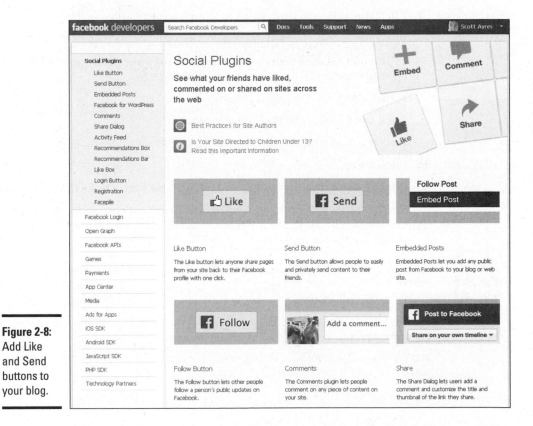

Figure 2-8: Add Like and Send buttons to your blog.

In most cases, social plugins don't require you to do anything to use them if you're signed into Facebook. Your browser can keep you signed in (you need to select the Keep Me Logged In check box when you first log in to Facebook). These plugins include the following:

✦ **Like or share button:** Share links to articles or pages directly to your personal Facebook timeline.

✦ **Share button:** Add a personal message to links before sharing them on Facebook.

✦ **Send button:** Send content directly to your friends.

✦ **Embedded posts:** Place a public post from a business page or person on Facebook into the content of your website or blog.

✦ **Follow button:** Subscribe to the public updates of others on Facebook.

✦ **Comments:** Comment on any content on a site.

✦ **Activity Feed:** See what your friends are doing on a site.

✦ **Recommendations box:** Display the most recommended content on your site based on Likes by your friends or other people on that site.

✦ **Recommendations bar:** Like content, get recommendations, and share what you are reading.

✦ **Like box:** Like a business page and view its stream directly from its website.

✦ **Registration:** Sign up for a website by using your Facebook account.

✦ **Facepile:** Display the pictures of people who have Liked a business page or registered for a site.

✦ **Login button:** Log in to a site by using your Facebook account. (Facebook Login is not considered a social plugin any longer.)

Using social plugins such as the Share, Like, and Recommend buttons makes your site more social. Facebook's social plugins are great for giving your visitors a way to recommend your site to their friends. You might want to use social plugins in the following places:

✦ **Individual posts/article:** By providing fresh, interesting content, blogging drives new traffic to your site. Asking your readers to click Share is an easy way to increase that traffic to your blog entry. Using the share button as social proof also tells the reader ahead of time how interesting the article may be because social-sharing buttons show how many people have already shared the article. If others see that your link has been shared a lot, they may click through (and share) as well because so many others have done so.

✦ **Individual products in an online store:** If you sell products on your site, getting referrals from other customers is the best way to get new business. That's the beauty of the Like and share buttons. Those who share your product are instantly sharing your product with all their friends. The best sales pitch for your product is a recommendation from a happy customer.

Increasing traffic by giving your loyal readers and visitors an easy way to share with their friends is important. People are more likely to do what's easy, so Facebook's social plugins can help increase your website's popularity! The Facebook social tools allow you to share in Facebook in two primary ways:

✦ **As a Like or a Recommend:** These show up in your activity feed. A Like or Recommend may appear in news feeds, if your friends have the broadest view settings, and on your timeline, as shown in Figure 2-9.

Figure 2-9: Likes show up on your timeline.

✦ **As a status update:** Readers click a button like the one shown in Figure 2-10, which prompts them to share an article as a status update or add it to their timelines.

Figure 2-10: Sharing as a status update.

Where should you put your share button? Some say that putting the share button at the top of the blog enables readers to instantly see the social proof if the story has been read. Others say that people don't want to scroll to the top to share an article or blog post they've just read. Scott thinks that the top and the sidebar are usually the optimal places for the share button.

Another option is to put one share button at the top of the article showing, for example, how many people have already Liked the article, and put the rest — such as share buttons for Facebook, Twitter, and Google+ — at the bottom of the article. When you put the social proof (how many people Like the article) at the top, you encourage others to read the article. And when you also put the other share buttons at the bottom, readers can quickly share the article to multiple social media platforms without scrolling back to the top. You can see how Scott positions share buttons on the Post Planner blog site, at `http://postplanner.com/blog`. The site uses the Flare plugin for WordPress to display social-sharing icons.

The bottom line? Put the share button wherever you feel is best, but make sure you consider the two schools of thought when setting up your site.

Using Facebook Badges for Social Proof

Badges are add-ons that you can place on your site to show a little bit of information from Facebook, such as text from your business page or your favorite Facebook photos. (See Figure 2-11.) You can use badges as a way to attract friends, followers, or interaction on Facebook. For example, a badge on your personal site can show how many people have Liked your business page as proof to visitors that they should as well.

Figure 2-11:
Add
Facebook
badges to
your site.

You can add the following types of Facebook badges to your site:

✦ **Profile badges** link directly to your timeline and show information about you, as shown in Figure 2-12.

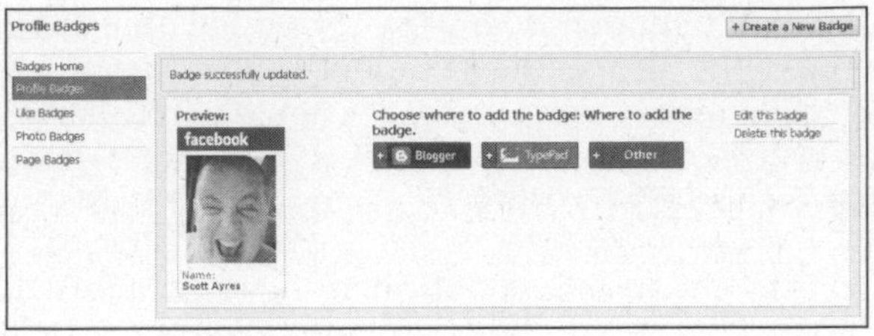

Figure 2-12:
Profile
badges
include your
Timeline info
on your site.

✦ **Like badges** show off business pages that you Like.

✦ **Photo badges** showcases your favorite pictures on Facebook on other sites.

✦ **Page badges** promote your business page on other sites (see Figure 2-13). They display your picture and how many people Like your business page.

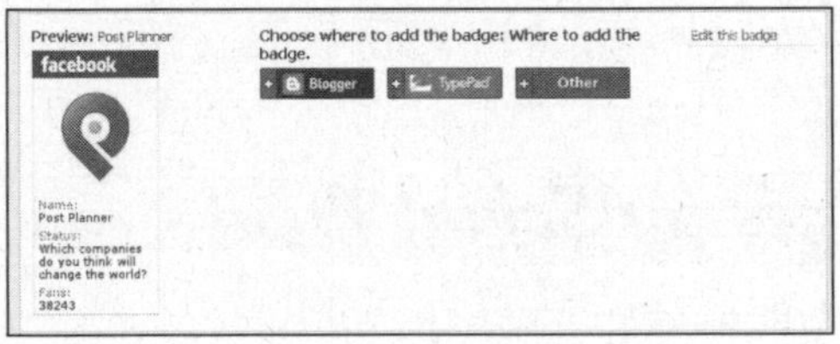

Figure 2-13:
Page
badges
shows off
your busi-
ness page.

Integrating Facebook with Marketing Efforts for Your Business

To get the most out of Facebook, you have to take it a step further and integrate it into all your other marketing efforts. Connecting a business page to your blog or website, and other social networks such as Twitter, is one way to broaden your reach when using Facebook as a marketing tool.

Facebook provides brands and networkers a way to extend the relationship with their customers beyond limited in-person interaction. Often, when customers have another way to communicate with you, however simple it may be, the value of that relationship increases. The following sections discuss a few ways to foster that relationship and invite your customers, friends, and those you network with to connect with you on Facebook as well.

Business cards

In the business world, you hand your business card out to nearly everyone you talk to. Business cards are obviously designed to provide someone the details of how they can contact you at a later time. Include your Facebook username on your business card so that when people are connecting with you for business, you're offering them the opportunity to connect with you socially as well.

Some fear that the mix between business and personal is not a wise idea. Scott disagrees. If you enjoy and believe in what you do, you should be more than happy to offer that to your friends. Also, when you reach out to someone in a friendly manner (by friending them on Facebook), you add a friendship factor to the relationship that in many cases increases the chances that people will buy from you. On the other hand, you might prefer to invite people to connect with you on your business page if they're interested in doing business with you. For example, although Scott has the follow feature enabled on his personal timeline, he only friends people he knows well. He likes to keep a personal space for himself and his family and friends.

Website or blog

If you own a business or blog, put a link to your business page on your website. Sometimes, giving people the opportunity to connect involves simply letting them know that you'd like to be connected on Facebook.

Sign or QR code in store or print materials

If you own a retail business, people can't click a button to connect with you on Facebook in your store to Like your business page on Facebook. However, many people carry smartphones, so you can use QR codes to direct customers to your business page. A *QR code* is a barcode that directs a device to your site of choice using a barcode scanner app. (We like the QR Reader app for iPhone or Android.) The QR code in Figure 2-14 directs a smartphone to Scott's personal timeline. Feel free to give it a try and follow Scott.

Figure 2-14:
QR codes direct people to Facebook.

 QR codes are a great way to make it simple for people to find your business page when they're not likely to write down the URL and visit it later. Make sure that you create a sign that explains what people will find when they scan the code!

Wherever you had your phone number in the year 2000

Today, Facebook is one of the most common ways of communicating. But only a few years ago, the best way to reach people was by phone. Remember when you used to write down your phone number on a gum wrapper when you wanted to give someone a way to reach you? Well, put your Facebook username there instead! The same goes for your business page. If you provide yard work, for example, wouldn't it be great if everyone who saw the logo on your truck also saw the URL of your Facebook business page?

Chapter 3: Flying on Autopilot

In This Chapter

✓ **Automating your Facebook marketing**

✓ **Scheduling posts to Facebook with third-party tools**

✓ **Setting up notifications**

✓ **Connecting a WordPress blog**

*W*ith all the third-party tools designed to manage your social media activity, the Facebook developer API (Application Programming Interface) has opened the door to great efficiency and automation. Automation is most interesting to those who manage social media for marketing because in that field it's important not to miss a beat. Marketing types should be on Facebook all the time to make sure they reach as many customers as possible. Because there's no way for that to happen, they need to turn to some Facebook productivity tools to make sure that they have the furthest reach without maintaining a nonstop connection.

Facebook's API allows third-party sites and web services to help you make your Facebook activity more manageable. In this chapter, we explain some of the ways that you can make it easier to keep your business pages and personal timeline active without having to sacrifice all your time.

Automating Facebook to Achieve Marketing Goals

Because you can't be online all the time to post updates, respond to comments, add friends, or suggest Likes, you may decide to automate some Facebook tasks. Before you start, however, consider the purpose of automating your Facebook marketing. Think about your goals.

If you're a marketer, you probably want to accomplish some or all of the following goals:

✦ Increase business page Likes

✦ Deliver quality content to followers and friends

✦ Drive traffic from Facebook to your blog or website

✦ Monitor the public use of keywords using search

✦ Maintain engagement with customers and followers

These goals aren't accomplished through a "set it and forget it" mentality. Flying on autopilot works only with these important points in mind: You must have great, consistent content and activity that engages your consumers and followers. In other words, you have to connect with your supporters so they will continue to connect with you. Here are some ways to automate with such goals in mind:

✦ Synchronize and schedule content to decrease the number of times you have to log in to post recurring or predetermined updates.

✦ Set up alerts so that you know when you need to respond to a comment (or not).

✦ Be sure that each one of your blogs is posted on Facebook to drive traffic to your other sites.

Scheduling Updates with Post Planner or HootSuite

Scheduling updates using a third-party tool such as HootSuite or Post Planner is a great way to consolidate your marketing activities and be more efficient. Some reasons why you might want to do this are

✦ You have an event you're promoting and need to share updates throughout the week.

✦ You have a blog or contest you want to share now and also later, when other viewers may be online.

✦ You want to increase your efficiency for general status posts by creating several at one time, but you want to schedule them to post intermittently.

✦ You want to share several things but don't want to flood your readers all at once.

Post Planner and HootSuite are useful tools for users at any level. You'll find one of these tools useful if you're sharing information on multiple social networks or if you want to be more productive by sharing specific marketing messages planned throughout the week, month, and so on.

HootSuite allows you to manage both your personal timeline and your business page, as well as Twitter accounts and other social networks. Post Planner focuses on posting content to Facebook profiles and business pages. See Figures 3-1 and 3-2 for examples of the screen view of HootSuite and Post Planner, respectively.

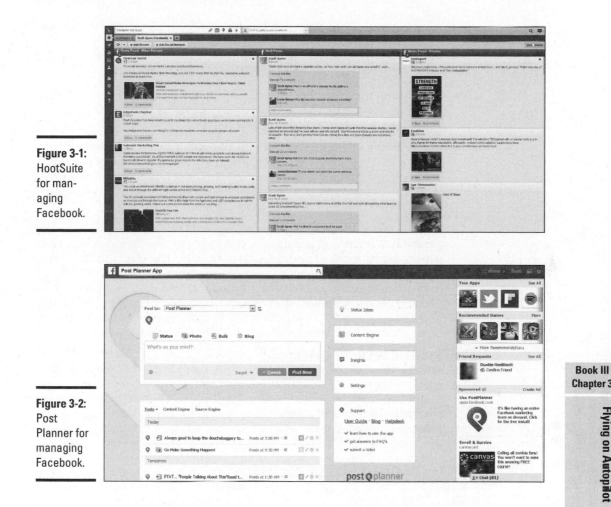

Figure 3-1:
HootSuite
for man-
aging
Facebook.

Figure 3-2:
Post
Planner for
managing
Facebook.

We find these tools most useful for creating updates that you want to share
on multiple social networks. Both are free, and you can access them online
through a browser. Post Planner is an app used inside the Facebook platform, whereas HootSuite can be used by logging in to their site or as an
extension in your browser or on your mobile device.

HootSuite and Post Planner both enable you to post and to plan posts, but
HootSuite also allows you to post to Twitter and respond to posts. On the
other hand, Post Planner allows a huge array of content curation methods
that HootSuite does not. Both allow multiple accounts, allow scheduling, and
can be accessed through the web. Both applications also work with one or
more business pages as well as personal timelines.

Following are some of the Facebook functions you can manage from these tools:

✦ **Posting status updates:** The core function of any Facebook user is posting an update. You can do this in HootSuite or Post Planner.

✦ **Scheduling updates:** Post Planner and HootSuite offer post scheduling, including a batch upload through a `.csv` (comma separated values) spreadsheet for bulk uploading of updates.

✦ **Commenting on your own and other people's posts:** HootSuite displays content in vertical streams. Your news feed column is one of the standard column options, and you can create others. When you see a friend's update in the news feed column, you can comment on it in HootSuite. Post Planner doesn't have this capability.

✦ **Finding status ideas:** Along with being a tool to schedule posts to your personal timeline and business pages, Post Planner also supplies users with many methods of finding content to post. The Status Ideas engine has tons of categories and ideas to choose from, such as questions, fill-in-the blanks, seasonal posts, and Facebook contests. You simply choose one and post to your accounts. You can also find trending content in the Content engine, which contains feeds from blogs all around the globe based on keyword. HootSuite doesn't offer this functionality.

✦ **Creating keyword searches:** Creating a keyword search based on your brand name or topics related to your industry is one of the most interesting ways to learn about your market or find out when someone is asking about the services you provide. HootSuite can perform keyword searches, as shown in Figure 3-3. Post Planner doesn't offer keyword searches for Facebook.

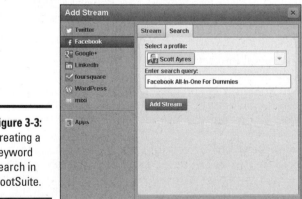

Figure 3-3: Creating a keyword search in HootSuite.

When you schedule posts to your personal timeline or business page, don't forget to interact with the post. It's one thing to plan and schedule your content, but if you're not going to interact with and engage with those following you, there's no point in posting.

If you're updating a business page and a personal timeline at the same time, consider the audience of each. If many of your Facebook friends are also followers of your business page, they are likely to see the same post back to back. We highly recommend separating these by at least a few minutes. It might also be wise to differentiate the content so that it comes across as fresh.

Setting Up Notifications for Business Pages

When you're flying on autopilot, you need to make sure that you still personally respond to comments on your business pages. Notifications are a great way to be alerted when you need to respond to a comment.

To set up notifications for your business page, do the following:

1. **Click the gear icon on the far-right side of the blue navigation bar and choose Account Settings.**

2. **Choose Notifications.**

   The Notifications Settings page appears, as shown in Figure 3-4.

3. **In the What You Get Notified About section, find the Pages You Manage row and click its Edit link.**

4. **Select the check box next to each business page from which you want notifications, as shown in Figure 3-5.**

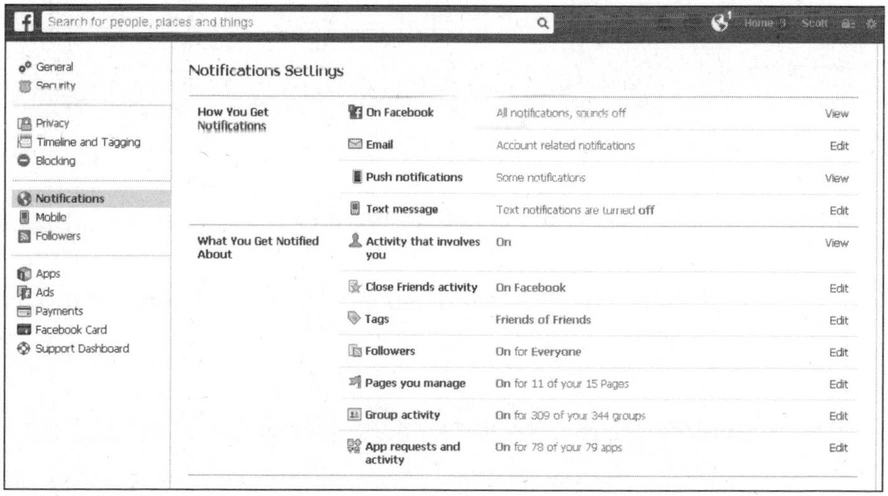

Figure 3-4:
Set up notifications on this page.

How You Get Notifications	On Facebook	All notifications, sounds off	View
	Email	Account related notifications	Edit
	Push notifications	Some notifications	View
	Text message	Text notifications are turned off	Edit
What You Get Notified About	Activity that involves you	On	View
	Close Friends activity	On Facebook	Edit
	Tags	Friends of Friends	Edit
	Followers	On for Everyone	Edit
	Pages you manage	On for 11 of your 15 Pages	Edit
	Group activity	On for 309 of your 344 groups	Edit
	App requests and activity	On for 78 of your 79 apps	Edit

Notifications Settings

General
Security
Privacy
Timeline and Tagging
Blocking
Notifications
Mobile
Followers
Apps
Ads
Payments
Facebook Card
Support Dashboard

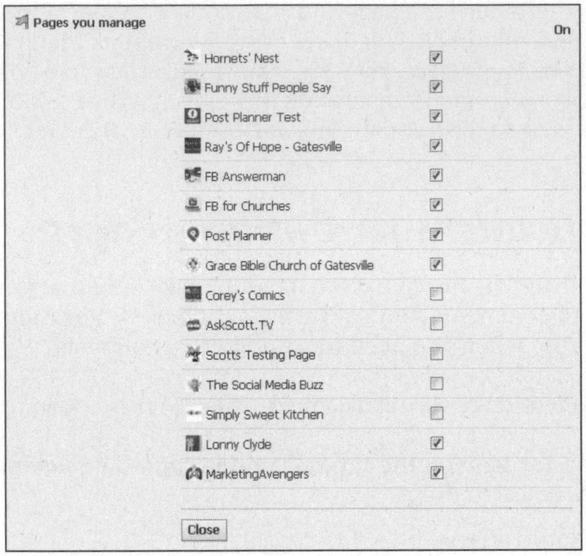

Figure 3-5:
Select the business pages.

5. **Click Close.**

   The Notifications Settings screen reappears.

6. **In the How You Get Notifications section, find the Email row and click its Edit link.**

   The screen shown in Figure 3-6 appears.

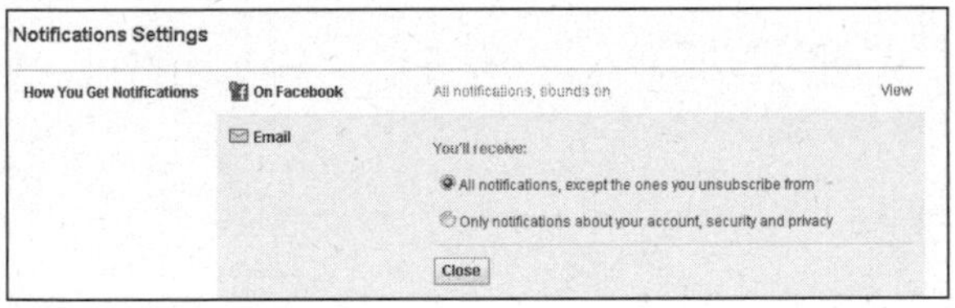

Figure 3-6:
Turn on or off e-mail notifications.

7. **Select the first radio button to receive all notifications, and then click Close.**

Connecting Your WordPress Blog to Facebook

Often times, the biggest source of traffic to a blog or website is social media sharing. You can post your blog on a page tab through an RSS feed (see Chapter 2 of this minibook), but this doesn't drive traffic to your blog site. If you're trying to drive traffic, perhaps to monetize your blog, you may want to use a third-party tool that automatically shares your blog posts to Facebook.

Avoiding automation blunders

The two primary functions of any Facebook automation are to syndicate content that you're posting on other sites or social networks and to schedule posts.

It's important to keep tabs on that content, because when you post automatically rather than manually, it's easy to forget that you have content posting from third-party apps. The result can be that you mistakenly post the same content manually or fail to respond to comments.

When scheduling updates, be conscious of the date and time that your update will be going out. It's important to revisit your scheduled content and adjust as necessary. For example, if you have an automatic post going out that says something like "Looking forward to a great day," but it happens to be the day that there's a major disaster, you'll look extremely insensitive.

If you're syndicating updates from other sources such as a blog or Twitter, be aware of the balance of content coming from that source in addition to any updates you may post directly to Facebook. Otherwise, you could risk updating too much and lose interest from your readers.

If you have a WordPress website (a common blogging platform), you can choose from any number of plugins to connect your blog to Facebook.

Some plugins or services require a Facebook developer application because Facebook uses the Facebook developer platform to connect to other sites. To create an application, go to `https://developers.facebook.com/apps`, and click the Create New App button at the top of the screen. This application is the foundation used for all types of ways of connecting to Facebook features on other sites.

Following is a brief description of a few popular plugins:

✦ **Simple Facebook Connect:** This plugin consists of a framework and a series of subsystems to add any kind of Facebook functionality with much less code writing. We recommend this plugin for the more expert user who's looking for a lot of Facebook features (including but not limited to sharing blogs on a business page).

To use this plugin, first you have to install it on your WordPress site and activate it, and then you need to create a Facebook page tab so that you can enable individual features that it provides as you choose. Simple Facebook Connect provides the following features:

- Users can comment using Facebook credentials.
- You can automatically publish new posts to Facebook.
- You can integrate comments made on Facebook back into your own site.
- Open Graph tags are implemented automatically.

**Book III
Chapter 3**

Flying on Autopilot

✦ **Wordbooker:** This plugin enables you to cross-post your blog posts to your business page and personal timeline. Wordbooker is easy to install and easy to authorize.

After you've downloaded and installed the plugin on your blog, go to the plugin settings page, where you're prompted to authorize Facebook to connect to the plugin. Then you're ready to go. Check the Wordbooker settings page for other customizations. If you're the administrator of more than one business page or group, you can select, with each post, which one you'd like to publish to.

You can always take the shorter and simpler route and use share buttons on your blog. Then the reader (or you) can share the blog easily to Facebook by clicking a button. The post is sent to your timeline but not to a business page.

Follow these steps to set up an application to connect your WordPress blog to Facebook:

1. **To create an app, point your browser to** `https://developers.facebook.com/apps` **and click the Create New App button.**

2. **If you haven't registered as a developer, click the green Register button and complete the registration process.**

3. **Type the app name.**

   The app name can be anything you want it to be, as long as the name isn't already taken.

4. **Click Continue.**

5. **Type the CAPTCHA in the text box, and then click Continue.**

   CAPTCHA is simply words and other characters that appear on your screen to manually verify you're a real person.

   The app's Basic page appears. Make sure your contact e-mail is accurate.

6. **In the App Domains field, type your site's domain and press Enter.**

   The site domain is the simple address without the `http://` prefix (such as `example.com`).

7. **Save your changes.**

   Scroll down and click the Save Changes button.

You can now see the completed page tab after you save your changes. You can find it also by pointing your browser to `https://developers.facebook.com/apps`.

Typically, when you're connecting your blog with a plugin, it will ask for the app ID and app secret. You find these on the app home page, just below the app's name.

Book IV
Building a Business Page

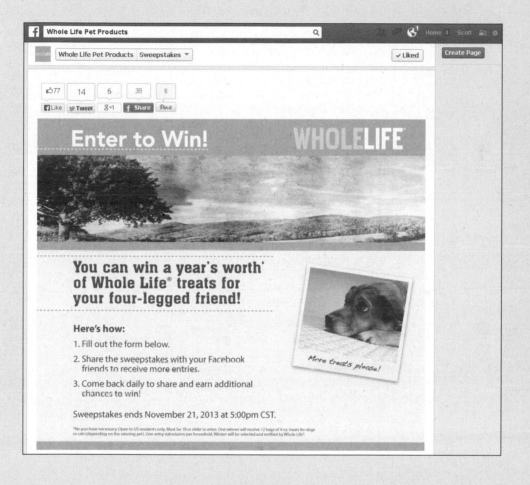

Visit www.dummies.com/extras/facebookaio for a recap of details that will affect the appearance of your Facebook business page.

Contents at a Glance

Chapter 1: Creating a Business Page 269

Deciding to Create a Business Page 269
Creating Your Business Page 271
Creating a Vanity URL..274
Understanding the Importance of Cover and Profile Pictures....................276

Chapter 2: Customizing Your Business Page 283

Adding Information about Your Business Page..283
Customizing Your Business Page Settings 285
Creating Admin Roles...289
All about Apps 290
Suggestions from Your Followers 293
Choosing Featured Business Pages..293
Sending Updates on the Go 294

Chapter 3: Touring Your Business Page 295

Reviewing the Overall Business Page 295
The Admin Panel..295
The Admin Panel Toolbar...297
Page Info Section 300
Apps Navigation..303
Your Timeline 307
Reviewing the Right Sidebar...313
Using Facebook as Your Business Page or Personal Timeline.....................313

Chapter 4: Building Your Community 319

Determining Your Goals and Objectives 320
Establishing Your Authority 321
Establishing Social Proof...322
Creating Shareable Content..323
Targeting Updates 332
Handling Customer Service 334

Chapter 1: Creating a Business Page

In This Chapter

✓ Understanding business pages

✓ Creating your business page

✓ Adding a vanity URL

✓ Choosing cover and profile images

"*B*ut I already have a website. Do I really need a Facebook business page?" In most cases, yes, you do. Facebook has proven to be an outstanding marketing tool. By integrating Facebook into your overall strategy, you expand your reach by millions. Consider these numbers:

✦ Facebook is the number two site on the Internet (only Google has more visitors).

✦ Over 1.2 billion people have active Facebook accounts.

✦ Over 727 million people log in to Facebook every day.

✦ The average user has 130 friends and is connected to 80 community pages, groups, and events.

Those are *your* customers. Your customers are on Facebook *looking* for ways to interact with you. Why not meet them where they are? Facebook business pages are an easy way to connect with your followers (and introduce yourself to new followers!).

This chapter explains how a business page works and how you can create one in just a few minutes.

Deciding to Create a Business Page

Before we show you how to create a Facebook business page, let us explain the options you may see on Facebook. Facebook has three types of pages, but businesses can use only business pages to create and interact with a community. The three types of pages on Facebook are

✦ **Personal timeline:** This type of page is a personal Facebook page that relates to your private life. (See Book I for a full discussion of personal timelines.) You can't use a personal timeline page to promote a business; personal timelines are strictly for personal use.

✦ **Business page:** Facebook created business pages to give businesses, products, services, celebrities, artists, and causes their own space on Facebook.

✦ **Generic community page:** This Facebook-generated page is not owned by anyone in particular (except Facebook), so you can't control the information shared. This type of page is generally populated by Wikipedia information and related status updates from business pages and personal timelines. Few Facebook users refer to generic community pages with any consistency.

Generic community pages should not be confused with creating a business page for a community or cause. If you choose to make your own business page dedicated to a community or cause, you have control over how that business page looks, which applications are installed, and how information is shared.

Business pages weren't part of the initial Facebook options. The result is that some businesses created personal timelines rather than business pages for their businesses. Now that business pages are mainstream and fully integrated into the Facebook experience, using a personal timeline for your business is against Facebook policy. This separation is actually a good thing. Facebook is aware that personal timelines and business pages have different needs, and they've addressed those by giving business pages more marketing functionality than personal timelines. If you're contemplating marketing your business, service, or product on Facebook, you probably want as much exposure as possible for your product or business. Table 1-1 shows that a personal timeline simply doesn't offer the marketing flexibility that a business page does.

Table 1-1   Personal Timelines versus Business Pages

Personal Timeline	Business Page
Limited to 5,000 friends	No limit on followers or Likes
Not allowed to install custom page applications	Allowed to install multiple applications to streamline your social media efforts
Only searchable in Facebook	Fully searchable inside and outside Facebook

Keeping your personal timeline and your business page separate enables you to connect with your friends personally while keeping your business contacts separate. Although there may be some overlap, your everyday friends will appreciate that they aren't being subjected to your business discussions, promotions, and information. Likewise, your business associates or followers won't be subjected to your personal status updates or to cute photos of your puppy and kids.

Make Facebook a component of your strategy

Facebook has a lot of features and opportunities for branding and customization. You can customize your business page so completely that you may be tempted to ditch your blog or website to focus your energy on your Facebook presence. We strongly advise against that.

All your social media efforts should work together. Think of your website as your hub. From there, you may have spokes (links) out to your Facebook business page, Twitter account, YouTube channel, and LinkedIn communities. Each of those spokes is owned by a third party; only your website is fully owned by your company.

You don't own your space in Facebookland — Facebook owns it and can evict you if it sees fit. Eviction (that is, deletion of your business page)

doesn't happen often, but if your business page violates Facebook's terms of service or any of the numerous guidelines, Facebook can and will remove your business page. The awful thing is, you don't have a say. Facebook doesn't contact you to warn you; it doesn't e-mail or call to discuss your options. Your business page (and all you've built — community, content, trust, *everything*) is erased. You'll have to rebuild from scratch because Facebook will not reinstate a business page it deleted.

It's never a good idea to put all your eggs in one basket for the simple reason that your audience doesn't gather in a single venue. Many people may look for you on Facebook, but others will seek out your website or blog or follow you on Twitter.

Creating Your Business Page

Setting up a business page is simple. With a few clicks, you'll be up and running. To get started, follow these instructions:

1. **Use your browser to navigate to** `http://facebook.com/pages/create.php`.

You see six boxes representing different categories, as shown in Figure 1-1.

Figure 1-1: Choose one of these six broad categories for your business page.

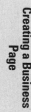

Many of the main categories offer similar options for your business. For instance, if you're creating a business page for a bookstore, you could choose Local Business or Place⇨Book Store or Entertainment⇨Book Store. The result is the same.

Here is an overview of each category to help you choose which one best fits your needs:

- **Local Business or Place:** Best choice if you have a single bricks-and-mortar store. This type of business page focuses on the location instead of product. You can share business hours, parking information, and so on.

- **Company, Organization, or Institution:** Best choice if your business has multiple stores. You still have the option to include addresses. Note that the business page you create will be a representation of your brand, not each store. Facebook isn't offering that functionality to the masses yet. You can make individual business pages for each store, but it may be confusing for your customers and you can only use your business name once as your username (discussed later in this chapter).

- **Brand or Product:** Best choice if you don't have a bricks-and-mortar storefront or want to focus on your product. You can share your website address, products, company overview, and so on. If you're a blogger creating a business page, this category is an excellent choice.

- **Artist, Band, or Public Figure:** Best choice if one of those descriptors fits you. You must be the official authorized representative (not just the biggest fan) of the artist, band, or public figure to create a business page.

- **Entertainment:** Best choice if your business is movies, theater, books, sports, music, and so on.

- **Cause or Community:** Best choice if you're creating a business page for a cause (such as Kids with Food Allergies) or a community (such as Points of Light).

2. **Click the box that best represents your business, product, or service.**

   A drop-down list to narrow the category and a text box for your business page name appear.

3. **Use the drop-down list to choose the subcategory for your business page.**

4. **In the Name text box, type the title for your business page.**

   The name is the title of your business page and is searchable both inside and outside Facebook.

Depending on the type of business page you chose, the Name text box may be labeled as follows:

- Business or Place
- Company Name
- Brand or Product
- Name
- Cause or Community

Until you have 100 followers, you can change your business page title, but only once. When your 100th follower Likes your business page, your title becomes permanent. Facebook figures that as you grow, it's important to keep your brand intact and not confuse your readers with changing information.

5. **If you're creating a business page for a local business or a place, type your street address, city, state, zip code, and phone number in the relevant text boxes.**

6. **Select the I Agree to Facebook Pages Terms check box.**

7. **Click the Get Started button.**

   The Set Up page for your business page appears.

8. **In the first text box, type a description of your business page. In the second box, add your blog or website URL, your Twitter handle, or another pertinent link.**

9. **(Optional) Upload an image to serve as your profile picture from your computer or import one from your website and click Save Photo.**

   If you don't set your profile image at this point, you can add it later (we tell you how later in this chapter). If you upload a picture, this image appears any time you post as your business page. We provide advice on choosing your profile image later in this chapter.

10. **To add your page to your favorites, click Add to Favorites. Otherwise, click Skip.**

11. **(Optional) Promote your page.**

    You can create an ad to promote your page. We recommend that you get your page completely set up before running ads. To find out more about marketing your business on Facebook, see Book V.

12. **If you don't promote your page, click Skip.**

    Your business page appears, similar to the one shown in Figure 1-2. If you are new at creating a business page, Facebook walks you through the important parts of your page.

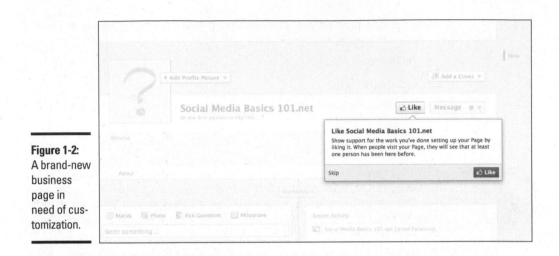

Figure 1-2:
A brand-new business page in need of customization.

Creating a Vanity URL

When you initially create your Facebook business page, it has a fairly long and ugly URL (or address), such as

`https://www.facebook.com/pages/Post-Planner/1234567890`

An address like that makes it hard for people to remember how to find you on Facebook. Luckily, as soon as you have 25 followers, you can create a vanity URL. A *vanity URL* is a custom address for your Facebook business page, such as `http://facebook.com/PostPlanner`. Although most people refer to these customized URLs as vanity URLs, Facebook calls them *usernames*. Also, you don't always need 25 followers to secure your vanity URL; sometimes you have that option as soon as you create your business page.

You can create a vanity URL for your personal timeline; see Book I, Chapter 2 for more information.

We have a few tips to share with you about vanity URLs:

✦ When you create your vanity URL, it's set. If you make a typo or change your mind, you're out of luck. Carefully check your spelling before you click the Save button!

✦ Try to match your vanity URL to your business page title, because people will find it easier to remember the address. If the vanity URL you want is taken, it's okay if the title of your business page is a little different from your vanity URL. When people search for your business page on Facebook, your title is what counts.

✦ Think of at least three vanity URLs for your business page. You may not be able to claim your first choice if someone else is already using that vanity URL.

✦ Facebook does not allow you to use the word *Facebook* in your vanity URL. The company doesn't want you to infringe on any Facebook trademark or imply that you're affiliated with it in any way.

✦ Vanity URLs can only use alphanumeric characters or periods, and can't contain spaces, hyphens, or other special characters — and if you use a period, it can't come at the end of the name.

✦ When a vanity URL is used, no one else can use it. This is true even if the vanity URL is abandoned. The only way to claim a used vanity URL is to prove you own the trademark.

✦ If you have trademarked your company name, but the vanity URL is not available, you can contact Facebook to help you obtain the correct vanity URL. Point your browser to `http://on.fb.me/InfringingUsername` and complete the form. Facebook usually helps you within 48 hours.

You can follow these instructions to create a vanity URL for your business page:

1. **In your browser, go to** `http://facebook.com/username`.

    The Username page appears with two boxes. The top box allows you to create a username (vanity URL) for your personal timeline; the bottom box allows you to create a username for your business page.

2. **In the bottom box, use the drop-down list to choose the business page for which you want to set the vanity URL.**

    If you're the admin for more than one business page, you see each of those pages listed in the drop-down list. If you are the admin for a single business page, that page will be the only one listed.

    A text box appears.

3. **In the text box, type the name you'd like to use for your vanity URL, and then click the Check Availability button.**

    If the name is available, you can set it; if it's not, try another name.

4. **When you have a vanity URL you want to use, click the Save button.**

TIP

You can shorten any Facebook URL even more by replacing `facebook.com` with `fb.com`. For example, `http://facebook.com/PostPlanner` becomes `http://fb.com/Postplanner`. This trick comes in handy when you're including your Facebook URL on a business card or other small space!

TIP

It may be tempting to link to your website and try to convert your readers into customers when they arrive there. Our experience is that people interacting in Facebook don't want to leave Facebook and are less likely to click links that take them away. If you think about it, you don't want your visitors to leave Facebook either. Isn't one of your goals to convince new visitors to Like your business page? If you're sending them away from Facebook, they may not Like your page before they click away. Instead of linking away from your business page, give a specific call to action (such as "Like our business page and receive a free chapter of our book!").

Understanding the Importance of Cover and Profile Pictures

Just like on your personal timeline, your business page also has a profile picture and a cover photo. These two images should work together to reinforce your brand, product, or business to your audience. We like the way KLM (`www.facebook.com/KLM`) uses its cover photo and profile picture, as shown in Figure 1-3.

Figure 1-3: KLM uses both the cover photo and the profile picture to reinforce its brand.

Both pictures work together to convey the KLM brand. The cover photo makes use of the large space, is visually appealing, and highlights KLM's logo (which is repeated in the profile picture). By displaying a blue sky and an airplane, you know immediately what their brand is all about. The profile picture is easily recognizable in the news feed and uses the KLM logo so followers can quickly scan and find updates from KLM.

We recommend using a strongly branded image as your profile image (the smaller image) because this image is attached to all updates and comments you make while using your business page. Don't change your profile picture regularly, unless that's part of your business's image. Your followers will appreciate having a standard picture to associate with your business. In social media outlets such as Facebook and even Twitter, your followers' streams move quickly, and they often scan that stream rather than read it word for word. A static, strong profile image becomes familiar to your followers and helps them quickly find your updates.

Your cover photo, on the other hand, can change as needed. In fact, Facebook encourages you to change it regularly and use it as a means of engaging your followers and bringing them back to your business page.

Why looks matter

In the most general sense, the overall look of a business page and personal timeline is simple and consistent. As you dig deeper into the capabilities of a business page, you discover how to leverage some of Facebook's page customizations to create a stronger message.

When someone visits your business page, you have a matter of seconds to capture their interest. Some studies say that within four seconds, visitors judge your company, and over 75 percent of visitors are judging your company by the look of your site alone. Your business page is an extension of your web presence, and a well-designed web presence is representative of a better company.

One important consideration is the outcome you're looking for. The appearance of your business page plays a big role in the ultimate results. For example, say you want to get people to take a customer survey. This survey will enable you to collect customer data such as e-mail addresses and will help you get information about your customer base so that you know the items they're interested in. A simple, clean design with a clear call to action (such as a button that says Take Survey) will have better results than a complicated design with only text links.

To put it simply, if your design is aesthetically pleasing and your message is clear and simple, you're sure to get better results!

Choosing a profile picture

People will come to associate your profile image with your presence on Facebook. We (and Facebook) suggest using your logo or a company symbol. The image you choose should be recognizable and consistent with the other business branding you do outside Facebook. By branding yourself consistently across platforms (Facebook, Twitter, your website, and so on), you make it easy for followers and potential followers to recognize your brand and engage with you.

You can use the profile picture area to highlight a special campaign or contest, but keep it simple because this area is small. Too much detail won't stand out in the news feed. Unlike tabs, no additional functionality is allowed in profile pictures. This area is limited to a simple image only.

We suggest using an image that is 180 x 180 pixels for your profile image. Facebook will scale it down to 32 x 32 pixels in the news feed. You can use a larger image, but it may not look as good. Experiment with what you have to see what you like best. As you consider what image to use for your profile picture, remember that you don't have a lot of real estate. Choose something that is easily recognizable (and readable if necessary) when shown in the smaller size.

**Book IV
Chapter 1**

Creating a Business Page

Choose an image that reinforces the brand you're trying to create and share. Figure 1-4 shows some examples of profile images; they provide little information but have a big effect. You can see how the profile images in the figure look when paired with their cover photos here:

✦ For Dummies: www.facebook.com/fordummies

✦ HyperArts: www.facebook.com/hyperarts

✦ HubSpot: www.facebook.com/hubspot

✦ Short Stack: www.facebook.com/shortstacklab

Figure 1-4:
Smaller
profile
images that
still have an
effect.

Before you upload your profile image, check to be sure it matches this criteria:

✦ **Your image should be at least 180 x180 pixels.** Page profile pictures are square and are displayed at 160 x 160 pixels. The photo you upload must be at least 180 x 180 pixels. If you upload a larger image or a rectangular image, Facebook will crop the image to fit in the square. It's important that your image is 180 pixels wide (or wider). If it's less than 180 pixels wide, Facebook won't allow you to upload it. If by chance you can upload it, Facebook will stretch your image to make it fit the space and you may end up with a distorted picture that looks blurry.

✦ **You must own the rights to the image you use.** If you use an image that you don't own, you risk losing your business page.

✦ **Your image should be saved as a PNG (.png) file.** These files tend to upload better to Facebook and they have the added bonus of being small files! You can also use .jpg files.

✦ **If you import your image from your website, know the exact URL for the image you want to use.** You can enter the main URL for your site (http://www.*domain*.com) and Facebook will pull an image from the site. However, this image may not be the one you want to use. To ensure Facebook pulls the correct image, use the image's URL.

To find the URL for an image from your site, right-click the image. Depending on your browser, you have these options:

• *Firefox:* Choose View Image from the menu. A new page appears showing the image. Note the new URL in your browser's address bar. That's the URL you'll need if you want to import your image to Facebook from your website.

- *Google Chrome:* Choose Copy Image URL from the menu.
- *Internet Explorer:* Click the Properties option to find the image URL.

Uploading your profile picture

You can upload a profile image when you create your page or at any time. You can choose from photos you've already uploaded to albums (which you probably haven't done yet if your page is new), you can take a photo with your webcam, or you can upload an image from your computer.

To upload a profile picture while on your business page, follow these instructions:

1. **Click the Add/Edit Profile Picture link.**

    A dialog box appears giving you a few choices.

2. **Choose Upload Photo.**

3. **Choose the file you want to upload to Facebook.**

4. **Click Open.**

    Your image immediately appears as your profile image.

Changing your profile picture

If you later decide to change your profile picture, just do the following:

1. **From your business page home screen, hover your cursor over the profile picture space.**

    An Edit Profile Picture link appears.

2. **Click the Edit Profile Picture link.**

3. **Choose from the following options:**

    - *Choose from Photos:* Select an image from photos currently uploaded to your business page.
    - *Take a Photo:* Use your webcam to take a picture to use as your profile picture.
    - *Upload Photo:* Select a photo from your computer and upload it to your business page.
    - *Edit Thumbnail:* Use your mouse to center the portion of the image you want to display.
    - *Remove:* Remove the current profile picture.

    After you select a photo, you're prompted to drag the image into the desired position.

4. **Click Save Changes.**

Use your page's real estate

Facebook has a limited area that you can customize, and that customization is valuable when you're trying to get a branding or marketing message across to your Facebook audience. Your use of the space should be meaningful and effective. You should use every bit of space available but in a way that doesn't clutter your page. A well-designed business page can attract more traffic simply because more people share it, especially if the design is particularly innovative.

Function is important too. Giving people a compelling reason to visit your business page will bring more traffic than a cool design. For example, if your business page merely shows a static graphic, one visit may be all you get from someone. However, if you regularly post new videos, visitors will return to see the latest one.

To make the most of your business page design, consider the following:

- Make the application images shown directly below the cover photo intriguing. Entice people to click to see more.

- Consider the use of white (blank) space to make images in a tab or a profile pic stand out more.

When you're just starting out designing your page, simple is better than a more complicated and not well executed design. If you can, hire a designer to put together some professional graphics for your business page.

Don't change your profile image frequently. As we note throughout this book, Facebook moves quickly and users scan information instead of reading it thoroughly. Your followers come to associate your profile picture with your updates. When you change the picture, followers may miss your updates because the picture isn't familiar.

Choosing a cover picture

Online, looks are everything. A great design can make or break your success. The more professional your web pages appear, the more authority you're perceived to wield. Your Facebook business page is no exception. Because your cover photo is likely a visitor's first interaction with your page, it can set the tone and expectation of your business page, as well as reinforce your brand.

Figures 1-5 and 1-6 show the cover photos for two of our favorite business pages, HyperArts and HubSpot, respectively. Note how the cover and profile images work together. When you first visit the business page, you have a sense of how things fit together, but when you see the profile image by itself in your news feed, there is no doubt which page it belongs to.

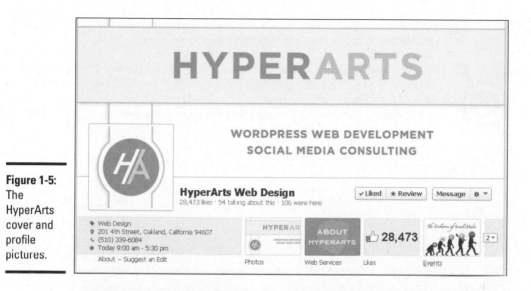

Figure 1-5:
The
HyperArts
cover and
profile
pictures.

Figure 1-6:
The
HubSpot
cover and
profile
pictures.

The rules regarding what can and cannot be included on a cover picture
have changed. Gone are the rules that disallowed ads, calls to action, and
contact information. Facebook simply encourages you to be creative and not
post any cover photo that misleads, is deceptive, infringes on anyone else's
copyright, or violates the page terms.

Even with the relaxed rules, we recommend that you keep the cover picture simple and use the space to properly brand yourself.

Facebook encourages business page admins to change out the cover picture as often as you like to keep things interesting for your followers. The actual dimensions for a cover picture are 851 pixels wide and 315 pixels high. You can upload a picture with a minimum width of 399 pixels, but your image will be stretched to fill the 851-pixel space and will likely be distorted.

Chapter 2: Customizing Your Business Page

In This Chapter

- ✓ Including company information
- ✓ Customizing the settings on your page
- ✓ Making a friend an admin
- ✓ Adding apps
- ✓ Getting updates from followers
- ✓ Featuring a business
- ✓ Showcasing an update
- ✓ Going mobile

*A*fter you create your business page, you want to customize it, or *brand* it. Marketing starts with good branding, and your business page is an important part of communicating that brand. We show you how to do these tasks in this chapter.

Adding Information about Your Business Page

In this section, you provide the information about your company that you want to share publicly. Navigate to your business page. Your Admin panel may or may not be visible above your cover photo. If it isn't, click the Show button in the top-right corner of your business page to reveal it. See Figure 2-1 for an example of an Admin panel.

Near the top of the page, click Edit Page to reveal a drop-down list and then select Update Page Info. The material you share on the Page Info page appears publicly on your business page. The options you see depend on the category you chose when you created your page.

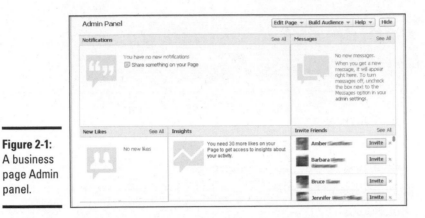

Figure 2-1:
A business page Admin panel.

We don't have room to explain every option (given that there are six main page categories and approximately 30 subcategories for each category), but the following list does describe the most common and important options:

✦ **Category:** Use the two drop-down lists here to change your business page's subcategory and group, respectively. Choosing the correct subcategory and group will help people find your business page.

✦ **Page Address:** When you've accrued 25 followers, you can change your Facebook page URL from a long, hard-to-remember address to a shorter, easier-to-remember address. We discuss usernames (also called *vanity URLs*) in the next section. We want to point out that you don't always need 25 followers before you can claim your username. Sometimes you can claim it immediately after you've created your page; other times you need 25 followers. We wish we had a better answer for you about why that is, but sometimes Facebook doesn't lend itself to easy answers.

✦ **Short Description:** The information you provide here appears on your business page's About Page (you find the link just above your timeline updates). The About box is a good place to share your website address or a link to your Twitter handle (provide the URL to your Twitter page — `http://twitter.com/`*username* — so your followers can click and connect rather than trying to find you themselves).

Any time you add a web address, be sure to include `www.` so that the link is clickable. For example, type `www.`*postplanner.`com* instead of *postplanner.com*.

✦ **Company Overview:** Write a paragraph about your company. You could include how you started or your business philosophy. Alternatively, you could include your contact information (e-mail, phone number, Twitter handle, or website address). It's up to you what you include here.

✦ **Long Description:** Include more information about your company, products, or niche. The description doesn't need to be as long as your company overview. In fact, you may not need both a long description and a company overview.

✦ **Products:** List your products or services in this text box.

Your business page and its contents are searchable outside Facebook. We suggest using keywords associated with your company, product, or niche as appropriate in the About, Description, Company Overview, and Products sections. *Stuffing* (overusing certain keywords or including irrelevant keywords) your descriptions with keywords is considered bad form. Instead, see how you can use keywords seamlessly with your existing marketing content.

✦ **Address, City/Town, Postal Code:** If you have a bricks-and-mortar location that customers and followers can physically visit, type the necessary information. Doing so allows your customers to check into your venue and find you quickly on a map.

✦ **E-mail:** Type your e-mail address here. Be aware that this information will be publicly available when followers click the About link. Instead of sharing your personal e-mail address, it's a good idea to create a general e-mail address (info@yourcompany.com or facebook@yourcompany.com).

✦ **Website:** Type the URL of your website in this text box. Remember to type the entire address, including http://.

The information you share on the Page Info link appears on the About Page for your business page. This information is publicly available — both inside and outside Facebook.

Customizing Your Business Page Settings

As you market your business through your Facebook business page, you'll discover that there is more to setting up your page than simply creating it and filling out the basic information. Every marketer should be aware of a few elements in the business page makeup. Knowing the flexibility of pages and how you can manipulate each aspect can open up ways to get better marketing traction out of your page.

In this section, you determine the settings you want for your business page. From the top of your Admin panel, click Edit Page➪Edit Settings. The Settings page shown in Figure 2-2 appears.

You use the many entries on the Settings page to determine the way your business page functions for you as the admin and for those visiting your page. This section describes them all.

To review any of these settings, either click the setting name (for example, Messages) or click the setting's Edit link, which appears on the far right.

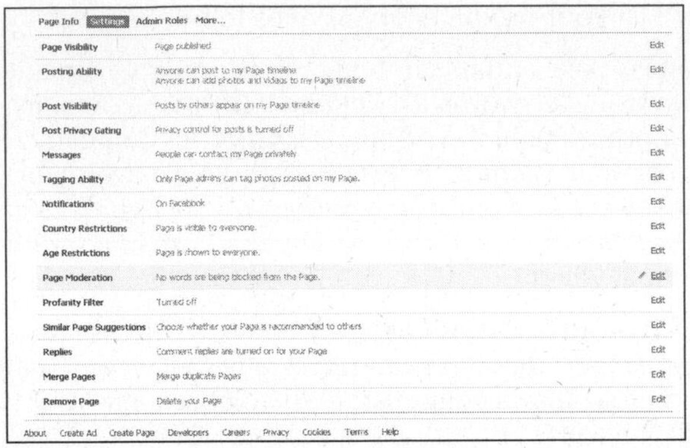

Figure 2-2:
Customize the settings for your business page.

Page Visibility option

Click the first option on the Settings page, Page Visibility (or click its Edit link on the far right). If your page isn't ready for public consumption, select the Unpublish Page (Only Admins Can See This Page) check box. Now your page is private and visible only to admins. When you're ready to interact with followers and expand your community, deselect the check box and your page will be published publicly.

The default for new business pages is to publish automatically, so if you want to keep your page under wraps until you have it just right, be sure to visit this option first.

Posting Ability option

For the Posting Ability option, we suggest allowing everyone to post to your page and to add photos and videos to your page. You may have to remove some comments occasionally, but you'll be building community.

People love to see themselves in print and have your attention directed to them. They want to interact with you. Make it easy for them to do so. If you find that you're dealing with too much spam, you can change these settings for a while and explain your actions to your followers. They'll appreciate that you're keeping the space professional.

Post Visibility option

If you've allowed others to post to your page, the Post Visibility option enables you to decide whether you want other people to see those posts. You can allow the posts or hide them from your page.

In addition, you can choose to highlight recent posts by others in a box at the top of the page. We recommend this feature because it's a great way for others to see what people are saying about your business. But make sure you monitor this section in case someone is overposting or posting spam.

Post Targeting and Privacy option

The Post Targeting and Privacy setting allows you to choose who sees posts on your page. If you leave the box deselected, whenever you post as your page, everyone who has Liked it or Followed it will see your posts. If you select the box, you can choose a target audience for each post. You'll be able to target by location and by language.

Messages option

To make customer service even easier for brands and Facebook users, Facebook allows people (both followers and nonfollowers) to send a private message to a business page. Select the Messages option to turn on the feature; deselect it to turn off the feature. When the feature is on, the Message button appears below your cover photo.

When you receive a message, you see a notice in the Messages section of your Admin panel above your cover photo. (For more on the Admin panel, see Chapter 3 of this minibook.) When you click the new message, you can type a reply. Remember that your reply will always appear from your business page, not your personal timeline, regardless of how you set your posting preferences (discussed earlier in this chapter).

Tagging Ability option

Select the Tagging Ability option to allow people to tag themselves in photos you share. We like to allow our followers full access to our pages, including the capability to tag themselves. In that way, we make it easy for those followers to interact with us.

If you meet some of your followers, take pictures with them and share those photos on your page.

Notifications option

You use the Notifications option to choose how you get notifications when people post, comment, or send a message to your page. You can receive notifications on Facebook, by e-mail, or by both methods. We recommend getting notified on Facebook because it is easier to know when your page has new activity.

If you use the e-mail option and have an active page, you will quickly become overrun with e-mail messages. Scott has set up a folder in Gmail that handles only Facebook e-mails.

Country Restrictions option

If you want to restrict which countries can see and interact on your page, click the Country Restrictions option and then type the name of the country in the text box provided.

Next, choose whether you want to hide your content from users in these countries or exclude all countries but that one. For instance, if you want to show your business page to users only in the United States, type **United States** in the text box, and select the Only Show This Page to Viewers in These Countries option. If you want your page to be visible to all countries *except* the United States, type **United States** in the text box, and select the Hide This Page from Viewers in These Countries option. Note that users must be logged in to Facebook to see your page.

Age Restrictions option

If your products and content are not appropriate for underage users, select the Age Restrictions option and use the drop-down list to choose the age restrictions for your page. If you choose Anyone 13+, you're publishing your business page to everyone using Facebook (except those you may have restricted based on country). If you choose to restrict your page to users who are 17+, 18+, 19+, or 21+, you're publishing your page to Facebook members who are that age or older. If you're creating an alcohol-related business page, you must choose the Alcohol-Related option from the drop-down list. Facebook notes that the Alcohol-Related option sets the restriction for your business page based on the user's location. For instance, in the United States, your page would be restricted to users 21 and over; in Canada, your page would be restricted to users 19 and over. Note that users must be logged in to Facebook to see your page.

Page Moderation option

If you don't want specific words appearing on your business page, select the Page Moderation option. Type those words in the Moderation Blocklist text box that appears. Use a comma to separate words and phrases. Be aware that any comment or post that uses the words listed here will be automatically marked as spam and removed from your timeline.

Profanity Filter option

Select the Profanity Filter option and then use the drop-down list to select Off (no filters; it's possible you or your audience will use or see profanity), Medium (mild profanity is not filtered), or Strong (almost no profanity allowed).

Similar Page Suggestions option

Select the Similar Page Suggestions option if you want your page to be suggested to people when they Like a page that is similar to yours. In addition, when someone Likes your page, he or she may see a unit on your page suggesting similar pages.

Replies option

The Replies option, which is selected by default, enables people to reply to new comments on your page in threaded comments. With *threaded comments,* someone can reply directly to a comment, which makes it easier to figure out what people are replying to in an active thread. This feature is not supported on mobile devices.

Merge Pages option

You see the Merge Pages option if you have two pages with similar names. this option enables you to merge pages you manage if they have similar names and represent the same thing. The Likes and check-ins from these pages will be combined.

Remove Page option

Use the Remove Page option to delete your page. If your page is new and has no Likes, it will be deleted immediately. Otherwise, you'll have 14 days to restore it in case you change your mind. After that, you'll be asked to confirm whether to delete the page permanently. You could simply choose to unpublish the page instead; in that case, only admins will see the page.

Creating Admin Roles

As the admin of your business page, you have the capability to add others to your admin list as well as delete them. We strongly suggest adding at least one other admin to your business page as a security measure. That way, if you're locked out, you have someone you trust who can reinstate you as an admin.

To add people as admins for your business page, you either need to be friends with them or know their e-mail address in their Facebook profile. Then, from the top of your Admin panel, click Edit Page➪Edit Settings➪Admin Roles. The screen shown in Figure 2-3 appears.

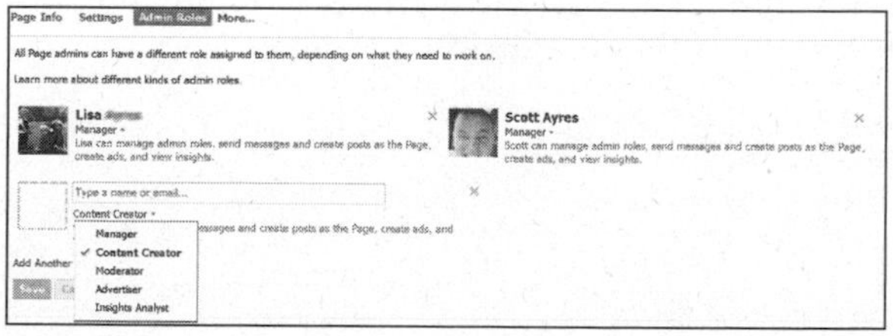

Figure 2-3: The Admin Roles page.

Book IV
Chapter 2

Customizing Your
Business Page

Start typing the person's name in the provided text box. A list of your friends appears, and you can either finish typing or select a name from the list. If you aren't friends with the person, simply enter the person's e-mail address.

Click Save. When requested, enter your password to confirm the changes, and then click Confirm. Facebook sends the person an e-mail and a notification on Facebook.

To remove an admin, simply click the Remove link next to the name of that person. When you click Save Changes, you'll be asked to enter your password. After you enter your password and click Confirm, that person will no longer have administrative privileges for your business page.

If you click the Remove link accidentally, click Cancel. A dialog box appears, asking if you want to leave this page with unsaved changes. Click Leave This Page. You'll end up on your business page timeline, instead of on your Admin panel.

Five levels of admins are available, making it easier to assign tasks. Only managers can change a person's admin type. By default, all admins are content creators. For a breakdown of admin roles and duties, see Figure 2-4.

Figure 2-4: Facebook page admin roles.

	Manager	Content Creator	Moderator	Advertiser	Insights Analyst
Manage Admin Roles	✔				
Edit the Page and Add Apps	✔	✔			
Create Posts as the Page and Delete Posts	✔	✔			
Respond to and Delete Comments	✔	✔	✔		
Send Messages as the Page	✔	✔	✔		
Create Ads	✔	✔	✔	✔	
View Insights	✔	✔	✔	✔	✔

All about Apps

Facebook apps provide additional functionality for a page. The Apps tab lists all the applications (or *apps*) you have installed on your Facebook business page. At the top of your Admin panel, click Edit Page⇨Edit Settings⇨Apps. The screen shown in Figure 2-5 appears.

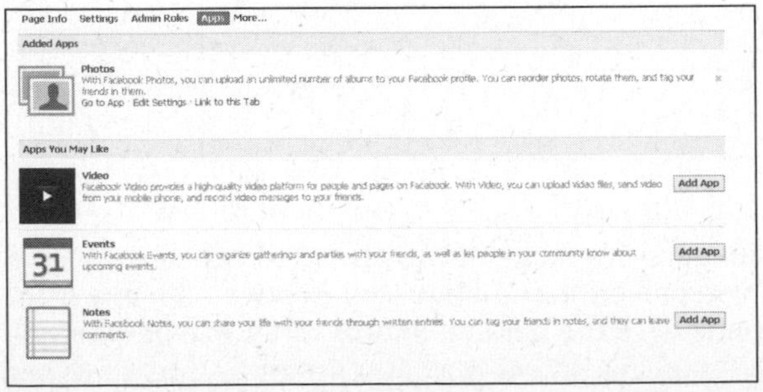

Figure 2-5: The Apps tab lists all installed apps.

By default, all business pages have the following apps installed and ready to use:

✦ **Photos:** Upload and share images with your friends and followers. Book II, Chapter 3 provides instructions on how to share and hide photos, as well as sort them into albums.

✦ **Events:** Create a special page to promote an event you're hosting. Book II, Chapter 7 explains how to find and create events; it also explains the etiquette behind event invitations.

✦ **Notes:** Write longer posts for your audience. Notes allow limited formatting, and you can include photos.

✦ **Videos:** Create video messages from your business page and keep them stored on your Videos tab. Find out more about using video with Facebook in Book II, Chapter 4.

Under each app listed on the Apps tab, you see links. Depending on the app, you may see a link for the following options:

✦ **Go to App:** Click this link to go directly to a page that allows you to choose the settings for your app. These settings vary greatly, depending on the app.

✦ **Edit Settings:** This sparse tab usually has just one or two options and tells you if the app is added as a tab on your business page or not. If you want to remove an app from your page, click the Remove link, and that tab is removed from your main business page navigation but remains in your list of apps on the Admin panel. You aren't deleting the app from your business page, so you can reinstate it later if you want.

To delete an app from your business page, click the X to the far right of the app. A dialog box appears, asking if you're sure you want to remove this application. Click Remove. When you remove an app in this manner, it is no longer associated with your business page and it no longer appears in your business page navigation nor in your list of apps. If you want to use it again, you need to reinstall it. (See Book VI, Chapter 3 for instructions on how to install an application on your business page.)

If the app is not currently active, the Edit Settings window displays Available (Add). Click the Add link to include the app in your business page navigation and make the app live.

Some apps may have another tab besides the Add/Remove option labeled Additional Permission. Click this tab to set any additional permissions for this app. These permissions generally include what the app has permission to access.

✦ **Link to This Tab:** Every app you install becomes a tab on your business page below your cover photo. Each tab has its own URL or *permalink*. This feature is handy, for instance, if you want to link directly to a note you shared or want to remind followers about a promotion you're running on your business page and provide a link to the entry form.

You can write a status update directing your followers to the link for that tab instead of sending them to your general timeline with the hope that they'll find the link. When you click the Link to This Tab link, a dialog box appears with the permalink for that tab.

Don't worry if you don't see a Link to This Tab link under an app. You can still find its permalink. Navigate back to your business page, look at the App thumbnails below your cover photo, and click the app to which you want to link. When the new page appears, copy the URL and paste it wherever you need to place your link (in a status update, an e-newsletter, your blog, and so on).

Each application tab link has its own URL. That's a great feature because you can write a status update with a call to action and provide a link to complete the action. For example, if you want to remind followers to sign up for your e-newsletter, you can share a status update like this:

> Sign up for our monthly newsletter to receive exclusive discounts and coupons at `www.facebook.com/postplanner/app_158086484245654`.

Note that the preceding link takes the reader directly to the newsletter signup tab on the business page.

Apps for a business page

The capability to install applications is one of our favorite things about Facebook business pages. Here are two of our favorite general applications for new Facebook business pages:

✔ **A contact form:** Although Facebook offers your audience the option to send you a message directly, you may want to design your own contact form that collects specific information (for example, e-mail address, name, or whether the person is a returning customer). You can create a contact form via ShortStack, TabSite, or Heyo.

✔ **E-mail newsletter sign-up form:** If you're trying every which way to increase your e-list, here's one more way. If people are visiting your business page, they might also sign up for your newsletter. Or, because every tab has its own permalink, you can link directly to your newsletter sign-up with a strong call to action in your status update. People hate to leave Facebook, so link to a sign-up housed on your business page. If you're using MailChimp (`http://mailchimp.com`) or Constant Contact (`www.constantcontact.com`), you can use their apps. If you use a different service, contact the help desk and ask if the service has a Facebook application you can install.

Suggestions from Your Followers

The audience of your page can click a link just below your About section and suggest an edit. This feature is meant to help you improve your page's information. As the page's admin, you can review these suggestions and accept or decline them.

Choosing Featured Business Pages

The Featured setting allows you to showcase specific business pages you have Liked as your business page. You can use the setting also to feature admins of your business page if you want. (Later in this chapter, you find out how to Like a business page as your business page — it's not as confusing as it sounds!)

In general, you can Like as many business pages as you want, and five of those pages appear randomly on the right side of your business page, as shown in Figure 2-6. To see the Featured page, go to your Admin panel and click Edit Page⇨Edit Settings⇨More. Then select Featured from the drop-down list.

Figure 2-6: Other business pages your page Likes.

Likes	See All
RazorSocial 8 friends also like this.	
Jon Loomer Digital 28 friends also like this.	
The Nonprofit Facebook Guy 12 friends also like this.	
Inbound Zombie • New media for nonprofits 16 friends also like this.	
ShortStack 27 friends also like this.	

You can also showcase specific business pages instead of a random sampling of all the business pages you Like. *Note:* If you haven't yet Liked other pages as your page, you won't to be able to change this setting.

Then follow these steps:

1. **In the Admin panel, click the Edit Featured Likes button.**

   If you haven't previously selected other business pages to feature, you may see the Add Featured Likes button. Click that to get to the Edit Featured Likes button.

The Edit Featured Likes window appears with a list of all the business pages you've Liked as your business page.

2. **Select the check boxes next to the five business pages you want to showcase.**

3. **Click Save.**

The business pages you selected will appear in random order each time your business page is visited or refreshed in the visitor's browser.

You may want to share who your admins are with your followers, especially if you're mostly interacting as your brand (your business page) instead of as your personal timeline. By featuring your admins on your About page, any followers visiting your business page can put a personal face to status updates and comments.

When you feature an admin timeline, the admin's name is listed on the business page's About page and linked to his or her timeline. Visitors (whether or not they are followers) can click that link to view the timeline and send a friend request to that timeline. It's important to consider your privacy settings and how you'll respond to friend requests. You are under no obligation to accept requests. If you'd like to keep your timeline private, you can respond by thanking the person for the request and explaining that you reserve your personal timeline for family and friends you've met in real life; if they'd like to connect with you, they can do so on your business page.

Sending Updates on the Go

You don't have to have your computer handy to post updates to your business page. You can send status updates via e-mail, mobile web, your smartphone's Facebook application, or text.

Open a browser on your smartphone and go to `https://m.facebook.com` to use Facebook in your mobile browser. Flip to Book II, Chapter 6 for further instructions and explanations of your mobile Facebook options.

Chapter 3: Touring Your Business Page

In This Chapter

✔ Understanding how a business page is laid out

✔ Familiarizing yourself with business page tools and options

✔ Using Facebook as a personal timeline or a business page

After you set up your business page, one of the first things you may notice is that business pages look a lot like personal timelines. However, several features of personal timelines (list of friends, summary of personal information, and so on) have been replaced with features related to interacting with your followers, tracking your followers, and more.

This chapter explains how a business page differs from a personal timeline, what each business page feature does, and how you can manage your page presence on Facebook.

Reviewing the Overall Business Page

Your business page is laid out in sections: the blue Facebook navigation bar at the top of the page, the Admin panel, your cover photo, basic page info, apps, and your timeline, as shown in Figure 3-1. The following sections explain what is included in each area of the page and how you can use the links and information to manage your business page.

The Admin Panel

If you don't automatically see your Admin panel, click the Show button, above your cover photo. The Admin panel includes five sections, as shown in Figure 3-2:

✦ **Posts and Notifications:** See a list of the most recent interactions and posts you made on your business page. When viewing a post, you can link directly to it to engage with your followers, as well as see its total reach and paid reach. In addition, you can run an ad specifically for the post. Click Notifications to see recent comments or replies on your posts. Click See All to see more interactions by date.

Figure 3-1:
The impor-
tant parts of
a Facebook
business
page.

✦ **Messages:** See whether any followers have sent you a private message (and whether you or another admin have replied). Click See All to go to your Messages page, where you can see all the messages your business page has received.

✦ **Get More Likes:** Promote your page to others to get more Likes. For more on Facebook ads, see Book V.

✦ **Insights:** Get a glimpse of how your business page is performing. Click See All to view your complete Insights data. Some pages will have different features in this space as Facebook tests new features.

✦ **Invite Friends:** Invite your friends to Like your page. Scott recently started a local business page and invites only friends and potential customers who are local to the business. If your page is new, you may see the Create Username option here (see Book IV, Chapter 1 to find out more about usernames). Some users may also see page tips in this space.

Figure 3-2:
The Admin
panel pro-
vides an
overview
of how fol-
lowers are
interacting
with your
page.

The Admin Panel Toolbar

In addition to the five sections described in the preceding section, you see
a toolbar at the top of the Admin panel with five options: Edit Page, Build
Audience, See Insights, Help, and Show (or Hide). Click each one to manage
different aspects of your business page.

Edit Page option

When you click Edit Page, a drop-down list appears with options for the
following:

+ **Update Page Info:** Click this option to edit information about your page
  and business. We explain this functionality in Chapter 1 of this minibook.

+ **Edit Settings:** Change who sees your page and who can post on it. For
  more on this feature, see Book IV, Chapter 2.

+ **Manage Admin Roles:** Edit who manages your page and how.

+ **Use Activity Log:** Click this option to go to your Activity Log page, where
  you can see a list of all the activity on your business page. The activity
  log for your business page functions similarly to the activity log for your
  personal timeline.

  You can control how content appears on your business page by choosing to allow, highlight, hide, or delete content. You can also report or
  mark content as spam, and change the date of the post. To control content, click the pencil icon next the update you want to manage and make
  a selection from the drop-down list, as shown in Figure 3-3.

You can manage content from the past as well. On the right side of the Activity Log page, click the year and month for which you want to see posts. You can filter your activity log also by choosing one of the options in the left sidebar, such as Photos, Videos, or Comments.

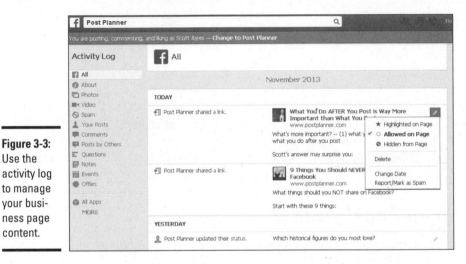

Figure 3-3:
Use the activity log to manage your business page content.

✦ **See Banned Users:** Click this option to see a list of the followers you've banned. You can click the Unban button to reinstate a follower's privileges. You can also click the Banned button in the top left of the dialog box to see a list of people who Like your page, other pages that have Liked your page, and subscribers and people who have administrative rights for your business page. When you're done, click the X in the upper-right corner of the box.

✦ **Use Facebook as *[your business page name]*:** You can use Facebook as yourself (your personal timeline) or as your business page. We explain this feature later in the chapter in the section, "Using Facebook as Your Business Page or Personal Timeline."

Build Audience option

When you click Build Audience on the toolbar, a drop-down list appears with the following options:

✦ **Invite Email Contacts:** You can invite contacts to your page from e-mail lists you've collected. You can upload a contact list file saved to your computer, or load an e-mail list from Constant Contact, MailChimp, and VerticalResponse. Clicking Invite Contacts for each of these will give you a list of instructions on how to import your contact list. If you choose Skype or iCloud, you'll need to provide your user login and password. You can import contacts from Outlook by providing your e-mail address. You'll also see Email Service, where you must log in with your e-mail address and password to import and invite those contacts.

✦ **Invite Friends:** Invite specific people to Like your page. When you click Invite Friends, the Invite Your Friends to Like *[your page name]* dialog box appears. Use the drop-down list in the top-left corner to target people to invite. You can also type a name in the text box. Click Close when you're done.

✦ **Share Page:** Share your business page on your personal timeline, a friend's timeline, in a group, on another page you admin, or through a private message. Type a quick status update introducing your business page or explaining why you're sharing the page. (A call to action, such as *Like our page so you never miss another sale!,* works well here.) Then click the Share Page button.

✦ **Promote Page:** Create a Facebook ad to introduce your business page to more followers. We explain how to craft a Facebook Ad in Book V, Chapter 4.

See Insights option

Clicking the See Insights option opens Facebook Insights for your page. Insights is a collection of data that shows you the performance of your page and posts on your page. You also see detailed demographics regarding those who are following your page. Anyone running a business page should become familiar with Insights. We go into more detail about Insights and its importance in Book V, Chapter 3.

Help option

When you click Help on the toolbar, a drop-down list appears with the following options:

✦ **Visit Help Center:** Go to the Facebook Help files. In Book I, Chapter 5, we explain how to use these files to find the answers you're looking for.

✦ **Facebook Help Community:** See user-generated questions and answers on various topics. The questions and answers are from users of Facebook, so the information might not be accurate.

✦ **Getting Started:** View a page that provides details on filling out your page, building an audience, and posting engaging content. This option is a great reference when you're just starting out.

✦ **Send Feedback:** Tell Facebook your thoughts about business pages. When you click the Send Feedback link, the Your Feedback about Pages page appears. Answer the questions and type your feedback as required.

You can also attach a screenshot to further explain your feedback or issue. Click the Send button when you're done.

Show (or Hide) option

Click the Hide button to hide your Admin panel. Your cover photo appears at the top of the page. Remember that only admins can see the Admin panel, so you don't have to hide it unless you just like a less cluttered look.

Page Info Section

Below the cover photo, you see some basic information about your page, as shown in Figure 3-4. This information serves as an overview of your business page, as well as provides basic navigation.

Figure 3-4: Basic info on your page.

The basic page information has the following:

+ **The title of your business page** was determined by you when you created your page.

+ **Your Number of Likes** is a public display of how many followers, or *Likes*, your page has. This number counts individuals (that is, personal timelines) that have Liked your page. If another page Likes yours, that Like doesn't count toward your total number of Likes. We explain how to create community and increase the number of followers throughout Book IV, but particularly in Chapter 4.

+ **The Number of People Talking about This** is the number of interactions your business page content has had in the last seven days. These interactions include Likes, comments, shares, answers to polls or questions, mentions in other status updates, tags, venue check-ins, and so on. You won't see a Talking about This number if you haven't had any interactions on your business page in the last week.

✦ **The Like button** allows you to become a follower of a page. You see the Like button only if you aren't currently a follower of the page you're viewing. (If you are a follower, the button says Liked.) If you want to see the business page's updates in your news feed and support the brand, click the Like button and become a follower of the page.

✦ **The Message button** allows followers and nonfollowers to send the admins of a business page a private message. If you turned off this option in your Settings, you (and your followers) won't see this button.

See Chapter 1 of this minibook for instructions on how to implement the Message button. We encourage you to keep this feature turned on because it allows customers to contact you directly if they have an issue rather than sharing their comments publicly on the timeline.

✦ **The gear icon** provides a drop-down list. The items you see depend on your relationship to the page. For instance, if you're an admin for the page, you see options that followers and nonfollowers won't. You'll also see different options based on your admin level, as discussed in Chapter 2 of this minibook. When you visit someone else's business page, whether as a follower or not, you see a different set of options. The options include quick access to the following:

   • *Create an Ad:* Only admins can see this option. Click this option to set a Facebook ad. We explain the process of creating ads in Book V, Chapter 4.

   • *Send Feedback:* Everyone can see this option. You can contact Facebook about an issue you're having or suggestions you have.

   • *Visit Help Center:* Only admins can see this option. If you have a question about how to use Facebook (either for your personal timeline or your business page), the Help Center is the place to start. You can find more information about the Help Center in Book I, Chapter 5.

   • *Share:* Both followers and admins see this option. Any time you come across a page that shares interesting content, it's easy to let your friends know about it. Click Share to post an update on your personal timeline, on a friend's timeline, to a group, or directly to your business page, depending on which audience you want to share with. You can also share the link via private message.

   • *Unlike:* You see this option if you already Like a page. Sometimes you think a page will be a fit but it isn't. No problem. You can click Unlike, and you'll stop receiving updates from the business page. The page admin can't tell who Unliked the page.

   • *View Insights:* Only admins see this option. Insights is Facebook's analytics program. A quick glance at your Insights page shows you how many active users you have and whether your interactions are up, down, or holding steady. Flip to Book V, Chapter 3 for information about how to use Insights and interpret your Facebook analytics.

- *Add to My Page's Favorites:* Everyone sees this option and it does just what it says it will. When you click this link, you can add the current page to your own page's favorites, and it will appear under Likes on the right side of your timeline. This may be a Facebook glitch, but you can add a page to your favorites without Liking the page. If this link doesn't show up for you, you've probably already added the page as a favorite. See Chapter 2 of this minibook for instructions on how to feature specific business pages in your Like section.

- *Remove from My Page's Favorites:* Everyone can see this option. Not feeling the love anymore? No problem. Go to the business page you want to remove from your favorites and click this link. The page no longer appears in your list of Likes in your timeline.

- *Report Page:* This link is visible only if you are not the admin of a page (because you wouldn't report your own page, would you?). If you aren't the admin of the page, you can see this link whether you Like the page or not. Click this link if you want to report a page as sharing inappropriate content. When you click the link, a dialog box appears with a list of violations. Select the page's infraction. You can choose from Spam or Scam, Hate Speech or Personal Attack, Violence or Harmful Behavior, Sexually Explicit Content, or Duplicate or Miscategorized Page.

- *Add to Interest Lists:* Select this option and then, in the drop-down list that appears, make your selection.

- *Like as Your Page:* You can Like another business page as your business page. When you select this link, a drop-down list appears so you can select the page.

- *Create a Page:* This link provides a shortcut to starting a business page. Click here and go directly to the section to start your page. See Chapter 2 of this minibook for more information on creating a business page.

- *Privacy:* Click here to find out more about Facebook's privacy policies.

- *Terms:* Click this link to go to the legal terms all users must follow when creating a Facebook account.

The options for reporting a page change, depending on the type of page.

You also have the option of reporting theft of your intellectual property. To do that, click the Is This Your Intellectual Property? link in the bottom-left corner of the dialog box. The Facebook instructions for reporting infringement claims appear.

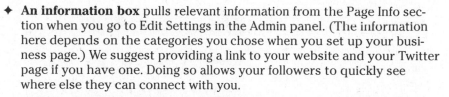

+ **An information box** pulls relevant information from the Page Info section when you go to Edit Settings in the Admin panel. (The information here depends on the categories you chose when you set up your business page.) We suggest providing a link to your website and your Twitter page if you have one. Doing so allows your followers to quickly see where else they can connect with you.

To create a usable link, be sure to include www. with any URLs you share in this box. For example, if you type *Shop our online store at postplanner. com*, that link won't be clickable. You can fix that by typing *Shop our online store at www.postplanner.com.*

+ **The About link** takes you to the About page, which displays the information you shared in the Page Info section when you go to Edit Settings in the Admin Panel. (See Book IV, Chapter 1 for more information.) Your followers will generally click this link if they're looking for store hours, directions, or more information about your company. Be sure you've provided the information your followers want.

In Chapter 2 of this minibook, we explain each link on your business page Admin panel. One of those links is the Featured setting. From there you can choose to feature the admins of your page. If you do so, the featured admins appear on the About page for your business page.

When you feature admins, their personal timelines are listed as links on your business page's About page. In addition, the business page that lists the featured admins also appears on that person's personal timeline in the About section.

+ **A list of apps installed** on your business page (we discuss apps more thoroughly in the next section).

Apps Navigation

If you refer to Figure 3-1, you see four pictures under the cover photo. These pictures depict apps installed on the page to enhance its functionality.

You can have many apps installed on your business page: a newsletter sign-up, a contact form, links to downloadable content, custom applications . . . the options are endless. Facebook displays apps in rows of four, and by default only the first row is displayed. Users can click the small number at the end of the row (the number at the end of the row indicates how many more apps are hidden) to expand the apps box to show more rows of apps (up to 12), as shown in Figure 3-5.

**Book IV
Chapter 3**

**Touring Your
Business Page**

Figure 3-5:
You can showcase up to 12 apps on your business page.

As the admin of a business page, you can see all your apps when you expand the apps box — you aren't limited to seeing the top 12.

You can choose the order in which your apps are displayed. The only exception is that the Photos app must always appear first.

The Photos app is populated by the images you upload to your business page and photo albums. For more information on how to add and delete photos to your timeline, flip to Book II, Chapter 3.

You can also create and display your own images for each app, as described later in this chapter.

When you click an app, you go to a new page with that app's functionality. For example, if you click a newsletter sign-up app, you leave the business page and end up on a page with the newsletter sign-up form. As you design your application landing page, it's helpful to know that the page is 810 pixels wide. That's a lot of screen real estate, and you can create some snazzy stuff with third-party application builders such as ShortStack, North Social, and Tabsite.

Changing the order of displayed apps

You can change the order in which your apps are displayed. The only exception is that the Photos app must always appear first; you can't move it. That means you really have space to showcase only three apps on the first row of apps under your cover photo. We suggest showcasing your most important apps (such as a newsletter sign-up) in the first row of displayed apps so they aren't overlooked.

To change the order of your displayed apps, follow these instructions:

1. **Navigate to your business page and click the arrow to see the full list of apps.**

2. **Move your cursor over the app you want to change and click the pencil icon that appears.**

3. **Choose Swap Position With, and then select the app with which you want to swap positions.**

   The apps swap positions. You can continue to tweak the order of your apps until you're satisfied.

Using your own images for displayed apps

You can also create and display your own images for each app. To do that, you need to create an image that is 111 pixels wide by 74 pixels tall. These images need to catch people's attention and have a clear call to action. For example, if you want people to sign up for your newsletter, create an image that reads *Join Our Newsletter!* We're sure you can come up with many creative ideas for customized application images.

When you have your image ready to install, follow these steps:

1. **Navigate to your business page and click the arrow to expose a full list of your apps.**

2. **Move your cursor over the app you want to edit and click the pencil icon that appears.**

3. **Choose Edit Settings from the list.**

   A dialog box appears with several options.

4. **Click the Change link next to Custom Tab Image.**

   The Upload a Custom Image page appears.

5. **Hover your cursor over the existing image, and click the Edit link that appears.**

6. **Click Choose File and select an image from your computer.**

   The image must be 111 x 74 pixels and will become the thumbnail for your custom page app. After you choose the image, it is uploaded and the screen updates.

7. **Close the browser window.**

   Your page opens in another window.

Choosing highlighted apps

Highlighted apps are the top four page tabs that appear below the cover photo on the right side. These apps are built in to all pages by Facebook, such as a map to your location or the number of Likes your page has.

You can also put up to three custom page tabs in this area. To do so, click the down arrow to the right of the Highlighted Apps area (the row containing Photos, Likes, Map, and so on) to reveal other applications or available spaces, as shown in Figure 3-6. Click the plus sign at the top-right corner of any blank area to add an application to your list. Only the top three appear at first glance on your business page. Users have to click the down arrow to reveal all the other applications you've installed on your business page.

Figure 3-6:
Applications
installed on
your page.

Photos is always the first app on your Highlighted Apps. You can't move this one. All your latest photo uploads are here, with the most recent one displayed in the box. Upload great photos that people will want to click!

When you can see all the applications on your business page, hover your mouse cursor over the top right, and you see a pencil icon, indicating that you can edit the application. Click the pencil icon to edit the settings as follows:

✦ **Remove** the app from your favorites.

✦ **Swap** its position with another application (the top three are visible on landing on your business page).

✦ **Link to This Tab** links the tab to the page tab.

✦ **Uninstall** the application.

✦ **Edit** the application's settings.

Editing the settings allows you to change the name of the application, as well as change the image that appears on your business page. The image acts like a button that leads to the page tab from your business page.

Your Timeline

The timeline portion of your page houses status updates and community interaction. The timeline is where you interact with your followers and where they interact with you.

Just like on your personal timeline, your business page has a line down the middle and information on the right and left sides. On your business page, though, the top-right side displays what other people are saying about your business page, friend activity, and Likes (the other pages you've Liked as your business page).

The timeline provides you with an opportunity to tell the story behind your business. Because you can add updates and assign them to a specific year, you're able to start with your first product sold and mark each milestone throughout your business history. Two companies that do a good job taking advantage of this feature are Red Bull (www.facebook.com/redbull) and Fanta (www.facebook.com/fanta). Each gives a complete history of their growth with fun pictures and interesting facts.

You (and your followers) can filter the content on the timeline by clicking the drop-down list under Basic Page info, as shown in Figure 3-7.

Figure 3-7: Filter the content on any business page by using the Filter list.

The list choices are self-explanatory. When you click a choice, the timeline shows only posts highlighted by the business page owners (usually milestones, but can be any highlighted content), posts by the business page (usually general status updates), or posts by others (anyone who has interacted with the business page — whether as a follower or not).

The following sections explain each timeline component.

Status update box

At the top left of your timeline, you see the status update box. Just like with your personal timeline, the status update box is where you type and share your status updates for your business page. Your business page status update options are

✦ **Post:** Type a status update.

✦ **Photo/Video:** Upload a photo or video from your computer, take a photo with your webcam, or create an album. See Book II, Chapter 3 for instructions and advice about using photos on Facebook. You can also use this option to upload or take video. See Book II, Chapter 4 for instructions and advice about using video with Facebook.

✦ **Offer, Event +:** Post an offer, an event, or a milestone to your page. (We discuss offers in Book V, Chapter 4.) Events are, well, events that pages can schedule and encourage others to attend. The milestone option allows you to create date-specific updates relating to major milestones for your business.

When you click Milestone the first time, you'll see an Invalid Date error, as shown in Figure 3-8. Go to your Admin panel, select Page Info, and add the date when the page Joined Facebook or the company started.

You can't create a milestone if you're trying to post to your business page as your personal timeline. Below the search box on your page, you can change between posting, commenting, and Liking as your page or as yourself.

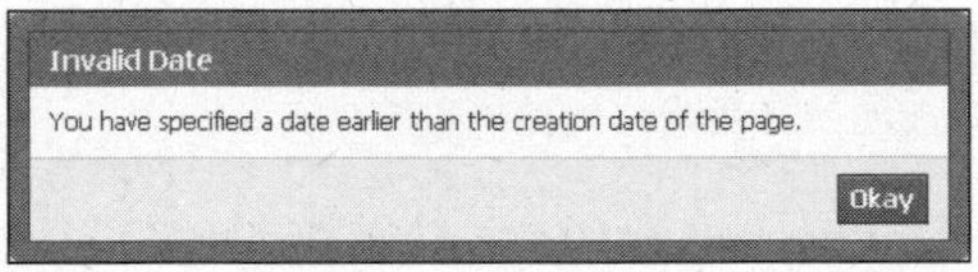

Figure 3-8:
Create a
milestone
for when
your busi-
ness,
product,
or service
began.

Invalid Date

You have specified a date earlier than the creation date of the page.

Okay

For information on targeting your status updates, see Chapter 5 of this minibook.

Creating a milestone update

If you'd like to add a milestone (either now or later), click the Offers, Events+ option and then choose Milestone in the status update box. The Milestone dialog box appears, as shown in Figure 3-9.

With the Milestone dialog box open, follow these steps to create a new milestone:

1. **In the Event text box, type the name of the milestone.**

2. **(Optional) In the Location text box, type the location of the event.**

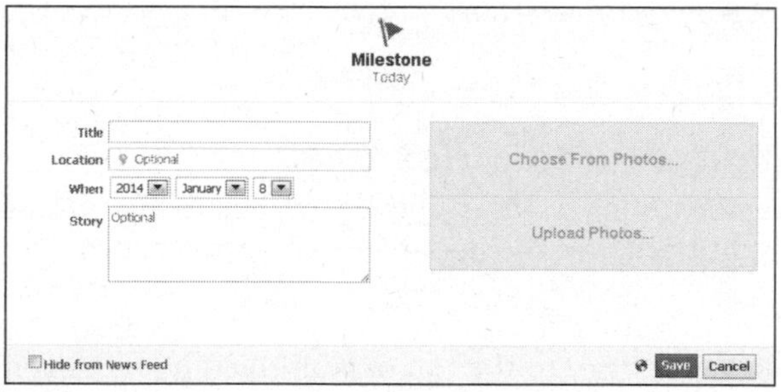
Milestone
Today
Title
Location
Optional
When
2014
January
8
Story
Optional
Choose From Photos...
Upload Photos...
Hide from News Feed
Save
Cancel

Figure 3-9: Use the Milestone box to create and highlight important updates to your business page.

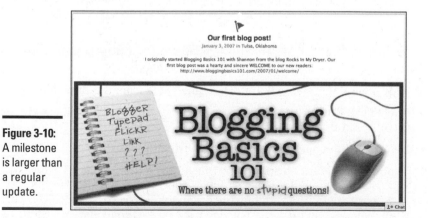

3. **Use the When drop-down list to choose a year for your milestone.**
4. **(Optional) If you want to include the month:**
   a. *Click the +Add month link.* If you choose to add a month, Facebook then gives you the option to add a specific date to your milestone.
   b. *If you want to include a specific date for your milestone, click the +Add Day link.*
5. **(Optional) If you don't want this milestone to appear on the news feed of your followers, select the Hide from News Feed check box.**
6. **(Optional) To add a photo to your milestone, click Upload Photo and select a photo.**
7. **Click Save to complete your milestone.**

When you create a milestone, it spans both the left and right columns of the timeline, as shown in Figure 3-10.

Our first blog post!
January 3, 2007 in Tulsa, Oklahoma
I originally started Blogging Basics 101 with Shannon from the blog Rocks In My Dryer. Our first blog post was a hearty and sincere WELCOME to our new readers:
http://www.bloggingbasics101.com/2007/01/welcome/
BLOGGER
TypePad
FLICKR
LINK
???
HELP!
Blogging
Basics
101
Where there are no stupid questions!
Chat

Figure 3-10: A milestone is larger than a regular update.

Milestones take up more screen real estate, so it's easy for your audience to notice them. Make your milestones pop by including relevant and interesting images.

Editing updates and milestones

You can edit a milestone or status update by clicking the drop-down arrow in the upper-right corner of the update. From here you can choose from the following:

✦ **Pin to Top:** Pin a story to the top of your timeline for seven days. Facebook limits the time to seven days to encourage business pages to create new content at least each week. After seven days, the story returns to its dated place on the timeline. Pinning a story to the top of your timeline helps draw attention to it and ensures that it's not buried as you create new updates throughout the week. For example, if you're hosting a giveaway on Facebook or offering a special discount to new followers, you may want to pin the post with that special information to the top of your timeline so it's easily viewed by everyone who visits. If you don't pin the story to the top of your timeline, it will move down the timeline each time you post a new story.

One of the best ways to get the most out of a pinned post is to use a strong call to action in your update, and then provide the means to complete that action (such as including the link to a specific page).

✦ **Change Date:** When you click this option, the Change Date dialog box appears, and you can change the year, month, and day of the story. This option appears only for regular status updates, not milestones.

✦ **Highlight:** The update will take up the full width of your timeline. It's a great way to make a video or an important update stand out. Some page owners don't like the left and right, back and forth setup of the timeline and have chosen to highlight every post so that things are easier to read.

✦ **Edit:** This option appears if you're editing a milestone. When you choose this option, you can change the milestone's event title, location, date, or story text. You can also add or delete an image.

✦ **Hide from Page:** Hide your story or milestone from the timeline.

✦ **Boost Post:** Run an ad using this post. For more about running ads, see Chapter 4 in Book V.

✦ **Delete:** Delete your story or milestone from the timeline.

✦ **Report Story/Mark as Spam:** The title of this option depends on whether you're editing a regular story or a milestone. Use this option to tell Facebook if a story is violating the Facebook Terms of Service (TOS) or if your intellectual property is being used by someone else. We think it's odd that this would be an option for your own stories, because you're unlikely to report your own milestone for a TOS infringement. It's possible that by the time you see this book, this option will have disappeared.

✦ **Embed Post:** Embed any post into a website or blog post. When you select this option, a box appears with embed code. Copy and paste that code into your blog post or your website.

Finding friends who Like this page

When you visit a business page, at the top right of the timeline is a list of your friends who also Like that business page. The purpose of this is to provide *social proof.* In other words, the hope is that if you see that your friends Like a brand, you'll take that as an endorsement and also Like the brand. We discuss the idea of social proof and how it works with Facebook throughout this book. Facebook and businesses both realize the power of word-of-mouth, and they take full advantage of it by reminding you that your friends are on board — and encourage you to come on board too.

Finding recent posts by others

When a follower or nonfollower posts on a business page, those posts appear in the Recent Posts by Others box. Because these comments don't show up in the main timeline as individual updates, it can be difficult for page admins to see at a glance who has posted a question or comment directly to the timeline. We suggest using your Admin panel to see new interactions. Click the action and you go directly to the update so you can respond.

Use your business page Admin panel to control whether the Recent Post by Others box appears on your business page.

Reviewing liked pages

Just as you can Like a page as yourself (your personal timeline), you can also like other business pages as your business page. Any pages you Like when you're using Facebook as your business page will show up in the Likes area. If you Like more than five business pages, the displayed pages will rotate each time the page is refreshed.

You can control which pages are displayed by going to your Admin panel and clicking Edit Page➪Edit Settings➪More and choosing Featured in the drop-down list. Then click the Edit Featured Likes button. Use the list to choose the five pages you want to feature. When you assign featured pages, those five pages are displayed randomly each time the page is refreshed. Other pages you've Liked will not appear.

Managing third-party posts

Most business pages allow their followers and other pages to share information on the timeline. The idea is that an open community is an inviting community. Usually people are respectful and are truly interested in engaging with your brand.

Sometimes, though, you'll find a spammy or otherwise inappropriate post on your business page. You can manage posts by others by moving your cursor over the post you want to address and clicking the X to the right of it.

When you click the X on someone's post, it becomes hidden and you see the following options:

+ **Default (Allowed):** This option is available for posts. Facebook allows anyone followers and nonfollowers, to write on your timeline. The default for these posts is Allowed.

+ **Highlighted on Page:** This option is available for posts. If you want to highlight a post by a follower or nonfollower, choose this option. The post will appear as a milestone (spanning both the right and left columns of your timeline). You may want to highlight a post if it's a particularly glowing accolade of your business, product, or service.

+ **Allowed on Page:** This option is for timeline posts by a follower or nonfollower.

+ **Delete Post:** This option is for timeline posts by a follower or nonfollower. You can remove the post from your timeline. The post cannot be reinstated.

+ **Report/Mark as Spam:** This option is for timeline posts by a follower or nonfollower. When you mark a post as spam, you remove it from your timeline. To reinstate a post (unmark it as spam), click Undo or visit your activity log and use the filter in the top-right corner to display your spam. Click the icon to the far right of the post and choose either Delete Post or Unmark as Spam from the list. If you click Report/Mark as Spam, you can ban that user from your page.

   If you want to delete the post, click the icon and choose Delete Post. The Delete Post dialog box appears and you have three choices: Delete, Delete and Ban User, and Cancel. If you choose Delete and Ban User, the person who posted can't interact with your business page again. A warning appears, asking if you're sure you want to delete the post and permanently block the person or business page from posting to your timeline. If you're sure, click Remove Post and Ban Page (User).

When you click X on someone's comment, it becomes hidden to everyone but that person and their friends and the following options appear:

+ **Unhide:** If you change your mind and want to display the comment, just click Unhide and the comment is live on the page again.

✦ **Delete:** You can delete the comment so that no one, not even the person who left the comment, can see it. Should you change your mind, you can choose Undo to restore the comment. If you click Undo after clicking Delete, the comment remains hidden from everyone but the person and his or her friends.

✦ **Report:** When you report a comment, a dialog box appears that enables you to choose whether the comment is harassing, spam, hate speech, sexually explicit, or violent.

✦ **Ban:** Ban a person from commenting or posting on your page again. The person will still be able to see your page and updates but can't comment on them.

To make it easier on you and your followers, create a set of posting guidelines for your page. Explain exactly what is and isn't appropriate for others to post to your timeline and what the consequence will be if the guidelines are ignored. Remember, you want to build community and encourage others to share and discuss, but this is still your page and you can set your expectations. If you have clear guidelines available and occasionally remind your followers where to find them, you may be able to stem some uncomfortable situations. For example, PETCO shares rules on their Info tab about what is and isn't appropriate to post. You can see it in action at `www.facebook.com/PETCO?sk=info`.

Reviewing the Right Sidebar

The right side of your business page has two items: a navigation button and a clickable list of years. At the top right of any business page is a button that changes depending on whether you're an admin or not. If you're an admin, you see a Promote Page button, which takes you to Ads Manager, discussed more in Book V. If you're not an admin, you see the Create a Page button, which takes you to the main page for creating your own business page.

Below the button is a list of years associated with posts from the business page. The number of years (and which years) listed depend on how the business page has updated its timeline. As we discuss earlier in this chapter, it's possible (and encouraged) to create stories associated with years that predate Facebook. (Again, the timeline on the Fanta page at `http://fb.com/Fanta` was updated to reach as far back as the 1950s.)

Using Facebook as Your Business Page or Personal Timeline

People have both personal and professional relationships. Sometimes those relationships overlap; sometimes they are unrelated. The same is true on Facebook. You may choose to keep your personal timeline focused on friends, family, and a few colleagues, and use your business page to connect with other businesses and to interact with your customers.

Because your personal timeline and your business page are separate but connected, the Facebook folks thought it would be a good idea to give you the choice of how you'd like to interact on Facebook and your business page — either as yourself (your personal timeline) or as your brand (your business page). That means you have the option to post comments to other business pages either as yourself or as your business page!

The idea of switching back and forth between timelines may be confusing at first, but after you get the hang of it, you'll see how useful this feature can be.

Your personal and business pages are connected to you. When you use Facebook as your personal timeline, the people and pages you interact with see the image and name associated with your personal timeline (such as Scott Ayres). When you use Facebook as your business page, the people and pages you interact with see the image and name associated with your business page (such as Post Planner).

Table 3-1 shows how your personal and business pages differ.

Table 3-1	Personal Timeline versus Business Page
As a Personal Timeline	*As a Page*
You can interact with friends on your timeline, in groups, in chat, and so on.	You can interact with individuals in the confines of your business page. Your business page can't post to an individual's personal timeline.
You can make new friend requests.	You cannot make friend requests.
You can Like a business page. This Like counts toward the total number of Likes for a page.	You can Like a business page. This Like does not count toward the total number of Likes for a page.
You can tag individuals in status updates, photos, video, and so on.	You cannot tag individuals in status updates, photos, video, and so on.

You can't post comments to someone's personal timeline while using Facebook as your business page. Allowing businesses to post on personal timelines could get spammy quickly, as you can imagine.

Switching from one to the other

To use your Facebook account as yourself (meaning as your personal timeline), just log in to Facebook as you normally do. When you'd like to switch to your business account, click the gear icon in the top-right corner of the blue toolbar. From the menu, choose Use Facebook as *[Your Page]*. (The menu lists all the pages you are associated with as an admin.)

You can easily switch back to using your personal timeline by clicking the gear and choosing Switch Back to *[Your Name]*.

Being able to switch between appearing as your brand (business page) or yourself (personal timeline) allows you to do a few things:

✦ **You can post as yourself on your own business page.** On your business page, just below the search box, is a note that reads *You are posting, commenting, and liking as your page.* You can change to your profile by clicking Change to *your name.* The wording of the note changes and Facebook lets you know you are now posting, commenting, and Liking as yourself.

✦ **Your page can Like other pages.** You have to Like a page before you can tag it in an update. When you're using Facebook as your business page (not your personal timeline), you can go to a business page and Like it, but that action won't clutter your personal news feed.

When you Like a page while using Facebook as your business page, that Like does not count toward that page's overall Likes. Facebook counts only Likes received from a personal timeline. In other words, if Scott uses the Post Planner business page and Likes the business page for ShortStack, that Like is not recorded as part of the overall number of Likes for the ShortStack page. But if he switches back to using his personal timeline, and then heads over to the ShortStack business page and clicks Like, that Like is recorded in the overall number of Likes for that business page.

✦ **You can interact with other business pages as your brand instead of as yourself.** If you want to comment on another business page as your business instead of as yourself, just be sure you're using Facebook as the timeline for your page.

The Facebook toolbar when using Facebook as your business page

When you switch to using Facebook as your business page, your Facebook experience is similar to when you're using your personal timeline, but everything is now focused on your business page instead of your personal timeline page.

In this section, we describe how the elements on the Facebook toolbar differ, depending on whether you're using Facebook as your personal timeline or as your business page.

Facebook link

When using Facebook as your personal timeline, the Facebook link takes you to your main news feed, where you see top stories, recent updates, updates from your Facebook friends, pages you've Liked, and groups to which you belong.

When using Facebook as your business page, the Facebook link takes you to a news feed for your business page. Because a business page can't connect with individuals and is restricted to Liking other pages, this news feed displays only updates from the pages you have Liked while using Facebook as your page.

Pages you Like with your personal timeline do not show up in this news feed unless you have also Liked the page as your business page.

Friend requests

When using Facebook as your personal timeline, the friend requests icon (silhouette) displays a list of people who have requested to become Facebook friends.

When using Facebook as your business page, this icon displays a list of Facebook users who have recently Liked your business page. You may click their names to see their personal timelines, but you may see only limited information, depending on their privacy settings.

Facebook business pages can't be friends with individuals. If you want to friend someone, you'll need to switch back to using Facebook as yourself and then make a friend request. We don't suggest friending your followers unless you know them in real life. Respect that your followers have connected with you on your business page because they support your brand.

If you'd like to see a list of all your followers, click the silhouette icon, and then click See All at the bottom of the list. The People Who Like *[Your Page Name]* dialog box appears. Unfortunately, Facebook does not make it easy to find specific followers — you have to scroll through the list one by one.

The People Who Like *[Your Page Name]* dialog box also displays other business pages that have Liked your Page, who you've made an admin of your page, who is subscribing to your page but hasn't Liked it, and who you've banned from your page. Just click the down arrow next to People in the top-left corner, as shown in Figure 3-11, and choose which list you want to see.

You can grant administrative privileges to any follower by clicking the Make Admin button next to the person's name (see Chapter 2 of this minibook for instructions on how to grant admin privileges). Alternatively, you can ban a specific follower from your business page by clicking the X next to the person's name.

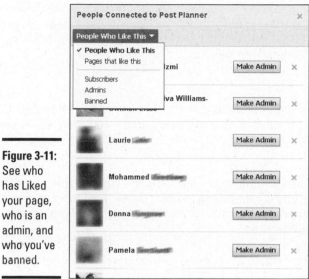

Figure 3-11:
See who has Liked your page, who is an admin, and who you've banned.

Personal messages

When using Facebook as your personal timeline, the messages icon (two speech bubbles) displays a list of personal messages various people have sent to you. Depending on your privacy settings, you may also receive personal messages from people to whom you are not directly connected (such as friends of friends). You can read more about managing your privacy settings in Book I, Chapter 4.

When using Facebook as your business page, the messages icon displays a list of personal messages followers have sent. Facebook allows followers to send you private messages as a way to handle communication away from the public timeline. Although followers can send a private message to a page, a page cannot initiate private messages to followers.

The Message feature for pages is turned on automatically. You can turn it off by going to your Admin panel and clicking Edit Page⇨Edit Settings⇨Settings⇨click Messages. Then deselect the option that allows people to contact your page privately by showing the Message button.

Notifications

When using Facebook as your personal timeline, the notifications icon (globe) displays a running list of people who have mentioned you in status updates, posted updates related to your actions (for instance, Liking a photo you shared or commenting on a status update you already commented on), and so on.

When using Facebook as your business page, the notifications icon displays a list of your followers who have recently interacted with your page either by Liking a status update or link, tagging your business page in an update, or commenting on a status update or link.

Search text box

When using Facebook as your personal timeline, you type search terms in the Search text box to find people, pages, groups, apps, and events. You can also find basic web results, posts from friends, posts published publicly, and posts to public groups.

When using Facebook as your business page, you can still use the Search tool. However, your results are limited to people, pages, events, general web results, and posts by everyone. Because a business page can't join a group, you don't see results for groups.

Profile link

When using Facebook as your personal timeline, the Profile link goes to your personal timeline. When using Facebook as your business page, the Profile link goes to your business page.

Home link

When using Facebook as your personal timeline, the Home link sends you back to your main news feed.

When using Facebook as your business page, the Home link sends you back to your business page's news feed. However, your business page news feed displays updates by other pages, not friends associated with your personal timeline.

Account menu

When using Facebook as your personal timeline, the gear icon provides the following options: Switch to Using Facebook as Your Business Pages, Create a Page, Manage Pages, Your Ads, Create Ads, Mange Ads, Create App, Manage Apps, Settings, Log Out, Help, and Report a Problem.

When using Facebook as your business page, the gear icon provides the following options: Switch to Using Facebook as Your Personal Profile, Use Facebook as Page (this could be another page for which you are the admin), Create or Manage Pages, Facebook Ads, Log Out, Help, and Report a Problem.

Chapter 4: Building Your Community

In This Chapter

✔ Understanding how your readers use Facebook

✔ Knowing your goals (so you know when you've met them)

✔ Using different kinds of updates to appeal to your followers

✔ Taking care of customer service

Using social media as an extension of your marketing strategy is mandatory these days. If you don't use Facebook or Twitter or at least a blog, you're missing out on key engagement with your customers and potential customers. Your business page can be an important part of your marketing strategy and must fit with other efforts to attract followers. When people become followers and are welcomed into your community, they are more likely to convert to paying customers.

By setting up your business page, you recognize that you need to market where your audience is . . . and they're on Facebook. Your business page can reinforce your brand and bring a new level of interaction to your customer relations. In fact, some businesses are so excited about using Facebook that they see only the potential for broadcasting their message. After all, your business and its products are phenomenal, and now you can tell everyone in the world! One of the key things to remember about Facebook is that although you own your page, your followers own the space. You control what you share, but your followers control how they consume it. If followers decide that you're sharing too often or not sharing content that interests them, they can hide your status updates from their news feed (or, worse, Unlike your page).

In Book IV, Chapters 1 and 2, we show you how to create your business page. What you do when you have your business page set up matters, and it's not a "set it and forget it" deal. One mistake some marketers make when including Facebook in their strategy is expecting a fast return on investment. Social media (whether it's Facebook, Twitter, a blog, LinkedIn, or another tool) requires time to develop a community. Any time you use social media, your space needs attention and interaction; otherwise, it loses its value.

In this chapter, we show you a few tips and tricks to interact with your followers so you both see value. We give you some advice about keeping your audience engaged and some things to think about for the future of your business page.

The marketing advice we offer throughout this book is solid, but it's just an overview. If you want to delve into Facebook marketing tactics, we suggest you check out *Facebook Marketing All-in-One For Dummies,* 2nd Edition, by Amy Porterfield, Phyllis Khare, and Andrea Vahl (John Wiley & Sons, Inc.), a comprehensive guide to building a business presence on Facebook.

Determining Your Goals and Objectives

You shouldn't assume that your business page isn't as important as your other advertising and marketing venues. You're building community and loyal followers here; in some cases, Facebook allows you to introduce your product to a much wider audience than you may have had access to previously. Before you interact with these existing and potential customers, you need to have a plan — just as you have a plan for your other advertising and marketing efforts.

Your plan should include a set of specific goals, a means to achieve those goals, a deadline for the goals, and a measurement for how well your efforts worked. Goals are useful when they are specific:

Vague Goal: Get more people to Like our page.

Specific Goals: Gain 25 Likes in one week. Have 50 new Likes on our page by the end of the month. Have five comments on posted status updates this week.

The goal of wanting more Likes is too broad. How do you know when you've achieved your goal? When you've had one more person Like your page? By being more specific, you make one vague goal into several specific goals that allow you to build on your successes. With specific goals in mind, you know exactly what you're working toward and how long you have to achieve those goals.

The next step is defining a strategy for reaching the goal in the allotted time. That strategy is what the rest of this chapter is about.

As you determine your goals, consider the following questions:

✦ How do you or your company want to use your business page?

✦ What are you hoping to achieve by using Facebook? For example, do you want to become an authority in your niche? Increase sales? Introduce yourself to a new market?

✦ How do you want to engage with followers?

✦ How do you want followers to engage with you?

✦ Will you share industry-specific information from many sources?

✦ Will you promote your products or services?

You want quality, not necessarily quantity, when it comes to Likes. It's better to reach 10 people who really want to buy than 1,200 who just don't care. As well, you need to define *why* you want followers. You can have thousands, but if they aren't interacting or buying, what's the point?

Marketing goals generally equal sales, but people using Facebook (and social media in general) don't like to be bombarded with sales pitches. Although Facebook is a public forum, users consider it their private space. Users choose who they interact with and how. If those interactions become uncomfortable (for a business page, that means spammy or intrusive), users can Hide, Unfriend, or Unlike the person or page making them uncomfortable.

Does that mean you shouldn't market or sell your products or services on Facebook? No. You can sell, but make your pitches relevant and don't make every status update a pitch.

When you do pitch, provide a call to action and provide a link that allows the reader to complete the action. In some cases, you may also want to include a picture, and provide context in your status update of how to use the product or show why it's relevant to your followers.

Establishing Your Authority

To build your community, you need to give people a reason to come to you. One way to do that is to establish yourself as an authority in your niche. To build authority, you need to fulfill a need for your audience: Solve a problem for them, entertain them, or educate them.

When users trust you to give them relevant information, they begin to look to you regularly for that information. As you share the information, they interact with it by clicking the Like button or commenting. If the information is particularly relevant, readers will also share the information with their own networks — essentially giving the content their stamp of approval. When followers do that, their friends see that they are endorsing your content, and they may be more likely to engage with (and possibly share) your content too.

Developing a large, loyal community takes time, but it's not necessarily hard. The bottom line is respect. If you respect your followers and their needs, they'll appreciate you. As you nurture your community, consider this advice:

✦ **Build trust.** As you build your community, keep in mind that you are building trust. You can gain your readers' trust by making your interactions primarily about them. Before you start any marketing campaign, know your target audience, know what they want, know how you can help them, and know how you can use that interaction to further your own goals as well. Use this information to craft status updates that address your audience's needs, include a call to action, and then provide a way to complete the action.

✦ **Pitch genuinely.** Use the 80/20 rule: Spend 80 percent of your time listening and 20 percent talking, or 80 percent sharing information that is relevant to your audience and 20 percent asking them to buy. Asking your readers to buy isn't a problem — your followers are probably coming to you because they like your product or service. Selling is a problem when you *only* ask your followers to buy and don't give anything in return.

When you do sell, not giving your followers a way to complete a transaction is also a problem. Take advantage of the followers who are interested in your product. Give them a chance to purchase your goods or services by linking directly to a product in your online store or website.

✦ **Listen.** Ask for your readers' opinions and pay attention to what they reference when they comment on your updates. Listen to your audience in other venues such as Twitter or your blog as well, and introduce interesting conversations from those venues to your followers on Facebook.

Establishing Social Proof

When your followers come to rely on you for a specific purpose, you've gained authority. When you have authority, you have earned your followers' trust and they're likely to offer social proof of acceptance to their friends and others. *Social proof* occurs when members of a community see others engaging with and sharing content, check it out for themselves, and — if they like the content — share it with other communities of which they're a part. If people are consistently commenting or sharing on your business page, that's proof that other people like your product or service. When a new follower arrives, that social proof reinforces the person's decision to be there and interact with you.

When people visit your business page, one of the first things they look at is the interaction there. If people only see posts from the page admin and no interaction (Likes or comments), the page appears one-way. On the other hand, if people see conversation (even limited interaction with a few Likes or comments spread out), that tells the visitor that people are indeed reading what's being shared and are investing their time in the community. One of the best ways to increase your social proof is to provide shareable content, which we go over in the next section. (See Chapter 2 of this minibook for directions on how to set your timeline to show posts from everyone, not just your business page updates.)

Creating Shareable Content

An unattended business page leaves a negative impression on your visitors — and they are less likely to Like it — because they assume it's not relevant or cared for. Updating your business page status regularly is important. How often you update your page depends on your audience and your niche.

You don't want to litter people's news feeds with irrelevant information multiple times a day. Instead, focus your updates on topics relevant to your niche (and your audience's needs) and post them as needed. Some days may see more updates; other days will see fewer updates. We find that one or two posts per day seems to be ideal, but small businesses can sometimes get away with three or four updates a day. (Scott posts to the Post Planner page at least six times per day, with different types of posts, and sees great engagement.)

To figure out when your followers are most likely to interact with your updates, check your Facebook Insights to see which updates are garnering the most engagement. (Book V, Chapter 3 explains how to use Insights.) Experiment with posting in the mornings, afternoons, evenings, and on weekends, and then check your Insights again. Did you see a difference in how or when your followers engaged with your content? Consider when your audience is most likely to be on Facebook. They're probably on Facebook before work, possibly during their lunch hour if Facebook is allowed through their work firewall, and again in the evenings after dinner. We've found that Sunday evenings can be interactive as well, but not all companies are willing to work on Sunday night.

Studies have shown that most people Like or follow a brand because they want exclusive deals, discounts, and promotions. When you're thinking about ways to interact with your followers, consider rewarding customers for being followers by giving them periodic perks.

Sharing instead of broadcasting

When visitors Like your page, they almost never go back to your actual business page (unless you provide a specific link or call to action in a status update; we cover that later in the chapter). Instead, your followers rely on their news feed to see status updates from friends as well as business pages. You can imagine how important those news feeds are and why you don't want to be hidden from anyone's stream.

Most users agree that they don't see Facebook as a place for businesses to market to them. Rather, they see Facebook as a place to connect with a business they enjoy. Your followers don't want you broadcasting your message to them all the time, which can be hard for a marketer to hear. Your main goal as a marketer is to share a message with others, and broadcasting is an efficient way to achieve that goal. Social media is changing the way you reach that goal by putting the power in the audience's hands instead of yours.

As you share content, remember to make it relevant to your audience. Put the information in context as it relates to them. Present the information in such a way that your readers feel like you found this information specifically for them. Your audience will eventually look to you as an authority in your niche.

To build a loyal community, you must offer quality content relevant to your audience's needs. If your content is good and truly meets the needs of your audience, you'll find that they often share it with their friends. When you consider what to include in your status updates, think about sharing the following:

✦ Links

✦ Photos and video

✦ Questions

✦ Calls to action

Sharing links

RSS feeds have been popular for many years. *RSS,* which stands for Real Simple Syndication, is a way for people to be alerted when new content is published on a blog, for example. In the past few years, however, people have come to rely less on RSS feeds and more on links to content shared by their friends and colleagues via platforms such as Facebook and Twitter.

Links shared by people you trust provide social proof — you believe the link has worth because someone you trust shared it with you. When you establish your business page as an authority in your niche, your followers come to believe the links you share have worth. If they also see colleagues or friends sharing or commenting on those same links, the social proof intensifies.

Here are a few best practices for sharing links on your business page:

✦ **Take the time to provide context.** Give your readers a reason to click the link by explaining how they can benefit from the information shared in the linked article. Without context or a short note from you, you're just posting a link — and that appears spammy. With so much questionable content floating around, links by themselves are suspect and your readers are less likely to click them for fear of spam.

✦ **Remember your goals.** If your goal is to encourage your followers to interact with your content, don't send them away from your business page. A link takes people away from Facebook, and they may or may not return after they've read the article. If they do return to Facebook, they may not return to your update to Like it or comment.

On the other hand, if your goal is to share information to gain authority as the go-to page for your niche, it's not as important if followers don't come back to comment or Like. Your job in this instance is to provide the tools for your audience to stay updated on niche-specific information. Plus, if you're trying to drive traffic to your own website, your first goal is not interaction on the Facebook content but getting people to go to your website.

✦ **Use a link-shortening and -tracking tool.** This point dovetails with the previous point. If your goal is to educate or disseminate or curate information for your followers, you may find yourself sharing many links that take followers away from your business page. When you send people away from your page to read an article, they may not return to your page. If they don't return, they won't comment or Like the link, and it's hard to tell if anyone interacted with your content.

You can check your Insights (see Book V, Chapter 3) to track how many clicks a link received. If you want more data, consider a link-tracking service. By using a link-tracking service such as bitly (`http://bit.ly`), you can see how many people click your links. Many times, we've seen no comments or Likes on a status update with a link only to check bitly and find that the link got 30 clicks. That information tells us that followers are using the content and interacting with it, even though we can't see that on Facebook.

Figures 4-1 and 4-2 show a business page and a bitly dashboard, respectively. You must be logged in to your free bit.ly account to see analytics. The link shared on the business page doesn't appear to have any interaction. But if you look at the bitly dashboard, you see that that link has had ten click-throughs, which means ten followers interacted with that content.

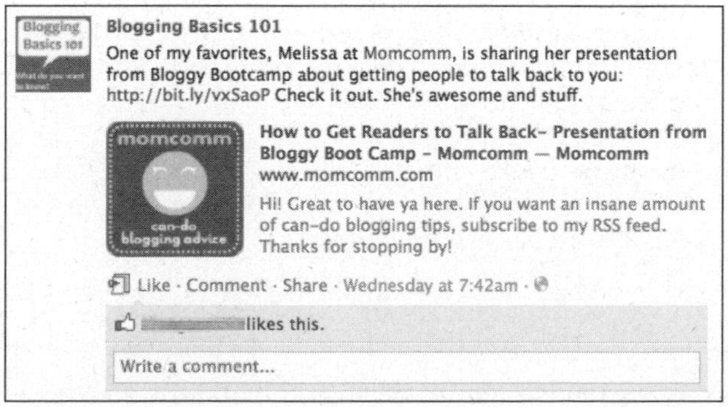

Figure 4-1:
A business page doesn't show whether people click your links.

Blogging Basics 101
One of my favorites, Melissa at Momcomm, is sharing her presentation from Bloggy Bootcamp about getting people to talk back to you: http://bit.ly/vxSaoP Check it out. She's awesome and stuff.

How to Get Readers to Talk Back– Presentation from Bloggy Boot Camp – Momcomm — Momcomm
www.momcomm.com
Hi! Great to have ya here. If you want an insane amount of can-do blogging tips, subscribe to my RSS feed. Thanks for stopping by!

Like · Comment · Share · Wednesday at 7:42am ·

likes this.

Write a comment...

Using photos and video to encourage sharing

If you think about how you interact on Facebook, which posts are the ones that inspire you to click most often? The answer is probably updates that include video or pictures.

Facebook displays photos nice and big so followers can see product pictures easily. And with videos right there in your news feed, you don't have to click around and later try to resume your place in the news feed.

Sharing visual content is easy! If you share interesting photos and video your followers love, they can just click the Share link and their friends will see the content as well. As more and more users become mobile, only users' photos and videos stand out and catch attention. For more information on how to use photos and video with Facebook, flip to Book II, Chapters 3 and 4, respectively.

Asking questions

When people use Facebook, they scan and click quickly. Anything that takes more than a few seconds to consider may be lost in the shuffle. As a result, you should interact in specific ways to ensure that you have a high rate of engagement.

Asking questions is an excellent way to engage followers, but only if done correctly. Because Facebook readers move from one update to the next quickly, you have to make your questions scannable and easy to answer. Here are some tried and true options:

+ **Yes/no questions:** These short questions require a one-word answer, but leave room for your followers to expound on their point of view if they desire. Consider these two questions:

  Question 1: Do your kids earn an allowance?

  Question 2: What do you think about kids earning an allowance?

  The first question is a simple yes-or-no answer. It's easy and it's fast. Followers can choose to expand on their answers, but yes or no will suffice. The second question requires a little more thought. If followers see that question in their stream, they may answer it in their heads but probably won't take the step of crafting a response because they have more complex thoughts on allowances in general.

✦ **Either/or questions:** Similar to yes/no questions, an either/or question requires only that your followers respond with their preference. They don't have to include an explanation if they don't want to.

✦ **Fill-in-the-blank questions:** Give your followers a prompt and ask them to share a word or two to complete a sentence. Add your own answer as well! Your followers will appreciate that you're interacting with them.

✦ **Polls with limited answers:** A great way to get people talking is to pose a question to your followers and provide specific answers for their feedback. It doesn't get any easier than that. If you keep your choices limited to around two to three, your followers can scan the question and answer and then quickly comment with their preference before they move on to the next status update.

If you're looking for an easy way to come up with questions to ask, check out the Status Ideas Engine from Post Planner, at www.postplanner.com. It contains thousands of ready-made questions and ideas to post to your page.

Don't be afraid to stray from your normal topics or to use humor in your questions. Scott's audience on Post Planner is primarily the social media marketing crowd. However, posting only information about Facebook would get boring, so Scott mixes in humorous posts or motivational posts that don't require much thought but cause people to react and engage, as shown by the number of Likes, comments, and shares in Figure 4-3).

Figure 4-3:
Don't be afraid to stray off-topic to encourage new interaction.

Integrate your Facebook efforts with your entire marketing strategy

Remember that Facebook is just one part of your marketing initiative. Facebook pretty much owns your content and can decide at any time to take down your business page if it's judged to violate the Facebook terms of service, so you should not get rid of your website or blog. Instead, integrate everything into a social media strategy.

Recognize that different parts of your audience will find you on different platforms. And each audience on each platform may have different expectations. How do you know what those expectations are? You ask your audience. Do a poll in your e-newsletter or ask your followers on Facebook. Not getting a great response? Narrow the choices. Sometimes people can't come up with an answer because there are too many options. Instead, ask whether they'd like to see Option 1 or Option 2 on the business page next week.

Another way to build your community is to include a Facebook plug-in on your website or blog. You can find several to choose from. Visit `http://developers.facebook.com/docs/plugins` to see your options.

Sometimes the best way to know what your audience wants is to ask them. When you know what your audience expects, needs, or wants, you can better determine which type of information to share and which products to promote. To begin, you may want to ask your followers questions such as

✦ Which social media networks do you use?

✦ How do you use your product or service?

✦ What information would you like to see?

✦ What other pages do you Like and interact with frequently?

Make note of how your followers respond, and use that information to help plan your page updates and blog articles (if you keep a blog).

Using calls to action

As we state earlier, Facebook users move quickly from one update to the next, skimming and clicking and occasionally commenting. If you want to bring attention to a status update and have your followers complete a specific task, place a strong call to action in the update and provide the means to carry out the action.

If the task is buying a product or service, you need to provide a link to your online store. Or you may just want to increase engagement on your business page for this update; in that case, you can ask followers to comment or click the Like button for your status update. For instance, if you've added or changed something (such as a product's functionality), ask your followers to click the Like button if they think the change is a good one.

As you create strong calls to action for various campaigns, consider using a version of this workflow:

1. Provide a call to action.

2. Provide a path to action (such as a link created with a trackable bit.ly link).

3. Measure the performance (record the number of click-throughs for your link, how many sales you made, and so on).

4. If necessary, figure out where the campaign broke down and fix it.

Part of giving followers what they want is showing them where to find it. As you create status updates, consider how you can help your followers complete an action that not only helps them but also helps you reach your goals.

Suppose that you own a successful knitting shop, and you have a website with a shopping cart and an active business page. Most of your business is conducted in your bricks-and-mortar store, but one of your goals is to increase online sales at your website by 10 percent this month.

Our first suggestion is to create strong calls to action for your followers. If you want to sell more, you need to tell your followers that you want them to buy something, and then give them the means to buy it. For example, the next time you post a picture of a finished project, provide direct links to your website's store where followers can buy the pattern, needles, and yarn needed to complete the project. Consider the following status updates (imagine both accompanied by a picture of someone showing off the scarf she just knitted):

> Update 1: Lisa is modeling her latest knitting project, the Beginner's Scarf!

> Update 2: Lisa is modeling her latest knitting project, the Beginner's Scarf. Are you looking for a quick project? Buy the pattern from our shop (`http://bit.ly/patternlink`) — it takes two skeins of Irish Lass cotton (`http://bit.ly/yarnlink`) and size 9 needles (`http://bit.ly/needlelink`).

Adding highlighted updates

A highlighted update is the full width of the timeline, so it's a great way of showcasing certain status updates. This feature is great for milestones and calls to action for your visitors.

To make a status update a highlighted update, hover your mouse cursor over the status update on your business page, click the arrow in the right corner of the update, and then click the Highlight option (star icon).

The first update explains the picture but doesn't really offer actionable information for followers. If readers really love that scarf and are considering starting a quick project, they're left to their own devices to find the pattern, the yarn, and the needles. If the store happens to be nearby, they can hop in the car and head over, but that's a pretty big step to expect a Facebook follower to take. (What if your store isn't close by, but another craft store is? You may have lost a sale to another store.) Instead, the second update provides a subtle call to action and provides several options (links) for completing the action. The update makes it easy for followers to buy everything they need to start a new project.

If you want to involve your followers even more, ask them to upload pictures in which they model their own projects and tell you what pattern and yarn they used. Then, when you comment on the photo, provide links to your online store so followers can purchase the supplies.

 You can install a Facebook shopping cart app on your business page to allow followers to purchase goods right from your business page! Or ask your webmaster to pull in your online store with the help of iframes (see Book VI, Chapter 1).

Creating content only for followers

When someone visits your business page and hasn't yet Liked it, that person sees the same view as any follower, including all your updates. You have to give the visitor a compelling reason to want to Like your page. One great way to do this is to provide interesting content that's available only to followers, something they can get right at that moment.

Page tabs (also called *application pages*) allow you to create separate content for followers and nonfollowers. Use this method to encourage new visitors to Like your business page to gain instant access to special information.

When you build this tab, you can create it with two versions: One for followers and another for nonfollowers. Most visitors arrive at your business page from a direct link outside Facebook, such as a link in an e-mail message or on your website. When placing this link for marketing, consider using the URL that leads to your page tab.

Anything that can be built into a website can be built into a page tab. Facebook marketers can create exciting additions to make their business pages more engaging and branded to the company. For example, a common use of a page tab is to hold contests, as shown in Figure 4-4 via an app created with TabSite (www.tabsite.com/). Figures 4-5 and 4-6 show examples of what a nonfollower sees versus what a follower sees.

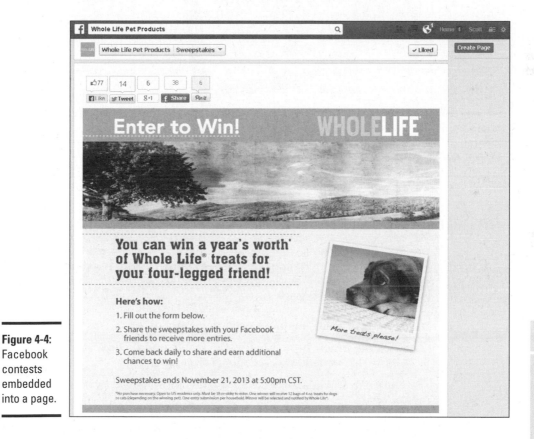

Figure 4-4: Facebook contests embedded into a page.

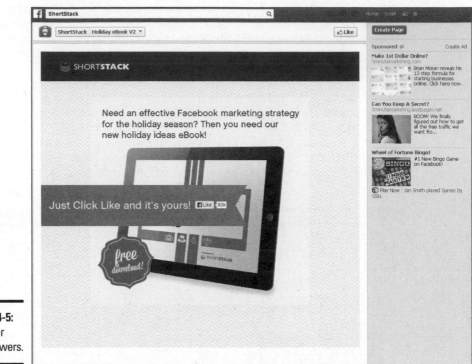

Figure 4-5:
A tab for nonfollowers.

Targeting Updates

You may find that some updates aren't relevant to your entire audience. In those cases, you can customize who sees your updates. First turn on Post Targeting and Privacy, as discussed in Chapter 2 of this minibook. Then follow these instructions:

1. **Type your status update as you normally do.**

2. **Click the Public button below the status update box, as shown in Figure 4-7, and choose Location/Language.**

   The Control Who Can See Your Post window appears.

3. **In the Location text box, type a country name.**

   New choices appear below the Location text box. The choices are dependent on which country you enter and may include Everywhere, By State/Province, and By City.

4. **Select the option you'd like to target and enter any required information.**

   If you select By State/Province or By City, a new text box appears. Enter the state, province, or city here.

5. **(Optional) In the Language text box, type a language.**

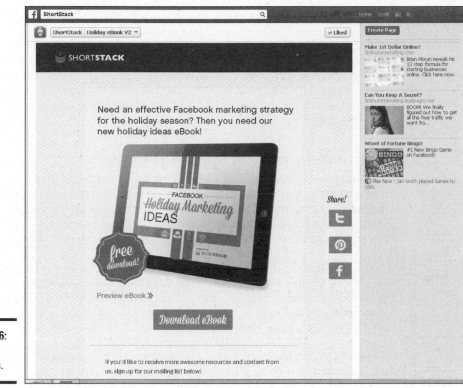

Figure 4-6:
A tab for
followers.

Figure 4-7:
Target
your status
updates
to specific
followers.

You can target a specific country, state/province, or city without specifying a language. You can also target a specific language without specifying a specific country, state/province, or city.

6. Click Save Post Settings.

You're returned to your original status update.

7. Click the Post button.

Your post is shared only with followers who meet the criteria of your customization.

Handling Customer Service

If you're monitoring your business page and interacting regularly with your followers, you're probably building a community in which people feel comfortable asking questions, praising your brand, and sometimes airing a grievance or two. The way you handle your customer interactions — both good and bad — has an immediate and lasting effect on how people talk about your company.

Interacting regularly with followers

The more you engage, the more likely people are to comment. Why? Because if they see that you're on the business page regularly, they feel like they're more likely to be heard. You wouldn't walk into an empty room and start talking to yourself, would you? You'd be more likely to go into a room with several people who are welcoming and ready to converse.

Taking the time to respond to comments or questions from your followers reinforces the fact that you take your Facebook community seriously and value your followers' opinions. On your business page, consider not only responding to a comment but also clicking Like on the comment so that the person knows you've seen it.

If you're looking for a way to expand your community, establish your authority, and interact regularly with your followers, try setting up a specific time to interact with them. On many Fridays, Social Media Examiner (`http://fb.com/smexaminer`) invites an industry expert to host a Q&A session on its Facebook timeline. This works well because followers show up not only to ask questions but also to offer answers to questions because the host can't always get to everyone.

Addressing negative comments and reviews

Engaging doesn't mean controlling the conversation or the message. Your role as a community manager is to give your followers a way to express themselves; let the conversation flow. Step in only if a specific question is directed to you or if you need to delete an inappropriate or rude comment.

If you do see a negative comment, address it professionally and let it stand. Consider how you can turn the negative into a positive with your response. Acknowledge the follower's frustration, address the specific issue (or find out what the issue is), and apologize. Many times people just want their frustration to be recognized and acknowledged. You can't always fix the issue, but you can give followers your attention, let them know you've listened, and tell them that you're sorry they're upset. You may occasionally run into a *troll* (someone whose sole purpose is to cause trouble), but usually people just want to know that their concerns are being heard.

If you're managing your community effectively, you're probably visiting your business page several times a day to address comments and share content. Invariably, you'll come across some spam. Although it's perfectly okay to delete spammy content, you can curb spam and inappropriate comments by establishing some guidelines for what is and isn't acceptable content to share on your business page. You can list these rules on your Info page.

Every month or so, depending on how much spam you're seeing, you can remind your followers of the rules by linking directly to the Info page or by noting the location of your community guidelines. If you have to delete a comment or status update or block a user, you can justify your decision based on your existing community guidelines.

Book V
Marketing Your Business

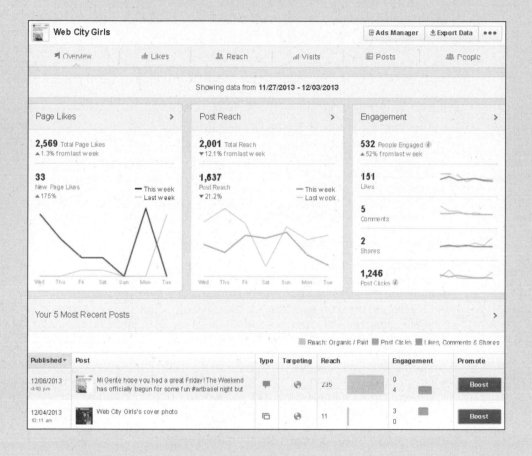

Contents at a Glance

Chapter 1: Building a Network of Influence 339

The Importance of Engagement..339
Integrating Facebook in Marketing Campaigns 344

Chapter 2: Running a Social Marketing Campaign 349

Understanding What Makes Social Marketing Campaigns Work 349
Types of Facebook Campaigns...351
Implementing Sharing Contests...352
Marketing a Facebook Contest 355
The Power of Crowdsourcing...357
Preparing Your Business Page for the Campaign 358

Chapter 3: Using Insights to Track Your Success.................363

Tracking Your Facebook Stats with Insights 363
Touring the Likes Page...366
Understanding Reach Page Data...368
Finding Friends by Using the Visits Page 369
The All-Important Posts Page..370
Understanding the People Page 371
Getting to Know the News Feed Algorithm..372

Chapter 4: Ads, Promotions, and Offers 377

Finding Facebook Ads...377
Deciding Whether Facebook Ads Are Right for You..............................378
Creating Your Facebook Ad...382
Finding and Using the Facebook Ads Manager......................................390
Generating a Report 392
Adding or Deleting an Ads Account Administrator................................393
Closing Your Facebook Ads Account 394
Using Facebook Promotions to Market Your Business 395
Using Apps to Create Customized Giveaways and Contests 401
Creating Best Practices for Your Facebook Promotion........................403
Using Facebook Offers to Reach New Customers.................................405

Chapter 5: Identifying Your Target Audience.....................407

Using Insights to Identify Your Audience...407
Understanding Why Online and Traditional Marketing Are Necessary................408
Marketing Facebook Offline...409
Online Marketing Resources 411
Integrated Campaigns...414

Chapter 1: Building a Network of Influence

In This Chapter

✔ Building a loyal following for your business

✔ Connecting with friends and followers

✔ Adding Facebook to marketing campaigns

✔ Getting more business page posts from friends and followers

Social media is about connecting with friends and followers. When marketing a business in the Facebook world, people often focus on how many friends and followers they have. The fact is, if you have friends and followers but have no influence over them, you might be wasting your time and marketing dollars.

Success on Facebook is about building an audience that is listening. Better yet, it's about building a network of influence, in which you influence not just the people in your own audience but their friends and connections as well. In the following sections, we give you practical advice on how to increase engagement with your current customers and how to attract new customers.

Although this chapter focuses on building your business using your business page, much of our advice is useful for individuals who are just looking to up their game on Facebook and have a more popular personal timeline. We want to be clear, though, that if you're promoting your business or branding your business on Facebook, you should abide by the Facebook terms of service and create a business page instead of using your personal timeline for your business.

The Importance of Engagement

When people Like your business page, they value a connection with your company, at least to some degree. That connection has to have some meaning. The more you can humanize your brand, the more value you will get out of your marketing efforts. This is achieved through engagement.

You can't build engagement without some human effort behind your Facebook marketing. You can automate a lot, but at the end of the day, people are looking to connect with other people. When customers feel that your company values the personal connection to them, they are more likely to do business with you.

Don't forget about being top of mind. If customers have several choices when buying a product or service, all things being equal, whoever they remember gets the business. This is one big reason why engagement on your business page is so important. Consumers tend to have a higher level of trust for a brand if they're more familiar with it by name or experience. This certainly presents a good case for having a presence on Facebook, but all the more for having an active presence where you engage with your consumers. Figure 1-1 shows an example of how Amy's Kitchen reached out to its customers to meet a need. Customers commented and felt connected to the brand.

Figure 1-1: Creating meaningful connections.

Amy's Kitchen
September 27

Tomorrow is Good Neighbor Day. We help get regular food deliveries to our neighbor, COTS (Committee on the Shelterless, in California), a nonprofit that cares for the homeless in our town. Any good deeds happening in your neighborhood?
http://pinterest.com/pin/135319163777135273/

BE KIND TO OTHERS

Like · Comment · Share   138 2 31

138 people like this.   Top Comments

Write a comment...

Joy Lynette   Yep! Tomorrow at our county fairgrounds (at Girard, KS) is a day-long benefit for a friend's child who has a congenital heart defect. To accommodate the medical equipment she requires, the family has to remodel their home - not cheap! Lots of local businesses donated raffle prizes, local bands are donating their time, and members of the community are volunteering to staff the gate and booths. Live music all day, a bake sale, t-shirts and games for kids and adults. Free-will donation admission. It is going to be a great time, for a great cause! There is rain in the forecast but it is a rain or shine event.
Like · Reply · 2 · September 27 at 11:49am

Jane
Like · Reply · September 27 at 2:35pm

Facebook and other social media sites have fostered a social media–driven world where people expect to be able to interact with their favorite brands. Some of this will happen automatically if you have wide enough name recognition. Some will happen only as you nurture your customer connections. When you nurture those customer connections, they become better customers and recommend you to their friends.

Building friends and followers for your business

We're sorry to tell you that you won't have a successful experience with Facebook for your business if you don't make the effort to build an audience. Building an audience starts with inviting people to Like your business page. The next steps are to get some interaction from the people that Like your business page and turn them into loyal followers who will tell their friends about you.

Here are a few ways to start building a following for your business:

✦ **Start in house:** When you first launch your business page, one of the most important things to do is get the ball rolling. People like to be where the party is, and having a starting group helps! Look to the people already involved with your company. Start by inviting everyone in your company to Like the business page. From there, each employee or partner can ask their personal friends to Like the business page as well.

✦ **Ask and invite:** No one is going to find your business page if they don't know to look for it, so it's a good idea to take every opportunity to share Facebook with your customers. It seems too easy, but a simple "Please Like our business page" really does work. Incorporate a link to your business page in your e-newsletter reminding your customers to Like your business page on Facebook. You'll get a good number of people who are happy to click the Like button and be the first among your Facebook audience. If you hand customers a receipt, put your Facebook address on the receipt, or hand them a card with your Facebook address. At the very least, remind them verbally to find you on Facebook and be sure to Like the business page.

Keep the ticker in the back of your mind, too. When you have several people Liking your business page at the same time, the ticker shows more Facebook Like activity, increasing the chance that a friend of someone who Likes your page will also Like your business page.

✦ **Use custom tabs:** A custom static HTML iframe tab enables you to have content that is only for people who Like your page. When you create a custom iframe tab, you have the opportunity to create more incentives for becoming a friend or follower (find out more about creating custom tabs in Book IV, Chapter 4). For example, you can create a tab that invites potential fans to Like your business page and then download a coupon, a white paper related to your niche, or even a short e-book. Giving potential friends and followers a reason to Like your business page is easy with a custom tab.

✦ **Use contests and sweepstakes:** By giving something away, or asking a question with the winner receiving a prize, or using games or any other creative way to get engagement, your friends and followers feel more involved with your brand and business. And those who don't already Like your page may be drawn in when they see the activity of their friends who do Like your business page in their news feed or ticker.

Facebook has strict guidelines for hosting contests and sweepstakes on its platform. Be sure and read Chapter 4 in this minibook to become familiar with the guidelines. Breaking the rules could mean losing your business page!

✦ **Make a difference:** A business was launching a business page for the first time. In an effort to create some buzz and get a burst of new followers, the customer launched a campaign to donate a dollar to a local charity for every Like on its business page within a certain time. The charity was promoting the campaign, and so were all the company's employees. The customer increased his Facebook audience by giving potential followers a compelling reason to Like his business page.

Connecting with your friends and followers

You need to connect with your friends and followers, but how do you keep up if you have a large audience? You can connect with your Facebook friends and followers in many ways; you're not just limited to making comments and posts.

The following list provides a few ideas that you can use to connect with your friends and followers:

✦ **Ask questions.** It's not about you; it's about your audience. The best thing you can do for your Facebook engagement is to ask questions of your Facebook friends and followers. When you give them a chance to talk, not only do they take a step in engaging with you, but their activity shows up in their friends' ticker. When their friends see that activity, they may be more likely to check out your business page and become a follower.

✦ **Encourage them to check back later.** You want your friends and followers to be repeat visitors. Sometimes it's just a matter of letting your fans know that more is coming tomorrow. How about posing a riddle of the day, and offering the answer the next day, along with a new riddle? With your business page's Pin feature, you can pin the daily riddle, question, or discussion to the top of your business page. Or you could create a new cover photo each week with a new question. If your fans come to expect a new cover photo on a certain day each week, you encourage them to visit your business page regularly.

✦ **Comment on other business pages as your business page.** A one-sided conversation isn't much fun, is it? It's important to remember that if you want people to interact with you, you also need to interact with them. You can even comment as your business page rather than your personal timeline. See Book IV, Chapter 2 for an explanation of how to do that.

Figure 1-2 shows how Jamie commented on another business page's status update as his company Crowdshifter. By commenting as his business page instead of himself, he's introducing his brand to potential followers.

REMEMBER You can't comment on personal timelines when you're using Facebook as your page; you can interact only on another business page. (We know it sounds confusing, but once you see it in action, you'll get it! Book IV, Chapter 2 explains this feature in detail.)

The value of commenting as your business page is making mutual connections by connecting with other businesses and building connections with some of their followers. This may lead to some of their followers choosing to check out your business page to find out more about your business.

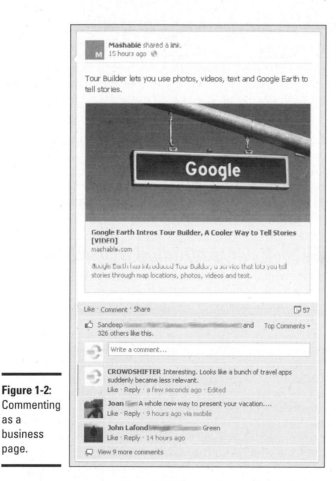

Figure 1-2:
Commenting as a business page.

✦ **Be a real person.** It's okay to let your personality shine through on your business page. Be funny, be serious, be professional. We're sure you know your goals and your audience and know what they can handle. Bring a little of yourself to your business page!

If you have multiple people in your office who update the business page, have them sign their updates with their name. Your followers will start to recognize your employees (and their personalities) and will feel a stronger connection with your entire company.

If you have a large audience, you can't always talk one-on-one with them all. Start by focusing on the influencers and those who are most engaging. You'll still project a human brand to your audience, even to those who aren't commenting directly with you.

Integrating Facebook in Marketing Campaigns

If you own a business, you know that finding and increasing your audience is essential for long-term success because those connections are the ones that lead to repeat business and referrals. As your Facebook audience grows, take advantage of the opportunity to build loyalty with those who connect with your company.

With a successful Facebook marketing strategy, you still use traditional marketing tactics. If Facebook proves to be a strong platform for your company, use outside marketing campaigns as a tool to drive new connections to Facebook. Do this by making Facebook the ultimate call to action. If your primary goal is to build an audience for long-term sales and customer loyalty, a call to action that leads them to Facebook is ideal.

Promoting Facebook via traditional advertising

You can advertise your company or product in many ways. With traditional advertising, your goal is to be seen by potential customers so that they know who you are and will choose to buy your product. Advertising is always more memorable if the person you reach takes some kind of action.

In addition to creating a memory, creating a database is important too. Advertising can be expensive. Not only do you want customers to buy your product today, you want them to buy again tomorrow. For example, after a car dealership sells a car to a customer, the next challenge is to get the customer to refer new customers to the dealership. And the next challenge is to get the customer back for service on his or her vehicle. If you can convince this loyal customer to connect with your business page, the person becomes part of your database from which you can ask for repeat business or encourage referrals. This is why promoting your business page within your traditional marketing is so valuable.

The following list gives tips to promote your business page using traditional marketing:

✦ **Billboard ads:** If your marketing campaign is going to reach a broad audience in a concentrated city (or several cities), a billboard may be part of your marketing strategy. Driving people to your business page from a billboard is challenging. Billboards only allow for a simple message, and a long URL might be difficult. If your company name is unique, it might be more effective to invite people to find you by searching your company name. Do this by telling people, "Search for us by name on Facebook." A more common name may make that difficult though. For example, blazefly might be fairly unique and therefore easy to find in a search. On the other hand, something like Bob's Car Care may be the name of several places and it may be difficult to find the correct one in a Facebook search.

Keep in mind that Facebook search is literal. If you search for *blaze fly* instead of *blazefly,* you won't find the business page. The capitalization isn't important, but the spaces are. As a business page owner, you want to be sure to title your business page in the way that you think people will search for it.

✦ **Print ads and handouts:** Someone who discovers your company in a favorite magazine or receives a handout has a little more time to read your message. Print ads and handouts are perhaps the easiest ways to get a message across because you can provide ample information. Often times, incorporating the Facebook logo and colors helps to make it more clear that your business page can be found on Facebook.

✦ **Get your free sample:** People love getting free samples before they decide to make a purchase. One really powerful way to build a database is by offering a free sample to anyone who requests it. You can create an iframe tab that hosts a contact form where people submit their contact information to receive a free sample.

Make sure that the actual form is just in the Like-only section, so that people have to Like your business page to access it. (You can find out how to do this in Chapter 4 of this minibook.)

✦ **The secret password:** If you've found a website that makes sense for you to advertise on, driving people with a good call to action is critical. You don't just want them to see the ad; you want them to click and take action. Imagine your company is a credit counseling service, and you're offering a free initial credit evaluation session. Your advertisement could say, "Click to go to our business page and get the secret password to redeem your free initial session." With this, you have the opportunity to use a fans-only iframe tab that provides the password. You get people who are interested in your services, and they become Facebook followers at the same time.

Having a memorable URL

When you share your Facebook URL as a call to action, it needs to be memorable. For example, if you are advertising on a billboard, your audience has a few seconds to read your ad. If the URL is a long destination, you may not get any traffic.

Make sure that you have a custom Facebook username (also called a vanity URL) for your business page. Book IV, Chapter 1 shows you how to create your own vanity URL.

After you have a vanity URL for your business page, it's a lot easier to tell people where to find you. If your company name is not conducive to being memorable in the form of a Facebook URL, try a typical web URL and redirect it to your business page. You can even redirect the URL to a specific tab, because Facebook tabs each have a unique URL.

You can buy a URL from NameCheap (`www.namecheap.com`), among other places. These services always have a simple function to allow you to direct your web address to any other page.

When creating your marketing materials, use the proper URL address. Make sure it's the URL you see when looking at your business page the way your fans view it, not your home screen where you look at your news feed.

Using apps to build influence

Using third-party apps can help strengthen your engagement with your friends and followers because you can customize specific functions and characteristics into your business page. Apps can provide a variety of functions if you have the resources to develop them. (You can discover the basics of developing apps in Book VI.) For example, if you provide efficient heating and air equipment, you could build a home efficiency calculator app that allows users to find out how they can lower their heating bills. The idea with this is to generate more influence with your fans by providing value.

Apps should, of course, be relevant to your business and the people you want to attract. For example, if your business is an arcade, how about having a game that fans can play right on your business page? If you aren't ready to invest in developing (or even repurposing) a customized app, you can use several simpler apps to customize your business page and provide value. You can find out about some of the ways to customize your business page in Book IV, Chapter 4.

Outsourcing your Facebook management

When running a business (especially as the owner), you have to balance your many tasks and determine the best use of your time. The question comes up frequently, "Is it okay to outsource social media to an expert?" You will always be best at serving your customers, but there are arguments for both sides of this conversation.

Outsourced social media marketing

When you outsource your social media (such as content creation and daily management), your biggest benefit is that you can hire someone who is familiar with the tools and how to effectively use them. Social media consultants usually end up in the business because they enjoy social media and are natural at executing social networking and communications.

The negative is that they are likely serving several clients at the same time and can't spend all their time on your company. Another negative is that they may not be fully familiar with your company, its culture, and its goals. It may take an outside resource weeks or months to learn the nitty-gritty of your business and your audience the way you do.

Finally, be sure you're working with a person or agency that truly understands the space. We've seen many agencies that say they can handle a social media campaign but either aren't aware of Facebook's basic terms of service or ignore them because they've seen others ignore them. If you're building a reputation on Facebook, you want to be sure the people helping you aren't hurting your brand's integrity.

In-house social media marketing

In-house people often find that their jobs can call them to many different activities. It's rare when someone can direct his or her full attention to just social media engagement, especially if the responsible party is the owner of the business. A business owner almost always has more immediate "fires" to put out, so social media management gets put on the back burner. For this reason, in-house Facebook management needs to come with discipline.

The connections and influence you build yield great long-term value. The biggest benefit of managing social media in-house is that you are always your best advocate and the best person to connect with your customers.

Chapter 2: Running a Social Marketing Campaign

In This Chapter

✔ Implementing Facebook campaigns

✔ Marketing a campaign

✔ Crowdsourcing to promote your contest

✔ Building your business page for the campaign

✔ Understanding Facebook's promotion rules

When starting your Facebook marketing, you'll probably find out how to build your audience, make connections with your audience, and nurture those connections so that they become loyal friends and followers.

After you've built a foundation with your business page audience, you likely need to give it a boost to get things to a higher level. A little shaking of the trees is required to let people know that it's worth connecting with your company on Facebook. Social marketing campaigns are a great way to do this. A social campaign enables you to reach people who you will not likely capture the attention of through daily interaction.

Campaigns tap into *crowdsourcing,* or using the resources that the public (the *crowd*) can provide to accomplish more than what you or your team can do with the resources you have. The word is a play on the word *outsource,* which is to look for a service provider outside your organization to deliver a service.

In this chapter, you find out how to start a social marketing campaign. You also discover how to build your business page to best show off your campaign and draw in fans to enter your promotion.

Understanding What Makes Social Marketing Campaigns Work

The goal of a social marketing campaign is to increase your business page engagement, followers, and awareness. The most successful campaigns are interesting enough to your followers that they're willing to do more than just read your status updates in their news feeds. Both Fanta (`www.facebook.com/fanta/posts/285086828227700`) and Red Bull (`https://apps.facebook.com/red-bull-tt/`) used their business pages to create complicated but fun scavenger hunts that rewarded interaction. We want to point out, though, that the rewards weren't always physical prizes. Often just completing a task — if it's interesting or challenging enough — is enough. In the case of Fanta, fans worked together to help a cartoon character find her way through the business page time warp. Red Bull followers had to follow intricate clues to win prizes. Both companies were promoting awareness about their brand by enticing friends and followers to explore their business pages, but the tasks kept followers' attention.

Another type of campaign that businesses often use on Facebook is a *promotion* (this is what Facebook calls contests and giveaways). Facebook has specific guidelines in place for promotions. You can find them at `www.facebook.com/promotions_guidelines.php`. We also explain them in detail in Chapter 4 of this minibook.

Regardless of the type of campaign you choose to run, we want to share some of the defining characteristics that make a social marketing campaign work:

✦ **Interactivity:** In many instances, the audience you want to reach isn't the audience you already have; it's their friends. To reach that audience, you need to entice your current friends and followers to share your content with their friends. Most Facebook users share only funny, useful, or interesting content. Regardless of the type of campaign you intend to implement, the content associated with it must be worth sharing.

Another interactive option is to include a voting component in a promotion. For instance, if you host a contest that requires each contestant to get votes to win, they are incentivized to invite people to your business page to help them win. You should note that contests should always be hosted on a third-party application (for details, see Book IV, Chapter 4).

✦ **Incentive:** Giving people an incentive to take action is a must. As we said earlier, if your campaign is engaging enough, the act of completing a task or solving a problem may be enough. On the other hand, your friends and followers will likely be motivated if they have the opportunity to win something exciting.

The nature of the prize can depend on the type of campaign, your goals for the campaign, and your desired reach. For example, invite your followers to submit a video of themselves interacting with your product. You aren't likely to get people to create their own dramatic video (and edit it) if there is only a chance that they could receive a prize worth $250. However, people would certainly upload a simple picture for such a prize. As with everything, it's important to know your audience. The value of the prize varies with different types of product industries and people.

✦ **Followers-only content:** When you offer followers-only content, you require that the visitors Like your business page before they can access the content, for example, a video or a white paper. For example, Figure 2-1 is a Welcome page you see if you haven't Liked the Microsoft business page. After you click Like, an animation plays.

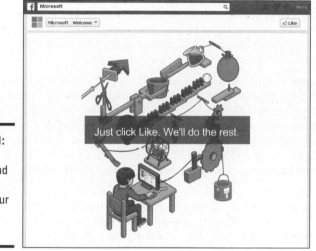

Figure 2-1:
Invite friends and followers to Like your business page.

✦ **Data capture:** One of the most important goals from a business perspective is to capture data. That data may simply be Likes or more specific information such as a name, an e-mail address, or demographics. The purpose of acquiring this information is to understand your current audience and build a larger audience with whom you can continue to connect. When you know your audience and can cater to their needs and interests, you can build the relationship.

Types of Facebook Campaigns

When you decide that you want to conduct a Facebook campaign, the next step is to determine the campaign's structure. If your sole goal is to earn space in the mind of current and potential customers, just about any form of campaign might work. A more specific goal requires a particular campaign concept.

We explain some of the most common features of Facebook campaigns in the following list:

✦ **Voting contests:** A voting contest is based on people entering a contest — usually by producing something — and getting votes for their entry. Photo contests are a common, time-tested concept for voting contests. Facebook requires that you use a third-party app to conduct this contest.

Facebook's terms of service state that you can't require anyone to take a specific Facebook action to participate in the contest. For example, you can't define Liking a post as a form of voting.

✦ **Sweepstakes:** In a sweepstakes, participants enter the sweepstakes and a winner is determined by a random drawing. The downside is that the sharing component is not as strong in this format. With other sorts of contests (especially voting contests), you often rule out some participants simply because they aren't confident that they have a chance to win. In a sweepstakes, each contestant has an equal chance of winning in most cases. For this reason, you could attract more entries, even if you don't get as much voting traffic to your business page.

✦ **Fundraisers:** A fundraising campaign is not necessarily a competition. Fundraisers promote the opportunity to do good by giving to a charity and inviting others to do the same. For example, you might offer to donate $1 for every Like your business page receives in a certain period of time. Fundraising through Facebook campaigns helps you spread the word in a lot of the same ways that contests do. Sometimes charities will form teams to encourage a little friendly competition in raising funds.

✦ **Facebook as a landing page:** Almost any marketing campaign benefits from having a landing page. A *landing page* is where you direct people with your call to action. For instance, you could direct visitors to a page where they can request free samples or sign up for your e-mail newsletter. Because the web is such a critical part of marketing, a landing page should be part of any campaign. E-mail marketing messages often have a corresponding landing page (or several, depending on the content of the message).

Using Facebook as a landing page simply puts the leads or customers you attract with your advertising in the path of your business page. This technique could be a simple way to increase your Facebook audience while targeting another goal. The best way to execute this is by directing a customized web address directly to your Facebook page tab. Create a unique URL that you place in your advertising message (something like "Find out more at `www.ourlandingpage.com`"), and then direct that URL to your page tab. Each page tab has its own web address (something like `www.facebook.com/mypagename?sk=app_7146470129`). For details, see Book V, Chapter 1.

Implementing Sharing Contests

Facebook contests have many variations, but one thing they all have in common is an *ask,* or a call to action. The call to action might be to complete a form, upload a picture, or nominate a charity. If your ask is only to complete an entry form for the contest, implementation of the campaign might be easy. If participants must create a video, complete the form as they upload, and promote the contest to their friends and ask them to vote, your ask is clearly more complicated. If the latter is the case, you face the

Implementing Sharing Contests **353**

Book V
Chapter 2

Running a Social
Marketing
Campaign

potential of *abandonment,* when people begin to enter your contest but then abandon the process, presumably because the effort to enter outweighed the potential reward.

Photo and video contests are popular forms of contests. People often love to share their photos and videos, especially when they might win something. Here are some of the things you need to know about photo and video contests:

✦ **Get a third-party app to host the contest.** Facebook has strict rules about not using any Facebook features (such as clicking Like or commenting) as a means of entry. Third-party apps allow you to manage the entry and hosting of the contest. Some well-known third-party apps that follow the Facebook rules are Wildfire (`www.wildfireapp.com`) and Offerpop (`www.offerpop.com`). Both allow you to implement a video or photo contest for your business page.

Because Facebook requires that promotions be run within third-party applications, promotions can be run only on business pages and not on personal timelines. All third-party applications are installed on a page tab (also called an *application page*). Page tabs display content through iframes, which means that the content itself (like the contest app and images) is hosted on a separate site, and your page tab displays that content. You can find out more about creating page tabs for your business page in Book VI.

✦ **Include clear instructions for how to participate.** Demonstrating visually always helps, so use some visual aids. You could even make a video describing how easy it is to enter.

✦ **Market to the right crowd.** Video contests are more complicated than photo contests, because putting together a video is more work than taking a photo. Be sure that the people to whom you market are likely to have a video camera and are comfortable producing a video. Many can shoot some video with a smartphone; however, some people are still intimidated by the idea of shooting a video. Video contests also work best when you clearly describe what you want in a video. You don't want people to be overwhelmed with the challenge of scripting.

Photo contests, although simpler by nature, require the same clear concept as video contests. A cutest puppy contest is a simple concept. Make sure that your concept is something that people can easily understand.

✦ **Compare voting versus judges to select the winner.** Gathering votes is a great way to incentivize friends and followers to invite people to see the entries and select their favorite. This method is a great way to attract new followers; however, in some cases, it may not be the ideal method. Do you want people to vote by clicking a button or by entering information? If you ask for information (such as a nomination or an e-mail address), you're likely to get less traffic but more engaged traffic. Make your decision based on the goals of your contest.

Both Wildfire and Offerpop support all the preceding features. Several other services can help you run contests, but we don't have room to list them all. You can even build your own application; see Book VI for details.

Getting a good response

One of the biggest fears you may have at the beginning of a Facebook contest is whether you will get a good response. When you've invested a lot of time and effort (and sometimes money) in a Facebook campaign, it would be a big letdown if it falls flat. You never know what is going to be a bang-up success and what isn't, but if you follow some best practices, you can certainly start with confidence.

Consider the balance of effort versus reward. More appropriately, consider the *perceived* effort versus *perceived* reward. It doesn't matter how easy it is to enter your contest or how exciting you believe it is; if entering appears too difficult, you won't have a successful response. If the incentive or reward doesn't interest the people that you reach, you may not have the success you desire.

The following tips will help you find the right balance so you can be sure to get a great response for your contest:

✦ **Private information:** People are often willing to give their home address, phone number, e-mail address, and so on if there is context for doing so. For example, if you ask people to enter your promotion to have their profile pictures featured as the face of your company, and you also ask for a home address, you may have a lower response because people feel that the information you're asking for isn't necessary. If capturing home addresses is important, offer a prize that must be sent in the mail.

✦ **Relevant messaging:** When determining your contest concept, be sure that your contest message and your business message align. For example, if your company prides itself on providing the highest quality to discriminating buyers, any message that enforces discounts or free products is inconsistent with your business message.

Contests can be a great way to reinforce a brand message. The components of that message are often embedded throughout the entire contest and its marketing materials. Use contests to enforce a message you want to get across to your customers. For example, if you make paper products and want to position yourself as a company committed to green products, consider a contest that asks people to show how they too are green. In a photo contest, for example, you may ask participants to "upload a picture of you wearing all green" or "show us your best tips on being green."

✦ **Easy entry:** Instructions for entering the contest should be clear. Use a simple call to action and limit what activities you ask participants to perform. Every barrier you put in place has a potential of eliminating entries. For example, if you host your contest through a third-party Facebook contest application that requires users to allow the app access to their Facebook accounts, and then they have to complete an entry form, you will have fewer participants than you would if you eliminate one of those steps.

As a general rule, the best first action (other than clicking to your contest landing tab) should be filling out a basic information form. On this form, include fields for only the minimum amount of information that you need.

If additional steps are necessary, make the steps something participants can do after they've submitted the form. If you give participants a percentage of completion, they are more likely to complete the steps because it feels unfinished.

✦ **Simple messaging:** Share a clear message that leaves nothing to conjecture. The longer your contest description, the fewer people will bother to read it. Be aware that some of your audience is going to find out about the contest through someone sharing it on a Facebook status update or other channel (such as Twitter). Make sure that your concept is something that can be summed up in as few words as possible.

Avoiding a flopped contest

Sometimes, no matter what you do, you just don't get people to participate as quickly as you would like. One of the best ways to avoid this situation is to make sure that you don't launch a contest without a strong network to invite to participate. Sometimes personally asking your customers to enter is a great way to get the ball rolling. For example, an HVAC service company asked every one of their technicians to invite their customers to enter their Facebook contest after each appointment. Putting a little extra attention on promoting your contest at the beginning makes a big difference.

Some people feel that it's okay to ask a few customers or friends that you know personally to enter a contest to get things started. Others feel that this gives people an unfair advantage or otherwise less genuine entries. Regardless of your feelings on the matter, be sure that you never seed a contest with falsified entries to make it seem like there's lots of interest.

Marketing a Facebook Contest

Initially, you might think that posting status updates telling people about your Facebook contest is enough. It isn't. The primary reason to conduct a Facebook contest is to increase the interaction that you get from your friends and followers, as well as increase your audience by attracting new followers.

A Facebook marketing campaign in most cases involves more than just Facebook to make it happen.

Facebook works well with other forms of digital marketing. Sure, sometimes if you have a strongly engaged and interested audience, you might be able to post one status update and see it turn into a major success. Most times, however, you have to use other resources as well.

The following list provides advice on how to market your campaign and make it a success:

✦ **Announce your campaign to your e-mail list.** Suppose that you send out a monthly newsletter. The content of that newsletter should highlight your Facebook contest and drive people directly to it. The cross-promotion of e-mail to Facebook and Facebook to e-mail makes your connection to your audience much stronger and more effective.

Some best practices include putting a graphic right at the top of the e-mail and linking it to the desired landing page. Note that you can link directly to the page with its unique URL. Find this in your browser address bar when you view the tab on which your contest is hosted. You may have made it your default landing page, but that applies only for followers.

✦ **Pass out cards at the counter.** If your business is in retail or any other business in which you see customers' faces, give them a small card that promotes the contest. Include a hook that gets them interested in checking out the contest. They have to be interested enough to remember to check out the contest later.

Alternatively, you can place a QR code by the register so customers can scan it with their smartphones. See Book III, Chapter 2 for more on QR codes.

✦ **Post your campaign on your website.** Make sure an invitation to join the contest obviously stands out on the home page of your site, and remember to link directly to the contest page on Facebook. When people visit your website, the first thing they see should be a contest announcement. This way, you can convert some of your web traffic into engaged Facebook followers.

✦ **Find a partner.** Finding a partner (also called *comarketing*) is perhaps the most powerful method in promoting a Facebook contest. If you sell custom wheels and another company sells customized car parts, you can be pretty certain that you have nearly the same type of people in your target audience — people who take pride in their cars and may want to make their cars ready for show. You're lucky, because this audience is already interested in sharing with friends. The winner of the contest might get his or her car fully outfitted with the two companies' products.

By doing this, you promote the contest on both business pages, both e-mail lists, and so on. You'll likely expand each company's following just by cross-promoting.

The Power of Crowdsourcing

One of the greatest reasons to conduct social media campaigns is because of the power of crowdsourcing. Crowdsourcing can yield great ideas and help to expand your reach.

Using crowdsourcing to create a new product

Suppose that a company that sells T-shirts with clever puns wants to introduce a new design. However, the company doesn't have a new design to announce. So they put together a Facebook contest with the following two stages:

1. Invite Facebook friends and followers to help determine the new slogan for the T-shirt.

2. Invite Facebook friends and followers to help create a concept for the new shirt's graphic.

The new T-shirt is released in a few weeks at a big event that many customers attend. The contest was a grand success for a number of reasons:

✦ The company uncovered many new ideas for the new T-shirt design. Ultimately, the company was able to simultaneously test the design's popularity before printing the T-shirts.

✦ The company increased its Facebook following because it gave people a compelling reason to visit the business page.

✦ The new T-shirt design sold better because Facebook fans already had a vested interest in the shirt. The new product raised specific awareness and attracted new buyers.

✦ The crowd was part of the creation of a new product, which sent the message that the company values its customers.

Using crowdsourcing to determine your Facebook content

One of the greatest challenges is keeping your Facebook followers interested and engaged in the content that you provide on a daily basis. Discussion keeps people interested. Let your Facebook followers tell you what they're interested in, and allow them to lead the conversation. This is where crowd-sourcing comes in. A contest or campaign can help you attract the interaction that will launch that sort of activity with your Facebook followers.

People like to be valued, and people tend to like the idea of being featured or recognized. One way to do this is to ask your Facebook fans to start a conversation about your company on your business page. Maybe you could ask your fans for a new slogan for your company or what they like best about your business. This invitation to engage in conversation might prompt participation from your audience without requiring that you award a prize.

Preparing Your Business Page for the Campaign

Make sure that your business page is ready for any contest or campaign that you implement. Campaigns can be simple or structured. Regardless, the most important aspect is making sure that people know that you have a campaign. The following sections describe how you can prepare for your campaign. (To find out more about customizing your business page, see Book IV, Chapter 4.)

Your cover photo

If possible, the theme of your business page should match your branding. When you conduct a campaign, you may want to tweak the cover photo design to highlight a theme, but you'll still want to keep your branding. For example, a Christmas photo of the week contest might feature holiday colors or other images to give the campaign a holiday theme, but keep your brand's logo or other defining characteristic on the photo as well.

The cover photo is a great way to highlight your campaign while still branding the look of your business page. For example, you might include bells and holiday colors for a holiday campaign, or pictures of dogs and cats for a cutest pet photo contest. Remember that your cover photo is 851 pixels wide by 315 pixels tall. (Facebook prohibits calls to action on the cover photo, such as "Enter Now," so be sure to use the photo only for branding and design aspects.)

A custom tab

You host your contest on an page tab. It's best to have a custom page for the contest that shows only a preview to nonfollowers and the full version to followers (refer to Figure 2-1). When visitors click Like, they see another view of the tab. You can utilize this setting when you create a custom Facebook tab.

By setting up separate tabs for followers and nonfollowers, you save some content for followers, thereby giving nonfollowers one more reason to become a follower. More importantly, when your campaign attracts tons of traffic, you can gain more of those visitors as followers. It's important to note again that you can't have the entry come by way of visitors Liking your business page; the entry must happen in the third-party app. You can find out more about promotions in Book V, Chapter 4.

Contact forms

Using a contact form extends your lead capture beyond only people Liking your page. Facebook contests are a great way to increase your e-mail list as well.

You embed a contact form in your Facebook tab in the same way you embed HTML on most websites. Using the Static HTML app, you can simply place your code in the fields. You don't have to know how to create a form — several services offer easily built forms. We recommend Formstack (`www.formstack.com`) because its service has many functions that enable you to create lead capture forms, including database storage for the data, and connect it to your favorite e-mail marketing services.

Canvas apps

Canvas apps are different than the common page tabs that are part of your business page. (To discover how to set up your own canvas app, see Book VI, Chapter 2.) A canvas app enables the owner of the page to occupy the entire screen in the context of the application. This screen includes the ticker, which updates with activity from the application, as well as other similar applications.

Canvas apps are 760 pixels wide, which allows for a reasonable amount of content; however, it's just shy of the 810-pixel width of the page tabs in your business page.

Setting up a canvas app can enable an interactive experience between users. This feature is most useful when your contest involves a game or something that can display real-time activity in the app. One distinct disadvantage is that canvas apps redirect your fans to an alternate URL, such as `http://apps.facebook.com/wordswithfriends` instead of `www.facebook.com/wordswithfriends`. This means your visitors may have a few seconds of wait time as the canvas app loads.

Canvas apps are great when more page space is necessary (or when you need to enhance the quality of your campaign). Offerpop (`http://offerpop.com`) is a great third-party tool for setting up a canvas app–based campaign. Figure 2-2 shows the Scrabble canvas app. (Most games are hosted on a canvas app.)

Figure 2-2:
A canvas
app.

The ticker

One big benefit of a Facebook campaign is the additional visibility created through the activity feed. Specifically, the Facebook ticker, shown in Figure 2-3, displays your friends' activity on the top-right side of your home screen.

Expect the following activity in the ticker:

✦ **Status updates:** If your contest encourages people to post a status update, people will see it in their news feed, but it appears also in the ticker.

✦ **New business page Likes:** Often, contests result in new Likes for your business page. These appear in the ticker as well.

✦ **Likes and comments:** When people Like or comment on a post in your contest, the ticker displays it.

✦ **Real-time data:** All the data you see in the ticker can be seen elsewhere on Facebook. The ticker just displays the data as it happens in real time. This factor might encourage you to carefully time your campaign launch. When you launch a Facebook campaign and everything (your Facebook tab and profile picture) goes live at the same time as your e-mail announcement and Facebook status posts, you may attract more activity through the action showing up in people's news feeds.

Figure 2-3:
The ticker.

Chapter 3: Using Insights to Track Your Success

In This Chapter

✔ Using Facebook Insights to track your success

✔ Discovering

✔ Improving your News Feed algorithm

If you have a business page, you're probably interested in how the page is performing with your audience. You want to know if you're reaching as many people as possible and how you can encourage them to interact with your content more.

Facebook offers an analytics program called Insights that's available for business pages (but not personal timelines). Insights offers information about who your users are, when they visit your business page most often, which of your posts have had the most response, and much more. This chapter explains how Insights works and how you can use the metrics you find on Insights to improve the effectiveness of your business page.

This chapter also explains the News Feed algorithm (formally *EdgeRank*), which is Facebook's algorithm that determines what content is most relevant to each Facebook user. The News Feed algorithm is important because it decides whether or not content appears on a user's top stories. (Most Facebook users have top stories as their default news feed.) The News Feed algorithm considers how an individual interacts (or doesn't) with different kinds of content and weighs those interactions. The result is Facebook's best guess at what interests someone. In the latter part of this chapter, we explain the elements that the News Feed algorithm considers and how you can try to use those elements to your advantage on your business page.

Tracking Your Facebook Stats with Insights

Insights is Facebook's analytics software and is available for business pages. Insights allows you to see how people interact with the content on your business page. You can track the demographics of your audience, which posts receive the most engagement, and even how people are finding and

Liking your page. Insights helps you monitor important stats, understand your audience, and make better marketing decisions. Throughout the following sections, we explain the details of what you can expect to find in Insights.

First, though, you need to open Insights. To do that, go to your business page and, at the top in your Admin panel, click the See Insights link.

Reviewing the main Insights page

Your main Insights page looks similar to the one shown in Figure 3-1 and provides an overview of your business page's activity. You can also see how your posts have been performing, export your data, and take a tour to get more information about how Insights works.

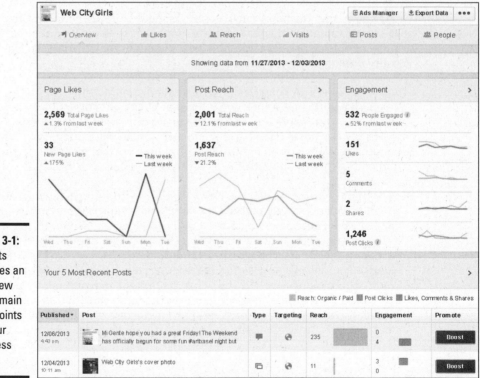

Figure 3-1: Insights provides an overview of the main data points for your business page.

The top of the page has six tabs: Overview (the current page), Likes, Reach, Visits, Posts, and People. We explore each of these tabs later in the chapter.

The three graphs on the Insights Overview page show the following data for one month at a time:

✦ **Page Likes:** The number of Likes your page has and how that number compares to the previous week. To dive deeper, click the Page Likes link or the Likes tab at the top of the page.

✦ **Post Reach:** The number of people who have seen your posts and how that number compares to last week.

✦ **Engagement:** The number of unique people who Liked, commented, shared, or clicked your posts and how that number compares to the previous week. You also see the number of people in each category.

At the bottom of the page is Your 5 Most Recent Posts section. You see the post's date, description, type, target (privacy setting), reach, and engagement. You can also boost, or promote, your post to get more exposure. To see additional posts, click the See All Posts link at the bottom.

Exporting your data

If you want to back up your data or just keep a copy on hand, you can export your Insights data and download it to your computer. To do that, navigate to your Insights page, and then follow these steps:

1. **Click the Export Data button, in the top right.**

   The Export Insights Data dialog box appears, as shown in Figure 3-2.

Figure 3-2: The Export Insights Data dialog box allows you to choose which data to export.

Export Insights Data

Insights export is changing to align with the new Insights. Learn more.

Export data directly to Excel (.xls) or comma-separated text format (.csv). Choose either Page level data or Page post level data. You may select any date range, with a maximum of 500 posts at a time.

SELECT DATA RANGE

Start Time: 11/6/2013

End Time: 12/4/2013

SELECT EXPORT
The new export is available to preview. You can use the old export through the end of the year.
◉ Old
◯ New

SELECT DATA TYPE
◉ Page level data
◯ Post level data

SELECT FILE FORMAT
◉ Excel (.xls)
◯ Comma-separated values (.csv)

Insights data is not available before July 19, 2011.

Facebook Page Terms   Download   Cancel

2. **Select the start and end dates to export.**

3. **Select the type of data.**

   Choose page-level data or post-level data. Page-level data just gives you numbers based on your business page's overall interactions (for example, overall Likes, Unlikes, and friends of followers). Post-level data includes numbers directly related to individual posts (for example, name of post, date posted, and total number of followers that the post reached).

4. **Select the file format.**

   Save your export file as an Excel spreadsheet (`.xls`) or a comma-separated values (`.csv`) file.

5. **Click the Download button.**

Export Insights data periodically as a backup. In 2010, Facebook changed the way it displayed Insights. When it made the change, you couldn't access any data from the previous version. If you hadn't exported it, you couldn't access it. Because Facebook periodically changes things, and it owns everything on the platform, we recommend keeping your own backups to reference, just in case.

Checking out your settings

The Settings button sports three dots and appears to the right of the Export Data button. When you click this button, a menu appears with the following options:

✦ **Send Feedback:** Send feedback about something that isn't working, questions you have, or suggestions to improve the data.

✦ **Take the Tour Again:** Discover the features in each part of your Insights page. This is a great option for visual learners.

✦ **Visit Help Center:** Go directly to the Facebook Help Center files related to Insights.

When you switch from tab to tab at the top of your Insights page, be sure to check your dates and reset them as necessary. For example, if you're looking at Likes for June 18–24, and then switch to looking at Reach, the dates may reset themselves.

Touring the Likes Page

After clicking the Likes link in the Insights navigation, the page shows you how many Likes your business page has and gives you details regarding each one. You can adjust the timeframe by clicking the calendar to the right in the first section. This change affects the other three sections as well.

The second section displays your total page Likes to date. You can also see the average number of Likes you're receiving over certain time periods by clicking the Total Page Likes link, as shown in Figure 3-3.

Figure 3-3:
Find the
average
number of
Likes during
a particular
timeframe.

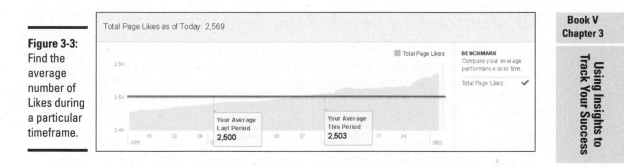

The third section shows you your net Likes, meaning how many Likes you've received minus how many people have Unliked you. You can also filter by Unlikes, Organic Likes, Paid Likes (through promoting and advertising), and Net Likes.

If one of your goals It to Increase Likes through Facebook ads, this section is a helpful way to see whether your ad dollars are working.

If you're receiving a large number of Unlikes over a short period of time, you should take notice and see what is driving people away. Perhaps you aren't responding to comments, or you've posted too much content in a short period of time. Also, if you have multiple people managing your business page, one may be practicing bad Facebook etiquette. Be sure to view this stat often!

The fourth and last section on the page shows the origin of your page Likes, as shown in Figure 3-4. Your graph may contain more or fewer options, depending on where you have your Facebook Like button and how you are promoting your business page.

Figure 3-4:
Discovering
the origin of
your busi-
ness page
Likes.

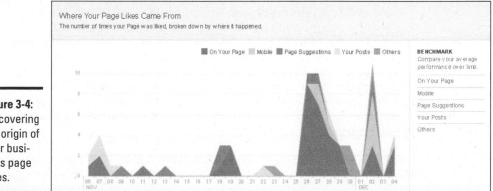

Understanding Reach Page Data

Facebook defines *reach* as the number of Facebook users who saw your content. Some users may have seen your content in their news feed because they're followers of your business page; because one of their friends Liked, commented, or shared your content; or due to a promotion, offer, or another form of Facebook advertising.

A Facebook user has an average of 229 friends. Any time a user interacts with content, the interaction is shared with their friends via the news feed, and those friends can also interact with the content if they want to. When you share compelling content, it has the potential to be seen by many, many more people than just your followers, thus increasing your reach.

The Reach page is where you find some of the most valuable data about how your business page is performing and whether you're meeting the goals you set. You can track the following information:

+ The number of people who saw your post

+ Your business page Likes, comments, and shares

+ The number of people that hid your page, reported it as spam, and Unliked your page

+ Your total reach, or the total number of people who saw any activity from your page

The next few sections explain these metrics further.

You can click the calendar and select the dates for which you want to view the information.

The first section deals with your post reach, which is the total number of people who saw your posts, organic (non-paid) or paid (promoted). You can sort by either option by clicking the appropriate link to the right of the graph. If you're using paid Facebook advertising, you can use this information to determine whether you are getting the expected results.

The second section shows the number of Likes, comments, and shares you received, as shown in Figure 3-5. You can sort by each of these categories, to determine whether you are meeting your goals and attracting a healthy level of engagement.

The Hide, Report as Spam, and Unlikes section helps you spot anything negative happening on your Facebook page. Monitor this section frequently. If the numbers continue to grow, you may have a problem that you need to address quickly. Just like the other sections, you can sort by clicking any of the links in the area to the right of the graph.

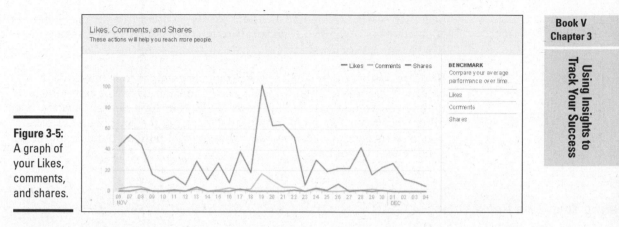

Figure 3-5:
A graph of
your Likes,
comments,
and shares.

Don't worry if you have a few Unlikes. If you see a large number of Unlikes, pay attention and try to determine the reason. Did the Unlikes occur after a specific post? Does your page contain offensive spam? Facebook gives you the date of the Unlike, which allows you to go back to your posts for that day and see whether you shared something controversial. Or maybe you posted too many times that day. You won't be able to know for certain what made a follower Unlike your business page, but you can use the data to help draw a conclusion. Similarly, if you have an influx of Likes on a specific day, you'll want to see what you posted that was so popular.

The last section on the Reach page is your total reach. The first section deals only with posts; this section contains the number of people who saw any of your activity, including posts, posts by other people, page Like ads, mentions, and check-ins. You can sort by organic or paid, to see whether one is a better option for you.

Finding Friends by Using the Visits Page

For the most part, after Facebook users Like your business page, they don't have to come back to your Page. Instead, followers rely on your content to show up in their news feeds. However, if you want to see just how many people are visiting your business page, look at the Page and Tab Visits graph on the Visits page. This graph includes every single time your business page was viewed for a given time period — even if the same person viewed the page multiple times. For example, if one person visits your business page five times, and three other people visit one time each, the total page views would be eight.

Along the right side of the graph, you will see the page tabs you've set up on your business page. Click one to isolate it and show only that metric in the graph.

Scroll a little further down the page to see the Other Page Activity section, which tracks the number of actions that each person took on your business page. These actions include mentions, posts by other people, check-ins, and claimed offers. Again, you can sort through each category by clicking the link to the right of the graph.

If you've ever wondered where your traffic is coming from, check your External Referrers section, which is shown in Figure 3-6. Not everyone is finding you from stories in their news feeds. Your blog, search engines, and other websites may be important lead generators for your business page. You may not see the section or see anything in it until an outside source sends a user to your page.

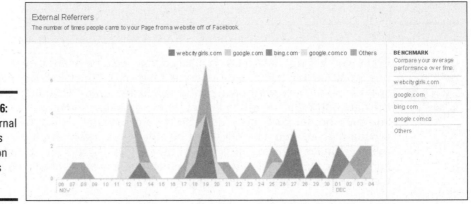

Figure 3-6:
The External Referrers section on the Visits page.

We encourage you to include a link to your business page on your blog or website, and even promote your business page on your business cards and in-store marketing.

The All-Important Posts Page

We think that the Posts page is one of the most important pages because it can help you learn what is attracting or repelling your followers and visitors. For example, if you share a video and it has a small reach and few comments, chances are the content didn't resound with very many people. On the other hand, a video that achieves a much higher reach and higher engagement is a sign that your audience likes that content and you should put out more of it.

If you have good content with little engagement, you might want to use the Boost feature to promote your post to a wider audience than just your followers. We will talk more about this Facebook advertising feature in Chapter 4 of this minibook.

At the top of the Posts page are two links: When Your Fans Are Online and Post Types. When Your Fans Are Online helps you identify the days and times when your followers are online, which can help you decide when to put out content. You should also consider being online at those times to engage right away with those who are interacting with your business page and content.

The Post Types link shows the average reach and engagement of each type of content on your page. As shown in Figure 3-7, video is by far the most popular medium on this business page. With the popularity of YouTube, Vine, and other video sites, video is probably the best delivery vehicle for communicating your message. Consider using video the next time you have something to say.

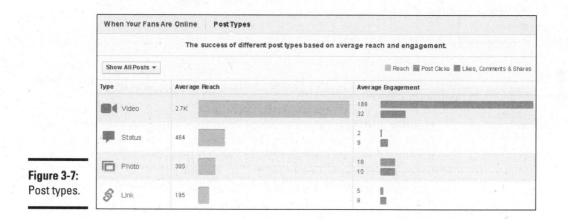

Figure 3-7:
Post types.

The rest of the Posts page displays your posts. You see the post's date, description, type, targeting (privacy setting), reach (organic or paid), and engagement (Likes, comments, and shares). You can also promote, or boost, your post.

Find which posts had the highest and lowest reach and engagement. Then create more of the former type of content and less of the latter.

Try changing your message and type of post if your posts aren't making a huge splash. For example, if you share a link to your blog post but it doesn't get a lot of click-throughs, consider making a short video summarizing your post content and share that instead.

Understanding the People Page

An important part of your marketing strategy is simply knowing your audience. The more you can find out about your readers and followers, the more you can customize your interactions with them. Facebook Insights doesn't give you specific data for individuals, but it does give you a helpful overview of who your audience is, where they're coming from, and what content they're interacting with the most.

The People page has three main areas: Your Fans, People Reached, and People Engaged, as shown in Figure 3-8.

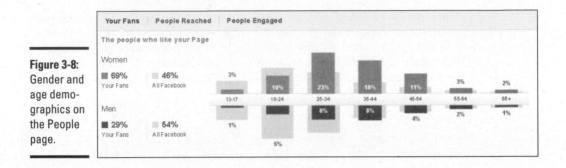

Figure 3-8:
Gender and age demographics on the People page.

You can access each area through links at the top of the page. Each area contains the following:

+ **Gender and Age:** Facebook shows you how your audience breaks down by gender and age, based on the information each business page shares. If a business page doesn't specify gender, it isn't included in this metric (which is why your percentages may not quite add up to 100 percent). Facebook also shows you how your audience compares to Facebook on average.

+ **Countries, Cities, and Languages:** You can see which countries and cities your followers reside in and which language they are using to view Facebook. You may be surprised at what you see here. The data shared for countries and cities is based on a follower's IP address, not what is listed in the person's timeline.

The demographic data for people talking about your business page requires that 30 people interact with your data within seven days of the dates you're viewing. If you can't see your demographic data, fewer than 30 people were interacting with your content. Try changing your date range to see if that helps. If it doesn't, it's time to integrate some new content-sharing tactics to promote more interaction. See Book IV, Chapter 4 for tips on building your Facebook community.

Getting to Know the News Feed Algorithm

You may have noticed that your news feed doesn't display items chronologically. This is because the News Feed algorithm ranks that content. Facebook uses that algorithm to determine whether specific content will be of interest to you. Facebook looks at how you interact with others and with content on Facebook and makes assumptions based on those actions. Those assumptions determine what content is filtered to your news feed in the highlighted stories.

Facebook is pretty closed-lipped about its News Feed algorithm, but as we researched, we found that Facebook appears to rank actions based on the level of effort it takes to interact, but it appears to rank content based on the number of interactions. For instance, Likes are easy to give and require little effort on the reader's part. Comments, however, take more effort and are rewarded accordingly.

Likewise, Facebook tends to reward certain content more than others. Facebook users are more likely to engage with photos or video than text updates. Facebook's goal is to have people share interesting content that elicits a response, so Facebook gives a higher ranking to video or photos. Facebook tends to rank content in this order:

✦ Photos

✦ Video

✦ Links

✦ Text

Understanding how the News Feed Algorithm works

Facebook users have their own algorithm for each bit of content they consume. As you can imagine, that can make it hard for your content to show up in everyone's news feed (especially if you're trying to have your business page updates appear). Each person interacts with content, pages, and people differently, and therefore, has his or her own version of ranking based on those actions.

The News Feed algorithm uses many variables. Following are three of the more important ones:

✦ **Affinity:** The relationship between a content creator and a content consumer. The affinity factor changes over time, depending on how a user interacts (or doesn't) with content. Affinity is determined by many things, such as how often a user

- Logs in to Facebook

- Interacts with content from another user or business page

- Clicks Like on content

- Types comments on content

- Clicks the Share option for content

Facebook keeps track of how a user interacts with content. When a user is consistently engaged with content from another Facebook user or business page, the affinity is high. If the user ignores content, the affinity begins to wane and can become low. When affinity is low, it's less likely that content from the ignored user or page shows up in the user's news feed as a highlighted story.

✦ **Weight:** Facebook determines the weight of an update and its engagement depending on how much effort it takes to complete. For example, it takes the most effort for a user to share a post created by someone else with his own audience, so shares weigh more than a Like. It takes a little more effort to post a video than a text update (and video is more likely to garner interaction), so video weighs more than a straight status update.

Facebook considers photos and videos as having the most weight, followed by links and then text updates. For engagement, shares have the most weight, followed by comments and then Likes.

Even though Facebook no longer calls its algorithm EdgeRank, you can still visit EdgeRank Checker (`http://EdgeRankchecker.com`), a website devoted to researching Facebook's News Feed algorithm. EdgeRank Checker found that comments appear to have four times the weight of Likes. What that means is that when a user took the time to leave a comment, the content had four times as many clicks than when the user just Liked the content. Of course, that helps a business page's ranking, but it also helps you see why it's important to try to engage your audience beyond a simple Like. If your audience is commenting, it's social proof to their friends that your article was worthwhile and they're more likely to click your content (and maybe also respond, thus widening your audience even further).

✦ **Time — decay:** How long an object has been out there. The older your post, the more decayed it is. Facebook moves fast. Each time you check your news feed, you see something new. Posts that are old lose their edge and weight and count less. You need to post more than once a day; otherwise, your posts (that is, objects) won't be seen by everyone, and they can't interact with your content. However, don't re-post the same information multiple times a day. Instead, post varied, relevant content throughout the day, especially at the peak times that the majority of your audience is online.

Check your Insights (discussed earlier in this chapter) to determine how time of day is affecting interaction on your posts. If you're posting at 6:00 am and not seeing a lot of interaction, try posting later in the morning. Or if you're posting at 4:00 p.m. and seeing many comments or Likes, try to post more around that time. You will likely need to experiment with several times of day to find the sweet spot for your audience.

Using rank to improve your news feed position

Facebook uses each of the three variables discussed in the previous section to ascribe a rank for each user. To make the most of your ranking, you need to do three things:

✦ **Determine who your audience is.** When you know to whom you're talking, you can customize your updates to meet their needs. By sharing content your audience wants, you increase your affinity with them.

✦ **Create and post content that encourages feedback and engagement.**
The kind of content you post is directly related to knowing your audience. When you know who your audience is and what they want from you, find new ways to give that content to them. If you usually post text status updates, try sharing video or photos. Regardless of the type of content you share, provide a specific call to action. If you tell your readers what you'd like from them, they're more likely to follow through for you.

✦ **Post when your audience is looking.** As mentioned, it doesn't do you much good if you're posting great content at times when people don't see it. You may have a great idea at 2:00 a.m., but if you post it then, few followers will see it. Instead, write it down and post it later in the day when more of your audience is on Facebook. Use your Insights to see whether you can find a pattern of when your audience is most active on your business page. What you find may surprise you! Keep in mind that not everyone has access to Facebook during the day because of firewalls or other restrictions at work.

To improve your audience engagement, you need to post content that people want to interact with. In Book IV, Chapter 3, we explain how to build your Facebook community. The keys to a loyal and interactive community are solving a problem, educating your audience, and entertaining your audience.

You need to have clear goals in mind and know how you're going to achieve those goals. Use calls to action, post links that promote sales, and tag other business pages in your status updates if it makes sense. When you tell your audience what you want them to do and provide a way for them to do it, they're more likely to follow through.

And if you're sharing a link to a post by another brand, tag its business page in your status update. Your update will be seen by that business pages' followers as well — which enhances your overall reach.

The bottom line is that you must know your audience and what they expect from you. If you give your audience what they want, you establish yourself as an authority and your audience comes back to you for answers and comes to appreciate the community you're building.

Chapter 4: Ads, Promotions, and Offers

In This Chapter

✓ Setting up a Facebook ad

✓ Using Ads Manager

✓ Creating a report

✓ Sharing administrative privileges

✓ Marketing your business through a promotion

✓ Finding the best apps to run your giveaway or contest

✓ Setting up best practices for a successful promotion

✓ Using offers to expand your business

One of the things Facebook does well is collecting demographic information about users. Facebook members share their likes and dislikes, brand loyalties, where they live, and so many other personal interests just by filling out their timelines, Liking business pages, and updating their status. Facebook doesn't sell this information, and each user controls what he or she shares or doesn't share with others. (Admittedly, though, it can be hard to *not* share on a platform such as Facebook.) What Facebook does do with that information is use it to allow advertisers to target users with their marketing. Because Facebook is and always will be a free platform, it makes money from advertisements.

If you run a business and are looking to get the biggest bang for your buck, Facebook ads aren't a bad way to go because you can reach a targeted audience. This chapter explains the considerations of setting up a Facebook ad and how to track your ad's success rate. We give you a pretty broad overview; if you really want to get into the nitty-gritty of Facebook advertising, we suggest getting a copy of *Facebook Marketing All-In-One For Dummies,* 3rd Edition, by Andrea Vahl (John Wiley & Sons, Inc.).

Finding Facebook Ads

Facebook ads appear in your news feed or in the right sidebar under your ticker, as shown in Figure 4-1. The ads you see are usually not too invasive and may have some interest for you. That's because Facebook and advertisers are trying to target the most useful ads for you based on the information you've shared in your personal timeline, your interactions with other pages in Facebook, or even who your friends are (and how they've interacted on Facebook).

Figure 4-1:
Facebook ads in the right sidebar.

> **Sponsored** 🖉 · Create Ad
>
> **Year-end referral bonus**
> Sprint ✈ — Switch a friend to Sprint by 12/31 and you'll get a $75 Reward Card. Restrictions
>
> **Verizon Wireless**
> verizonwireless.com
> New Nokia Lumia 928 — Buy the phone that lets you take photos worth sharing. Only on Verizon.
>
> **Great Wolf Lodge**
> greatwolf.com
> GREAT WOLF LODGE — Save up to 15% on a family getaway to our Indoor Waterpark Resort and experience Snowland!
>
> **Start Your Someday**
> bellevue.edu
> Earn your degree from Bellevue University. Private - Accredited - Non-Profit. Start Now!

You may see ads for external websites or Facebook pages such as business pages, events, and apps. Ads for Facebook-related items may also show which of your friends have Liked a business page or RSVP'd to an event. Seeing those connections with people you know provides *social proof* — reinforcement that your friends endorse something — and you may be more likely to complete an action (for example, Liking a business page).

Sometimes ads miss their mark. If you're seeing an ad you don't like or if an ad keeps coming up in your sidebar and you're tired of seeing it, you can remove it. Just move your mouse over the ad and click the X that appears. You have the option to hide the ad itself or hide all ads from the same advertiser. When you hide the ad, you can have a say in what kinds of ads you receive in the future. Unfortunately, you can't opt out of all advertisements.

If you're interested in seeing the types of ads Facebook thinks you would be interested in, go to www.facebook.com/ads/adboard.

Deciding Whether Facebook Ads Are Right for You

If you're looking to get the most bang for your advertising buck, Facebook ads may be just what you're looking for. We know at least some of your audience is using Facebook because it has more than 1.19 billion active users. And with that many users, just think of the new customers you can find!

Why is Facebook such a great place to advertise? Well, Facebook is in a unique position. It has access to specific demographic information for each user. Facebook allows advertisers to target ads to specifications regarding location (down to the ZIP code), gender, age, interests, education, and even employment. And, of course, you can use keywords as well. Heck, you can even target people whose birthdays are today! That kind of precise audience targeting means you should enjoy a healthy return on your investment.

Other benefits of using Facebook advertising include the ability to

✦ Target your audience in the following areas: post engagement, page Likes, clicks to website, website conversions, app installs, app engagement, event responses, and offer claims.

✦ Buy your ads based on cost per click (CPC) or cost per impression (CPM).

✦ See whether people completed an action within 24 hours of seeing your ad.

✦ Set your own daily or lifetime budget and pay only for what you use.

✦ Change any aspect of your ad (image, content, link, budget, and so on) during the ad's run.

✦ Stop the ad — even if the time isn't up yet.

If you've ever used other methods of advertising (online or offline), you know you don't always have this kind of flexibility.

Although you can advertise just about anything — business pages, groups, events, apps, and external websites — Facebook gives you two choices of ads: Facebook ads or sponsored stories.

Choosing an ad: Facebook ads

You can use a Facebook ad to attract interest for any page in Facebook (for example, a business page, a group, an event, or an app), or you can promote an external website. Any time you promote something in Facebook, it's called an *engagement ad,* and it includes two important parts:

✦ An opportunity to complete an action in the ad (instead of interrupting the user's flow by having to click over to your business page)

✦ Relevant actions by users connected to the viewer to help build awareness through social proof

For example, if a user sees your ad for your business page, the ad will include a Like button so that the person can Like the business page right from the ad and can see whether any of his or her Facebook friends Liked your business page as well. Figure 4-2 shows an example of an engagement ad.

Figure 4-2:
An engagement ad provides social proof and an opportunity to complete an action.

If you are using cost per click (CPC) for your ad, you're charged each time someone clicks Like or clicks through to your destination page.

Choosing an ad: sponsored stories

Sponsored stories (also called *featured stories*) are stories about a business page, a place, or an app that are already available in your news feed. A sponsored story may show a friend who Likes a business page, checks into a place, or Likes or shares a status update from a business page.

The interactions you see in a sponsored story (for example, Likes or shares) are interactions that already show up in your news feed or ticker. The difference is that a business or individual is paying for the sponsored story to be more prominent and less likely to be lost in the constant flow of information.

Figure 4-3 shows an example of a sponsored story ad that would appear in the right column. If the sponsored story ad were to appear in the news feed, it would look similar to the example in Figure 4-2. You decide in which position you want the ad to appear, as described later in the chapter, in "Text and Links section."

Figure 4-3:
A sponsored story ad.

Should you create an ad just to get Likes?

If you want to create an ad just to garner more Likes for your business page, you may do just that. But what use is it if you have a lot of followers, but no one is converting to a customer? It's more important to have followers who want to engage with your business, tell their friends about you, and eventually buy from you. To find those people, create your ad accordingly.

If you promote an ad that says you're giving away an iPad, you'll get a lot of traffic and Likes — but how many of those people are interested in your product(s) and how many just want to win an iPad? You may say, "But I just want to get as many eyes on my updates as possible!" We know, we know. Remember, just because someone Likes your business page, doesn't mean he or she sees your update. Users can hide your updates from their news feeds, stop interacting with your business page so that they don't see it as often in the top stories in their news feeds, or even Unlike your business page after they don't win the iPad.

Consider this: Having a bunch of followers who don't care about your brand could hurt you in the long run. Facebook uses an algorithm to determine how your business page performs in individual news feeds. That algorithm as well as the metric in Insights (Facebook's analytics program) called People Talking about This rely on your fans interacting with your shared content. If you have a hundred fans and many of them Like, comment on, and share your content, your ranking for your followers is probably high (meaning you're showing up in their news feeds regularly), and your People Talking about This number is high. If your People Talking about This number is high, it's likely that you have a wider reach because the friends of your fans see those interactions as well. That's all pretty good, right?

Now, say you have 100 Likes, and you run an ad that promises an iPad giveaway. You end up getting 1,000 total Likes. You just increased your fan base by 1,000 percent. But what if only the original 100 fans are still talking about you and the new fans are just ignoring you because they were only interested in the giveaway? Facebook looks at your overall fan base and the number of people interacting with your content, so it looks like you've had a huge drop in engagement. Consequently, your overall rank drops, and you aren't showing up as much in people's news feeds — especially the new followers who didn't really care about your brand or product and so aren't Liking, commenting, or sharing.

Which would you rather have? A smaller number of followers who are more likely to help you spread the word about your products and buy from you, or a large number of followers who do nothing at all?

You can enable sponsored stories by selecting the box on the left side of the Text and Links section if applicable. Not all ads offer this choice.

Knowing what you can't do with ads

Facebook has guidelines for everything. It has terms of service for your personal timeline and your business page, guidelines for giveaways and contests, and yes, guidelines for advertisements. Facebook must approve each ad you create, so it makes sense to know what you can and can't do with your ads. If you don't comply, Facebook rejects your ad.

You can read the guidelines in their entirety at www.facebook.com/ad_guidelines.php. Here are a few examples of what you are not allowed to advertise (again, read the guidelines for a full list):

✦ Pornography

✦ Alcohol, drugs, or tobacco

✦ Gambling or lotteries

✦ Pharmaceuticals and supplements

✦ Any site that uses domain forwarding (that is, you think you're going to one website and end up on another)

✦ Any site that contains spyware or malware

✦ Weapons and explosives

Facebook won't double-check your ad to be sure it's legal — that's completely up to you. If your ad doesn't comply with the law, you, not Facebook, are liable.

Creating Your Facebook Ad

You can start the ad-creation process in about eleventy billion ways. Okay, we're exaggerating. But Facebook does give you several opportunities to click and create an ad on just about every page you browse. We show you one of the ways. However, realize that whenever you see a Create Ad link, you can click it and the steps to create the ad will be largely the same.

To get started with a Facebook ad, go to www.facebook.com/ads/create. You see the Advertise on Facebook page, which offers all the options you need to create a Facebook advertisement. The page has the following sections:

✦ What Kind of Results Do You Want for Your Ads?

✦ Select Images

✦ Text and Links

✦ Audience

✦ Account and Campaign

✦ Bidding and Pricing

We explain each section more thoroughly in the next few pages.

What Kind of Results Do You Want for Your Ads? section

The main section of the Advertise on Facebook page is shown in Figure 4-4.

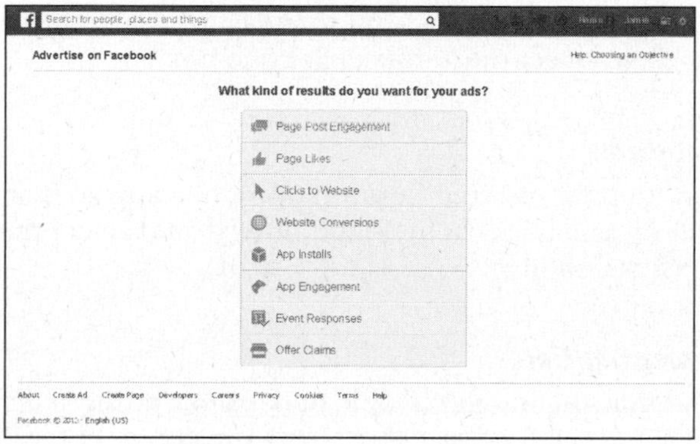

Figure 4-4:
Options
for creat-
ing your
Facebook
ad.

You have eight choices to help you focus your goals and results, as detailed next.

Page Post Engagement option

Select the Page Post Engagement option to expand the reach of your page posts to attract more comments, shares, Likes, and photo and video views. Then enter your business page or URL, and a menu appears listing the posts that you can promote. Select one and click Continue. If you do not want to select a current post, you can click the + button and create a new page post.

Page Likes option

If you want to promote your page to get more Likes, select the Page Likes option. On the right, enter the business page or URL, and you see the main advertising page.

Clicks to Website option

To drive traffic to your website, select the Clicks to Website option. In the box on the right, type the URL of the website, and the main advertising page appears.

Website Conversions option

A conversion-tracking pixel is code that will track desired conversions such as downloads, sign-ups, and sales on your website.

Select the Website Conversions option when you want to promote individual conversions on your website. On the right side of the screen, enter the URL that you want to promote. A drop-down menu appears with the types of conversions you can track: Checkouts, Registrations, Leads, Key Web Page Views, Adds to Cart, and Other Web Conversions.

Select the type of conversion you want to measure, and if desired, give it a custom name. Then select the Terms of Service box.

App Installs option

When you want to promote your desktop or mobile app so that users will install it, select App Installs. On the right, browse and select the app or enter its URL. Then click Continue.

App Engagement option

To create an ad that encourages people to use your desktop app, select App Engagement. On the right, browse and select the app or enter its URL. Then click Continue.

Event Responses option

Have an event that you want to promote? Select Event Responses, and then browse and select the event or enter its URL. Then click Continue.

Offer Claims option

Have you created an offer and want to promote it? Select the last option on the page, Offer Claims. On the right side, select the business page or URL that has the offer you want to promote. Then make a selection from the menu of posts that appears. If you want to create a new offer instead, click the + button.

Select Images section

After you select an option in the preceding section (you may or may not have to click Continue), your selection appears at the top of the Advertise on Facebook page. The next section on the page is the Select Images section, which is shown in Figure 4-5.

You can upload up to six images to create additional ads that Facebook will rotate at no extra charge. Whichever ad performs better will be shown, so it's to your advantage to use six images. Each image should be 600 x 225 pixels.

You have the option to upload new images, select images from your library, or choose a stock image courtesy of Shutterstock. After you upload the images, you can reposition them to your liking.

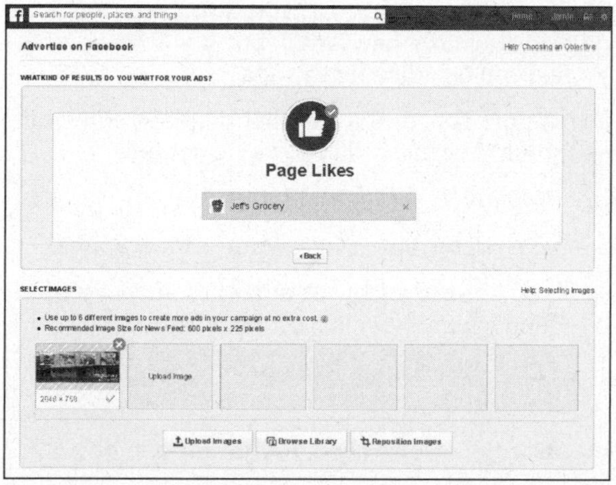

Figure 4-5:
The Select
Images sec-
tion of the
Advertise on
Facebook
page.

Text and Links section

Your ad appears to the right of the Text and Links section, as shown in
Figure 4-6, and the options appear on the left.

Figure 4-6:
Choosing
where your
ad will
appear.

Depending on the ad type you chose, you'll see some or all of the following
options:

+ **Headline:** Your main text goes here.

+ **Text:** Type supporting text here.

+ **Sponsored Stories:** Reach the friends of your friends.

✦ **Connect Facebook Page:** If you're promoting your website, this option will link to your site in the news feed, but it will be seen as one of your business pages. You can disable this feature.

✦ **Advanced Options:** This drop-down list displays some or all of the following, depending on which ad type you selected:

- *URL Tags:* Append or replace URL tags.

- *Ad Placements:* Determine where your ad will appear.

- *Landing View:* Choose a view or app on your page where you want people to land when they click on your link.

- *News Feed Link Description:* Explain why people should go to your site.

✦ **Ad Placements:** Select News Feed, Right Column, or both.

Audience section

One of the biggest draws for using Facebook ads is the capability to fine-tune who sees your ads. You can customize your audience right down to the ZIP code you want to reach, if you like.

Move down the screen until you see the next section, Audience, as shown in Figure 4-7.

Figure 4-7: The targeting information you choose determines your ad's potential audience.

Pay close attention to the Audience Definition section in the upper-right corner. As you customize your targeted audience by making selections on the left, the number for your potential reach changes.

If you haven't looked at your Insights data yet, now is a good time to check them out. (See Chapter 3 of this minibook for details on how to use your data.) Insights, Facebook's analytics program, provides important demographic and engagement information about your current audience. You can use that data to determine the target audience for your ad.

You can start targeting your audience based on location, age, gender, interests, and who they're connected to. You can go even further by including specific relationship status, language, education, and employment information. Each Facebook user has shared a certain amount of data pertaining to his or her life, and Facebook uses that information to help you reach the best audience for your business or product ads.

Account and Campaign section

The next step in setting up your Facebook ad or sponsored story campaign is determining how much you want to spend, when you want to run your campaign, and whether you want to pay for clicks or impressions (and how much you're willing to pay for each). These items are shown in Figure 4-8.

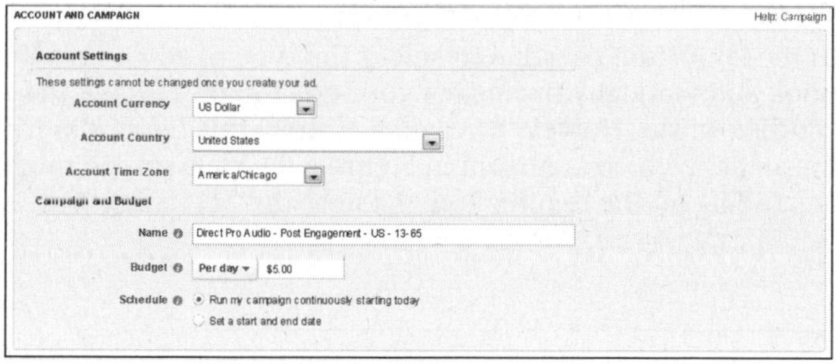

Figure 4-8: Determining the budget for your campaign.

ACCOUNT AND CAMPAIGN	Help: Campaign

Account Settings

These settings cannot be changed once you create your ad.

Account Currency	US Dollar
Account Country	United States
Account Time Zone	America/Chicago

Campaign and Budget

Name	Direct Pro Audio - Post Engagement - US - 13-65
Budget	Per day ▼ $5.00
Schedule	● Run my campaign continuously starting today
	○ Set a start and end date

First, under Account Settings, you need to set up the currency, country, and time zone for your account. After you create your ad, these selections cannot be changed, so make sure you choose correctly.

The second subsection is titled Campaign and Budget. Facebook allows you to group similar ads into *campaigns*. Each campaign can have multiple similar ads. This feature is useful when you want to see which ad works best. Each time you create an ad, you can put it in an existing campaign or you can create a new campaign. When choosing a name, you might want something that indicates your goals or distinguishes your different ads.

When setting your budget, you can choose to spend a specific amount per day or to set a lifetime budget. When you set a daily budget, Facebook will promote your ad until the ad has met its budget for the day. The next day, the process starts over. So if you have a budget of $50 per day, Facebook shows your ad until it meets that $50 parameter. Then tomorrow, Facebook shows the ad again until it reaches its $50 limit. Facebook continues to show the ad until the end date you set.

Be careful! If you want to spend $50 total, but want your ad to run for five days, you need to set your daily budget to $10 and set the dates accordingly. Otherwise, you may end up paying quite a bit more than you intended for a campaign. Pay special attention to your end date. Facebook automatically sets the end date a month from the start date, so you may have to change it.

By default, your campaign is set to run continuously. If you want to set specific dates for your campaign, click the Set a Start and End Date option. Start and end dates appear for you to set. Enter a starting and ending date and a time, adjusted for your own time zone.

Suppose you have a campaign that is set to run for five days. If you've limited your daily budget, Facebook will stop displaying your ad when you've reached that daily budget. Facebook won't continue to display your ad and then charge you more.

Bidding and Pricing section

One of the important reasons to select the type of ad you want is that Facebook automatically optimizes your ad. You don't have to understand how bidding works. However, you can control this feature in the Bidding and Pricing section, which is shown in Figure 4-9. (Your screen might look different, depending on the results you chose at the beginning.)

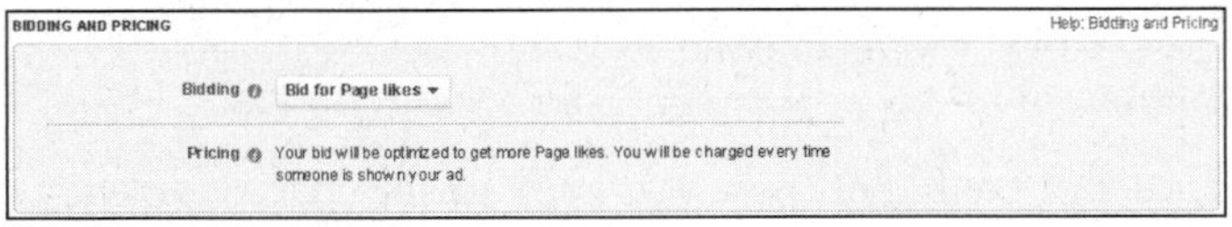

Figure 4-9: The Bidding and Pricing section.

> BIDDING AND PRICING   Help: Bidding and Pricing
>
> Bidding ⊘ Bid for Page likes ▾
>
> Pricing ⊘ Your bid will be optimized to get more Page likes. You will be charged every time someone is shown your ad.

If you want to optimize for something other than what Facebook suggests, you can select either Bid for Clicks or Bid for Impressions. The screen changes as shown in Figure 4-10.

Ad pricing is based on either cost per impression (CPM) or cost per click (CPC). *CPM* stands for cost per *mille* (which is French for 1,000; M is the Roman numeral for one thousand — CPM seems to make sense in every language except English). When you choose the CPM model, you're choosing to pay for every thousand times the ad is seen. Choose this option if it's more important for your ad to be seen than for people to click it. CPM works well when you're trying to build brand awareness.

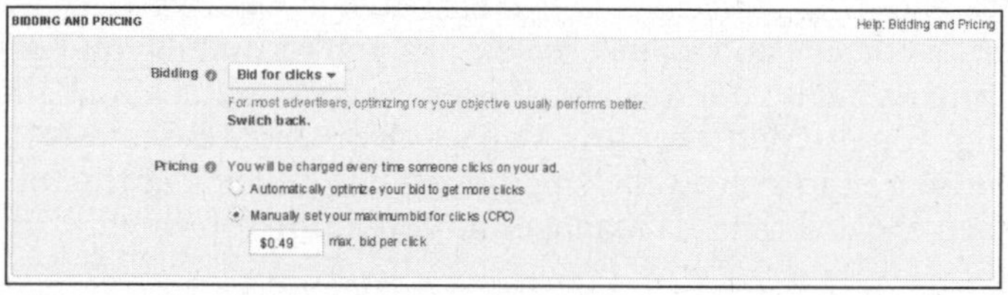

Figure 4-10:
Customized
pricing
options.

BIDDING AND PRICING   Help: Bidding and Pricing

Bidding ⓘ   Bid for clicks ▾

For most advertisers, optimizing for your objective usually performs better.
Switch back.

Pricing ⓘ   You will be charged every time someone clicks on your ad.

⚪ Automatically optimize your bid to get more clicks

⦿ Manually set your maximum bid for clicks (CPC)

$0.49   max. bid per click

CPC stands for cost per click. You pay only when someone clicks your ad — this action can include clicking the Like button, submitting an RSVP to an event, clicking through the ad and landing on the destination page, and so on. Choose this option if it's more important for people to complete an action.

When you set your bid, you're determining what you're willing to pay for a click or an impression. The least amount you can pay for CPC is $0.01 and the least you can pay for CPM is $0.02. However, it's unlikely that ads with those bids would ever be seen. Facebook uses an auction-type system to determine which ads are shown. Basically, all ads and sponsored stories are competing for the same ad space. When you place your bid, it's wise to use the maximum amount you're willing to pay for CPM or CPC. Facebook will calculate the least you would have to pay to "win" your ad space. That price may be lower than the maximum price you submitted. For instance, if you say you'll pay $5 for each click, but the next lowest bid is $3, Facebook sees that you have a higher maximum and will sell the space to you for, say, $3 instead of the $5 you bid. On the other hand, if you're in a competitive niche, you may end up paying that full $5 (but not more than your bid; if you want to raise your bid later, you can).

Facebook gives you a suggested range for your bid based on your target audience, your keywords (that is, interests), and so on. You don't have to bid more than the minimum of a penny or two, but you'll have more success if you make a reasonable bid based on Facebook's suggestions.

Review

After you've designed your ad, targeted your audience, and determined your budget, click the Review Order button. A page appears, showing you what your ad will look like. You have the opportunity to edit the page as needed. When you're ready to go, click Place Order. If you don't have a payment option set up in your account, you will be asked to select one. Otherwise, you see the Facebook Ads Manager page.

It can take up to 24 hours for Facebook to approve your ad.

Finding and Using the Facebook Ads Manager

The Facebook Ads Manager, which is shown in Figure 4-11, is the command center for the ads and sponsored stories you're running on Facebook. From here, you can edit your ads and stories, as well as track how they're performing. You can find your Ads Manager by navigating to www.facebook.com/ads/manage or by clicking the See Insights link at the top of the page and then clicking the Ads Manager button at the top right.

Figure 4-11: The Ads Manager page gives you an overview of your campaign's performance.

Understanding the left navigation options

Your main Ads Manager page has links in the left column that allow you to quickly move from one page to another to manage various aspects of your account:

✦ **Campaign and Ads:** If you click the Campaign & Ads link in the left sidebar, you see a page similar to Figure 4-12, with two sections: Notifications and Daily Spend. *Notifications* are updates on the status of ads (for example, whether they've been approved or whether Facebook charged your credit card on file). *Daily spend* is how much your ads cost you on a daily basis.

Under the Notifications and Daily Spend sections are your campaigns along with ten metrics: Your Campaign name, Status, Results, Cost, Reach, Start Date, End Date, Budget, Remaining Budget, and Total Spent.

If you're not reaching enough of your target audience, tweak your campaign. You may need to raise your bid so that your ads appear more frequently.

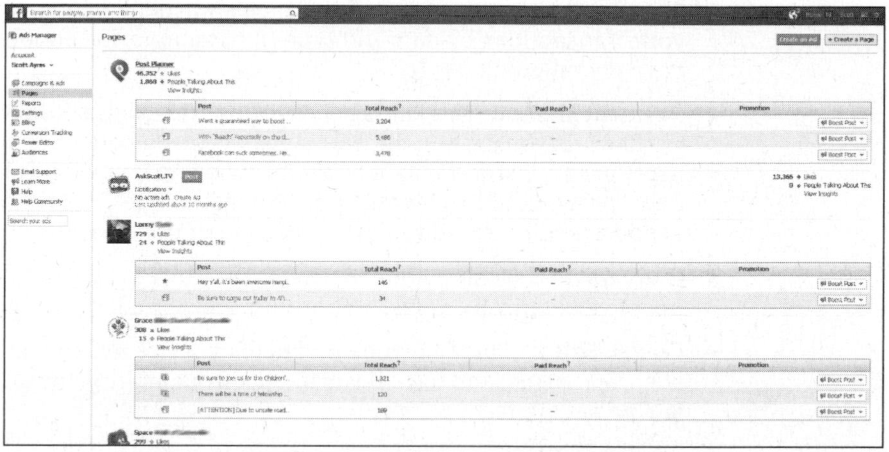

Figure 4-12:
The Pages link in the left navigation allows you to see stats and promote your posts.

✦ **Pages:** Click the Pages link to see a list of business pages you own or are the administrator of. You can quickly see how your business pages are doing, and you can promote or boost a post right from here. You can see page notifications, when you last updated, total page Likes, and weekly activity.

If you click the name of a business page, you navigate to that page. If you click the gear icon in the upper-right corner and select a business page in the Use Facebook As section, you switch to using Facebook as that business page. (See Book IV, Chapter 2 for an explanation of how to use Facebook as a business page instead of as yourself.)

✦ **Reports:** You can run reports about how your ads, stories, and campaigns are performing so you can decide if they need to be tweaked or are fine as is. The reports include data such as impressions, clicks, connections, and spend. We explain more about reports in the next section.

✦ **Settings:** Click this link to see your Ad Account Settings page. On this page, you can find your account ID, close your ad account, and set your business name and address. If you're located in the European Union, you can enter your EU VAT number here as well. This is also where you can set your permissions and e-mail notifications.

✦ **Billing:** Your Billing page provides an overview of any outstanding balances, your daily spend limit, and your account spend limit. Your daily and account spend limits are the maximum Facebook will allow you to spend — not necessarily the bid or limit you set when creating your ad or story.

Facebook won't charge you more than the limit you set, but it lets you know what your limit is if you'd like to change your settings. For instance, if you set the daily spending limit at $25, your Facebook daily limit may be $250. Facebook knows that you set the limit at $25 and won't allow you to spend more than that in a given day. However, you can up the limit as high as necessary up to $250.

In addition to monitoring your balance and spend limits, you can check your transactions by date and type (for example, Facebook coupons, PayPal, and credit card).

✦ **Payment Method:** This link is below Billing. This page shows you which credit cards you have on file. You can add a credit card or debit card, connect your PayPal account, or add a Facebook Ad coupon by clicking the Add New Payment Method button in the top-right corner. Follow the directions to add a credit card, add a PayPal account, or use a Facebook ad coupon.

✦ **Conversion Tracking:** Here is where you can keep track of actions that people take on your website after they view or click through your ads.

✦ **Power Editor:** This Facebook tool helps you create, edit, and manage ads, campaigns, and page posts in bulk from multiple business pages and ad accounts.

✦ **Audiences:** Manage groups of people that you want to view your ad. You can save these groups and use them for different campaigns in the future.

✦ **Learn More:** Facebook has an extensive library of help files for Facebook ads. Click the Learn More link to start finding the answers you need. Here are few additional resources you may want to check out:

- *Facebook's business section:* www.facebook.com/business

- *Facebook help files for advertising:* www.facebook.com/help/ads-and-business-solutions

- *Facebook advertising guidelines:* www.facebook.com/ad_guidelines.php

Generating a Report

The data Facebook collects for your ads, stories, and campaigns can be an invaluable resource for you as you gauge whether your ads are working. To run a report, click the Full Report button below the Notifications section on the Ads Manager Campaigns page or click the Reports button in the left navigation. With either method, the Facebook Ads Reporting page appears, as shown in Figure 4-13.

This page has four buttons at the top of the page:

✦ **Schedule:** Run a weekly report and receive it through e-mail. To schedule reporting, click the Schedule button. In the Schedule Report window that appears, complete the form and then click Schedule.

✦ **Save:** Save the report in Facebook.

✦ **Share:** Create a link to the report so you can send it to others. You may shorten the link through Facebook's link shortener.

✦ **Export:** Run a report and save it to your desktop as a .csv (comma separated value) or .xls file that you can open in Excel or Numbers.

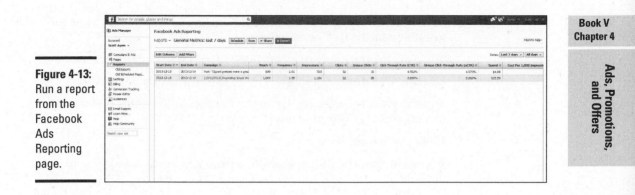

Figure 4-13:
Run a report
from the
Facebook
Ads
Reporting
page.

Adding or Deleting an Ads Account Administrator

It's always a good idea to have a back-up plan. Jamie likes to have at least
one other trusted person as an admin on his business page and his Facebook
ads account. That way, if he's locked out for some reason, he still has a spare
key, so to speak.

When you add someone to your Facebook Ads account, the person may
have access to your credit card information. It's important to grant privileges only to someone you trust.

To add an administrator to your Facebook ads account, follow these steps:

1. **Navigate to** www.facebook.com/ads/manage or select the Ads
   Manager button at the top of the Insights page.

2. **Select the account in the left sidebar.**

3. **Click the Settings link in the left navigation and scroll down the page
   until you see Ad Account Roles, as shown in Figure 4-14.**

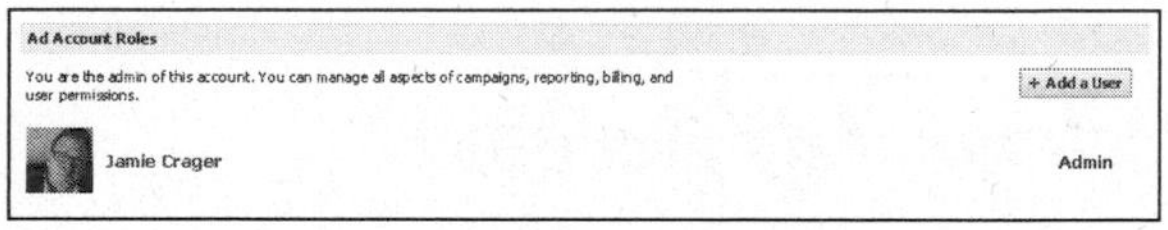

Figure 4-14:
The Ad
Account
Roles sec-
tion on the
Settings
page.

> **Ad Account Roles**
>
> You are the admin of this account. You can manage all aspects of campaigns, reporting, billing, and
> user permissions.   **+ Add a User**
>
> Jamie Crager   Admin

4. **Click the +Add a User button.**

   The Add a New User to This Ads Account window appears.

5. **In the text box, type the name of the person to whom you want to grant administrative permissions.**

   You can type the name of a Facebook friend or an e-mail address.

6. **Use the drop-down list to determine the new user's permissions.**

   You can grant the user access to the full account settings (General User) or only reports (Reports Only).

7. **Click the Submit button.**

   A window appears stating that the person has been added to your account.

8. **Click Okay.**

   The new administrator appears under Ad Account Roles on your Settings page.

Someday, you may need to delete an administrator. Follow these steps:

1. **Navigate to** `www.facebook.com/ads/manage` or select the Ads Manager button at the top of the Insights page.

2. **Select the account in the left sidebar.**

3. **Click the Settings link in the left navigation and scroll down the page until you see Ad Account Roles.**

4. **Click the X next to the user's permission status (for example, General User).**

   A window appears, asking if you want to remove this person from your account.

5. **Click Remove.**

   A window appears confirming that the person is removed from your account.

6. **Click Okay.**

   The person is removed from your account and no longer appears in your Ad Account Roles area.

Closing Your Facebook Ads Account

If you decide Facebook ads just aren't for you, no problem. When you close your Facebook ads account, any active ads, stories, and campaigns will cease and you won't be able to create new ones. Facebook will charge any leftover balance to your credit card on file and then delete the card from your account.

TIP

If you think you may want to return to Facebook ads later, pause your account instead of closing it. To pause your account, click the Campaign and Ads link. From there, change the status of each ad, story, and campaign to Paused.

To close your Facebook ads account, follow these steps:

1. **Navigate to** www.facebook.com/ads/manage or select the Ads Manager button at the top of the Insights page.

2. **Select the account in the left sidebar.**

3. **Click the Settings link in the left navigation pane.**

4. **Click the Close Ads Account link at the bottom-right corner.**

   The Close Ads Account window appears.

5. **Select the reason(s) you're closing your account (or type a reason in the text box labeled Other).**

6. **Click the Close Ads Account button.**

   It may take up to two days for Facebook to completely close out your account.

Using Facebook Promotions to Market Your Business

As a business page admin, you'll be interested in creating ways to encourage new visitors to become followers. One way to convert visitors is to offer them the chance to win something.

In this section, we explain why you may want to host a Facebook promotion and how to interpret the Facebook promotions guidelines (fb.com/promotions_guidelines.php) so you don't run the risk of losing your business page and its community. We also explain the concept of Like-gating content and help you find some great tools to administer your promotions.

Running a Facebook promotion is an excellent way to promote your business page, bring attention to a specific product or service (especially a new launch), and possibly garner more Likes for your page. First, some Facebook definitions:

✦ A *promotion* is either a contest or a giveaway.

✦ A *contest* is a promotion in which users are asked to submit something that will be voted on, either by the public, the business page owner, or a panel of judges. The winner of a contest is whoever receives the most votes.

✦ A *giveaway* (also called sweepstakes) is a promotion of chance. Users are asked to complete an entry form, and a winner is chosen at random.

It's okay to use the words *giveaway* and *sweepstakes* interchangeably, but you wouldn't use *giveaway* and *contest* interchangeably because they are different beasts.

Giveaways and contests are fun and easy ways to drive traffic to your business page. They aren't expensive to run (depending on what you're giving away), and your fans love to win something! The benefits for you as a company could include

✦ Bringing more people to your business page

✦ Increasing your business page Likes by Like-gating the entry form (as discussed later in the chapter)

✦ Increasing your e-mail list by collecting e-mail addresses on the entry form (which are needed to contact the winner)

✦ Recording important demographic information or product feedback by incorporating a short survey as part of the entry form

✦ Inspiring followers and customers to share their own experiences related to your brand via a story, a photo, or a video contest

You must be clear about what information you're gathering and how you'll use the information. For example, if you're collecting e-mail addresses, let followers know if you're going to automatically subscribe them to your newsletter — and give them an opt-out option.

Getting the word out

When you create your Facebook promotion, remember that you need to get the word out. It stands to reason that you'll tell your Facebook followers about your promotion, but you may be interested in reaching beyond your current followers. To reach a wider audience, you need to integrate your Facebook promotions with all your other outlets: Twitter, a blog or website, an e-mail newsletter, and even offline in your store.

People won't know about the promotion unless you tell them. Write status updates on Facebook and Twitter that include a link directly to your Facebook promotion entry form, publish a blog post explaining the promotion and its purpose (and the prize, of course). Take advantage of your e-newsletter list and send out an alert that you're having a promotion on Facebook, and then suggest that people forward your newsletter to their friends so they can enter as well. If you have a bricks-and-mortar venue, ask employees to remind your customers to find your Facebook page online and enter to win.

Using a strong call to action

When you're hosting a Facebook promotion, you'll probably be posting status updates telling people about it. Unfortunately, many people do this task half-heartedly, so they don't see a great response. A strong call to action is important in all your marketing efforts — and most important on Facebook. Facebook visitors move fast. They skim their news feeds for video, pictures, and links. In other words, they're looking for action. Consider this sample status update:

> One day left to enter our giveaway! Win a full pass to our conference!

The previous status update looks interesting, but it has a weak call to action and doesn't offer a way to complete the action. Instead, try a status update like this one:

> Enter to win a full pass to the International Marketing Conference! Just complete the entry form at http://bitly./link! Good luck!

Note that this status update tells you exactly what you can win (a pass to the International Marketing Conference), has a clear call to action (complete the entry form), and tells you how to complete the task (with a link to the form).

When you include a link in your status update, don't send your followers to your business page! If you do, they may not know how to find the entry form, and even if they can find the entry form, it's an extra step. Every navigation tab on your business page has its own URL. Send followers directly to the entry form tab. This method is more efficient and will give you a higher rate of completion. To find the URL for any custom tab on your business page, follow these instructions:

1. **Use your browser to navigate to your business page.**

    Below your cover photo, you see your apps.

2. **Click the app to which you want to send followers (in this case, the app for your giveaway).**

    If you can't see the app you want to use, click More next to the fourth application box to reveal the rest of your apps.

3. **Copy the new URL from your browser's address bar.**

4. **Click the** *(Your Page Name)* **link next to your profile picture at the top left of the page to return to your business page.**

5. **Paste the URL in your status update box, and then type a status update with a strong call to action.**

6. **Click the Share button to share your update with your followers.**

If you want to track how many people click the link in your status update, use a link-shortening and -tracking tool such as bitly. Visit `http://bitly.com` and create an account, and then return to your Facebook business page and follow these instructions:

1. **Copy the URL of the destination tab.**

   To find the URL, see Step 3 in the preceding set of instructions.

2. **Navigate your browser to** `http://bitly.com` **and log in.**

3. **Paste the URL in the text box.**

4. **Click the Shorten button.**

5. **Copy the resulting shortened link.**

6. **Return to your business page and copy the bitly link into your new status update.**

When you want to see how many people have clicked your link, return to bitly and check your dashboard. You may be surprised how many times followers clicked your link!

You can see how many people have clicked your links also via your business page Insights.

Understanding the promotions guidelines

Many businesses and bloggers running Facebook promotions don't realize that Facebook has guidelines regarding how you can (and can't) administer a promotion on Facebook. As a result, many businesses run the risk of losing their business pages because they run improper giveaways or contests. You can find the guidelines at `http://facebook.com/promotions_guidelines.php`.

The Facebook promotions guidelines are pretty self-explanatory. Be sure to follow them and you shouldn't have any problems.

Before you create a Facebook promotion, it's important to understand the federal and state laws that govern sweepstakes, contests, and lotteries. It's a good idea to talk to a lawyer before you start your promotion (and that goes for promotions on your website, blog, Facebook, or anywhere else you're holding one) to ensure that you're in compliance with the law. "Everyone else was doing it" won't help you should someone bring a lawsuit against you.

Because you can't install third-party apps on your personal timeline, you won't be able to run a giveaway or contest on your personal timeline.

One of the applications we discuss later in this chapter is ShortStack. If you use ShortStack to create your promotion, it provides some nice verbiage you can include in your giveaway that adheres to the Facebook rules. The text is placed clearly on the promotion and ensures that you're adhering to promotion guidelines. Figure 4-15 shows how your giveaway may look using ShortStack's verbiage.

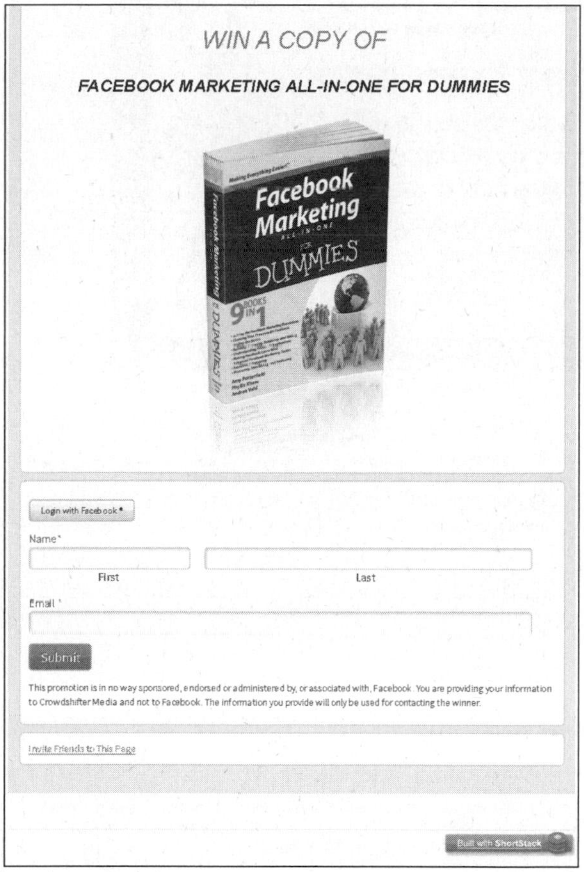

WIN A COPY OF

FACEBOOK MARKETING ALL-IN-ONE FOR DUMMIES

Figure 4-15: Be sure to include a notice releasing Facebook of liability related to your promotion.

ShortStack also enables you to create content that only followers can see. Figure 4-16 shows a promotion that has been Like-gated. Note that the gate page asks the user to Like the page to reveal the entry form. Figure 4-17 shows what users see after they click Like and reveal the entry form. From here, they can enter the promotion and hope for a win!

Figure 4-16: A Like-gated promotion page.

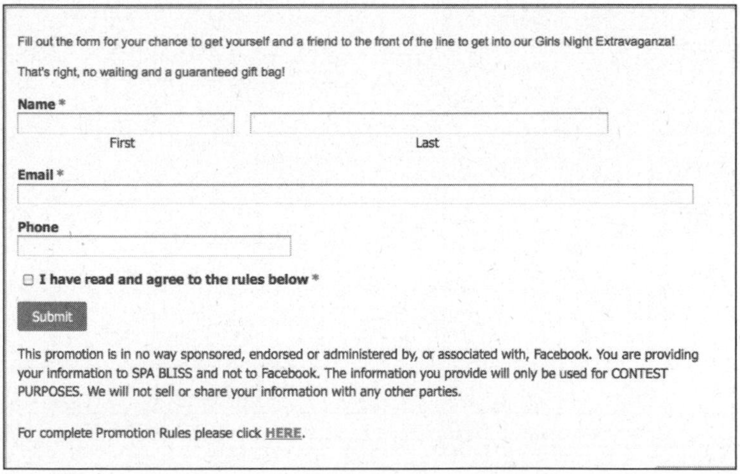

Figure 4-17: The entry form is revealed after the user clicks the Like button.

Fill out the form for your chance to get yourself and a friend to the front of the line to get into our Girls Night Extravaganza!

That's right, no waiting and a guaranteed gift bag!

Name *

First   Last

Email *

Phone

☐ **I have read and agree to the rules below** *

[Submit]

This promotion is in no way sponsored, endorsed or administered by, or associated with, Facebook. You are providing your information to SPA BLISS and not to Facebook. The information you provide will only be used for CONTEST PURPOSES. We will not sell or share your information with any other parties.

For complete Promotion Rules please click HERE.

Using Apps to Create Customized Giveaways and Contests

The biggest complaint we hear about the Facebook promotions guidelines is "But it's just so easy to do it on the business page. I don't want the hassle of setting up an application! That sucks the fun out of it."

We suspect what these complaints mean is that the page admins think setting up a promotion via a Facebook application will be hard and they'd rather just post a status update because that's easy and they already know how to do it. We have good news for you: The companies who create Facebook promotions applications understand the need for an easy way to set up promotions. In the following sections, we list a few of the most popular apps so you have a starting place.

With most of these tools, you can be up and running with a promotion in less than 15 minutes. It's true that setting up a promotion via an app is still not as fast as creating a simple status update, but this way, you don't risk losing your business page!

ShortStack

ShortStack (http://shortstack.com) offers Facebook applications that allow you to create custom tabs for your business page. The one that concerns you in this chapter is the app that allows you to create a Facebook promotion (including Like-gating if you want; note that ShortStack calls it "fan only" content). You could also create a printable coupon or a contact form. Or you could share images and video from an external site or pull in PDF documents using www.scribd.com and a ShortStack app. ShortStack has five plans, ranging from free up to $300 a month, depending on the features you choose.

A few things to know about ShortStack:

✦ You can use ShortStack for free if your Business Page has fewer than 2,000 Likes.

✦ You can Like-gate content on a custom tab with the click of a button.

✦ You can schedule your promotion to auto-publish in the future, and ShortStack takes care of everything.

✦ You can include custom CSS or templates featuring your logo or design in ShortStack widgets to reinforce your brand.

✦ You can manage multiple client sites with a single account.

WARNING!

If you disregard the promotions guidelines . . .

So what happens if you don't follow the rules? You could lose your business page. Think about that. If you lose your business page, you lose your

✔ Content (images, video, notes, status updates . . . *everything*)

✔ Community (all your followers)

✔ Credibility (trust is what social media is built on)

The applications we describe in the "Using Apps to Create Customized Giveaways and Contests" section all have point-and-click interfaces that are easy to use. Those tools were built with a firm understanding of the

Facebook promotional guidelines and have a few built-in features to make it easy for you to adhere to the rules. It doesn't make sense to risk losing your hard-earned Facebook community when it's easy to create a promotion that adheres to the Facebook promotions guidelines.

If you do lose your business page, you can head over to the form at `www.facebook.com/help/contact/183000765122339` and complete it to try to reinstate your business page. We warn you, though, that reinstating a business page is difficult. Most companies who have lost a business page have had to start it from scratch and rebuild their community.

Wildfire

Wildfire (`http://wildfireapp.com`) has a robust cache of applications to help you create a contest or giveaway as well as to customize your business page. Wildfire is social marketing software for enterprise companies.

A few things to know about Wildfire:

✦ You can publish your campaign to multiple outlets at the same time.

✦ You can run several types of promotions, including sweepstakes; coupons; user-generated photo, essay, and video contests; and quizzes.

✦ Use the dashboard to publish campaigns and view analytics, leads, and results.

Strutta

Strutta (`www.strutta.com`) enables you to create promotions that can stand alone or live on Facebook. It's a premium tool, and pricing starts at $399 for sweepstakes and $999 for contests. If you want to customize your promotion, you need to upgrade to the Pro version. The interface is very user friendly, which makes creating your promotion a breeze.

A few things to know about Strutta:

✦ You can optimize your promotion for mobile devices.

✦ You can use Strutta's analytics or your Google Analytics tracking code to track your promotion's success.

✦ You can use Strutta's promotions tools outside Facebook. Embed your contest or giveaway on your blog or website.

✦ The basic templates are clean and attractive.

Creating Best Practices for Your Facebook Promotion

Following Facebook's promotions guidelines is the first step to hosting your contest or giveaway. Beyond adhering to Facebook's rules, though, you need to make sure your promotion is fulfilling your own goals. Do you want to increase your e-mail list? Do you want to draw attention to a specific product or service? Are you interested in expanding your base of followers? Do you want your Facebook community to participate more? Whatever your goals are, be sure you know how you're going to reach them. To that end, it makes sense to create your own set of best practices. In this section we offer some ideas to get you started.

Know the goals of your promotion

How can you determine whether a promotion is a success if you don't know what you want to achieve? Write down measureable goals (for example, "Our business page will garner 150 new Likes" is better than "increase the number of Likes"), and then decide two things:

✦ What do you need to offer your audience (the prize) to entice them to share information (via the entry form)?

✦ What information do you need to collect from your entrants to meet your goals?

The more valuable the prize, the more participants are willing to share their information. If you're offering a $25 gift card, don't expect your entrants to complete a lengthy survey. If you're offering a vacation, though, people are more willing to answer some questions for you or jump through some hoops.

Keep hoops to a minimum

Our experience with running promotions is that people want free stuff, and they don't want to put a lot of work into entering a promotion. On the other hand, as the business owner, you have certain goals you're trying to reach. The key to balancing both is keeping the barrier to entry commiserate with what you're offering for a prize. If you're offering something small as a prize, your followers are less likely to do more than Like your business page. However, if you're offering an iPad or a trip as a prize, your followers will be more forgiving of the hoops you make them jump through for entry.

In general, the barrier to entry as it relates to likelihood of entry is as follows:

✦ Completing an entry form is the easiest form of entry and will probably result in the most entries and traffic. People are most interested in promotions in which they don't have to exert a lot of effort but have a reasonable expectation of payoff.

✦ Liking a business page to access an entry form (that is, like-gating your entry form) is the next highest barrier to entry and may or may not decrease the traffic to your promotion. However, be aware that you may see a drop in Likes after the promotion ends because those who didn't win may Unlike your business page.

✦ User-generated content is the highest barrier to entry. Although you may have fewer entries in this type of promotion, those entering are usually brand enthusiasts or serious about sharing their own information to enhance their visibility to your audience. Examples of user-generated content for a promotion could be inviting entrants to share original recipes or a story about your product, or submitting photos or video based on specific criteria.

Provide the what, why, and how

Tell entrants what information you require, why you require it, and how you'll use it in the future. If you need both an e-mail address and a street address, tell your entrants why. Are you going to add those addresses to your database and send them periodic notifications via e-mail and snail-mail? Or will you add their e-mail address to your newsletter or e-mail list, but only use their street address for shipping purposes and then delete it from your database?

Your audience needs to know these details when deciding whether to participate in your giveaway. The way you plan to keep and use their information may determine whether they choose to enter the giveaway.

Go beyond your current followers

If you're running a Facebook promotion on your business page, it stands to reason you'll tell your followers about it. But if the purpose of your promotion is to spread the word about a specific product or service, to create buzz around an idea, or even to increase your page Likes, you need to garner attention beyond your existing fan base. You can do that by

✦ *Using a Facebook ad with your Facebook promotion.* You can target Facebook ads to specific audiences based on interests, location, or even friends. Be sure to create your Facebook ad with a strong call to action and include a direct link to your Facebook promotion.

✦ *Promoting your contest or giveaway on other social channels.* Facebook shouldn't be your only social media outlet. More likely than not, Facebook is just one of the ways you're creating community. Use your Twitter, website, and blog outlets as well as QR codes or signs in your bricks-and-mortar store to spread the word.

Using Facebook Offers to Reach New Customers

You can post an offer on your business page for your targeted audience. When people claim your offer, they receive an e-mail message that they can bring to your store or business to redeem.

Your business page must have 50 or more Likes to create an offer.

To create an offer, follow these steps:

1. **In your business page's status update box, click the Offer, Event+ link, as shown in Figure 4-18, and then select Offer.**

    A pop-up box appears.

Figure 4-18:
Creating a
Facebook
offer.

2. **Provide the following information about your offer: a headline, an image, an expiration date, the audience, the budget, and the reach.**

3. **Click the Create Offer button.**

Remember to follow Facebook's guidelines concerning offers. For details, go to www.facebook.com/page_guidelines.php.

Chapter 5: Identifying Your Target Audience

In This Chapter

✔ Marketing business pages offline

✔ Why online and traditional marketing are important

✔ Other online marketing tools used for Facebook

*Y*ou might be reading this minibook to get a better understanding of how you can use Facebook to market your business. If this is the case, we would be remiss if we didn't offer you balanced advice.

Facebook is one of the most important places to market your business in the Internet age for many reasons. The driving reason to use Facebook for marketing is not because of how dynamic and interactive you can get with your market. It's not because of the two-way conversation and the ability to respond to your customers in real time. These are secondary reasons. The primary reason is its user base. Millions of potential customers are on Facebook.

In this chapter, we discuss marketing your Facebook presence using a healthy mix of traditional and online tools.

Using Insights to Identify Your Audience

To effectively market to the right audience, you need to identify who that appropriate audience is — that is, the people who will buy your product and are a good fit to be your customers. The way to determine this might be to identify who your customers are today. In addition to looking at your company and customer list, identify your audience on Facebook by using the analytics tools in Insights, as shown in Figure 5-1.

Facebook Insights tells you not just how many people you reach with your business page but also their demographics. You can discover the balance of male versus female, the age range, and many more details. This data tells you who has shown an interest in your business page, but you can dissect the information even more and see the demographics of people who are talking about your business page.

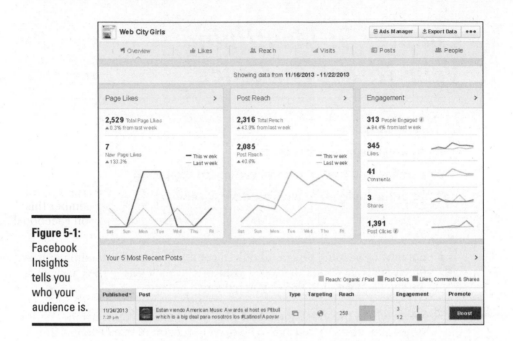

Figure 5-1:
Facebook Insights tells you who your audience is.

Insights is designed to give you a better understanding of your Facebook audience so that you can refine your marketing on and offline.

For example, if it's time to promote your Pilates studio and build your Facebook following by advertising offline, you don't want to buy an offline ad in a men's magazine if your Facebook Insights shows that women make up 70 percent of your Facebook audience. Furthermore, although 30 percent of your friends and followers are men, suppose you find that 100 percent of those talking about your business page are women. This statistic would suggest that your true target audience is women.

Although this example is simplistic, you can apply these principles across multiple demographic factors. If you get the right message to the right audience, you can attract the right kind of people to expand your business without wasting time and money on the wrong crowd.

You can read more about Insights and how to use its data in Chapter 3 of this minibook.

Understanding Why Online and Traditional Marketing Are Necessary

When your advertising method is more of an experience, your results are likely to be higher. And how can you offer a more interactive marketing experience? Online. Depending on your goals and campaigns, you can ask your audience to participate as you market to them (via polls, games, and other things). Of course, you can only get so many people to take that high level of action, but that's okay because in the end, you want to spend time reaching only those customers who are right for your business and who are going to buy your product or service.

With all this talk about reaching the right customers, it's important to remember that a healthy mix of marketing tactics will yield the greatest results. Traditional marketing (such as print, TV, and radio advertising) is tried and true. It's never going away, but it is changing. Traditional marketing is the foundation of your messaging. Choosing which forms of traditional marketing are right for your business (and which forms are worthless) is easy when you know your audience and their lifestyle. But remember this: No matter what their lifestyle, there is a good chance they are on Facebook!

Marketing Facebook Offline

Offline (or traditional) marketing has just as much room for innovation as online marketing. By including your business page information on your traditional marketing materials, you may expand your reach to those you have not been able to connect with on Facebook. This integration also enables you to add an interactive element to the traditional advertising campaign.

Facebook plays the role of a lead capturing method when it's integrated in traditional marketing. This means that every Like is a lead that you now have subscribed to further marketing messages.

Several studies have shown that when Facebook users Like a business page, they do not consider that action consent to be marketed to. Remember the advice we've given throughout this book, and don't overdo the hard sell. If your friends and followers feel like you're invading their space with too much marketing, they stop listening — by ignoring your updates, Unliking your page, hiding your updates, or possibly even reporting your updates as spam.

Offline marketing comes in many forms, and they all have their respective strengths and limitations. The way that you effectively use them to market your business page will vary with each example.

Direct mail marketing

Direct mail can be one of the most powerful or one of the weakest forms of marketing. The reason for the variation is that people ignore messages that appear to be an advertisement. When customers receive something from someone they trust, however, the story is different. Direct mail is always more successful when it has some context, meaning the recipients have some reason to expect what is sent to them. Using direct mail with this principle in mind can lead to powerful results.

The best use of a Facebook direct mail marketing campaign is giving people something worth responding to. Don't just direct people to a contest or ask for followers. Instead, consider that when people get their mail and look through it, they're at home. They may not be on the computer, but they likely have one close by. Getting someone to take a moment to log in to Facebook might be realistic if you give them a good enough reason. You may want to create follower-only discount codes via an application. (See Book VI for information about creating and using apps.) Just remember to make the discount large enough to entice your customer to stop what they're doing and log in to Facebook to find your page.

A permission-based marketing response always works best when you give the customer some value. For example, if the people you send a message to are already your customers, direct mail could be the contact they need to consider connecting with you another way (such as on your business page).

Always make sure that with any print campaign that you give customers an easy-to-remember URL. That way, you don't lose a potential opportunity because the web address is just too long to type. You may want to use a custom URL that forwards to a custom tab on your business page.

TV ads focused on Facebook

Some time ago, TGI Fridays created a campaign to increase its Facebook following. The restaurant did a series of TV commercials as well as other marketing tactics in which a fictional character named Woody asked friends to join him for a free burger. In the commercials, Woody stated he was the restaurant's biggest fan. This character fronted the commercials and print ads to implore you to become a fan so that the restaurant could give everyone a free burger. The company offered a burger to the first half million fans. This allowed the restaurant to increase its Facebook page followers to nearly one million. The restaurant realized the value of having a connection to its customers through Facebook.

The restaurant didn't hide the fact that it was trying to increase the number of Facebook business page fans: That was the topic of discussion. The approach was that if the restaurant's business page hit 500,000 fans, every fan would get a coupon for a free signature burger.

The restaurant's fanbase is over 1.3 million at the time of this writing. Each fan (eligible for the free burger) gave his or her e-mail address (via a third-party app) so that the restaurant could send the coupon. In this way, the restaurant created a strong database to regularly connect with customers, and it used Facebook as way to strengthen customer loyalty. Those who Liked the business page and shared their contact information considered it worth their time. (Even though Liking a business page and providing contact information isn't a big step, it's just enough that you're more likely to get a response from people who are in your true market.)

With a campaign like this, the restaurant made the best of its investment in TV commercials. With every advertising investment, make sure you get the most out of your investment by giving your audience a call to action with which you can bridge a sustained relationship with them. This philosophy also poses a significant argument for using both paid Facebook ads and your business page in tandem. This way, you're building your audience but also sustaining it with a continued connection.

Radio ads focused on Facebook

Radio can be the hardest tool to use to promote Facebook for many companies because you don't have the benefit of visual aids or the option of click-throughs. If you use the radio to promote your business page, make sure that you know how easy or difficult it is to find your business page for the first time, and prepare for that with your *copy* (the commercial's script). If your URL isn't easy to spell correctly, you should create a custom redirect URL that's easier to spell. You might even want to be sure that you have a prominent ad on your own website that links to your business page so that people have several ways to find you on Facebook.

You should take note of the way people search for you in the search box on Facebook. For example, if your business page name is A.B.C. Pilates Studio and people typically type ABC Pilates, they may have trouble finding you! If you haven't already set your name, change it to something that works well when searching.

Radio works best when the ads are frequent. Make sure that the station and time you choose is consistent and targeted at the right audience. Finally, make sure that your call to action clearly states how to find you.

Online Marketing Resources

Facebook is not a standalone online spot for marketing your business. Although Facebook is one of the most visited sites on the Internet, for many, it's a place to connect with people, discover interesting news, blogs, and more. Facebook acts as a portal to the rest of the Internet.

Don't forget to use other marketing tools on the web. When people are on the Internet catching up on TV shows, checking e-mail, searching for products, or even visiting your website, they're only a click or two away from becoming a fan of your business page. The following sections describe a few ways to use some of the most common tools for marketing your business page on the rest of the web.

E-mail marketing

Of all marketing channels, e-mail marketing is credited with delivering the highest return on investment. From our experience, we've found that the most successful Facebook promotions are supported by a permission marketing e-mail distribution list. This tells us that e-mail marketing must be a strong way to build your social media audience and drive them to engagement.

One of the biggest benefits of e-mail marketing is that you can communicate with your Facebook friends and followers directly, even if they miss your updates in the news feed. Figure 5-2 shows an e-mail newsletter that reminds subscribers to enter a contest on a business page.

Figure 5-2:
Pairing e-mail marketing with Facebook.

Your e-mail marketing software should allow you to efficiently track the success of your campaign. Tracking is what makes e-mail marketing so powerful; you can measure how many people opened your e-mail, as well as how many people clicked the links in it. E-mail marketing software is also generally required to deliver an e-mail in full HTML formatting. This means that you can send an e-mail message that has a fully designed layout, much like you see in Figure 5-2. E-mail marketing software also manages unsubscribes from people who do not want to receive your e-mails any longer. MailChimp (`http://mailchimp.com`), Constant Contact (`http://constantcontact.com`), AWeber (`http://aweber.com`), and ExactTarget (`http://exacttarget.com`) are some of the most popular options.

Although you can create e-mails in plain-text format, marketing e-mails tend to be more effective when they have images to help communicate your message in a simple manner. It's easy to create a template for your e-mail that resembles the design of a business page tab. We suggest including a distinctive graphical button in your e-mail (refer to Figure 5-2) that makes it easy to click directly to the destination.

E-mails typically have a short life span. Make sure that you follow two important tips in an e-mail marketing campaign:

✦ **Don't give away too much information in your e-mail.** Make sure you share just enough to get your readers interested. Make them visit your business page to get the rest of the details. If you satisfy their interest in the e-mail, they may forget to click over to Facebook later.

✦ **Send your e-mail when you have something notable to share with customers.** You will get more traffic if you offer something particularly interesting, so it's always better to tie e-mails to a specific campaign (such as a special promotion or contest) rather than just an invitation to check out your business page. With campaigns, it usually makes sense to send an e-mail at the beginning and another towards the end of the campaign as a reminder.

E-mail can be tied into your Facebook marketing in reverse as well. We suggest installing an app on your business page that allows your friends and followers to sign up for your e-mail list. (Most e-mail marketing software has an app; check their website's FAQ section.) After you install the app, you can post a status update reminding your friends and followers to sign up (be sure to provide the link to the signup tab). Or if friends and followers are perusing your business page, they may see your app and sign up on their own — but don't count on it; 90 percent of friends and followers don't return to your business page unless you tell them to.

Search marketing with PPC

PPC (pay per click) ads typically appear at the top of search results in Google and other search engines. These ads are paid out based on how many times the ad is clicked. In other words, the advertiser is charged when someone clicks the ad, not on how many times it's displayed. PPC is a great way to create advertising directed at the right audience (anyone who is searching for your product or service), and you can do it on almost any budget. With PPC ads, you define what you're willing to spend, and that amount is applied to ad appearances until the budget is exhausted.

Because all Facebook users are Internet users, it makes sense to use the Internet to promote your business page. In this case, you use search results to draw relevant traffic to your business page. (See Figure 5-3.) For example, if you owned a restaurant in the Old Market district of Omaha and people searched for *Omaha Restaurants Old Market* in a search engine, PPC allows them to see an ad at the top of their results page that links directly to whatever page is defined by the advertiser.

Figure 5-3:
Promoting
Facebook
with Google
PPC.

When people search for a product you sell, you don't want to miss the opportunity to capture their purchase. If you promote a business page with a PPC ad, make sure you can take orders in a custom tab or direct people to where they can place an order.

Integrated Campaigns

Using a mix of tactics including both online and offline channels is the ideal situation. If your goal is to increase your Facebook audience by drawing your customers there, make sure that your call to action is clear in every portion of your campaign. It helps to use the Facebook logo and colors in your advertising because the Facebook logo is easily recognizable.

Using custom page apps (tabs) is the most important element of your Facebook promotions, even if your initial goal is simply to increase Likes on your business page. All promotions are conducted on a Facebook tab. Giving your audience something to see that is unique to them is important. For example, BMW customized its business page with an interactive page app (tab) that allowed visitors to assemble a car with the custom options they prefer. Visitors had to Like the business page to use the interactive page app. For more information on business page apps, see Book VI.

Book VI
Developing Facebook Apps

web extras

For step-by-step instructions on creating a tab on your business page, go to www. dummies.com/extras/facebookaio.

Contents at a Glance

Chapter 1: Custom Apps for Business Pages .417

Using Apps for Facebook Marketing 417
Extending the Facebook Experience 419
Discovering iframes 421
Increasing Engagement with Apps...422
Avoiding the Reinvention of the Wheel..428

Chapter 2: Building Canvas Apps and Page Tabs. 429

Finding the Differences between Canvas Apps and Page Tabs....................429
Creating Your App...432
Getting to Know App Settings..435
Insights in Facebook Apps 442

Chapter 3: Creating Your Own Apps 445

Creating and Deploying a Facebook App 445
Authenticating Your App..453

Chapter 4: Tour of the Facebook API. 459

Finding Technical Information 459
Understanding Facebook's Core Concepts 462
Developing Apps More Easily with SDKs..466
Placing Facebook Objects on Your Web Pages with Social Plugins 470

Chapter 1: Custom Apps for Business Pages

In This Chapter

✔ **Using apps for Facebook marketing**

✔ **Extending the Facebook experience**

✔ **Discovering iframes, application pages, and canvas pages**

✔ **Finding out what apps can do to increase engagement**

If you're a Facebook marketer, you're likely always looking for ways to increase the engagement that you have with your customers. For many Facebook users, interesting status updates aren't enough to hold their attention. Facebook apps allow you to create a far more engaging Facebook presence. You're not just looking for more people to visit your business page and Like it; you also want to give followers more of a reason to interact with your brand or find other value.

In addition, a typical Facebook user does not want to leave Facebook to view content surrounding your brand. Because of this, having content outside Facebook can lead to fewer conversions and sales from your customers. Having an app right on your business page inside Facebook reduces your chances of Facebook users leaving your site and you losing the sale. This also provides a great landing page for any Facebook ads you may have created on Facebook.

Apps are designed to deliver all the interactive elements of Facebook to your followers in a custom way. With an app, you have access to Facebook features from the Like button to the ability to access the friend lists of your followers and incorporating those into your app experience. You can even prevent followers from seeing certain content until they Like your page! Apps can use just about any feature, person, thing, or relationship you see in the Facebook user experience. To write an app, you can use any web-enabled code (such as PHP, JavaScript, and other web software languages) to develop custom apps for Facebook.

Using Apps for Facebook Marketing

Companies that make apps for their business pages want to make Facebook a more engaging environment and extend the connection to their audience of followers. The most common appearance of an application on Facebook is the *page tab*. Within a business page, you can create any app and install it into a page tab, limited only by the capabilities of the web itself. Some apps are a simple aesthetic element, such as an image that appears at the top of your page (as a square below the cover photo) to enhance the look of your business page. Other apps are more complex, such as interactive elements your followers can use. Building an app gives you the opportunity to integrate more deeply into the core Facebook experience. Your app can integrate with the news feed as well as notifications, requests to a user's friends, and other features.

Here are a few of the things that apps can add to your marketing plan:

✦ **Share content in a new way.** Apps can use many, if not all, elements of the web by integrating elements of your web experience right in your Facebook page. You can view anything that can be created on the web through any web browser. The only limitation is your browser size — if you can write the code, you can do it. This model means that the content that you would host elsewhere (on another service or website) can be viewed in the tab on Facebook. This means that whatever you would like to share can be shared on Facebook as well.

Apps can also interact with other elements of Facebook if you build the features into the apps. For example, app participants can post content on their Facebook timeline.

✦ **Gain followers in a short time.** Apps enable you to put together powerful promotions, which allow you to create an interactive experience for your followers. Doing so can empower you to create promotions, contests, and more, which enable you to increase your Facebook audience in a short time.

Because apps can interact with Facebook features such as the news feed and notifications, a successful promotion can have a viral effect, drawing other participants through friends. With these features, you can catapult your audience to a new level.

✦ **Provide a valuable service.** The longest lasting and most effective apps provide value to the consumer, not just an interesting experience with your brand or business page. Games that offer a desired value to users will be used more and uninstalled less. This sort of value leads to strong audience engagement. It's fine to have a Facebook app that allows you to virtually pour your favorite soda and share it with your friends, but if you can use a Facebook app to get weather updates or create customized birthday cards, you can get so much more mileage out of the app.

For some, a "valuable service" may mean games. A successful game might lead to in-game purchases for new levels and features. More than half of Facebook users log in to games, and at least 20 percent of them have purchased in-game features. Aside from generating revenue through in-game sales, apps of this sort can be an advertising opportunity.

✦ **Maintain the Facebook experience.** Facebook users are more likely to interact with your company and the experience your company provides if they can remain on Facebook while doing it. Apps allow you to accomplish this by providing a custom experience for your company right on your company's Facebook page.

If you use Facebook ads, this feature improves even further. Those who click your Facebook ad can land on a specific tab you've created for your page. Because these people stay on your page, they are more likely to Like the page and get future updates from you, and they are much more likely to convert to real customers for your business.

Extending the Facebook Experience

Page tabs and other types of apps take connecting with an audience to new levels in several ways. In this section, you find some of the ways that all Facebook apps extend the capabilities of your Facebook marketing.

Screen real estate

One of the simplest things that you gain with a page tab is more space. The timeline and cover image for your page are pretty much all you have without apps. In addition, all design elements of your page must fit in a compatible format. Page tabs give you the capability to customize the look, feel, and experience of your page outside these boundaries.

A page tab can use up to 810 pixels of screen width. With the extra real estate, you can include more pictures, videos, and other content on your business page. Having that space is valuable to a marketer because you can offer more features or say more things — without the user leaving Facebook. The extra screen width also makes the sales experience more enjoyable, such as the Coca-Cola Store on their Facebook page, shown in Figure 1-1.

Canvas apps versus page tabs

Canvas apps and page tabs are different types of apps that you can create. A *canvas app* is unrelated to any specific Facebook page and is intended to be a custom experience that Facebook users can use and share. Many games you see on Facebook are canvas apps.

Page tabs are custom apps attached to an existing Facebook page. They appear linked from the top of the page in the header and are always associated with the page. The top of a page tab lists the name of the page it is associated with, and users have the ability to Like that page.

Figure 1-1:
More real
estate with
page tabs.

Social channels

Apps provide a great avenue for increasing the number of followers because
they easily move through the key social channels that make Facebook
interactive.

Imagine a friend is participating in a new fun game. While he plays, he may
be prompted to share his story relative to his Facebook experience on his
timeline as a status update. (See Figure 1-2.) Perhaps he will be asked to
invite other friends to enjoy the game. Inevitably, his activity in the app will
also appear in the ticker on each of his friends' home pages. This encourages
his friends to also play the game. Some may simply check it out but not play,
while others will play and share it.

Figure 1-2:
Social
channels.

Social channels allow Facebook apps to expand their coverage to a broader
audience.

Analytics

It isn't enough to know how many followers you have. Marketers need to know details about those people and how they can market to them. Business pages are all equipped with Insights, the Facebook analytics tool, as shown in Figure 1-3.

Figure 1-3:
Facebook
Insights
shows how
followers
interact with
your app.

Facebook Insights tells you how users interact with your app, what sites refer traffic to your app, and what user actions contribute to the active user count. Insights also provide demographics on your authorized users and active users. With this information, you can fine-tune your app, its content, and your marketing surrounding it to be sure that you get the most out of it as a marketing tool.

Discovering iframes

To offer apps on your business page, you will quite possibly need to do as much building off Facebook as you would on Facebook. Page tabs are blank spaces provided by Facebook in which you input an app URL that Facebook then displays through a simple web interface called an *iframe*. This means that much or all of your content isn't on Facebook — it's simply viewed through a window.

An iframe allows an HTML browser window to display the contents of practically any web page inside another. In a Facebook page tab, this feature means that you, the app creator, can create your own content on your own web server, and display that content inside a nicely polished Facebook interface right on Facebook.com itself. The iframe is simply a box inside your page that displays content from your own website.

To set up your page tab, go to `https://developers.facebook.com`, create your app, and specify the URL on your website that you want Facebook to load in your Facebook page. Install the app on your page, and — voila! — the content in the page is loaded every time your fans visit the app on your page. In Figure 1-4, for example, you can see and use the Post Planner app right inside Facebook by using `http://www.postplanner.com/` as the URL for your page tab. After the foundation of your app is built in Facebook, an iframe allows you to display any content on the web.

Figure 1-4:
Page tabs
can direct
someone to
any site.

Increasing Engagement with Apps

Apps have capabilities designed to increase the engagement of a Facebook user. You can deploy mechanisms in the programming of your app to increase an individual's use of the app, as well as increase the number of people using the app.

Draw people in with requests

Apps send notifications to the notifications bar in the same way that you receive other notifications on Facebook. Users can also send invites, or *requests,* to other users; these requests appear to users in the same manner. To send requests to a friend or receive notifications from the app, a user only needs to authorize the use of the app — no other extended permissions are required.

Notifications and requests can also deliver other features, such as a virtual gift. The requests feature creates another way to invite new users into the app experience through the network of the players' friends.

Requests and notifications are two different ways to notify users or their friends:

+ **Notifications:** This feature, which is currently in beta (meaning it is subject to change), allows the app to deliver user messages that appear in the notifications drop-down in the top bar of Facebook. Notifications can be used, for example, to inform the user when it's his or her turn in a game, to let the user know that something new was discovered, or to remind a user of a deal you're offering on your Facebook page.

+ **Requests:** Requests allow users to send things to other Facebook users. The things they send appear to Facebook users in their notifications drop-down in the top bar of Facebook. You might send an invite to play a game or a special offer on your Facebook page. A special dialog box initiated by your app lets the user select friends to whom to send the request. If you've received a Words with Friends invite, you've seen a request in action.

Publishing stories

When using an app, users can publish stories about what they're doing in the app, such as the Foursquare check-in shown in Figure 1-5. Your app can prompt users to publish these stories in the app. If the user chooses to publish the story, it will be published to the user's timeline and may appear in the news feed of the user's friends. Other examples of this could include sharing a special offer the user received or a contest the person entered on your Facebook page.

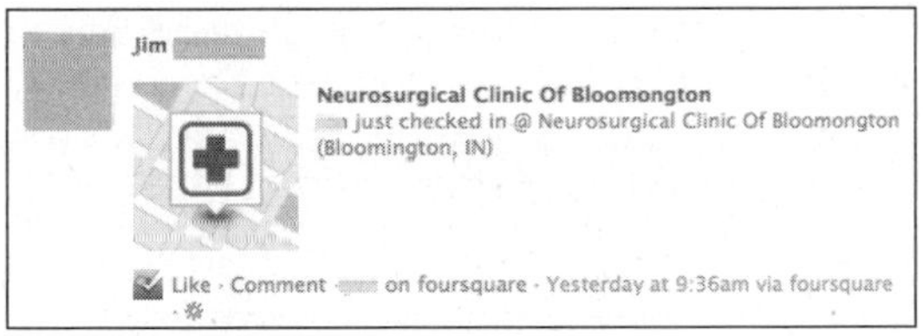

Figure 1-5:
Publishing
stories.

When stories are published from the app, they include a link to the app and can include an attachment, such as an image. Images often represent an accomplishment, such as a badge that the user earned. To publish content to your user's timeline, you use a small piece of JavaScript in your web page that prompts the user using Facebook's own dialog box for sharing. This dialog box pops up wherever you put the JavaScript, and asks the user to share your content to the user's timeline. This can be a great way to drive new fans to your Facebook page or to increase the use of your app.

News feed discovery stories

Discovery stories appear in the ticker (that little live feed that updates with everything your friends are doing) when someone begins using a new app, and also in the news feed of friends of the user, as shown in Figure 1-6. These stories are triggered when a user installs a new game or starts using an app.

Figure 1-6: Discovery stories in the news feed.

Because the first thing a user sees when logging in to Facebook is the news feed, these stories can be highly visible. However, because users have the ability to control (to some degree) what kind of content they see in their news feed, they may not see updates in the news feed about your app.

Users' permissions with apps

In most cases, apps access the user's timeline to use social features such as posting updates or displaying stories in the ticker. All apps require that users permit the app to access their timelines. To ensure that your app is a success, it's important to have a fair understanding of Facebook's authentication process. The permissions process typically contains more specific permissions for each part of Facebook that can be accessed by that application. The user sees each item and verifies his or her permission. Figure 1-7 shows the screen a user sees when granting permissions.

Figure 1-7: Granting permissions for an app.

Make sure you include the appropriate permissions in your app. Too few permissions might prevent your app from providing the necessary features it is intended to deliver for the user. For example, if the function of your app includes posting badges to the user's timeline, you need permission to access the user's timeline. The downside is that requiring too many permissions can deter users. Facebook recommends that you request permission only when you need it.

The quality of your app and the number of things you ask your users to reveal about themselves could affect the trustworthiness of your brand, so you'll want to measure the effectiveness of how many permissions you request from your users. At the same time, if the quality of your app and the demand to use it is high enough, you may discover that the required permissions are less of a concern for most people.

Facebook apps use a simple authentication protocol (called OAuth 2.0) to allow a user to authenticate an app and give your app permission to perform functions on the user's behalf. The Facebook authentication and authorization process has basically two steps:

✦ **User authentication:** Verify that the user is who he or she claims to be (the user is legitimately logged in to his or her own timeline). To authorize your app, users are asked to log in to their accounts using their login credentials (username and password), as shown in Figure 1-8. If they're already logged in, Facebook validates the login cookie in their browsers to validate their identities.

Figure 1-8:
Users must
log in to
authenticate.

✦ **App authorization:** Your application needs access to the user's timeline, such as permission to post updates on behalf of the user, or permission to invite friends through the app, or access to personal data such as an e-mail address or activities. App authorization ensures that users know what data and capabilities they grant the app access to.

Permissions in an app cover any type of access to the user's timeline. For example, if the user completes the post and clicks the button to post an update on the user's behalf, the app needs to have permission to post updates to his or her timeline. This process happens at the same time as the user authentication portion (refer to Figure 1-8). After the user allows the app, Facebook redirects the user to the destination site in the app and passes along an authorization code.

Apps that don't require user permissions

Apps that access data or features in someone's timeline must follow the Facebook authentication process. Many apps deliver only front-facing features such as playing a video or linking to a site. These apps still require a similar setup process but bypass the need for user authentication. Custom apps on pages are a great example. In most cases, apps are more of a customized business page, not a game or a tool that requires special access.

What you lose with an app that doesn't require permission is some of the features that often help the page or app grow virally. Depending on your goals, you may want to weigh this option.

Features that encourage sharing with friends

From a marketing standpoint, an app typically has two primary objectives. The first is to increase the engagement level with your current followers or users. The second is to build your audience by encouraging sharing.

The following sections describe some of the specific features that help to make your app more social and encourage users to share with friends: the news feed, requests, and automatic channels.

The news feed

The news feed, or home page, is the first thing that users see when they log in to Facebook. The news feed is where people find out what their friends are doing.

✦ **The Feed dialog** prompts users to publish updates to their news feed, as shown in Figure 1-9. Facebook recommends this approach when asking users to publish stories about your app. It doesn't require that the user log in to your app or grant it any special permission; it's essentially a shortcut to post a status update.

✦ **The Feed graph object** is for situations in which certain app activities trigger a post to the user's timeline. The app needs authorization with posting privileges through the OAuth process. The result is to post onto the user's timeline or on the ticker of the user's friends, without the Feed dialog box.

✦ **The Like button** allows users to share content from an app or a website (using Facebook social features) and post it on their timelines. This action shows up as an activity update on users' timelines and in their friends' news feeds. Updates may say something like "Bob Smith Likes My Great Website."

Figure 1-9:
The Feed
dialog.

**Book VI
Chapter 1**

Custom Apps for
Business Pages

Automatic channels

Automatic channels are those that are enabled by default. These features encourage more use and traffic to apps and Facebook. You don't need to do anything additional for these channels to be in place because they're part of all apps.

Here is a list of just a few automatic channels available to your app:

✦ **Bookmarks,** described previously in this chapter, enable people to quickly return to your app.

✦ **Notifications** let app users know when they have a request, an update, or anything else to respond to. These appear to the right of the bookmark.

✦ **Dashboards** are screens that show the bookmarked links of the apps that a user has used recently and those that friends have used.

✦ **Usage stories** are the activity updates that appear in the news feed or in the ticker. To attract new users, usage stories are typically targeted at people who haven't used your app.

✦ **App profiles** are similar to a business page or a personal timeline. App profiles include a timeline, an info tab, and configurable tabs.

Like-gating

Like-gating requires users to Like your page before they can see new content in your app. This feature can be an excellent way to offer a deal or something free. You implement a special code that "listens" for when a user Likes the page and then reloads the page with your new content after the Like.

Building a friendly experience

In every app you create, we strongly suggest integrating a user's friends into the experience. The Facebook API in apps allows you to build rich experiences centered around the user's friends. For example, if the user plays a game, he or she might see other friends who are playing that game. Or the user might see other friends who have taken part in a deal or a promotion your page offers.

Avoiding the Reinvention of the Wheel

After taking you through this chapter, you should have a pretty good grasp on what's possible with a Facebook page tab. However, you don't have to build a page tab on your own. Several services can do this for you. And with a simple WYSIWYG (What You See Is What You Get) editor, you can get started in no time with your own custom page tab.

A web search will reveal a list of available services, such as ShortStack. ShortStack, at www.shortstack.com, is a platform for building custom apps and for building promotions for your Facebook page through those apps. Its simple interface makes it easy to configure and create page tabs and other apps for your brand on Facebook.

The company provides a few prebuilt apps including ones for refer-a-friend and Like-gating. The WYSIWYG editor enables you to create your own experiences by pulling in simple elements of the Facebook APIs.

Chapter 2: Building Canvas Apps and Page Tabs

In This Chapter

✔ Seeing the difference between canvas apps and page tabs

✔ Building your dev app

✔ Defining roles for your app

✔ Facebook Insights

*I*f you're embarking into the app-driving marketing space, it's time to consider the format of your application. Facebook apps, like many other web apps, can be designed in a nearly unlimited number of formats. The sky is the limit. Facebook apps take on four major forms:

- ✦ Page tabs
- ✦ Canvas apps
- ✦ Social plug-ins
- ✦ Websites and mobile apps

A myriad of Facebook features can be embedded into other websites, apps, and web tools known as Facebook Platform. With Facebook Platform, you can create an app that integrates with the Facebook API to use various Facebook features. These apps can be created in the context of any of the preceding applications, and can bring Facebook features right into your own website or mobile app. You can find out more about Facebook Platform for Websites in Chapters 3 and 4 of this minibook. In this chapter, we focus on page tabs and canvas pages.

Finding the Differences between Canvas Apps and Page Tabs

When you develop an application, you need to know from the start whether the app will appear on a page tab or a canvas app. Page tabs and canvas apps have similar functionality, but they have enough differences (display size, for one) that one or the other may be better suited to house your app. The following sections describe page tabs and canvas apps to help you choose which is better for displaying your app.

Let us clarify the relationship among page tabs, canvas apps, and apps. All Facebook apps are built using Facebook Platform, which allows you to take the application you build (using any common web code language) and connect it to Facebook's features. When someone uses your app in the context of Facebook, the app needs to be displayed somewhere. Canvas apps and page tabs are your two choices on Facebook:

✦ **Page tab:** A page (sometimes called a *tab*) where your app can be displayed in the context of your business page, as shown in Figure 2-1. A page tab is simply an iframe space that's 810 pixels wide, in which your app is viewed within the context of your brand's Facebook page. Every Page tab has the name of the page and number of likes at the top.

Figure 2-1: Page tabs are part of your business page.

✦ **Canvas app:** A place where your app can be displayed in the context of its own space. Canvas apps have a different format; they take up the entire page and display, in a column to the right of the app, ads and other apps the user has used.

Page tab features

Page tabs appear in the center of a business page; shortcuts to page tabs appear as thumbnail images below the cover photo on the business page. Page tabs take up a width of 810 pixels and appear in the same relative area as the timeline on your business page.

In a page tab, you can have a completely functional, interactive application, or you can simply display an image to enhance the look of your page. Companies often treat page tabs as a way of personalizing their social environment on the web. An example of a page tab app is shown in Figure 2-2.

Figure 2-2:
A Facebook
page tab
app.

Because page tabs appear in the context of your business page, people can quickly find your app and use it instantly. If you want to increase traffic to your page to increase your Facebook audience, use page tabs to create a destination space. In this case, you may initially develop an app for short interactions (such as getting votes in a photo contest).

Canvas app features

A canvas app is 760 pixels wide by default. However, you have the option of making a canvas app a *fluid width,* in which the application expands to the width of the user's browser.

Canvas apps offer a few additional interactive components for users that page tabs lack. A defining characteristic of canvas apps is the blank canvas given to the app to do practically anything you want inside the Facebook.com website. Canvas apps have the Facebook logo and other header information at the top. Unlike page tabs, canvas apps are not associated with any page information at the top, such as the number of Likes or the page name. Canvas apps all have ads on the right, with a list of other apps that the user has used and other similar apps above the ads. You can find and discover new canvas apps by clicking Apps in the left column of your Facebook news feed.

Canvas apps and page tabs can work well together, if they are designed to complement each other.

Because a canvas app redirects users to another page, you may end up developing a custom page tab as well to direct the user to your app.

If you create a canvas app as a promotional tool for your business, you'll want to build a link in your business's Facebook page to promote the app and its function. One retailer used a page tab as a customized look for its page with a button linking to the canvas app that housed its catalog. This was a great use of these two options because the page presents the branding and information about the company. However, when someone decides to look at the catalog, they link to another area (the canvas app) that they may spend several minutes reviewing.

Choosing between a page tab and a canvas app

Depending on the app, it may be obvious whether a page tab or a canvas app is the better choice. Other times, it's not so simple to decide between the two. Table 2-1 gives you a rundown of the size and features of page tabs and canvas apps to help you decide which to use.

Table 2-1		Page Tab versus Canvas App	
Type	*Width*	*Features*	*Downsides*
Page tab	810 pixels	Shortcut on your business page	Offers a limited display width and always displays the name of your Facebook page at the top (this behavior may be positive as well)
Canvas app	760 pixels or fluid width	Flexible width, ticker, bookmarks	May require a page tab and permissions so that existing fans can find it

Creating Your App

The first step to building your own app is to set up your app inside Facebook's app builder. You take this step to become a developer on Facebook and to have a place to find all your apps.

Follow these steps to set up your first app:

1. **Point your browser to** `https://developers.facebook.com/apps.`

   An authorization screen appears, as shown in Figure 2-3. You need to allow the app to access basic information on your timeline to use it. This is all that's required to have developer capabilities with Facebook.

Book VI Chapter 2

Building Canvas Apps and Page Tabs

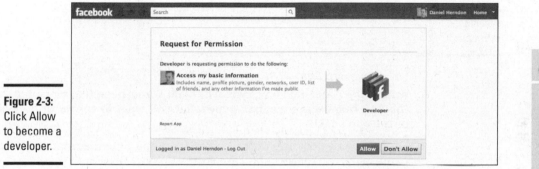

Figure 2-3: Click Allow to become a developer.

2. **Click Allow.**

   After you complete the authentication, you see the apps page. The first time you go to the apps page, you see a blank screen and the Create New App button, as shown in Figure 2-4.

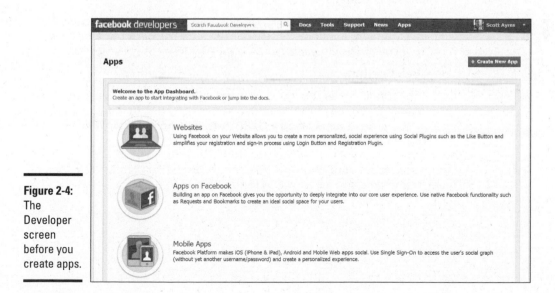

Figure 2-4: The Developer screen before you create apps.

3. **Click the Create New App button.**

   The Create New App dialog box appears, asking you to name the app. See Figure 2-5.

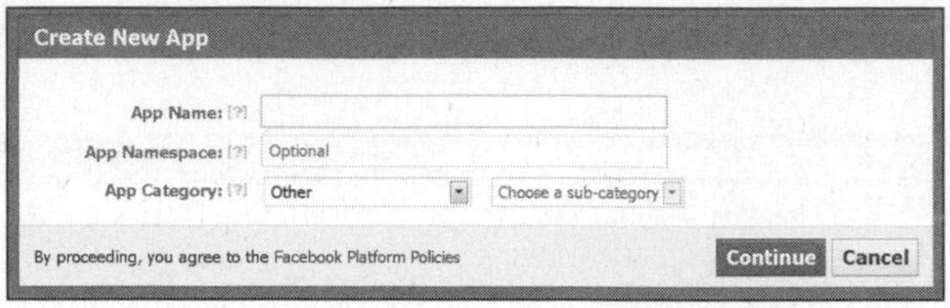

Figure 2-5:
Naming
your app.

Create New App

App Name: [?]

App Namespace: [?] Optional

App Category: [?] Other ▼ Choose a sub-category ▼

By proceeding, you agree to the Facebook Platform Policies   Continue   Cancel

Figure 2-5:
Naming
your app.

4. **In the App Name text box, type what you want the app to be called. In the App Namespace text box, type what you want to appear at the end of the app's URL.**

   You can name your app whatever you want, but note that the namespace can't have uppercase letters or symbols. For example, if you type **fordummies** in the App Namespace text box, your app's URL will be http://apps.facebook.com/fordummies.

   The App Namespace field must be filled in with a name that hasn't been taken by another app. If the name you chose is taken, Facebook will immediately indicate that it isn't available. (If you're having trouble finding a name that hasn't already been taken, you can always determine the namespace later.)

   Leave the other fields blank, and your app will be fine. If you want to learn more about all these fields, be sure to check out *Facebook Application Development For Dummies* by Jesse Stay.

5. **Click Continue.**

   If Facebook needs any more verifying info here, they will ask for it. For instance, you may have to enter a series of letters and numbers to prove that you're human (called a *CAPTCHA*). For most people, however, your app is created.

You just created your core app! You're now on the configuration screen of your brand-new app, as shown in Figure 2-6.

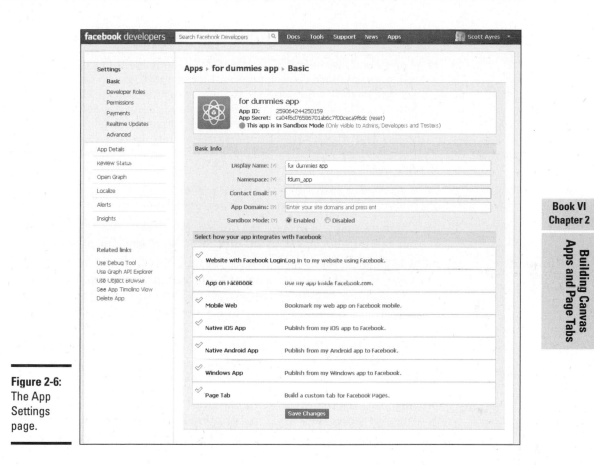

**Book VI
Chapter 2**

**Building Canvas
Apps and Page Tabs**

Figure 2-6:
The App
Settings
page.

Getting to Know App Settings

After you create the app, you have a little bit more discovery to do to move on to the next step, where you integrate your app into Facebook. This app is the foundation that allows you to plug in any type of apps, including those hosted on page tabs and on canvas apps, as well as all other Facebook integrations for websites.

Every app has a timeline similar to a business page. The first part of the App Settings page displays your app icon and profile picture, which will appear on the app timeline page. The app icon will also appear on the left column of the user's timeline if the user installs the app, as well as in the apps section of other canvas apps that the user runs.

From the App Settings page, you can change the following options:

✦ **App ID and app secret:** The App ID is a unique identifier of the app itself, sort of like a catalog number for the app. The app secret is a (yes, you guessed it) secret code that you use to authenticate the application when conducting an API call with another app. (An *API call* is when your app is calling upon the application programming interface of Facebook to use its features.) This older feature is rarely needed anymore. You'll probably never use the app secret if you use auth tokens to authorize API calls.

✦ **App Display Name and App Namespace:** These fields are the app name and namespace that you chose when you created the app.

✦ **Contact E-mail:** By default, the Contact E-mail is the e-mail address associated with your Facebook timeline. You can change this if needed.

✦ **App Domain:** Use this field to enable authorization on domains and subdomains. If your app is part of your website (and not necessarily on a business page or a canvas app), the core Facebook app will know to authorize that domain and subdomain, such as `example.com` or `anything.example.com`.

✦ **Sandbox Mode:** If you select this option, only app developers will be able to see and use your app. You need to deselect this option when your app goes live so that others can use the app.

You also need a server to host your app and a URL that points to the location on your server from which the app will load. This URL tells Facebook where to look for your app. You'll use this URL in the website and app sections mentioned next.

In the section of the App Settings page that was shown in Figure 2-6, you need to select the type of app that you want to launch. Facebook has seven types of apps to deploy with the Facebook developer tools:

✦ **Website with Facebook Login:** Facebook can be used to log in to a website in place of your website's separate login credentials. Select this section, and enter your domain name (website URL) in the text box.

✦ **App on Facebook:** An app on Facebook is any of those that we refer to most frequently in this book. This means that the app will be accessed somewhere in Facebook, through a canvas app. To use this feature, you select the App on Facebook section and enter two URLs. Make sure that you type the entire URL, including the `http://` portion.

In the Canvas URL text box, enter the URL for the web page where your app is hosted. The secure Canvas URL text box typically takes the same URL, only with `https` instead of `http`. Users have the option to enable secured browsing using HTTPS on their Account Settings page. To support these users, you need to set up your destination URL on a secured server using an SSL certificate. This is the default destination for users viewing your app. If a secure URL isn't available, users will be warned that they're about to enter unsecured browsing. Facebook requires you to have an SSL certificate but doesn't completely block out the unsecured version.

+ **Mobile Web:** If you redirect users to a mobile site, select this option and enter the URL. The Mobile Web option is applicable for games or other applications that are supported on both standard web and mobile web. When you use this feature, users can bookmark your app on Facebook Mobile, and your app will be seen in their friends' mobile news feeds.

+ **Native iOS App:** Use this feature to publish an iPhone app to Facebook. For example, if you have a shopping app, your app could have a feature that allows users to post products they're interested in on their timelines. To create an iPhone app, you need to fill in five fields. Refer to Apple's developer toolkit for further information about these fields:

  - iOS Bundle ID
  - iPhone App Store ID
  - iPad App Store ID
  - Single Sign On
  - URL Scheme Suffix

+ **Native Android App:** To publish a Facebook app on an Android phone, you have to fill in the following fields:

  - Package Name
  - Class Name
  - Key Hashes
  - Single Sign On

Please refer to the Android developer documentation to identify each of these.

+ **Windows App:** To publish a Facebook app on a Windows phone, you have to enter the Windows Store ID and, optionally, the Windows Phone Store ID (which is currently in beta).

+ **Page Tab:** The last option, Page Tab, is where you create a custom Facebook tab. Click this row and fill in the following text boxes:

  - *Page Tab Name:* Enter the name of the tab that will appear on your Facebook Page.

  - *Page Tab URL:* Enter the HTTP version of the URL you will be viewing in the tab.

  - *Secure Page Tab URL:* Enter the HTTPS version of the destination web application.

- *Page Tab Edit URL:* Enter the administrator edit link (if you have one available) to access the editing of the app.

- *Page Tab Width:* Select between Normal (810 pixels) or Narrow (520 pixels). This option sets the page width used when your app is displayed in a custom app tab.

- *Page Tab Image:* This image will represent your app in the list of apps at the top of your Facebook page. If your only goal is to enhance the look and feel of your Facebook page, as mentioned in Chapter 1 of this minibook, this image is the only thing you need.

App Details page

The App Details page, shown in Figure 2-7, is where you customize details provided to users, such as descriptions of the app and where to find your privacy policy. Users see an authorization dialog box when you use Open Graph for your app. (*Open Graph* is the integration feature that Facebook uses to share activity on your timeline; see the following section for more.) To get to the App Details page, click the App Details link in the left sidebar (refer to Figure 2-6).

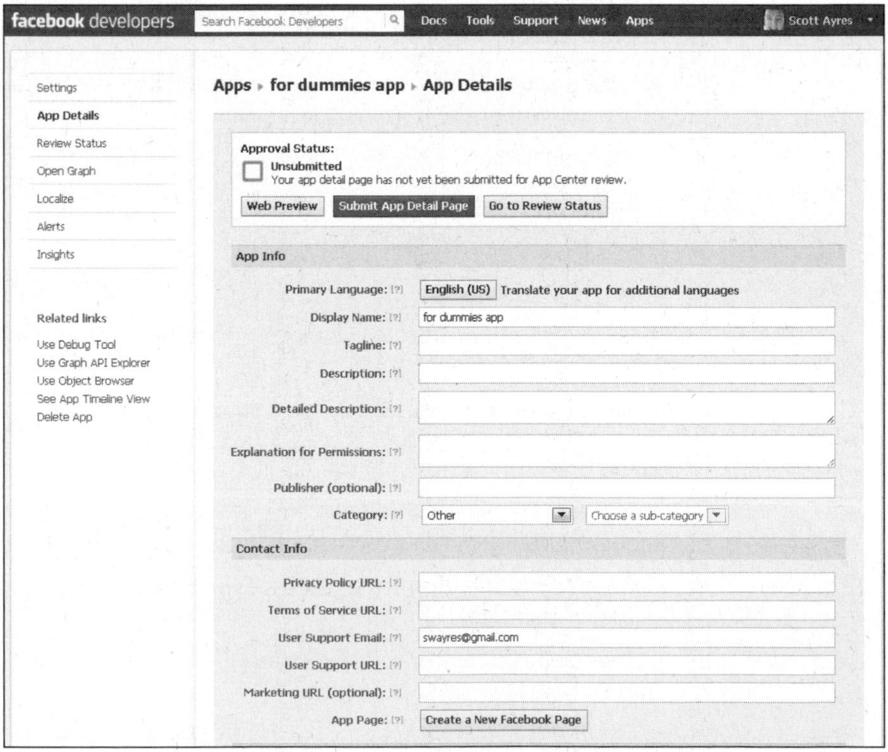

Figure 2-7: Customize the details.

As you complete the text boxes in this app, you can click the web preview button on your screen to see how the dialog box will appear. Each URL text box just directs users to the page on your site that you enter as the source for that information. For example, if your privacy policy is at `www.mycoolapp.com/privacy`, enter that URL into the Privacy Policy URL text box.

Open Graph

Open Graph is the integration of Facebook that makes your app more engaging. Using Open Graph allows you to deeply interweave the social elements of Facebook with your app and create a more social experience. Begin by clicking Open Graph in the left sidebar (refer to Figure 2-6).

**Book VI
Chapter 2**

The foundation of Open Graph apps are stories, which contain apps, actors, actions, and objects:

+ **Actor:** The person who published the story.

+ **App:** The app that publishes the story on the actor's behalf. Every story is generated by an app, and every story includes the app used to create it.

+ **Action:** The activity the actor performs, such as Finished Reading. Facebook provides a number of common actions that can be used to create stories, or you can create your own.

+ **Object:** The object with which the actor interacts. Objects are publicly accessible web pages hosted on the Internet. Almost any web page can be an object. Objects are public information.

In your app, you have an action that people do in your app and an object that people connect with by doing that action. For example, if your app allows users to track their movie experiences, the social activity that the users are sharing is watching a movie. In this case, the action is Watch. That action has the corresponding object, Movie.

An app like this would be targeted at making real-life experiences more social by sharing them with friends. These actions would be shared on the user's timeline, in news feeds, and in the ticker. This takes the social act of Liking a page or an article a step further by allowing a Facebook app to define more actions. You have complete freedom to define your actions and objects. To get started in creating an Open Graph story, click the Create a New Story button (see Figure 2-8).

You have to have added a namespace, mentioned in the "Getting to Know App Settings" section, previously in this chapter, to create an Open Graph story.

Building Canvas
Apps and Page Tabs

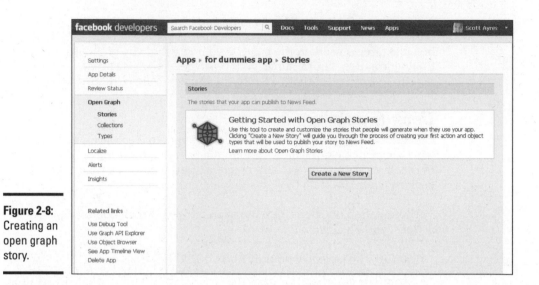

Figure 2-8:
Creating an
open graph
story.

When deciding how to implement an Open Graph app, don't think too much about the activities being done in the app itself. Instead, think about building apps to make activities more social. Open Graph apps are all about stories being shared on the user's timeline. For example, if your business is a gym and you want to engage people in your experience through Facebook, your app could contain tutorials giving people a routine to follow, in which they complete steps as they move through the routine. Your action might be Complete and your object might be Exercise.

Facebook has a strict approval process for Open Graph stories to ensure that certain standards are followed. The core of the matter is to create actions that make sense and protect the integrity of the Open Graph concept. Facebook wants to make sure that your app publishes actions that are simple, genuine, and not abusive. You can read these guidelines in the Facebook Developer help section at `http://developers.facebook.com/docs/opengraph/opengraph-approval`.

After clicking the Add Custom Story button, the dialog box shown in Figure 2-9 appears. You can add any action type you want and then associate it with a listed object type or create your own object type. When you're satisfied with your selection, click the Create button.

If your selection is incorrect, Facebook will tell you why and you'll need to adjust it to fit the parameters of Open Graph.

For each action type, your app settings page gives you a code that you use to build app functions around the action. You can add more actions and objects to your app.

After you create your story, you'll be able to see a summary of the objects that a person has interacted with in your app.

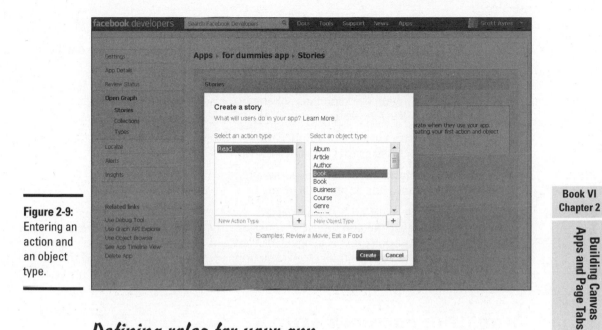

Figure 2-9:
Entering an
action and
an object
type.

Defining roles for your app

When developing an app, you might be working as part of a team. Depending
on the level of detail and the size of your team, you can add and remove
team members from your dev app. Just like business pages, apps have
administrators assigned to them who have rights to edit and manage the
page. A dev app has a few additional roles, as shown in Figure 2-10.

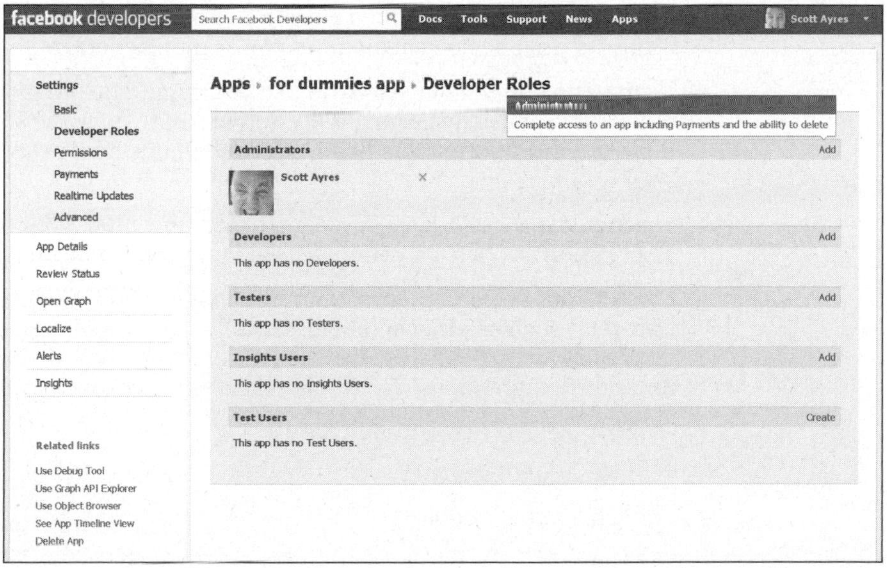

Figure 2-10:
Defining
roles in your
dev app.

The following list shows the roles assigned to a Facebook dev app:

✦ **Administrators** have complete access to the dev app. They can access all the app's settings.

✦ **Developers** can access all technical settings, but are restricted from changing the secret key, changing or adding additional users, and deleting the application.

✦ **Testers** can test the application in what is called *sandbox mode*. They can't make any changes to the app.

✦ **Insights users** can access Insights for marketing purposes but can't modify the application in any way.

✦ **Test users** are imaginary users that Facebook allows you to create to access the app to test its functionality. When you use the test user, Facebook creates a login URL that expires in two hours. You can access a user access token to take actions on behalf of the user and test API functions. You can create up to 500 test users for an app.

Insights in Facebook Apps

Insights, shown in Figure 2-11, tells you which users use your app and how they use it. Although Insights provides limited data, the data is invaluable if you intend to use the app as a marketing tool.

Insights has several areas that provide critical information to the app developer:

✦ **Overview:** A snapshot of your app's activity, including the number of users, data on sharing, and a measure of performance based on API requests (that is, how many times the app pulls data).

✦ **Users:** The number of users who use your app. The numbers are broken down into total active users, daily active users, new users by day, and demographic information. Lastly, the list shares how many users remove your app.

✦ **Traffic:** Statistics showing how much and how often your app is used. This option also allows you to access your app's performance.

✦ **Open Graph:** Open Graph details. You can see how much activity the app gets (such as Likes and comments), clickthrough rates of stories your app posts (the percentage of viewers who clicked), and ticker and news feed impressions. The subcategories for Open Graph are

• Story CTR (Click Through Rate)

• Likes and Comments

• Aggregation Activity

• Ticker

• Demographics

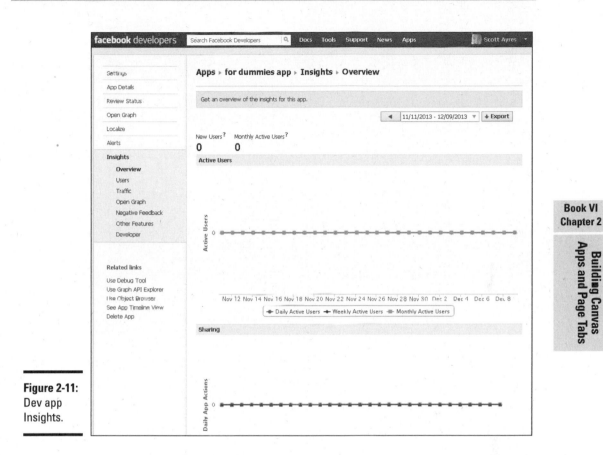

Figure 2-11:
Dev app
Insights.

✦ **Negative Feedback:** The negative feedback your app receives. You can use this feedback to improve your app.

✦ **Other Features:** Ratings and revenue. The App ratings section shows you the ratings that users have given your app. The Payments section tracks the revenue your app brings in and any chargebacks or refunds.

✦ **Developer:** The technical efficiency of your app and the activity the app gets. The latter detail can be different than the number of users because some users may perform a lot of activities but others may spend only a short time in your app. This section also assesses any glitches in the app — API errors, restrictions, and warnings — so you can keep your app working properly.

All these items can be viewed by week, month, or a specific date range. You also can export the data to an Excel spreadsheet or a .csv (Comma Separated Value) file. These analytics are critical in measuring the effectiveness of your app. You can use this data also for marketing purposes to measure one effort against another.

Chapter 3: Creating Your Own Apps

In This Chapter

✓ Understanding the types of Facebook core apps

✓ Creating a Facebook app

✓ Installing a Facebook app

✓ Authenticating a Facebook app

You can develop apps for all kinds of reasons. Some apps conduct surveys, other apps sell things. Some are marketing tools. Some collect charitable contributions. You're limited only by your ambition and imagination.

Facebook apps are, in effect, web applications that run inside the Facebook interface, and they can do most things non-Facebook web applications can do. The difference between standard web apps that don't use Facebook API and Facebook apps that do is that the latter also integrate with Facebook, allowing users to interface with their close friends and family in the app experience. A Facebook app can duplicate just about any piece of functionality you see on Facebook.

When developing Facebook apps, in many instances you're limited by your programming skills. Before getting deeply into this discussion of creating Facebook apps, realize that highly sophisticated games, marketing, and revenue-generating apps are usually developed by professional programmers. (But that doesn't mean you can't do it, too.)

Creating and Deploying a Facebook App

Facebook apps are little programs that run inside the Facebook environment. A simple way to look at it is that Facebook is your operating system, similar to Windows, Mac OS, or iOS. Apps run in the core environment — the Facebook program and the capabilities the folks at Facebook have built into the core.

At Facebook's core

When developing apps for Facebook, it's helpful to look at the Facebook platform as a group of core technologies. Depending on what your app does, it will integrate with one or more of these core technologies. The most commonly used core technologies are social plugins and platform dialogs.

Social plugins

Social plugins, discussed in Chapter 4 of this minibook, are some of the common objects you use in your daily interaction with Facebook. They include the Like button, the Send button, the Follow button, and Comments dialog boxes. When developing your Facebook apps, you can take advantage of these common objects and use them in your apps.

Platform dialog boxes

Facebook has lots of dialog boxes for posting to your timeline, posting to your friends' timelines, sending messages, and so on. Your apps can generate these dialog boxes and accept input from users. Platform dialog boxes are discussed in Chapter 4 of this minibook.

A basic app

Creating and deploying apps on Facebook is a huge, deep subject. To help you appreciate the possibilities and familiarize yourself with the process, we delve into setting up and installing a simple app. While creating apps can get complicated, installing them on your Facebook account isn't difficult, thanks to the great tools the folks at Facebook provide.

In this chapter, you install a basic little app in Facebook to walk through the process. This app doesn't exploit any Facebook objects, nor does it use social plugins or platform dialog boxes. You look at using these features in Chapter 4 of this minibook.

Creating and deploying an app on Facebook consists of two procedures, one on a non-Facebook server and the other inside the Facebook interface, as follows:

✦ **Create the app and save it on a web server.** This step is the hard part that usually requires web page design and programming skills, depending on the scope of your app. The process entails designing the app and making it available on the Internet, so that Facebook can find it and load it on a canvas page. Designing and developing apps is beyond the scope of this book, but you can find several examples of Facebook apps on the web; another resource is *Facebook Application Development For Dummies* by Jesse Stay (John Wiley & Sons, Inc.).

✦ **Deploy the app on Facebook.** This process entails going to Facebook's app developments pages, installing the app, and making it available to Facebook users. Facebook has several tools for making this part of the process fairly simple.

In this example, you take a simple mind-reading game app and install it on Facebook.

Before you can install apps on Facebook, however, you must first confirm your Facebook account.

App, app — who has the app?

Before you can install an app on Facebook, you need an app. Remember that an app is a separate file (or files, for more complex apps) located somewhere else on the Internet. The app itself is not installed and saved on Facebook's servers. A Facebook app is a web app that runs inside the Facebook interface. For this example, we created a simple app; if you're feeling adventurous, you can use your own app.

Because Facebook doesn't allow you to upload your apps to its servers, you need access to a web server. The following procedure to upload and save files on an external, non-Facebook server assumes basic knowledge of FTP and computer file directory structure. If you don't have this knowledge or access to an external server, Facebook partners with Heroku, an app-hosting service that integrates with the Facebook developers' pages. Get more info on Heroku at `https://developers.facebook.com/blog/post/558/`.

**Book VI
Chapter 3**

**Creating Your
Own Apps**

The following steps show you how to make an app available on a public web server:

1. **Using Dreamweaver, a source-code editor, text editor, or whatever you use for creating web pages, create a page consisting of the following code:**

```
<script type=text/javascript>
var iRandom;
function Restart()
{
iRandom = Math.floor(Math.random()*10)+1;
alert('Can You Read My Mind?');
}
function Go()
{
var read = document.getElementById('myRead').value;
if (read>iRandom)
    alert('Go Down!');
if (read<iRandom)
    alert('Go Up!');
if (read==iRandom)
    {
    alert('You Read My Mind!');
    Restart();
    }
}
</script>
<h2>Can You Read My Mind?</h2>
<hr />
<h2><img src="images/mindread.png" alt="Mind Reader" width="300"
    height="232" hspace="10" align="left" />Are You Psychic?</h2>
<p>I'm thinking of a number between 1 and 10. To test your mind-reading
    skills, type a number in the field below and click Go. If you guess
    wrong, you can try again until you get it right. To start the game
    over, click the Play Again button.</p>
<p>Good Luck!</p>
<p>I'm thinking of a number between 1 and 10:
  <input name='MyRead' type=text id='myRead' size="5">
  <input type='button' onClick='Go()' value='go'>
</p>
<p>
  <input type='button' onClick='Restart()' value='Play Again'>
</p>
```

```
<p><em>If this took more than one guess, you're probably not psychic.
    Sorry.</em></p>
<hr />
<script type=text/javascript>
Restart();
</script>
```

This is a simple HTML form with one field and two buttons, some accompanying text, an image, and some JavaScript. The user guesses a number between 1 and 10 and types it in the field. When the user clicks the Go button, the script matches the number to a number randomly chosen when the page loaded. If he or she guesses correctly, a dialog box confirms the correct guess. If the wrong answer is chosen, the dialog box tells the user whether the number is higher or lower than the randomly generated one, allowing him or her to guess again.

2. **Name the file `index.html`.**

3. **Create a subdirectory named `apps` in the root (main) directory of your public web server, and then create a subdirectory of `apps` and name it `images`.**

The root directory is the main directory of the site. On the web, subfolders are typically accessed by tacking the directory name onto the back of the site's domain name, as follows:

```
http://www.MyWebSite.com/apps/
```

4. **Upload `index.html` with an FTP client, such as Dreamweaver or whatever you have, to the `apps` subdirectory you created in Step 3.**

5. **Upload the image file (for example, `mindread.png`) to the `images` folder inside the `apps` folder.**

That's it! To test the app, navigate in your browser to the URL where you saved the page, for example:

```
http://www.mysite.com/apps/
```

You should get the mind reader app shown in Figure 3-1.

Figure 3-1:
Your web app prior to deploying it on Facebook.

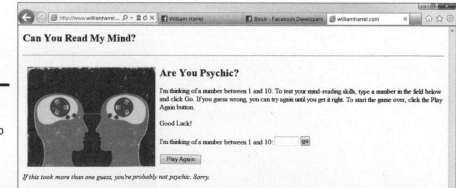

Go ahead and try it if you want. If you guess wrong, a dialog box will let you know. Simply enter another number based on the feedback the dialog box provides, telling you to go up or down in the number value. When you get it right, the dialog box tells you that you're a mind reader.

Installing the Facebook app

Getting the app to work on Facebook is fairly simple, after you know where to start:

1. **Start your web browser and log in to Facebook.**

2. **In the browser's address bar, type the following URL:** `http://developers.facebook.com/`.

   This takes you to the developers greeting page. From here, you can branch off to pages for building websites, building mobile websites, or building Facebook apps.

3. **Click the Apps link in the upper-right corner of the menu bar, and then click the Create New App button.**

   This displays the Create New App dialog box, as shown in Figure 3-2. From here, you can name your new app and give it an app namespace. The *app namespace* is the directory where Facebook saves data about your app. The namespace needs to be different from other namespace names on Facebook. We named ours *mymindread,* so you can't use that name.

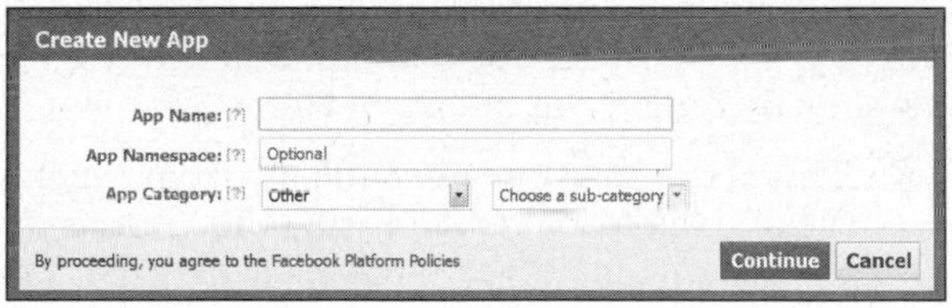

**Book VI
Chapter 3**

**Creating Your
Own Apps**

Figure 3-2:
The Create
New App
dialog box
for starting
the app
installation
process.

Create New App		
App Name: [?]		
App Namespace: [?]	Optional	
App Category: [?]	Other	Choose a sub-category
By proceeding, you agree to the Facebook Platform Policies		Continue Cancel

4. **Type a name for your app in the App Name text box.**

   You can name the app whatever you want; we named ours *Mind Reader*. You can use that name, too. Facebook saves apps with unique ID numbers that are generated when you save this dialog box.

5. **Type the App Namespace until you get one that works.**

   This field requires seven letters. The namespace can't be the same as any other namespace on Facebook. Also, the namespace can't have any spaces, uppercase, or nonalphabetic characters. After you type the namespace, a message beside the App Namespace text box displays either a green Available message or a red Failed, depending on whether you type a namespace already in use. Just keep trying until you get an Available message. (Or you can change it later in the process.) The category is optional.

6. **Click Continue**.

You see a security CAPTCHA.

7. **Type the security code and then click Continue.**

The Basic Settings page appears. The following describes each option on the page. You can leave most of these options as is, unless you want to customize your app further:

- *Display Name:* The name of your app.

- *Namespace:* The app's namespace.

- *Contact Email:* The e-mail address for the app to send data to.

- *App Domain:* The domain name on the server where you saved your app earlier — just the domain name — such as `yourdomain.com`.

- *Sandbox Mode:* Determines whether only app developers (selected) or everyone (deselected) can use the app.

8. **Select Add Platform.**

You are selecting the platform with which your app will be integrated. A dialog box appears.

9. **Choose App on Facebook as the type of app you want to create.**

10. **Scroll to the lower half of the page, and fill out the necessary fields.**

This is where you set up your app's integration with your external app located on the other server, as shown in Figure 3-3:

- *Site URL:* This is the base domain and path from which all calls to your web server will load. Including this URL ensures that Facebook always knows that your servers are making the call. Type the entire URL path of the app you just created on your web server here, including the page name.

- *Canvas URL:* The nonsecure location of the external app. This is the full URL that will be loaded when your canvas app on Facebook.com loads.

- *Secure Canvas URL:* The secure location of the Canvas URL (it should begin with https://). You'll probably want to include SSL on your web server so that you can load your app securely inside Facebook. Facebook runs in SSL mode by default, and you'll get errors if you try to load a nonsecure app.

- *Canvas Page:* The Facebook URL for your app. Facebook generates it according to the data you entered in previous fields. This is how users get to your app.

• *Mobile Web URL:* If you developed a separate version of the app for mobile devices, put that URL here, or use the same Site URL, if the app will run on mobile devices as is.

Note that Facebook filled in the Canvas Page URL text box, based on the information you typed in the other text boxes. This is the URL to the app itself in Facebook. You could place that URL in the address bar of your browser while logged in to Facebook and go straight to your new app, as could anyone else logged in to Facebook. Posting the canvas page URL on your timeline, in messages, and on other web pages is one way to provide access to users.

11. Click the Save Changes button at the bottom of the page.

Facebook checks the data you entered as it saves the app info. If any entries are not in the correct format, you're prompted to change them.

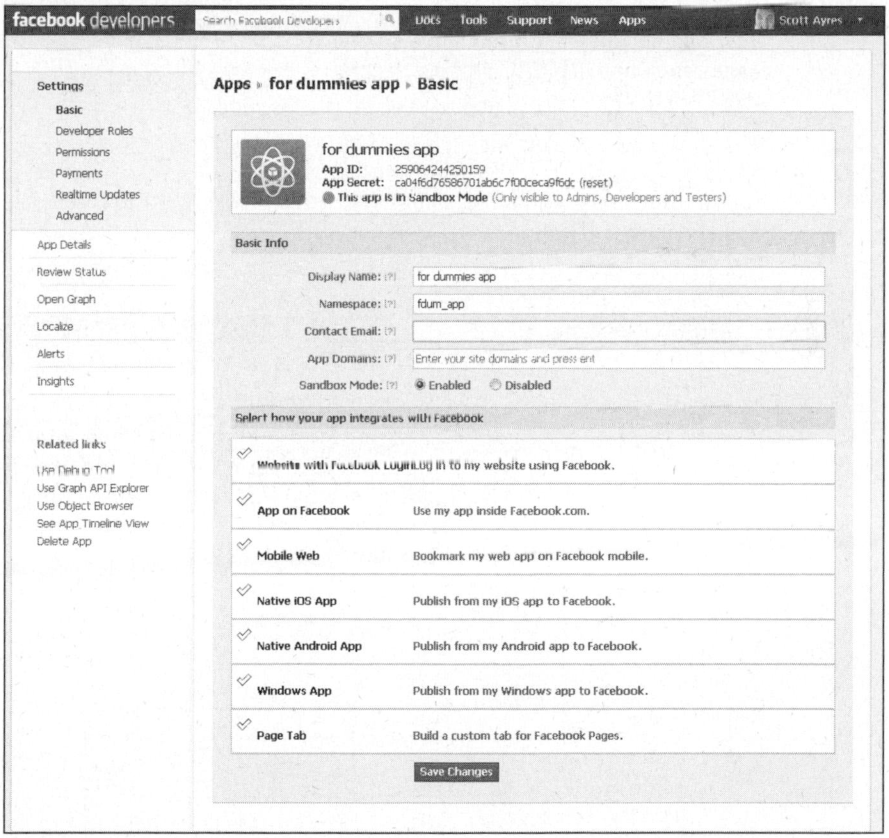

facebook developers

Search Facebook Developers | Docs Tools Support News Apps | Scott Ayres

Apps ▸ **for dummies app** ▸ **Basic**

Settings
Basic
Developer Roles
Permissions
Payments
Realtime Updates
Advanced

App Details

Review Status

Open Graph

Localize

Alerts

Insights

Related links
Use Debug Tool
Use Graph API Explorer
Use Object Browser
See App Timeline View
Delete App

for dummies app
App ID: 259064244250159
App Secret: ca04f6d76586701ab6c7f00ceca9f6dc (reset)
● This app is in Sandbox Mode (Only visible to Admins, Developers and Testers)

Basic Info

Display Name: [?]	for dummies app
Namespace: [?]	fdum_app
Contact Email: [?]	
App Domains: [?]	Enter your site domains and press ent
Sandbox Mode: [?]	● Enabled ○ Disabled

Select how your app integrates with Facebook

✓ **Website with Facebook Login** Log in to my website using Facebook.

✓ **App on Facebook** Use my app inside Facebook.com.

✓ **Mobile Web** Bookmark my web app on Facebook mobile.

✓ **Native iOS App** Publish from my iOS app to Facebook.

✓ **Native Android App** Publish from my Android app to Facebook.

✓ **Windows App** Publish from my Windows app to Facebook.

✓ **Page Tab** Build a custom tab for Facebook Pages.

Save Changes

Figure 3-3:
Use these fields to associate your external content with the Facebook core.

Adding your app to a business page tab

As discussed in Book IV, Chapter 1, you can create your own business page on Facebook. One of the ways to make your app available is to publish it as a tab. Tabs (also called apps) show up below your cover photo on your page.

Creating a tab on one of your business pages is a four-step process, as follows:

1. **While filling out the Basic settings form when installing your app in Facebook, select the Page Tab check mark to open that section of the form, shown in the following figure.**

2. **Fill in the Page Tab Name (the name of your app as you want it to appear on the page), the Page Tab URL, and the Secure Page Tab URL.**

   These last two should match what you typed for the Canvas URL and Secure Canvas URL in the App on Facebook section of the form. Save the form.

3. **While logged in to Facebook, go to the following URL (replace** `your_app_id` **with the Facebook ID for your app and** `your_canvas_url` **with the URL for your app on your web server):**

   ```
   http://www.facebook.com/dialog/
         pagetab?app_id=your_app_id
         & next=your_canvas_url
   ```

   The URL takes you to the Add Page Tab dialog box.

4. **In the Choose Facebook Pages drop-down list, choose the page from which you want to install the app, and then click the Add Page Tab button.**

   Facebook adds the tab to the requested page.

That's it! Although many apps require additional setup, the simple Mind Reader app does not. It doesn't require any permissions or other settings.

You can make your app available to users in many ways. In addition to the method described in Step 8, you can also create a link on your business page, as described in the "Adding your app to a business page tab" sidebar in this chapter. For a description of the differences between tabs and canvas pages, see Chapter 2 of this minibook.

 After Facebook has successfully saved the data, the app ID is displayed at the top of the page. The app ID is critical to several aspects of promoting your app. For an example, see the "Adding your app to a business page tab" sidebar. The app ID can be used also in your app scripts, inside the app itself.

Authenticating Your App

The Auth dialog box, shown in Figure 3-4, allows the user to install your app on the user's Facebook home page and authenticate the app. Authenticating an app grants it the permissions it needs to run properly. Permissions define which objects of a Facebook account the app needs. For example, if your app needs to post the user's timeline, the Auth dialog box requests this permission from the user.

The App Details

The App Details form is available by clicking App Details in the left sidebar of your app setup. Shown in Figure 3-5, the App Details section allows you to define which permissions the app needs to request from the users when they click the app from Facebook's App Center. (App Center is a directory of apps available when users click Apps in the left sidebar of the news feed). The App Details section enables you to configure exactly how your app will appear and work in App Center.

Here is a description of the options in this form and how they affect your app's appearance in App Center:

✦ **Primary Language:** Leave this option set at the default for now. This option determines basic defaults for the language that the user sees when they use Facebook features of your app.

✦ **Display Name:** Type the name of your app here. The name will appear across the top of the Auth dialog box.

✦ **Tagline:** Type a short tagline, up to 40 characters. The tagline will appear below your app's name.

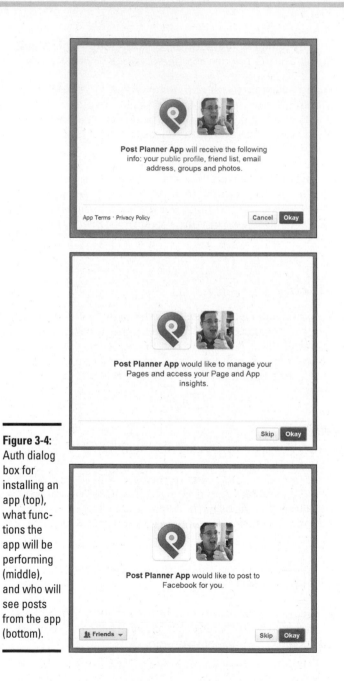

Figure 3-4:
Auth dialog box for installing an app (top), what functions the app will be performing (middle), and who will see posts from the app (bottom).

✦ **Description:** Enter a description of your app — what it does, why, and so on. You are limited to 130 characters.

✦ **Detailed Description:** Enter a detailed description of your app, up to 1000 characters. This description will help users decide whether or not to install your app.

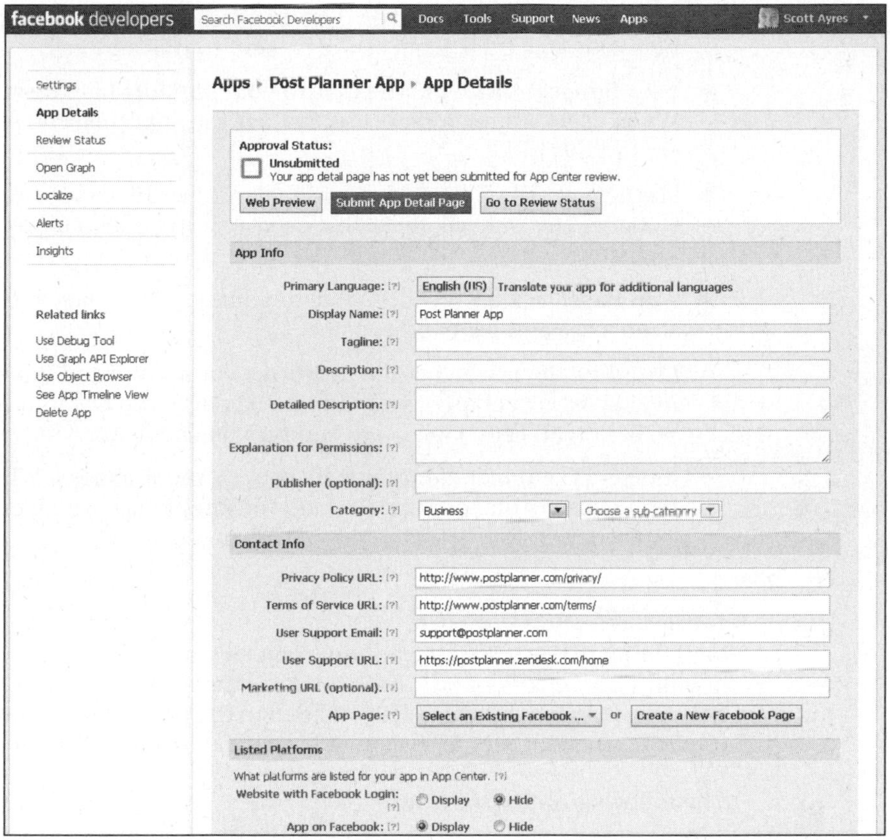

Figure 3-5:
Configure
how your
app will
appear in
App Center.

Book VI
Chapter 3

Creating Your
Own Apps

✦ **Explanation for Permissions:** Type the description of the types of permissions your app needs to get from the user's Facebook account. This description helps the user decide whether to authenticate the app.

✦ **Publisher:** This field is optional. You can add the name of the person or company publishing the app.

✦ **Category:** Choose the category and subcategory that best describe your app. This information helps users find your app.

✦ **Privacy Policy URL:** Create a link in the Auth dialog box that takes the user to a page on your web server describing your privacy policy. Because your app accesses personal information on Facebook, you can use this option to assure users that their data is safe with you.

✦ **Terms of Service URL:** Create a link in your Auth dialog box that takes the user to a page on your web server describing the rules or terms of service for your app.

✦ **User Support Email:** Add an e-mail address. When users report or contact your app, their request will be sent to this address.

✦ **User Support URL:** Add the URL to your support help desk or FAQ page. When users submit a report or contact the app, their request will be sent to this URL.

✦ **Marketing URL:** This field is optional. Add a URL to your promotional website. This link will be visible on your app detail page as Visit App Website.

✦ **App Page:** Link a Facebook page to your app. The page must be categorized as an app page for it to link.

✦ **Listed Platforms:** Select the platforms you want listed under the Available On section of your app detail page. You can choose between Website with Facebook Login and App on Facebook.

✦ **Images:** The remainder of this page is all about images. What you enter here depends on your app. Upload the images according to the sizing listed.

Request permission

In addition to the preceding options, you may need to tweak the permissions of your app. Click Permissions in the left sidebar. You see the Configuring Permissions section, which lets you define the permissions that Facebook requests from the user as well as set the default activity privacy.

The following options are available:

✦ **Default Activity Privacy:** Choose the default privacy setting for your app's activity. Users can change this setting in the Login dialog box. You can choose from Public, Friends, None (User Default), or Only Me.

✦ **User & Friend Permissions:** Include required permissions, permissions that typically just request information rather than make changes to the user's Facebook objects. Note that you must request access to each specific type of data. To get the user's birthday, interests, location, relationship data, and so on, you'll need a string in this field for each one.

To enter permission, start typing the permission string in the field, as shown in Figure 3-6. Facebook will then suggest available strings based on what you type.

✦ **Extended Permissions:** Typically, the Extended Permissions allow you to make changes to the user's Facebook objects, such as posting and uploading photos and videos. The user can also revoke any of these permissions after authenticating your app. In most instances, revoking permissions for an app will break it or change how the app works.

To enter a permission, start typing the permission string in the field. Facebook will suggest available strings based on what you type.

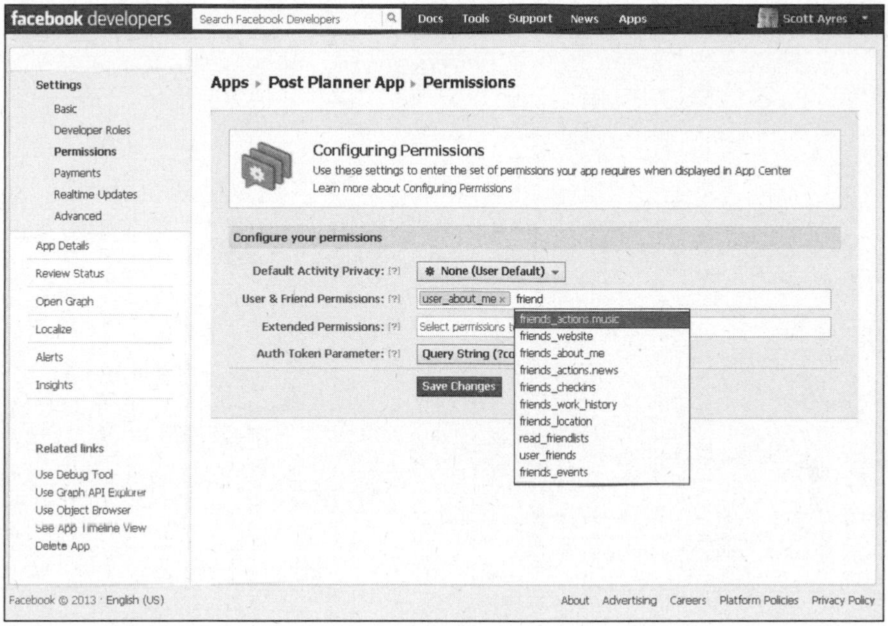

Figure 3-6:
Use these fields to request permissions from the user's Facebook account.

✦ **Auth Token Parameter:** Some apps interact with the Graph API. An auth token, or authorization token, is passed to the Graph API to allow the app to interact with it on behalf of Facebook users. This sophisticated concept is designed for use with intricate apps. You can get a full description of app authentication at `http://developers.facebook.com/docs/authentication/`.

Chapter 4: Tour of the Facebook API

In This Chapter

✓ Finding technical information

✓ Understanding the Facebook API core concepts

✓ Using Facebook SDKs

✓ Placing Facebook objects on your website with social plugins

Developing apps for the Facebook platform requires a little knowledge on two fronts. The apps themselves often consist of HTML and CSS for creating and formatting websites, as well as JavaScript, PHP, Python, or Objective-C programming. To deploy an app on Facebook and take advantage of all the various objects, such as news feeds and other Facebook features, you need to have an understanding of the basic Facebook application programming interface (API).

Facebook provides a well-developed API for creating apps, with plenty of tools to help you integrate your app into Facebook's social fabric, as well as extensive documentation. However, like most documentation (usually written by technogeeks), finding information isn't always easy. Using it can be difficult, especially if you don't know what to look for.

In this chapter, we take a look at the API and its core concepts, the various development tools, and the documentation — where to look for each tool and where to find detailed instructions on how to use them. In many instances, the Facebook documentation includes detailed deployment information, as well as online tools that create some of your app code for you — the parts of the code that integrate your app with the API, anyway.

Consider this chapter the tourist guide for using the Facebook API, including a map for finding the documentation for developing and deploying your Facebook apps.

Finding Technical Information

No matter how you slice it, just like creating apps for any other platform, developing Facebook apps is a highly technical undertaking — an expedition up Geek Creek. You know what they say about going up Geek Creek without a paddle, so remember that your paddle is Facebook's online developer's documentation, as well as a few other resources.

Like all aspects of information technology, Facebook changes frequently. The Facebook interface and features are under constant development, as is the site's app technology and developer interface. In many cases, sometimes the only current documentation is the site's online manual, which is usually updated with the site itself.

Facebook's online API documentation

Because Facebook apps can do so many things, and can run from the very simple to the highly complicated, writing a step-by-step tutorial isn't useful. The online documentation for the Facebook API is divided into topics; in this section, you discover where to find technical information on some of the more important app development topics.

Where to start

In Book VI, Chapter 3, we provide a step-by-step exercise on installing a simple app in the Facebook API. That exercise is basic. You can get more detailed information at the following locations:

✦ **Getting Started, Canvas Tutorial:** Complete with code samples, this section, shown in Figure 4-1, provides information on creating your app, installing it on Facebook, authorizing it, and exploiting social channels (such as the news feed and game stories). You can also find a link to a sample app that uses real-time updates as one of its Facebook integration features. You can get to this page at `https:// developers.facebook.com/docs/guides/canvas/`.

✦ **Getting Started, Apps on Facebook:** This page provides an overview of the app-creation process, describing the canvas page, social channels, and analytics. *Analytics* enable you to gauge the performance of your app in terms of how often it gets used, who is using it, and so on. This page is located at `https://developers.facebook.com/docs/ appsonfacebook/tutorial/`.

Advanced API documentation

The more sophisticated your apps become, the more you need to know about core concepts, Facebook's software development kits (SDKs), and other advanced topics, such as dialogs and ads. You can get detailed information on the following Facebook documentation pages:

✦ **Core concepts:** Core concepts include social plugins, social channels, and authentication. We talk more about these later in this chapter in the "Social channels" and "Authentication" sections. You can get detailed information about core concepts at `https://developers.facebook. com/docs/coreconcepts/`.

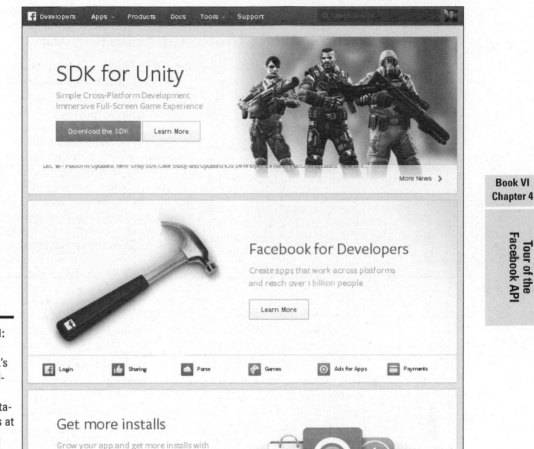

Figure 4-1:
Much of
Facebook's
app devel-
opment
documenta-
tion starts at
this page.

✦ **SDKs and other tools:** Facebook's SDKs enable you to add functionality through JavaScript and PHP, as well as write code specific to Apple iPads and iPhones and mobile devices that use Google's Android platform. Other Facebook API tools include the Developer App, debugging options, and a JavaScript test console. You can find a gateway page to these tools located at `https://developers.facebook.com/tools/`.

Helpful tutorials

In addition to the canvas tutorial described in the earlier section, "Where to start," the folks at Facebook provide several other online tutorials on topics such as creating page tabs and games. Here are a few that we found helpful:

✦ **Page tab tutorial:** You can get a more detailed description of this process in the tutorial located at `http://developers.facebook.com/docs/appsonfacebook/pagetabs/`.

Third-party technical information

In addition to Facebook's extensive developers' manual, several other publications and websites are available to help you in creating and deploying apps. Here are a few we have found helpful:

✔ ***Facebook Application Development For Dummies*** by Jesse Stay (John Wiley & Sons) covers Facebook app development from start to finish. It includes such topics as which scripting languages to use, OAuth 2.0, real-time objects, and the Search API, as well as how to develop and sell business apps. We found this book quite helpful.

✔ **Top 10 Facebook Apps for Building Custom Pages and Tabs** on Social Media Examiner (www.socialmediaexaminer.com/top-10-facebook-apps-for-building-custom-pages-tabs/) showcases several apps that help you with creating page tabs and Facebook pages. These apps create fancy pages and multiple tabs on pages, and write HTML and other code for you to help spruce up your Facebook pages. They install directly into your Facebook account and provide extensive help in these and several other processes.

✦ **Games tutorial:** Game apps are popular on Facebook. A well-designed game can drive traffic to your Facebook account. For a detailed explanation of creating game apps, go to `http://developers.facebook.com/docs/guides/games/`.

✦ **Fluid canvas tutorial:** A fluid canvas adjusts its size to the browser window and screen resolution. For a detailed tutorial on making your canvases fluid, try `http://developers.facebook.com/docs/fluidcanvas/`.

Understanding Facebook's Core Concepts

Building Facebook apps requires an understanding of Facebook's core concepts — the building blocks upon which you develop your apps. In this section, you take a quick look at these core concepts so that you can gain a broader understanding of app development.

One of the core concepts is social plugins. These Facebook apps are deployed *on* your website with links back to Facebook, instead of being deployed *from* your website *to* Facebook. Although Facebook lumps them in with the core concepts for app development, we discuss them in a separate section, "Placing Facebook Objects on Your Web Pages with Social Plugins," later in this chapter.

Open Graph versus Graph API

According to Facebook cofounder Mark Zuckerberg, the *social graph* is the network of connections and relationships between the people on Facebook.

The objects in the social graph are people, events, photos, pages, and so on. The network is the connection between these objects. Your apps exploit these objects from within and from outside Facebook.

Although highly simplistic, Figure 4-2 shows a visual representation of the social graph for one user's Facebook account.

Also called the *Open Graph protocol,* Open Graph started in 2010 allowing people to Like third-party, or non-Facebook, websites and pages. Perhaps the most common use for this protocol is the Like button on a blog post. Open Graph has been expanded to allow third-party sites and pages to interact with several Facebook actions and objects, as well as non-Facebook actions and objects within the app. Put simply, Open Graph is the social graph open to access from websites outside Facebook.

Graph API differs from Open Graph in that it represents objects within the Facebook API, such as people, events, and pages. Every object in Facebook — each photo, each person, each event, each app — is assigned a unique ID. Your apps can access and use these objects by referencing their IDs. Some objects have number IDs and are referenced like this: `"id":` `"19292868552"`. Other objects have alpha, or word, IDs, and are referenced as follows: `"username":` `"dannyt"`. In simple terms, the Graph API presents and represents objects on Facebook.

Book VI
Chapter 4

Tour of the
Facebook API

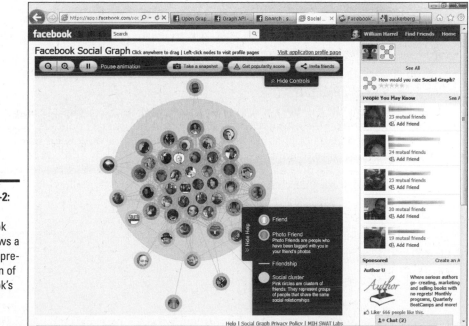

Figure 4-2:
This Facebook app shows a visual representation of Facebook's social graph.

Requesting access to and accessing objects

Before your apps can access a user's information and other objects associated with an account, the app must be granted access to these objects. Your apps request access to objects through authentication. Your app in turn accesses the objects and potentially shares them with the user's friends through social channels.

Authentication

The first time a user accesses your app, an Auth dialog box appears, as shown in Figure 4-3, asking the user for permission to actions and objects from the user's Facebook account. Which actions (writing to a timeline, uploading photos, and so on) and objects (news feeds, events, pages, and more) your app needs access to depends on what the app does inside the Facebook API — your app code dictates what permissions you need. You set up and deploy the Auth dialog box that your users see through the Auth Dialog settings form, as demonstrated in Chapter 3 of this minibook.

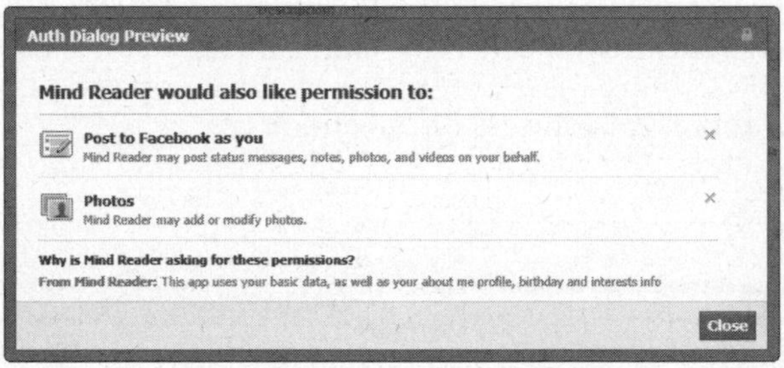

Figure 4-3:
Example
of the Auth
dialog box
requesting
permissions
from a user.

Social channels

Most social channels work in third-party websites, as well as in apps on Facebook. Note, though, that not all objects are social channels. A photo, for example, is an object, but because it isn't used as a vehicle for passing data from one user to another, it isn't a channel. The Like button, on the other hand, facilitates the flow of information from one user to another (or to many others), making it a social channel. Social channels include the following objects:

- ✦ Feed dialog box
- ✦ Feed graph object
- ✦ Like button
- ✦ Request dialog box
- ✦ Bookmarks
- ✦ Notifications

✦ Dashboards

✦ Usage stories

✦ Search dialog box

Cool core tools for creating advanced apps

Facebook provides several tools for creating highly sophisticated apps — apps that post to users' timelines, add tabs to user pages, prompt users to add friends, query and display information from databases, collect funds, initiate chat sessions, and many other functions. The following list takes a look at some of the more commonly used tools and what features they can add to your apps:

✦ **Ads API:** Part of the Graph API, the Ads API allows you to place advertisements in your apps or create apps that generate and manage ads on Facebook. To use this tool, you must apply and meet certain criteria. You can find out more about the Ads API at `http://developers.facebook.com/docs/reference/ads-api/`.

✦ **Chat API:** You guessed it. This tool allows you to integrate Facebook Chat into other chat applications, such as instant messaging apps, web-based chat apps, and mobile instant messaging apps. You must use the Jabber/XMPP service to make the connection between Facebook Chat and your application. To find out more, check out `https://developers.facebook.com/docs/chat/`.

✦ **Dialog boxes:** Dialog boxes are used for just about everything on Facebook, including apps that collect payments. You can use Facebook dialog boxes in your apps, on third-party sites, and so on. There are several types of dialog boxes, including Friends, Feed, Pay, Request, and Send, and you can display them as pages, pop-ups, and in iframes. Find out more at `https://developers.facebook.com/docs/reference/dialogs/`.

✦ **Facebook Query Language (FQL):** If you're familiar with database applications, you know about SQL. FQL differs from SQL in that it queries Graph API data instead of a SQL database. Most of the query language is similar to SQL, although it isn't nearly as robust in math and other functions. For a description of how queries are formatted and which Graph API tables you can query (and how), go to `http://developers.facebook.com/docs/reference/fql/`.

✦ **Internationalization API:** This API translates your app (or website) among the 70 languages Facebook supports. Pretty cool, right? Be forewarned, though: Even for apps built in Facebook canvas pages and iframes, the translation is not automatic and must be set up for each language you want to use. Find that information at `http://developers.facebook.com/docs/internationalization/`.

XFBML — the Facebook markup language

Similar to HTML, XFBML (eXtended FaceBook Markup Language) allows you to integrate Facebook functions into your apps and web pages. XFBML contains special tags that call up Facebook actions and objects, such as Like buttons and Comment dialog boxes. These special tags provide a more robust integration with Facebook than iframes, which are discussed in Chapter 1 of this minibook.

Why does XFBML provide a more robust integration with Facebook than do iframes? For example, if you deploy a Like button by using XFBML, you can also include a Send button, which allows users to send messages to selected users about your pages (or anything else they want). In other words, XFBML simply gives you more options than iframes.

To use XFBML, your apps and web pages must load the Facebook JavaScript SDK library (discussed in the "Developing Apps More Easily with SDKs" section in this chapter). To use XFBML in your apps and pages, you place the XFBML tags in your page and enter the code that loads the required Facebook JavaScript SDK. The SDK interprets XFBML tags for the browser, thereby allowing the page to perform Facebook actions and exploit Facebook objects.

The good news is that for many objects, you don't have to learn XFBML to use it. As discussed in the "Placing Facebook Objects on Your Web Pages with Social Plugins" section in this chapter, Facebook provides many code generators for most of the more common objects, such as Like buttons and Comment dialog boxes.

Developing Apps More Easily with SDKs

Facebook's SDKs perform two important functions. Depending on the SDK, they load libraries of scripting functions that browsers can use to execute script code not otherwise available to the browser, or they provide programming environments that make writing code for a specific platform, such as Apple's iOS mobile platform, easier. Some SDKs perform both functions.

Facebook has five SDKs, two for writing code in popular web-scripting languages (JavaScript and PHP), and two for writing platform-specific code for iOS (iPods, iPhones, and iPads), and Google's popular Android operating system (OS) used on many smartphones and tablets. For the sake of this discussion, we separate the SDKs into two categories, placing the web-scripting language SDKs in one group and the OS SDKs in the other.

Typically, web-scripting languages are used for web apps, and OS SDKs are used for creating *mobile apps,* or standard apps that don't usually require a web page to run in. You probably already have several mobile apps running on your smartphone or tablet.

Web-scripting SDKs

The two most popular scripting languages on the web are JavaScript, a client-side language, and PHP, a server-side language. Client-side scripts are executed by the browser, and server-side scripts are run by the server. Each has pluses and minuses. PHP, for instance, is better at data manipulation, such as querying databases and displaying data. JavaScript works better for visual and behavioral effects, such as simple animations, and displaying menus and buttons.

Another advantage to server-side scripts is that the server processes the code, removing much of the stress from the browser and device resources, which can be beneficial on mobile devices. In addition, JavaScript is not supported on all mobile devices, especially older smartphones and feature phones. Server-side scripts can help ensure that your pages and apps work on a wider range of devices.

Facebook's JavaScript SDK

The JavaScript SDK supports client-side calls to Facebook's server-side API, allowing your apps and web pages to take advantage of most Facebook features, including the Graph API and dialog boxes. It also processes XFBML for exploiting social plugins (discussed in the "Placing Facebook Objects on Your Web Pages with Social Plugins" section, later in this chapter), as well as providing a mechanism for your canvas pages to communicate with Facebook.

To use the Facebook JavaScript SDK, all you have to do is load it on top of your web pages and canvas pages. Your app can then use XFBML to interact with the Facebook API. Depending on what your app does inside Facebook, each application will require slightly different code to load the SDK. The basic script for loading it goes below the <body> tag in your pages and looks like Listing 4-1.

Book VI
Chapter 4

Tour of the
Facebook API

Listing 4-1: Loading the JavaScript SDK

```
<div id="fb-root"></div>
<script>
  window.fbAsyncInit = function() {
    FB.init({
      appId      : 'YOUR_APP_ID', // App ID
      channelUrl : '//WWW.YOUR_DOMAIN.COM/channel.html', // Channel File
      status     : true, // check login status
      cookie     : true, // enable cookies to allow the server to access
    the session
      xfbml      : true  // parse XFBML
    });

    // Additional initialization code here
  };

  // Load the SDK Asynchronously
  (function(d){
     var js, id = 'facebook-jssdk'; if (d.getElementById(id)) {return;}
     js = d.createElement('script'); js.id = id; js.async = true;
     js.src = "//connect.facebook.net/en_US/all.js";
     d.getElementsByTagName('head')[0].appendChild(js);
   }(document));
</script>
```

You can get detailed information on the JavaScript SDK from `http://developers.facebook.com/docs/reference/javascript/`.

PHP SDK

Because the PHP SDK loads server-side scripts, it consists of several PHP pages that you download from github (`https://github.com`) and upload to your web server (the server that hosts your app or web pages on which you want to include Facebook objects).

To use the PHP SDK, you need to acquire an app ID from Facebook's developer app, which we show you how to use in Chapter 3 of this minibook. You need a lot more info to set up and use this SDK, which you can find at `http://developers.facebook.com/docs/reference/php/`.

Mobile app–scripting SDKs

Facebook also provides SDKs for popular mobile devices, such as Google's Android operating system (OS), found on many of today's smartphones and tablets, as well as Apple's iOS, used on iPhones, iPod touches, and iPads.

iOS SDK

The iOS SDK allows you to create apps for Apple's handheld devices: the iPod Touch, iPhone, and iPad. Like the PHP SDK, the iOS SDK must be downloaded from github (`https://github.com`). You must also register it with Facebook and install it, which requires an app ID that you acquire from Facebook.

Technically, the iOS SDK is a Facebook app itself. As shown in Figure 4-4, it contains dialog boxes and debugging tools to help you through the app development process, but it does not completely eliminate the need for programming skills. The URL for the iOS Getting Started page, which contains links to multiple other iOS SDK technical documents, is at `https://developers.facebook.com/docs/mobile/ios/build/`.

Android SDK

The Android SDK allows you to develop Facebook apps for mobile devices (smartphones and tablets) that run on Google's popular Android OS, which powers hundreds of devices. You must download the Android SDK from github (`https://github.com`), register it with Facebook, and install it.

If you've used Google's Android SDK, you'll see some similarities in this one. As shown in Figure 4-5, the Android SDK provides several dialog boxes for walking you through the development process, including a code editor, a debugger, and a compiler. You can get full installation and usage details for the Android SDK at `https://developers.facebook.com/docs/mobile/android/build/`.

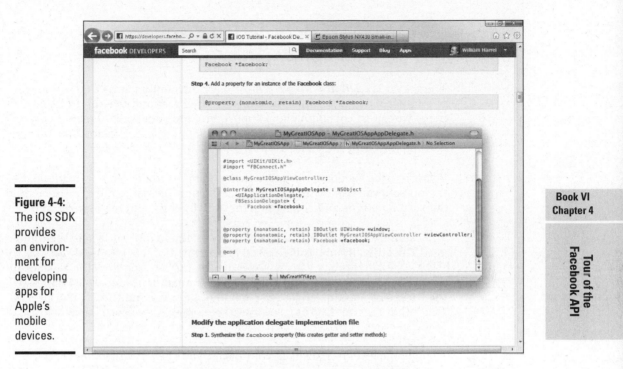

Figure 4-4:
The iOS SDK provides an environment for developing apps for Apple's mobile devices.

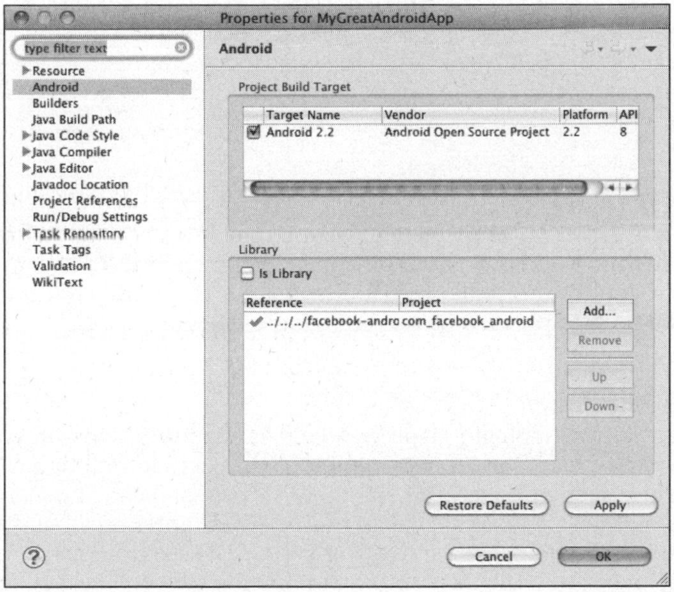

Figure 4-5:
The Android SDK provides an environment for developing apps for Android-based devices.

Placing Facebook Objects on Your Web Pages with Social Plugins

The Facebook API provides a platform for developing apps that integrate and interact with Facebook, both inside the Facebook API and from third-party websites. Social plugins allow you to add Facebook objects to your web pages. A common application for social plugins is placing Like buttons on blog posts.

If you've used Facebook for more than a minute, you're familiar with most of the objects you can control with social plugins, including the Like, Send, and Subscribe buttons and comments, the activity feed, and recommendations.

You can implement most plugins with either the XFBML or iframe technologies. The latter, iframe, is discussed in Chapter 1 of this minibook. Similar to HTML, XFBML formats your app web pages. (XFBML requires the JavaScript SDK.) For an explanation of XFBML, see this chapter's sidebar, "XFBML — the Facebook markup language." To find out more about the JavaScript SDK (and other Facebook SDKs), see the "Developing Apps More Easily with SDKs" section, earlier in this chapter.

To implement social plugins in your pages, you need to write some code. Facebook provides code generators for most social plugins. All you have to do is provide some basic information in the code generator forms, click the Get Code button, and copy and paste your code into your page. Figure 4-6 shows the Like button code generator. The page located at `http://developers.facebook.com/docs/plugins/` provides links to pages containing social plugin code generators.

Embedded Posts

The embedded posts plugin allows you to share any post on Facebook on a website or a Facebook app. This plugin can be useful for sharing a notable post in your blog or when you are trying to drive more engagement to a Facebook page post from your company's website.

Activity feed

The activity feed plugin displays recent Facebook activity on your site. The activity feed can contain information about users interacting with content in your site, such as Like, Read, and Play. Comments also show up in the activity feed. What the user sees depends on whether he or she is logged in to Facebook. When logged in, the user sees activities from his or her friends. When logged out, the user sees recommendations (discussed later in this section) from your site and is provided with an opportunity to log in to Facebook.

Figure 4-6:
Facebook's
code
generators
automati-
cally create
the code for
deploying
social
plugins in
your pages.

Comments button

The Comments box allows users to, you guessed it, comment on your page.
If the user doesn't deselect the Post to Facebook check box, the comment is
posted to news feeds of the user's friends, which is a terrific way to promote
your site.

Facepile

The Facepile plugin displays profile pictures of Facebook users who have
connected with your page in one way or another. You can configure it to
display the pictures of people who have signed up for your site, people who
have Liked your site, and so on. The images are tiled in your Like box.

Like box

The Like box, which appears on external web pages, differs from the Like
button in that the Like box provides information about your web page,
such as how many users have Liked this web page, as well as which of their
friends have Liked it. Users also see recent posts from the web page and can
Like the web page from within Facebook without having to go to the page.
You can include several options, such as faces and profile streams, as shown
in Figure 4-7.

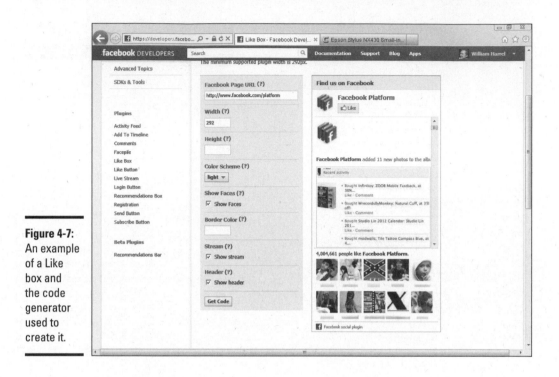

Figure 4-7:
An example
of a Like
box and
the code
generator
used to
create it.

Like button

When the user clicks the Like button for your external web page, a connection is created between your web page and the user. Your web page will appear in the Likes and Interest section of the user's timeline. You can also target ads to the people who have Liked your web page.

Share button

The Like button shows that the user liked your web page on Facebook, but the Share button actually shares a new entry on the person's timeline that links back to your website. This feature can sometimes be more effective at driving traffic than a Like button. As always though, measure to see which one performs better.

Recommendations box

The recommendations box shows personalized recommendations to your users. Recommendations are generated by all the social interactions with URLs from your site. A recommendation might look something like this: "Your App Name," with a link to the app. The next line might read, "1,000,000 people recommended this."

Note that recommendations are generated by domain or multiple domains specified in the plugin. You can get an explanation of how to implement this feature at `http://developers.facebook.com/docs/reference/plugins/recommendations/`.

Recommendations bar

The recommendations bar works like the recommendations box but sends real-time updates of suggestions for users to a bar at the bottom of your website. With the recommendations bar installed, users can both Like each page of your website from the bar and get individualized recommendations for each page of the site. You can also configure the bar so that recommendations appear a few seconds after a person visits each page of your website.

Registration

The registration plugin allows visitors to your site to sign up for your pages with their Facebook accounts. As shown in Figure 4-8, the plugin creates a form on your page and prefills it with information from the user's Facebook account. You can choose to use several Facebook object fields for information or just a few. There's also an option to allow the user to sign up through *your* registration process, just in case the user doesn't want to use Facebook credentials, eliminating the need for separate forms.

Book VI Chapter 4

Tour of the Facebook API

Figure 4-8: An example of the Facebook registration form, which allows users to use Facebook credentials to register for your site.

Send button

Including a Send button on your external web page allows users to send content to friends. They can, for example, send the URL for your web page in a message or in an e-mail. The Send button differs from the Like button in that it allows users to send content to selected users, instead of to all their friends.

Follow button

Placing a Follow button in your web page lets users subscribe to your public updates. As part of the Follow button implementation (with JavaScript), you tell your app to listen in real time for clicks on the Follow button, which informs you immediately when a user subscribes.

Registration plugin

The registration plugin gives you a simple way to sign up users on your website using just their Facebook profile. The users log in to Facebook, and Facebook automatically detects their username and prepopulates fields that you can then use in your website either to store for later use or to customize the experience. To learn more about this plugin, go to `https://developers.facebook.com/docs/plugins/registration/`.

Index

Symbols

\# (hashtag)
  Instagram feeds, 119
  overview, 108
@ symbol, 109
+1 Add Friend button, 22
+Add Friend button, 19
+Create Group button, 146
+Find Friend button, 19

A

Account Balance setting, 43–44
account deletion, 48
account ID, 24
account menu, 51
account settings. *See also* security
  deactivating/reactivating, 33–34
  General account
    account ID, 24
    Ads, 43
    Apps, 40–42
    data downloads, 27
    Email, 25–26
    Facebook Card, 46
    Followers, 39–40
    Language, 27
    Mobile, 38–39
    Name options, 23
    network affiliations, 26–27
    Notifications, 36–37
    Password, 26
    Payments, 43–46
    Support Dashboard, 47
    Timeline and Tagging, 34–36
    username, 23–25
  overview, 22
Active Sessions setting, 33
activity applications, 56
activity feed (plugin), 470–471
Activity Log button, 59
+Add Friend button, 19
Add/Remove option (lists), 75

admin
  Admin Panel
    overview, 295–297
    toolbar, 297–300
  assignments
    account deactivation/reactivation
      issues, 33–34
    business pages, 65
    groups, 146, 148
    privacy settings, 65
  creating roles, 289–290
Adobe Photoshop, 128
Adobe Premiere, 141
Ads API tool website, 465
Ads Manager
  Ads account
    administrator management, 393–394
    closing, 394–395
    pausing versus closing, 395
    settings, 43
  left navigation sidebar, 390–392
  overview, 390
  report generation, 392–393
advertising. *See also* demographics
    tracking; marketing
  ad creation
    Account and Campaign section, 387–388
    Audience section, 386–387
    Bidding and Pricing section, 388–389
    goals and results section, 383–384
    overview, 382
    Review Order/Place Order buttons,
      389–390
    Select Images section, 384–385
    Text and Links section, 385–386
  ad types
    engagement ads, 379–380
    sponsored stories, 380
  Ads Manager
    Ads account administrator
      management, 393–394
    Ads account closing, 394–395
    left navigation sidebar, 390–392
    report generation, 392–393

Ads Manager *(continued)*
　alternative marketing integration
　　outsourcing management functions,
　　　346–347
　　overview, 344
　　third-party apps, 346
　　traditional promotion ideas, 344–345
　　URL name choice/acquisition, 346
　business importance, 339
　customer interaction, 242–243
　economical, 10
　engagement value
　　brand humanization, 339
　　brand interactions, 341
　　influencing followers, 339
　　'top of mind' benefits, 340
　Facebook advantages, 243, 407
　Facebook guidelines
　　forbidden items, 382
　　terms of service, 381
　friends/followers
　　building a following, 341–342
　　connecting, 342–344
　marketing campaigns
　　business page adjustments, 358–361
　　characteristics, 350–351
　　crowdsourcing, 356–358
　　overview, 349
　　sharing contests, 352–357
　　third-party hosting, 353–354
　　types, 351–352
　offers, 405
　promotions, contests, and giveaways
　　app benefits, 401
　　best practices creation suggestions,
　　　403–405
　　call to action links, 397
　　guidelines/rules/laws, 398–399
　　legal verbiage, 399
　　overview, 395–396
　　ShortStack use, 399–401
　　spreading the word, 396–397
　　Strutta use, 402–403
　　tracking responses, 398
　　Wildfire use, 402
　targeted ads
　　deleting, 378
　　flexibility, 379
　　location, 377–378
　　pricing/value, 378–379
　　reach value, 381
　　social proof value, 378
albums
　adding pictures, 124–125
　creating/organizing, 121–123
　editing, 123–124
　moving pictures between, 125–126
　overview, 120–121
　privacy settings, 123–124, 126–127
　types, 121
alerts
　business page notifications, 263–264
　settings, 260
AllFacebook (blog), 89
Android SDK websites, 468–469
API. *See* Facebook Platform API
App Center page
　accessing games from, 199
　game information display, 199–200
App Center website, 200
app ID, 453
application pages, 330–332, 353
Application Programming Interface (API).
　　See Facebook Platform API
apps. *See also* custom apps
　approval code issues, 31
　Apps headers list, 53
　blocking/unblocking, 67
　business pages
　　building influence with, 346
　　contact form, 292
　　default apps, 291
　　display image changes, 305
　　display order changes, 304–305
　　e-mail newsletter signup
　　　form, 292
　　highlighted apps editing, 305–306
　　link options, 291–292
　　navigation, 303–304
　　overview, 290
　　use of, 143
　calls to action, 292
　contacts, 67
　creating, 266
　definition, 198, 445, 447
　editing, 310–311

Facebook Platform, 245–246, 429
formats, 429
games
  accepting/declining/blocking
    invitations, 203
  brand sponsorship/advertising, 198
  credit-card management, 203–204
  finding friends' games, 199–200
  in-game purchases, 203–204
  inviting friends, 202
  overview, 197–198
  permissions, 200–202
invite blocking/unblocking, 67
overview, 40
passwords
  approval codes versus, 31
  automatic, 245–246
  generating/using, 32
  overview, 31
permissions
  automatic, 245–246
  OAuth service, 247, 425–426, 433
personal timeline restriction, 143
tutorials (online), 460–462
Apps settings
  overview, 40–41
  permissions viewing/editing, 42
Aquaintances list, 72
@ symbol, 109
audience
  engagement mechanisms, 428
  identification, 407–408
authentication. *See also* OAuth service
  App Details form, 453–456
  app secret code, 436
  Auth dialog settings form, 464
  overview, 453, 464
  permissions configuration, 456–457
authority establishment
  content
    relevancy, 324
    selection, 215
  cover photo choice, 280–282
  filling needs, 321
  gaining respect, 322
  resource provision, 103

automatic channels, 428
automation
  common mistakes, 265
  content delivery
    scheduling updates, 260–262
    synchronizing updates, 260, 263
  engagement issues, 339
  marketing goals, 259–260
  notifications
    business page alerts, 263–264
    third-party tools, 260–261
  primary functions, 267
  requirements, 260
  set and forget warning, 260, 262, 319
  update scheduling, 260–263
autopopulated lists, 72
avatar (profile photo)
  business use, 209–210
  changing, 58
  choosing/uploading, 17
  overview, 276
  Profile Pictures photo album, 125

B

backups, 27–28
badges, 255–256
benefits of Facebook
  community building, 9
  marketing options, 10
  news access, 9–10
  overview, 8
  relationship extension, 8–9
  research, 8
birthdays
  notices, 55–56
  synchronizing online
    calendars, 179
bitly (link tracking) websites, 325
blocking
  apps, 67, 227
  contacts, 224–225
  event invites, 67
  friend requests, 224
  people, 67

blogs
  automating
    scheduling updates, 260–262
    synchronizing updates, 260, 263
  brand-building, 101
  cross-posting, 250
  Facebook Newsroom, 101
  Instagram photo posting, 119
  linking to, 217
  microblogging, 237
  overview, 237
  RSS feeds, 101
  vioggers (video bloggers), 135
  WordPress to Facebook connections
    creating an app, 266
    overview, 264
    Simple Facebook Connect plugin, 265
    Wordbooker plugin, 266
brand-building
  business
    attracting customers, 101–102
    brand humanization, 339
    content authority reputation, 103
    content planning, 102
    customer interactions, 341
    customized applications, 101
    etiquette rules, 102, 104
    influencing followers, 339
    pages versus timelines, 101–102
    timeline restrictions, 101
    'top of mind' benefits, 340
  personal
    business page development, 100
    etiquette rules, 103
    online content sharing, 103
    profile photo (avatar), 101
    timeline content control, 100
  profile and cover photos, 276
  RSS feeds, 101
  social marketing campaigns
    business page adjustments, 358–361
    characteristics, 350–351
    crowdsourcing, 356–358
    overview, 349
    sharing contests, 352–357
    types, 351–352

business cards, 256–257
business networking. *See* professional
  networking
business page layout. *See also* timeline
  Admin panel, 295–297
  Admin panel toolbar, 297–300
  Apps navigation/management, 303–306
  campaign adjustments
    canvas apps use, 359–360
    contact form embedding, 359
    cover photo tweaks, 358
    custom contest tab, 358–359
    ticker use, 360–361
  Page Information section, 300–303
  personal timeline versus, 313–315
  personal/business switching, 314–315
  right navigation sidebar, 313
  tab creation, 452
  timeline management, 307–313
business page settings
  age restrictions, 288
  company information editing, 283–285
  country restrictions, 288
  merging, 289
  messages selection/deselection, 287
  moderation/profanity filter, 288
  notifications, 287
  overview, 285–286
  post targeting and privacy, 287
  posting options, 286–287
  removal, 289
  similar suggestions, 288
  tagging notifications, 287
  visibility, 286
business pages. *See also* status updates
  administrative rights issues, 34, 65
  apps usage
    custom app publishing, 452
    forms, 292
    link options, 291–292
    overview, 290
  audience engagement
    mechanisms, 428
  automatic notifications, 263–264
  brand-building, 101–104
  calls to action, 277

campaign adjustments
  canvas apps use, 359–360
  contact form embedding, 359
  cover photo tweaks, 358
  custom contest tab, 358–359
  ticker use, 360–361
comment permissions, 110–111
creating, 271–273
customizing
  admin role management, 289–290
  apps use, 290–292
  clickable URL links, 284
  editing options, 283–285
  featured pages, 293–294
  page settings, 285–289
  suggestions from followers, 293
deletion/eviction, 271
design
  cover photo, 280–282
  cover photo ads, 281
  layout suggestions, 280
  profile photo (avatar), 277–280
  simple and consistent, 277
Facebook Tips website, 87
Followers option versus, 39
guidelines/rules, 216, 313, 335
importance of, 320
interest list additions, 76–78
left navigation sidebar display, 51
Liking, 11, 217–219
logo use, 104
mobile updates, 294
overview, 269–270
personal timeline switching
  advantages, 315
  overview, 314–315
  toolbar differences, 315–318
personal timeline versus, 270
photo uploading, 117–118
promoting
  e-mail contact invites, 219
  inviting friends, 217–218
  sharing, 217–218
searching, 50, 69
shopping cart app, 330
tab creation, 452
tagging rules, 109–110
ticker pane responses, 57

timeline information
  Like pages review, 311
  managing others' posts, 312–313
  milestones, creating, 308–310
  milestones, editing, 310–311
  overview, 307
  pinning stories, 310
  recent posts, 311
  social proof, 311
  status update editing, 310–311
  status update posting, 307–308
types, 269–270
Unliking, 226
URL clickable links, 303
video use, 133–135, 143

C

calls to action
  apps use of, 292
  authority establishment, 321
  business page use, 277
  cover photo use, 281
  customer involvement, 330
  example of use, 329–330
  image inclusions, 305
  Like buttons, 275
  necessity of, 328
  planning workflow, 329
  share page use, 299
  trust-building, 322
Camera+ app website, 132
campaigns. *See* social marketing
    campaigns
canvas apps
  definition, 430
  features, 431–432
  `https://` versus `http://`, 436–437
  overview, 359–360
  page tab combinations, 431–432
  page tabs versus, 419, 432
  redirection links, 432
  settings, 436–437
  SSL certificates, 437
  URL links
    app settings, 436
    Facebook posting suggestions, 451

Chat API tool website, 465
chats
  limiting availability/hiding, 72, 194
  settings, 193–194
Close Friends list, 72
Code Generator
  left navigation sidebar access, 161
  overview, 31
  social plugin generator website, 470
comments
  building engagement, 217
  business pages, 110–111
  customer service
    interaction/response regularity, 334
    negative comment/review management,
      334–335
    spam management, 335
  editing/deleting, 111–112
  etiquette, 102–104
  Facebook Platform benefits, 248
  feedback options, 113
  Follow option, effects of, 69
  mobile devices, 159–160
  multi-site commenting, 248
  news feed, effecting, 94
  permissions, 110–111
  photos, adding, 120
  privacy settings, 69
  searching, 100
  spam reporting, 88
  threads, 289
  videos, 142
  wall postings, 178
Comments box (plugin), 471
community forum, 86–87
contact forms, 292, 359
contacts
  accumulating, 236
  blending personal and professional
    approach suggestions, 211
    respecting differing opinions, 209
  e-mail
    business page invitations, 219
    searches, 15–16, 18
    uploads, 215
  initial setup, 16

managing
  blocking/unblocking, 67, 224–225
  hiding updates (unfollowing), 222–223
  overview, 221–222
  reporting inappropriate behavior,
    224–225
  unfriending, 223–224
professional
  e-mail contact list, importing, 212–215
  meaningful connections, 215–216
  nurturing relationships, 216–217
smart list updates, 72
Trusted Contacts setting, 32
content
  automation
    common mistakes, 265
    scheduling updates, 260–262
    synchronizing, 260
    synchronizing updates, 263
  delivery methods
    broadcasting versus sharing, 323–324
    Like-gating, 428
    link sharing, 324–325
  filtering, 94–95, 236
  link sharing, 103
  planning, 102
  relevancy, 324
  sharing
    broadcasting versus, 323–324
    community building, 324
    links, 324–325
    photos/videos, 326
    share settings, 70
  timeline control, 100
conventions used in book, 2
core concepts
  core tools, 465–466
  Facebook Connect access, 197
  overview, 445, 460, 462
  social plugins
    button location options, 254–255
    discussion, 252, 446, 462
    social graphs, 462–463
    types, 253
    usage recommendations, 253–254
  website, 460

core concepts websites, 460
cover photos
  business use, 210
  call to action use, 281
  changing, 60
  Cover Photos album, 125
  overview, 58, 276
  specifications, 282
cross-posting
  blogs, 250
  Google+ integration, 251–252
  overview, 249–250
  Twitter integration, 250–251
crowdsourcing
  definition, 10, 237
  overview, 349
custom apps. *See also* apps
  app settings
    app type selection, 436–438
    developer information, 436
    overview, 435
    server URL, 436
  app types
    Android, 437
    canvas, 436–437
    iOS, 437
    Mobile Web, 437
    Page Tab, 437–438
    Website with Facebook Login, 436
    Windows, 437
  audience engagement mechanisms
    discovery stories (news feed), 423–424
    games attraction, 418
    Like gating, 428
    notifications (beta), 422–423
    publishing stories, 423
    requests/invites, 422–423
  authentication
    App Details form, 453–456
    app secret code, 436
    OAuth service, 247, 425–426, 433
    overview, 453
  canvas apps
    bookmarks, 432
    definition, 430
    Facebook logo, 431
    fluid width option, 431
    page tab combinations, 431–432

    page tabs versus, 432
    redirection links, 432
    ticker pane, 432
  configuration, 456–457
  creating
    App Details page, 438–439
    app namespace directory creation, 449–450
    app naming, 449
    App Settings options, 435–436
    authenticating, 433
    developer role assignments, 441–442
    Facebook developers page access, 449
    Heroku app-hosting service, 447
    installation, 449–453
    naming restrictions, 434
    Open Graph implementation, 439–440
    platform dialogs, 446
    platform selection, 450–451
    server upload, 448
    social plugins, 446
    type of app selection, 436–438
  definition, 198, 445, 447
Facebook Platform
  app creation, 266
  automatic permissions/logins, 246–247
  blog posting updates, 249–250
  business page alerts, 263–264
  cross-site bookmarking, 248–249
  games and apps access, 247
  marketing goals, 259–260
  multi-site commenting, 248
  multi-site sharing/liking, 249
  overview, 245–246, 259
  requirements, 260
  scheduling updates, 260–262
  secure online access, 245–247
  synchronizing updates, 260, 263
  tweet cross-posting, 249
  update scheduling, 260–263
Insights implementation, 442–443
installation
  app namespace directory creation, 449–450
  app naming, 449
  external app integration, 450
  Facebook developers page access, 449
  platform selection, 450–451

custom apps, installation *(continued)*
language translation, 465
marketing appeal
audience engagement, 418
Insights analytics access, 421
remaining on Facebook, 419
revenue generation, 418
social channel connections, 420
Open Graph implementation
advantages, 439
custom app use, 439–441
definition, 438
Facebook approval process, 440
overview, 439
Simple Facebook Connect benefits, 265
overview, 417, 445
page tabs
advantages, 418–420
business page shortcuts, 432
canvas apps versus, 431
fixed width, 430
instant access, 431
interactive application space, 430
page name displayed, 432
tutorials, 461–462
permissions
checking, 42
configuration, 456–457
OAuth service, 425
optional, 202, 426
request considerations, 245–246, 425
requirements, 424
user authentication, 425
security
https:// versus http://, 29, 65, 436–438
SSL certificates, 437–438
sharing-encouragement features
automatic channels, 427
integration of friends, 428
Like-gating, 428
news feed mechanisms, 426–427
tutorials (online), 460–462
user access, 451
customer service
interaction/response regularity, 334
negative comment/review management, 334–335
spam management, 335

D

data
account deactivation/reactivation issues, 34
account deletion issues, 48
backups, 27–28
downloads
information copied, 28
overview, 27
Insights statistics tracking
algorithm variables, 373–374
backups, 366
data exporting, 365–366
Likes page review, 366–367
main page layout, 364–365
News Feed algorithm, 372–375
overview, 363–364
People page review, 371–372
Posts page review, 370–371
Reach page review, 368–369
settings, 366
statistics tracking, 363–364
Visits page review, 369–370
deactivating/reactivating issues, 33–34
Delete List option, 75
demographics tracking. *See also* Insights
ad targeting value, 379
Ads Manager use, 390–392
business content decisions, 216
e-mail responses, 412
example of use, 94
game progress, 197
importance of, 363
Insights statistics, 387, 407–408
life moments (timeline), 62
link tracking services, 325
News Feed
algorithm rankings, 390–392
issues, 71
overview, 363–364, 372–373, 377
people
Lists feature, 71
smart list use, 72
People page (Insights), 371–372
photo/video ranking, 373
privacy issues, 63

Purchase History, 44
rank management options, 374–375
reach statistics, 368–369
survey use, 396
dialog boxes
app generated, 446
Auth dialog, 464
documentation for, 460
JavaScript SDK support, 467
login, 456
social channel use, 464–465
types, 465
user input, 446
website, 465
XFBML tags, 466
dialogs website, 465
digital footprint. *See* privacy
discovery stories (news feed),
    423–424

E

EdgeRank. *See* News Feed algorithm
e-mail
  calls to action, 299
  contacts
    business page invitations, 219
    searches, 15, 18
    uploads, 212–215
  Facebook e-mail
    address changes, 196
    limitations, 196
    overview, 189
  group addresses, 151
  limitations, 196
  marketing
    format recommendations, 412–413
    tracking responses, 412
    value of, 412
  newsletter signup form, 292
  sending pictures and posts, 167–168
  settings editing
    adding addresses, 25
    download allowing/preventing, 26
embedded posts (plugin), 470
emoticons, 106–107

engagement nurturing
  commenting, 217
  humorous posts, 216
  multimedia, 217
  short postings, 216–217
etiquette
  brand-building, 102–104
  commenting, 102–104
  photos
    profile photo (avatar), 17, 104
    tagging, 129
  posting/updating, 103
  tagging, 110
Events
  calendar synchronizations
    all events, 179–180
    description, 173
    overview, 179
    single events, 180
  changes, 184–185
  creating/editing, 173–174, 181–182
  guest list viewing, 177–178
  invitation viewing, 176
  invitations
    friends, 183–184
    friends of guests, 182
    notifications, 171–172
    viewing, 174
  left navigation sidebar access, 173
  link location, 176
  link postings, 174
  overview, 171–172
  permissions, 174–175, 181–182
  photos, 182–183
  promotion ideas, 185
  public versus private, 174
  responding
    response buttons, 174
    RSVP, 176–177
  searching, 175–176
  wall postings
    commenting, 178
    posting options, 174
eXtended FaceBook Markup Language
    (XFBML). *See* XFBML

F

Facebook
  overview, 7, 56
  Terms of Service agreement, 11–13
  websites
    terms of service agreements, 13
    updates, 1
Facebook AIO FD websites, 3
Facebook apps. *See* apps; custom apps
Facebook e-mail
  address changes, 196
  limitations, 196
  overview, 189
Facebook for Websites. *See* Facebook
    Platform API
Facebook Mobile
  game play, 205–206
  website, 206
Facebook Mobile websites, 206
Facebook Newsroom (blog), 89
Facebook Platform API
  advantages
    automatic permissions/logins,
      246–247
    blog posting updates, 249–250
    cross-site bookmarking, 248–249
    games and apps access, 247
    multi-site commenting, 248
    multi-site sharing/Liking, 249
    OAuth services, 247
    tweet cross-posting, 249
  app creation
    App Details page, 438–439
    App Settings options, 435–436
    authenticating, 433
    developer role assignments,
      441–442
    Heroku app-hosting service, 447
    installation, 449–453
    naming restrictions, 434
    Open Graph implementation,
      439–440
    platform dialogs, 446
    server upload, 448
    social plugins, 446
    type of app selection, 436–438

app installation
  app namespace directory creation,
    449–450
  app naming, 449
  Facebook developers page access, 449
  platform selection, 450–451
automation
  business page alerts, 263–264
  marketing goals, 259–260
  overview, 259
  requirements, 260
  scheduling updates, 260–262
  synchronizing updates, 260, 263
  update scheduling, 260–263
definition, 445
OAuth service, 247
online documentation
  apps on Facebook, 460
  canvas tutorial, 460
  overview, 245–246, 459
  secure online access, 245–247
Facebook plugins. *See* social plugins
Facebook Query Language (FQL), 465
Facebook smartphone app
  code generator, 30–31
  commenting, 159–160
  game searching, 206
  Likes link, 159
  limitations, 164
  navigation, 161
  news feed screen, 159
  notifications, 161
  overview, 37, 132
  status updates, 161–164
  updating business pages, 294
  video creating/uploading, 136–137, 161
  video uploads, 136–137, 161
Facebook Touch Mobile website, 164–165
Facebook websites. *See* websites
Facepile (plugin), 471
Family list, 72
Family Safety Center, 224
Favorites list
  editing, 52
  lists, adding to, 73–74
  overview, 51
  rearranging, 74

feed readers, 11
filters
  friend requests, 66
  news feed content, 94–95
Final Cut Pro, 141
+Find Friends button, 19
Find Friends link, 19–20
Flipboard, 9
fluid canvas
  canvas app feature, 431–432
  tutorial, 462
Follow button (plugin), 474
Followers settings
  options, 39–40
  overview, 39
following
  friending versus, 20
  overview, 11, 114
  people, 115
  settings, 114–115
  videos, 142
forms
  contact form, 292
  e-mail newsletter signup form, 292
FQL (Facebook Query Language), 465
friction, 64
frictionless sharing, 64
friend requests
  allowing/filtering, 66
  blocking, 224
  business versus individual, 314
  e-mail contacts, 212–213
  following versus, 20
  mobile settings, 37
  notifications, 161
  overview, 69
  personal versus business pages, 314, 316
  responding
    confirming, 20–21
    ignoring, 22
    Not Now, 22
    pending notifications, 21–22
  sending
    +1 Add Friend button, 20
    adding to lists, 75
    mass-adding warning, 104
    mutual friend posts, 212

friend requests icon, 50
friending definition, 9
friends
  choosing, 8
  connecting/reconnecting, 8
  definition, 17–18
  finding/inviting
    Insight Visits page, 370–371
    overview, 17
    signup process, 15–16
  searching methods
    +Find Friend button, 18–19
    existing contacts, 18
    friends of friends, 19
    Graph Search box, 19, 100
    topic page reviews, 20
    websites/blogs, 20
friends list. *See* contacts

G

games
  App Center page
    accessing from, 199
    game information display, 199–200
  brand sponsorship/advertising, 198
  credit-card management, 203–204
  Facebook Mobile website, 206
  Facebook Platform benefits, 247–248
  finding friends' games, 199–200
  in-game purchases, 203 204
  gameplay information gathering, 201
  invitation management, 203
  inviting friends, 202
  overview, 197–198
  permissions
    OAuth service, 247
    requested information, 200–202
  privacy settings, 204–205
  timeline postings, 206
  tutorial, 462
Gear icon, 59, 301–302
gift cards
  displaying, 46
  lost/stolen reports, 46
  overview, 208

gifts
  finding/sending, 207
  overview, 206
  purchasing, 208
GIMP website, 128
github website, 466–467
GLMPS app website, 132
Google+
  Chrome browser extension, 252
  Facebook integration, 251–252
  overview, 241
GPS
  Location Services use, 157
  security concerns, 96
Graph Api
  Ads API tool website, 465
  Authorization token use, 457
  FQL queries, 465
  Open Graph versus Graph API, 463
Graph Search
  accessing, 50
  overview, 19, 98–99
  search techniques, 100
groups
  advantages, 145–146
  creating, 146–147
  deleting
    documents, 155
    entire group, 156
  document collaboration, 154–155
  image displays
    changes, 150
    graphics, 149–150
    member profile pictures, 148
  inviting members, 148
  leaving groups, 225–226
  listing, 146
  members
    inviting, 152–153
    leaving groups, 155–156
  overview, 11, 145
  posting
    permissions/approvals, 151–152
    update methods, 154
  privacy settings, 147, 151
  public versus private, 145, 153

reporting inappropriate behavior, 155–156
  settings modifications, 150–152
  unfriending, 223
Groups section, 52

H

hashtag (#)
  Instagram feeds, 119
  overview, 108
Help Center
  business pages, 305–306
  gear icon use, 301
  individual query issues, 87–88
  left navigation sidebar access, 161
  overview, 83–84
  searching methods
    community forum, 86–87
    keywords, 84–85
    left sidebar topics, 85–86
  website, 84
help resources
  Admin Panel Toolbar options, 299–300
  blogs, 89
  Community Forum link, 86–87
  Facebook Help Community, 299
  Facebook Tips news feed, 88
  gear icon use, 301, 318
  web pages, 88
Heroku (app-hosting service), 447
highlighted updates, 330
Highlights, 61
Hike website, 143
home link, 50
home page. *See also* timeline
  algorithm management, 71, 94
  chat pane, 56
  content
    automation, 260–265
    delivery methods, 323–325
    filtering, 94–95, 236
    link sharing, 103
    planning, 102
    relevancy, 324
    share settings, 70
    timeline control, 100

Event notifications, 175–176
filtering content, 94–95
navigation options
  left navigation sidebar, 51–53
  right navigation sidebar, 54–55
  top navigation toolbar, 50–51
overview, 49, 93
status updating, 53
story list editing, 53–54
targeted ad location, 377–378
ticker pane
  activity applications, 56
  business responses, 57
  hiding, 56
  overview, 55
top navigation toolbar, 50–51
unfollowing, 222–223
video viewing, 133
HootSuite
automation tools, 262
overview, 260–261
https:// versus http://
canvas app use, 436–438
privacy protection, 65
secure browsing, 29

I

icons used in book, 2–3
iframes
definition, 422
online store access, 330
overview, 421–422
page tab displays, 353
XFBML versus, 466
iMovie, 141
Inside Facebook (blog), 89
Insights
app developer benefits, 442–443
audience identification, 407–408
backups, 366
business versus personal use, 363
custom app access, 421
data exporting, 365–366
Likes page review, 366–367
main page layout, 364–365
News Feed algorithm
  importance of, 363
  overview, 372–373
  photo/video ranking, 373
  ranking management options, 374–375
  ranking variables, 373–374
overview, 363–364
People page review, 371–372
Posts page review, 370–371
Reach page review, 368–369
settings, 366
statistics tracking, 363–364
Visits page review, 369–370
Instagram app
album restrictions, 125
blog posting, 119
Facebook purchase, 242
overview, 242
picture posting, 119
website, 131
Instagram Feed tab, 119
InstaTab, 119
interest lists
creating, 76–78
following, 76–77
managing, 78–80
overview, 76
searching for, 77
sharing links from, 113–114
sharing options, 80–82
Internationalization API, 465
Internationalization API websites, 465
iOS SDK websites, 468–469
iPhone camera app, 132

J

JavaScript SDK (client-side)
overview, 467
PHP versus, 466–467
website, 468
.jpg files, 119

L

Language setting, 27
language translation, 465
left navigation sidebar
  Blocking link, 67
  business page display, 51
  customizing, 51
  Events access, 173
  Favorites list, 51
  Groups list, 52, 146
  Help Center topics, 85–86
  options, 51–53
  overview, 50–53
  Privacy settings, 65–66
  rearranging, 11
  timeline actions, 51
legal documents websites, 13, 88
life events, 106. *See also* status updates
lifecasting, 96
Like box (plugin), 471
Like button (plugin), 472
Like-gating, 428
Likes page (Insights)
  evaluating ad success, 367
  overview, 366–367
Liking
  ads, 16–17
  business page promotion, 217–219
  business versus individual, 314
  call to action button, 275
  choosing interests, 16–17
  compelling, 330
  Insights statistics tracking, 366–367
  Like button use, 253
  mobile device use, 159
  multi-site methods, 249
  photos, 130
  quality versus quantity, 321
  social proof value, 311
  videos, 143
LinkedIn
  connection requirements/
    limitations, 239
  online resume/endorsements, 240

links
  blogs, 106, 217
  business
    blog posts, 102
    page updates, 168
    sharing, 217
  business page apps, 291–292
  context provision, 324
  Events postings, 174
  Facebook logo, 50
  hashtag (#) use, 108
  link tracking services, 325
  phishing/spam warning, 104, 192
  sales pitches, 321–322
  search engine access, 66
  security concerns, 104, 192, 324
  sharing
    best practices, 324–325
    blog posts, 102
    resources, 103
    RSS feeds, 324
  status page use, 185
  status update use, 105–106, 185
  tagging, 109
  tracking tool, 325
  URL copies, 85, 180
  video uploading versus, 135
  virus issues, 228–231
lists
  Aquaintances and Close Friends, 72
  autopopulating, 72, 77
  catalog view, 71
  chat availability control, 72
  creating, 19, 73
  deletion restrictions, 73, 75
  favorites
    adding to, 73–74
    rearranging, 74
  friends, 75
  interest lists
    creating, 76–78
    following, 76–77
    managing, 78–80
    overview, 76
    searching for, 77
    sharing, 80–82

managing
  Add/Remove Friends option, 75
  Delete List option, 75
  overview, 74
  Renaming option, 74
  Update Types option, 75
  News Feed algorithm versus, 71
  Notification Settings, 80
  overview, 52
  sharing links from, 113–114
  smartlists (autopopulated), 72, 77
  timesuck avoidance, 10
Location Services
  Facebook Places use, 168–170
  overview, 157
  smartphone access, 168–169
  smartphone permissions, 168
Login Notifications
  overview, 29
  privacy protection, 65

M

marketing. *See also* advertising;
    demographics tracking; social
    marketing campaigns
  alternative marketing integration
    outsourcing management functions,
      346–347
    overview, 344
    third-party apps, 346
    traditional promotion ideas, 344–345
    URL name choice/acquisition, 346
  audience identification, 407–408
  automation
    business page alerts, 263–264
    common mistakes, 265
    engagement issues, 339
    goals, 259–260
    requirements, 260
    scheduling updates, 260–262
    synchronizing updates, 260, 263
    third-party tools, 260–261
    update scheduling, 260–263
  blog page integration, 257
  business card integration, 256–257

business pages
  brand-building, 101–104
  cover photo design, 280–282
  creating, 271–273
  deletion/eviction, 271
  importance of, 320
  interest list additions, 76–78
  layout suggestions, 280
  logo use, 104
  overview, 269–270
  photo uploading, 117–118
  product launches, 7
  profile photo (avatar) design, 277–280
engagement value
  brand humanization, 339
  brand interactions, 341
  influencing followers, 339
  'top of mind' benefits, 340
Facebook
  advantages, 9–10, 243, 407
  integration, 256–257, 328
friends/followers
  building following, 341–342
  connecting, 342–344
importance of, 339
permission-based, 410, 412
pitches
  benefit provision, 322
  bombardment avoidance, 321
  call to action links, 321–322
  customer interaction/
    recommendations, 254
product launches, 7
QR code advertisement, 257
shopping cart app, 330
social media benefits
  customer interaction, 242–243
  interactive campaigns, 235
vanity URL
  clickable links, 304
  creating, 275
  naming restrictions/suggestions,
    274–275
  overview, 274
  URL shortcut, 275
Vocus platform, 143

marketing campaigns. *See* social marketing campaigns
marketing strategies. *See also* demographics tracking; Insights
  calls to action
    customer involvement, 330
    example of use, 329–330
    necessity of, 328
    planning workflow, 329
  content delivery
    customer rewards, 323
    link sharing, 324–325
    RSS feeds, 324
    updates timing experiments, 323, 374–375
  customer service
    interaction/response regularity, 334
    negative comment/review management, 334–335
    spam management, 335
  demographic information use, 377
  establish authority
    content selection, 215
    cover photo choice, 280–282
    filling needs, 321
    gaining respect, 322
    resource provision, 103
  Facebook
    as a component, 271
    integration, 328
  goal-setting
    interaction choices, 321
    quality versus quantity, 321
    questionnaire benefits, 328
    specific versus vague, 320–321
  integrated campaign benefits, 414
  Like-gating, 428
  overview, 319–320
  questionnaires
    options, 326–327
    overview, 326
    planning benefits, 328
    question sources, 327
  sharing
    broadcasting versus, 323–324
    community building, 324
    photo/video use, 326

shopping cart app, 330
social proof
  badges, 255–256
  establishing, 322–323
  Liking value, 311
  shared links, 324
  visitor interactions, 322
targeting
  followers versus nonfollowers, 330–331
  interest list use, 76
  market knowledge, 322
  Post Targeting and Privacy setting, 287, 332–333
  status updates, 332–333
traditional promotion ideas
  direct mail, 409–410
  e-mail, 412–413
  online resources, 411
  overview, 409
  PPC (pay per click) ads, 413–414
  radio ads, 411
  TV ads, 410–411
messages
  friend connections, 190–191
  nonfriend connections, 191–192
  overview, 188
messages icon, 50
microblogging, 237. *See also* blogs
milestones
  creating, 308–310
  definition, 57
  editing, 310–311
  highlighted update creation, 330
  pinning stories, 310
mobile devices
  cellphone access
    number changes, 167
    overview, 165
    pictures and posts, 167–168
    setup, 166
    status updates via text, 166–167
  Facebook advantages, 158
  Facebook smartphone app
    commenting, 159–160
    Likes link, 159
    limitations, 164
    navigation, 161

news feed screen, 159
photo transfers, 161
status updates, 161–164
video uploads, 136–137, 161
Facebook Touch Mobile website, 164–165
Location Services permissions/use,
168–170
photo transfers
Instagram use, 119, 125
Mobile Upload album, 125
smartphone app websites, 131–132
tablet access, 164–165
updating business pages, 294
video uploads, 136–137
Mobile settings
enabling, 38
options, 39
Mobile Uploads album, 125

N

NameCheap website, 346
navigation. *See also* left navigation sidebar
overview, 11
right navigation sidebar, 54–55
top navigation toolbar, 50–51
networks
affiliation confirmation, 26
business importance, 339
engagement value
brand humanization, 339
brand interactions, 341
influencing followers, 339
'top of mind' benefits, 340
friends/followers
building following, 341–342
connecting, 342–344
joining/inviting, 26–27
marketing integration
outsourcing management functions,
346–347
overview, 344
third-party apps, 346
traditional promotion ideas, 344–345
URL name choice/acquisition, 346
networking possibilities, 8–9

News Feed algorithm
business content decisions, 216
example of use, 94
importance of, 363
news feed issues, 71
overview, 372–373
photo/video ranking, 373
ranking management options,
374–375
news feed page. *See also* timeline
algorithm management, 71, 94
chat pane, 56
content
automation, 260–265
delivery methods, 323–325
filtering, 94–95, 236
link sharing, 103
planning, 102
relevancy, 324
share settings, 70
timeline control, 100
Event notifications, 175–176
filtering content, 94–95
navigation options
left navigation sidebar, 51–53
right navigation sidebar, 54–55
top navigation toolbar, 50–51
overview, 49, 93
status updating, 53
story list editing, 53–54
targeted ad location, 377–378
ticker pane
activity applications, 56
business responses, 57
hiding, 56
overview, 55
unfollowing, 222–223
video viewing, 133
news reporting
accuracy, 10
real-time information, 9
Notification Settings
interest lists, 80
options, 37
overview, 36
Support Dashboard screen, 47

notifications
business page alerts, 263–264
business versus personal,
317–318
choices, 37
custom app use (beta), 422–423
e-mail reports, 25
Event
invitations, 171–172
settings modifications, 185
Facebook smartphone app, 161
followers, 39
friend requests, 161
logins, 29, 65
mobile phone texts, 24, 37–38
posts from friends, 21
tagging, 34–36, 50
Notifications icon, 50
(hashtag)
Instagram feeds, 119
overview, 108

O

OAuth service, 247, 425–426, 433
Offerpop website, 353
Offers, 405
online persona, 8
Open Graph
activity details, 442
advantages, 439
custom app use, 439–441
definition, 438
Facebook approval process, 440
Graph API versus, 463
overview, 439
Simple Facebook Connect
benefits, 265
story creation, 439
outsourcing, 349

P

page tabs
advantages, 418–419
canvas apps versus, 419, 431

features
business page shortcuts, 432
fixed width, 430
instant access, 431
interactive application space, 430
page name displayed, 432
iframes interface, 421–422
Insights statistics tracking, 353
overview, 330–332
settings, 437–438
tutorials, 461–462
Pages headers list, 53
passwords. *See also* OAuth service
accessing/editing, 26
App Passwords setting
generating/using, 32
overview, 31
strength, 64
pay per click (PPC) ads, 413–414
Payments settings
account balance, 43–44
Payment Methods, 44–45
Preferred Currency, 45
Purchase History, 44
Shipping Addresses, 45–46
Subscriptions, 44
Payvment Shopping Mall website, 229
People page (Insights)
demographics tracking, 371–372
overview, 371
permission-based marketing, 410, 412
permissions. *See also* OAuth service
Ad Accounts settings, 391
admin status, 393–394
App Center settings, 291
app requests, 245–246
business page reply rights, 110
custom apps
app authentication, 425–426, 453–457
authenticating, 433
checking, 42
configuring, 456–457
optional, 426
request considerations, 425
user authentication, 425
Events access, 174–175, 181–182
games settings, 201, 204–205

group posting rights, 151, 153–154
Location Services, 169
optional, 202, 426
overview, 95
requirements, 424
persona development
audience assessments, 97
audience attraction/engagement, 98
brand-building benefits, 100–102
business use, 209
goal setting, 95
humorous updates, 98
lifecasting, 96
overview, 8
personal profile
initial setup, 16
picture etiquette, 17, 104
personal timeline. *See* timeline
phishing
mistyped URL, 230
suspicious links, 104, 192
photo-editing software, 128
photos
advantages, 117
albums
adding pictures, 124–125
creating/organizing, 121–123
editing, 123–124
moving pictures between, 125–126
overview, 120–121
privacy settings, 123–124, 126–127
types, 121
brand-building benefits, 101
business use, 209
commenting, 130
comments, adding pictures to, 120
editing
Edit Album page use, 124
Edit button, 130
limitations, 128–129
shared pictures of you, 131
software, 119, 128
engagement value, 217
Events
uploads, 183
wall posting, 185

events uploads, 183
Facebook smartphone app,
161–162
following other people, 115
GPS security concerns, 96
group image displays
display changes, 150
graphics, 149–150
member profile pictures, 148
Instagram use, 119
iPhone camera app, 132
.jpg versus .png, 119
Like/Unlike button, 130
location adding, 130
mobile device transfers
Facebook smartphone app, 161
Instagram use, 119
smartphone apps, 131–132
News Feed algorithm ranking, 373
privacy settings, 127
profile picture etiquette, 17, 104
sending, 130
sharing options, 130
tagging
album editing, 125
etiquette, 129
notifications, 36
privacy issues, 103
spamming, 129
status update method, 118
Tag Photo button, 128, 130
tag reviews, 35–36
untagging, 130
uploading images, 117–118
Photoshop Elements, 128
PHP SDK (server-side)
github download website, 468
JavaScript SDK versus, 466–467
Pinterest
cross-site bookmarking, 248
overview, 241
pitches
bombardment avoidance, 321
call to action links, 321–322
customer interaction/
recommendations, 254

Places
  Location Services permissions, 168
  overview, 168
  smartphone use
    finding friends, 170
    finding present location, 169
    tagging friends, 170
platform dialogs. *See* dialog boxes
plugins
  button location options, 254–255
  overview, 252
  Skype video calls, 195
  types, 253
  usage recommendations, 253–254
+1 Add Friend button, 22
+Add Friends button, 19
+Create Group button, 146
+Find Friend button, 19
.png files, 119
Post Planner
  automation tools, 262
  overview, 260–261
Post Planner website, 3
Post Targeting and Privacy setting, 287,
    332–333
posting/updating
  business versus individual, 314
  comment editing/deleting, 111–112
  cross-platform
    blogs, 250
    Google+ integration, 251–252
    Twitter integration, 250–251
  embedded posts, 470
  etiquette, 102–104
  hashtag (#) use, 108
  Insights statistics tracking, 370–371
  managing third-party, 312–313
  milestones
    creating, 308–310
    editing, 310–311
  mobile device use, 294
  recent posts viewing, 311
  social plugin use, 252–255
  status updates
    creating/uploading, 105–106
    editing, 310–311
    emoticons, 106–107

  icons used, 107
  overview, 105
  pinning stories, 310
  relevant content, 324
  timing strategies, 323, 374–375
  types, 106
  Twitter/Facebook integration,
    250–251
Posts page (Insights), 370–371
PPC (pay per click) ads, 413–414
Preferred Currency setting, 45
privacy. *See* professional networking
  admin assignments, 65
  authentication, 453–456
  chat settings, 72, 193–194
  comment controls, 69
  frictionless sharing issues, 64
  friend requests
    response options, 69
    visibility options, 68
  Friends Only setting, 64
  game permissions, 200–202, 204–205
  games settings, 201, 204–205
  groups settings, 151
  login notifications, 65
  overview, 63
  password strength, 64
  permissions access, 95
  personal choices, 97
  personal responsibility, 64–65
  photo tagging, 129
  photos, 123–124, 126–127
  posting etiquette, 103
  Privacy Policy URL setting, 439
  secure browsing option, 65
  settings
    activity log review, 66
    follow feature, 114–115
    friend request filter, 66
    groups, 147
    photo albums, 123–124, 126–127
    search controls, 68
    search engine access, 66
    status update hiding, 66
    status updates, 69–70
    View As option, 68
    visibility options, 65–66

shortcuts, 51
status update controls, 107
tagging concerns, 65–66, 69, 109, 129
timeline control, 97
tracking issues, 63
videos, 142
websites, 66
private conversation options
 chats
  going offline, 193
  initiating, 192–193
  limiting availability/hiding, 72, 194
  multiple friend conversations, 193
  overview, 188
 Facebook e-mail, 189
 group chats, 189
 messages
  friend connections, 189–191
  nonfriend connections, 191–192
  overview, 187–188
 pokes, 188
 video calls
  ending, 195
  Initiating, 194–195
  overview, 188
  Skype integration, 194
profanity filter, 288
professional networking
 affiliation confirmations, 26
 automation
  business page alerts, 263–264
  common mistakes, 265
  engagement issues, 339
  marketing goals, 259–260
  requirements, 260
  third-party tools, 260–261
  update scheduling, 260–263
 badge use, 256
 blending personal and professional
   contacts
  approach suggestions, 211
  respecting differing opinions, 209
 business contacts
  e-mail contact lists, importing, 212–215
  meaningful connections, 215–216
  nurturing relationships, 216–217
 business importance, 339

business page promotion
 badge use, 256
 inviting e-mail contacts, 219
 inviting friends, 217–218
business pages
 cover photo ads, 281
 cover photo design, 280–282
 creating/organizing, 271–273
 layout suggestions, 280
 profile photo (avatar) design,
   227–280
content
 automatic updating, 260–263
 building engagement, 216–217
 controversial topics, 216
 exclusive, authoritative, 215
cover photo, 210
engagement nurturing
 commenting, 217
 humorous posts, 216
 multimedia, 217
 short postings, 216–217
engagement value
 brand humanization, 339
 brand interactions, 341
 influencing followers, 339
 'top of mind' benefits, 340
friends list issues, 209
friends/followers
 building following, 341–342
 connecting, 342–344
joining/inviting, 26–27
LinkedIn platform, 239–240
marketing
 advertising, 243
 blog page integration, 257
 business card integration, 256–257
 customer interaction, 242–243
 Facebook advantages, 9–10
 Facebook integration, 256–257
 interactive campaigns, 235
 QR code advertisement, 257
 Vocus platform, 143
marketing integration
 outsourcing management functions,
   346–347
 overview, 344

professional networking, marketing
  integration *(continued)*
    third-party apps, 346
    traditional promotion ideas, 344–345
    URL name choice/acquisition, 346
  meeting/connecting
    business contacts, 212–215
    personal contacts, 209–211
  message filtering, 209
  networking possibilities, 8–9
  overview, 209
  persona development, 209
  personal conversation, 212
  profile photo (avatar), 209–210
profile. *See* timeline
profile photo (avatar)
  business use, 209–210
  changing, 58
  choosing/uploading, 17
  overview, 276
  Profile Pictures photo album, 125
promotions
  advantages, 396
  best practices creation suggestions
    advertising ideas, 404–405
    entry process, 403–404
    goal setting, 403
    required information explained, 404
  calls to action, 397
  contests versus giveaways, 395–396
  Facebook Offers use, 405
  guidelines/rules/laws, 398–399
  legal verbiage, 399
  spreading the word, 396–397
  third-party apps
    ShortStack use, 399–401
    Strutta use, 402–403
    Wildfire use, 402
  tracking responses, 397
Purchase History setting, 44

Q

QR code advertisement, 257
questionnaires
  options, 326–327
  overview, 326
  planning benefits, 328
  question sources, 327

R

Reach page (Insights), 368–369
Real Simple Syndication (RSS) feeds
  blog posting, 264
  brand-building, 101
Recognized Devices setting, 32–33
Recommendations box (plugin), 472–473
Recommendations button (plugin), 473
registration (plugin), 473–474
Renaming option (lists), 74
reporting inappropriate behavior
  contacts, 224–225
  groups, 155–156
  spamming, 88
requests, 422–423
right navigation sidebar
  business versus individual, 313
  options, 55
  overview, 54
  targeted ad location, 377–378
RSS (Real Simple Syndication) feeds
  blog posting, 264
  brand-building, 101

S

safety. *See* Family Safety Center
School list, 72
SDKs (software development kits)
  JavaScript SDK
    discussion, 467
    website, 468
  overview, 466
  tutorial, 461
searching
  crowdsourcing, 10, 237
  friend requests, 69
  Graph Search
    overview, 98–99
    search techniques, 100
  search engine access, 66
  visibility options, 68–69

sections
  past events, adding, 62
  stories
    editing, 61
    hiding/reinstating, 61–62
    highlighting, 61
    posting/updating, 61
secure browsing option, 67
security. *See also* permissions; privacy
  Active Sessions, 33
  activity log review, 66
  admin assignments, 65
  browser extension warning, 252
  Code Generator, 31
  Facebook advertising guidelines, 381–382
  Facebook Platform web access, 245
  game permissions, 200–202
  GPS concerns, 96
  `https://` versus `http://`
    canvas app use, 436–438
    privacy protection, 65
    secure browsing, 29, 437
  links concerns, 104, 192, 324
  Login Approvals
    code generation/use, 30–31
    overview, 29
  Login Notifications, 29, 65
  overview, 28
  password strength, 64
  permissions
    app authentication, 425–426
    OAuth service, 425
    optional, 202, 426
    request considerations, 425
    requirements, 424
    user authentication, 425
  Recognized Devices, 32–33
  Secure Browsing, 29
  SSL certificates, 436–437
  timeline control, 97
  Trusted Contacts, 32
  websites, 66
security and privacy websites, 66
Send button (plugin), 474
settings
  blocking/unblocking people and apps, 67
  Privacy
    activity log review, 66
    admin assignments, 65

frictionless sharing issues, 64
friend request filter, 66
friend request response options, 69
Friends Only setting, 64
login notifications, 65
overview, 63
password strength, 64
personal responsibility, 64–65
search controls, 68
search engine access, 66
secure browsing option, 65
status update hiding, 66
status updates, 69–70
tagging, 110
timeline, 110
View As option, 68
visibility options, 65–66
Security
  Active Sessions, 33
  activity log review, 66
  admin assignments, 65
  Code Generator, 31
  Login Approvals, 29, 30–31
  Login Notifications, 29, 65
  overview, 28
  password strength, 64
  Recognized Devices, 32–33
  Secure Browsing, 29
  Trusted Contacts, 32
  websites, 66
sharing. *See also* privacy
  audience assessments, 97
  audience attraction/engagement, 98
  business page promotion, 219
  controversial posts, 98
  feedback options, 113
  frictionless, 64
  hashtag (#) use, 108
  humorous posts, 98
  interest lists, 80–82
  links, 102–103
  list links, 113–114
  multi-site methods, 249
  news feed links, 113–114
  online content links, 103
  photos
    album privacy settings, 123–124, 126–127
    Instagram use, 119
    options, 130

sharing, photos *(continued)*
    sending, 130
    tagging, 125
  popular update types, 97
  relevancy assessments, 98
  security warnings, 96
  share button use, 253
  status update controls, 107
  status updates, 98, 113
  tagging
    @ symbol use, 109
    business versus individual, 110
    icons used with, 107
    overview, 109
    privacy controls, 109–110
    status update actions, 105–106
  videos
    computer uploads, 135–136
    exposure potential, 133–134
    phone uploads, 136–137
    Vimeo uploads, 139
    YouTube uploads, 138
Shipping Addresses setting, 45–46
shopping cart app, 330
shortcuts, 51
ShortStack website, 143
signing up
  choosing interests, 16–17
  finding/inviting friends
    e-mail account access, 15–16
    personal profile information, 16
  overview, 15
Simple Facebook Connect (plugin), 265
Skype
  contact uploads, 212–215
  video calls
    ending, 195
    initiating, 194–195
    overview, 188
    plugin download, 195
smartphone app websites, 131–132
smartphones. *See* mobile devices
SMS (text messages)
  pictures and posts, 167–168
  setup, 166
  status updates, 166–167
social channels, 420, 464–465

social graphs. *See also* Insights
  definition, 462
  Open Graph versus Graph API, 463
social marketing campaigns
  business page adjustments
    canvas apps use, 359–360
    contact form embedding, 359
    cover photo tweaks, 358
    custom contest tab, 358–359
    ticker use, 360–361
  characteristics, 350–351
  crowdsourcing
    advantages, 356
    content driving, 357–358
  Like-gating, 428
  overview, 349
  sharing contests
    contest advertising suggestions, 356–357
    effort versus reward balance, 354–355
    ensuring success, 355
    overview, 352
    posting status updates, 355
    third-party hosting, 353–354
    video and photo concepts, 353
  types, 351–352
social media
  definition, 235
  Facebook Platform benefits
    automatic permissions/logins, 246–247
    blog posting updates, 249–250
    cross-site bookmarking, 248–249
    games and apps access, 247
    multi-site commenting, 248
    multi-site sharing/Liking, 248
    OAuth services, 247
    tweet cross-posting, 249
  Facebook/Google+ integration, 251–252
  Facebook/Twitter integration, 250–251
  friends
    definition, 18
    finding/inviting, 17–18
    interactions, 18
  marketing
    advertising, 243
    attraction, 242
    customer interaction, 242–243
    gameplay information gathering, 201

other platforms
Google+, 241
Instagram app, 242
LinkedIn, 239–240
Pinterest, 242
Twitter, 238–239
Vocus, 143
overview, 235–236
Twitter/Facebook integration, 250–251
social plugins
activity feed, 470–471
button location options, 254–255
Code Generator use, 470
Comments box, 471
embedded posts, 470
Facepile, 471
Follow button, 474
Like box, 471
Like button, 472
overview, 252, 446
Recommendations box, 472–473
Recommendations button, 473
registration, 473–474
Send button, 474
types, 253
usage recommendations, 253–254
XFBML implementation, 470
social proof
badges, 255–256
establishing, 322–323
Liking value, 311
shared links, 324
targeted ad value, 378
visitor interactions, 322
software development kits (SDKs)
JavaScript SDK
discussion, 467
website, 468
overview, 466
tutorial, 461
spamming
avoiding, 104, 192
reporting, 88
tagging issues, 129
sponsored stories, 55
Statigram website, 119

statistics tracking. *See* Insights
Status Ideas Engine, 327
status updates
account deletion issues, 48
apps settings, 40–42
backups, 27
blog links, 106
calls to action
authority establishment, 321
business page use, 277
customer involvement, 330
example of use, 329–330
image inclusions, 305
necessity of, 328
planning workflow, 329
share page use, 299
trust-building, 322
creating/uploading, 105–106
editing/deleting, 112
emoticons, 106–107
feedback options, 113
follow feature settings, 114–115
following other people, 115
hashtag (#) use, 108
humorous posts, 216
icons, 107
individual content share settings, 70
interest list sharing, 80–82
length suggestions, 216–217
links, posting, 105–106, 185
microblogs, 237
overview, 105
photos
engagement value, 217
transfers, 161
uploading, 118
pinning stories, 310
privacy setting adjustments, 107–108
privacy settings
overview, 69
share settings, 70
shared app links, 7
sharing, 98, 113
Support Dashboard screen, 47
ticker views, 360–361
timeline posting control, 107
types, 106
unfollowing, 222–223

stories. *See also* status updates
  definition, 57
  discovery stories (news feed), 423–424
  hiding/reinstating, 61–62
  highlighting, 61
  posting/updating, 61
  publishing stories (custom apps), 423
Subscriptions setting, 44
Support Dashboard, 47
synchronizing
  automating, 260–263
  business page integration, 271
  events to calendars, 173, 179–180

T

tablet access. *See* mobile devices
tabs, 452
tagging
  @ symbol use, 109
  attracting readers, 97
  business versus individual, 110, 314
  etiquette
    general rules, 110
    photos, 129
    privacy issues, 103
  icons used, 107
  managing tags, 59
  monitoring/editing, 35
  notifications, 34–36, 50
  overview, 109
  photos
    album editing, 125
    uploads, 36, 118
    viewer page options, 128–131
  privacy concerns, 65–66, 69, 109–110
  rules, 110
  settings, 34–35
  status update actions, 105–106
  video, 142–143
targeting
  advertising, 10, 377–378
  followers versus nonfollowers, 330–331
  friend invitations, 299
  market knowledge, 322
  status updates, 332–333

Terms of Service agreement, 11–13
text messages (SMS)
  pictures and posts, 167–168
  setup, 166
  status updates, 166–167
third-party tools
  apps/websites, 353
  canvas apps, 359–360
  Facebook promotion requirements, 350–351, 353
  marketing campaign hosting, 353–355
threaded comments, 289
thumbnails
  editing, 103
  video, 142
ticker pane
  activity applications, 56
  business responses, 57
  hiding, 56
  overview, 55
  status update views, 360–361
timeline
  accessing, 57
  Activity Log button, 59
  adding events, 62
  brand-building, 101
  business pages
    content, 215–217
    Like pages review, 311
    managing others' posts, 312–313
    milestones, creating, 308–310
    milestones, editing, 310–311
    overview, 307
    personal timelines versus, 270, 313–315
    recent posts, 311
    restrictions, 101
    social proof, 311
    status update editing, 310–311
    status update posting, 307–308
    switching between, 314–315
    toolbar differences, 315–318
  Change Cover button, 60
  content
    professional, 215–217
    removing, 228

cover photo, 58
display options, 61
editing, 61
Facebook apps restriction, 143
game access permissions, 200–202
game activity postings, 206
Gear icon, 59
hiding stories, 61–62
life moments tracking, 62
links, 51
More link, 60
order of events, 60–61
overview, 7, 51
personal versus business pages, 270
photo uploading, 117–118, 125
picture choosing/uploading, 17
privacy control options, 97
profile photo (avatar), 58
sections
    editing stories, 61
    hiding/reinstating stories, 61–62
    highlighting stories, 61
    managing, 60
    past events, adding, 62
    posting/updating stories, 61
status update posting control, 107
timeline information, 312–313
unfollowing, 222–223
Update Info button, 58
updating events, 57
Timeline and Tagging settings
options, 35
overview, 34
photo tagging, 36
Timeline Photos album
overview, 125
photo uploading, 118
timesuck avoidance
feed reader use, 11
Follow feature, 11
groups, 11
lists, 10
navigation options, 11
top navigation toolbar, 50–51
tracking. *See also* Insights
ad targeting value, 379
Ads Manager use, 390–392

business content decisions, 216
e-mail responses, 412
example of use, 94
game progress, 197
importance of, 363
Insights statistics, 387, 407–408
life moments (timeline), 62
link tracking services, 325
News Feed
    algorithm rankings, 390–392
    issues, 71
overview, 363–364, 372–373, 377
people
    Lists feature, 71
    smart list use, 72
People page (Insights), 371–372
photo/video ranking, 373
privacy issues, 63
Purchase History, 44
rank management options, 374–375
reach statistics, 368–369
survey use, 396
translations, 465
Trusted Contacts setting, 32
tutorials
advanced API documentation
    core concepts, 460
    SDKs, 461
apps on Facebook, 460
canvas, 460
fluid canvas, 462
games, 462
page tabs, 461–462
third-party, 462
tweets (Twitter), 238
Twitter
character limitation, 238
Facebook integration, 250–251
features, 239
tweets, 238

U

unblocking
apps, 227
contacts, 67
event invites, 67

unfollowing
  friends, 222–223
  videos, 142
unfriending, 223–224
Unliking
  business pages, 226
  photos, 130
  videos, 142
Update Info button, 58
Update Types option (lists), 75
updating. *See* posting/updating
URL links. *See also* vanity URL
  advertising, 258
  canvas page postings, 451
  clickable, 303
  copying/pasting, 85, 180
  custom app installations, 450–451
  QR codes versus, 257
username. *See* vanity URL

V

vanity URL
  creating, 275
  naming
    availability check, 275
    choosing/acquiring, 346
    NameCheap website, 346
    restrictions/suggestions, 274–275
  overview, 23–24, 274
  setting/changing
    account verification, 24–25
    restrictions, 25
  unique number assignment, 23–24
  URL shortcut, 275
video calls
  ending, 195
  initiating, 194–195
  Skype integration, 194
video editing software, 141
video sharing app websites, 143
videos
  business uses, 134–135
  content ideas, 134–135
  creating
    Facebook smartphone app, 137
    production suggestions, 144
    webcam use, 135

editing
  button locations, 141–142
  finding on Facebook, 140
  options, 143
  software, 141
News Feed algorithm ranking, 373
overview, 133, 372–373
privacy issues, 142
production suggestions, 144
quality, 134
sharing
  computer uploads, 135–136
  exposure potential, 133–134
  Facebook apps, 143
  links versus uploads, 135
  smartphone uploads, 136–137
  Vimeo uploads, 139
  YouTube uploads, 138
tagging, 142–143
uploading
  computer sources, 135–136
  smartphone options, 136–137
  social media channels, 137–139
viewing on news feed page, 133
View As option, 68
Vimeo, 139
vioggers (video bloggers), 135
viruses
  avoiding, 229–230
  detecting, 228–229
  overview, 228
  repairing, 230–231
visibility options, 65–66
Visits page (Insights), 369–370
Vocus website, 143

W

websites
  Ads API tool, 465
  AllFacebook (blog), 89
  Android SDK, 468
  app authentication, 457
  App Center, 200
  bitly (link tracking), 325
  Camera+ app, 132
  Chat API tool, 465
  Chrome browser extension (Google+), 252

core concepts, 460
dialogs, 465
Facebook AIO FD, 3
Facebook developers page, 449
Facebook help, 84
Facebook legal documents, 13
Facebook Mobile, 206
The Facebook Newsroom (blog), 89
Facebook service agreements, 13
Facebook Tips, 87
Facebook Touch Mobile, 164–165
FQL queries, 465
github (PHP SDK downloads), 466–467
GLMPS app, 132
Inside Facebook (blog), 89
Instagram app, 131
Internationalization API, 465
iOS Getting Started page, 468
JavaScript SDK, 468
legal documents, 88
NameCheap, 346
Offerpop, 353
Payment Shopping Mall, 229
photo-editing software, 128
Post Planner, 3
security and privacy, 66
smartphone apps, 131–132
Social Media Examiner, 462
social plugin generators, 470
Statigram, 119

third-party tools, 353
tutorials
    apps on Facebook tutorial, 460
    canvas tutorial, 460
    core concepts, 461
    fluid canvas, 462
    games, 462
    page tabs, 461–462
    SDKs, 461
    third-party, 462
updates, 1
video sharing applications, 143
Wildfire, 353
Wildfire website, 353
Wordbooker (plugin), 266
Work list, 72

X

XFBML (eXtended FaceBook Markup
    Language)
    iframes versus, 466
    JavaScript SDK processing, 466, 470
    plugin implementation, 470

Y

Your City list, 72
YouTube, 135, 138

About the Authors

Jamie Crager is the founder and CEO of crowdshifter.com and Crowdshifter Media, a digital marketing company that helps businesses use digital and social media to expand their companies. Crowdshifter Media provides "done for you" digital services, consulting, training, and speaking. He is also launching blazefly, a new patent-pending mobile application that will be a social and digital ecosystem for consumers and businesses. You can sign up for the beta at blazefly.com. Jamie also teaches social networking and digital marketing classes in the Continuing Education Department of Iowa Western Community College and sits on the advisory board of several companies. Some of his most recent achievements are Voted Best Social Media Consultant 2011 by Omaha Businesses via B2B Magazine, Google AdWords Qualified Individual, 2011 Stevie Awards Finalist for National Accounts Manager of the Year, and Miller Heiman Certified. Jamie lives in Papillion, Nebraska, a suburb of Omaha, with his wife, Jen, son, Joshua, and daughter, Katelyn.

Scott Ayres is a professional blogger and social media consultant who currently blogs and heads up training for the Facebook scheduling app Post Planner (www.postplanner.com) as well as podcasts on the popular "Facebook Answerman" show (www.FacebookAnswerman.com). He became addicted to social media even before MySpace (the first time around). He's a horrible Internet marketer because he's more concerned about teaching than turning a quick buck. On any given day, he spends 20+ hours on Facebook! He's been married for 20 years and has three kids that are his world. Scott grew up in a tiny community of about 150 in Flat, Texas, far away from the hustle and bustle of big city life. He now lives in Gatesville, a small country town in Texas.

Dedication

Jamie Crager: I dedicate this book to my mother, Ann, who would say this and previous versions were written just for her. Although she is no dummy, she, like many others, finds technology and the online digital world a challenge. I hope this book helps make that world a little easier. My mom is a true example of selflessness, strength, and love. She is a two-time cancer survivor and, at the time of this writing (December 2013), will defeat it one more time in the coming months. I would not be who I am today without her. I'm very grateful for her sacrifices through the years, including watching our kids for five years, and for her example of what a great mother is. Thank you mom and I love you always! I would also like to dedicate this to my dad, Guy, who has always supported me and given his time, resources, and love to make things better for our family — for that I will be always thankful.

Scott Ayres: I dedicate this book to my best friend and wife, Lisa. We've been together for over 23 years and I can't imagine doing life with anyone else. Who would have thought I'd be writing a book someday about my online addiction! This book also goes out to my three great kids, Madison, Macee, and Nathan, who are too young to be on Facebook yet! I love you guys. To my two brothers, Loney and Corey: We've been through a lot and the best is yet to come. Dad, even with your disabilities you inspire me every day, and I'm so proud of you. Mom, I miss you. You always pushed me to swim against the current; being a part of this book is testament to that. Thanks.

Authors' Acknowledgments

Jamie Crager: My contribution to this book would not have happened if it weren't for the wonderful people in my life and those who helped me on this project. I'd like to thank Jen, my beautiful wife, for her support, love, and encouragement. Her dedication to our family — along with watching our kids while I worked on this book late into the night and on weekends — is one of the biggest reasons I could do this project. I love you and am so blessed to have you by my side. To my son, Joshua, and daughter, Katelyn: You inspire me to be a better person and to do more. But at the end of the day, regardless of who I am or what I do, I'm content just being your dad. Of all my titles, this is my favorite and the most important one to me. I love you both, and you're always in my thoughts and prayers.

I'd like to thank my editor on this project, Susan Pink. Her encouragement, patience, and help were above and beyond the call of duty. I'd also like to thank my sister-in-law, Kate McCabe, and her husband, Tim. Thank you for the research and contributions that helped me on this project. I'd like to thank my wife's parents, Al and Wendy McCabe, for their love and support and for all they have done for our family. I'd also like to note that the bulk of this project was done while visiting their home in Ontario. I have too many others to acknowledge, but I'd like to thank Ken Power, Chris and Jenn Carlson, Jason and Jen Crager, and the rest of my family and friends for being there and helping me in more ways than I could list. Also thank you to my coauthor, Scott, for his contributions on some of the figures and for moral support as we navigated this project together. To everyone else I know, personally and professionally, I'm grateful that you're in my life.

Scott Ayres: I'd like to thank Andrea Vahl, author of *Facebook Marketing All-in-One For Dummies,* for recommending me to Wiley as a coauthor of this book. I'm forever in your debt. Thank you to Amy Fandrei, for allowing me to be involved in the project, and to Susan Pink, for keeping us on track and making sure we completed our work.

Big props to Josh Parkinson of Post Planner for allowing me to set aside some time from my responsibilities to write this book. Thanks bro! To Rosh Khan, thanks for being a quiet inspiration to me via Skype and always challenging me to think bigger of myself. Chris Brogan, what can I say? You inspire me through your public messages but hundreds of times more through your private e-mails and messages to me. Your persistent message of being brave and taking risks motivated me to accept the book deal, and I thank you for it.

Publisher's Acknowledgments

Acquisitions Editor: Amy Fandrei

Project Editor: Susan Pink

Copy Editor: Susan Pink

Technical Editor: Michelle Krasniak

Editorial Assistant: Annie Sullivan

Sr. Editorial Assistant: Cherie Case

Project Coordinator: Patrick Redmond

Cover Image: ©iStockphoto.com/YinYang

Math & Science

Algebra I For Dummies,
2nd Edition
978-0-470-55964-2

Anatomy and Physiology
For Dummies,
2nd Edition
978-0-470-92326-9

Astronomy For Dummies,
3rd Edition
978-1-118-37697-3

Biology For Dummies,
2nd Edition
978-0-470-59875-7

Chemistry For Dummies,
2nd Edition
978-1-1180-0730-3

Pre-Algebra Essentials
For Dummies
978-0-470-61838-7

Microsoft Office

Excel 2013 For Dummies
978-1-118-51012-4

Office 2013 All-in-One
For Dummies
978-1-118-51636-2

PowerPoint 2013
For Dummies
978-1-118-50253-2

Word 2013 For Dummies
978-1-118-49123-2

Music

Blues Harmonica
For Dummies
978-1-118-25269-7

Guitar For Dummies,
3rd Edition
978-1-118-11554-1

iPod & iTunes
For Dummies,
10th Edition
978-1-118-50864-0

Programming

Android Application
Development For
Dummies, 2nd Edition
978-1-118-38710-8

iOS 6 Application
Development For Dummies
978-1-118-50880-0

Java For Dummies,
5th Edition
978-0-470-37173-2

Religion & Inspiration

The Bible For Dummies
978-0-7645-5296-0

Buddhism For Dummies,
2nd Edition
978-1-118-02379-2

Catholicism For Dummies,
2nd Edition
978-1-118-07778-8

Self-Help & Relationships

Bipolar Disorder
For Dummies,
2nd Edition
978-1-118-33882-7

Meditation For Dummies,
3rd Edition
978-1-118-29144-3

Seniors

Computers For Seniors
For Dummies,
3rd Edition
978-1-118-11553-4

iPad For Seniors
For Dummies,
5th Edition
978-1-118-49708-1

Social Security
For Dummies
978-1-118-20573-0

Smartphones & Tablets

Android Phones
For Dummies
978-1-118-16952-0

Kindle Fire HD
For Dummies
978-1-118-42223-6

NOOK HD For Dummies,
Portable Edition
978-1-118-39498-4

Surface For Dummies
978-1-118-49634-3

Test Prep

ACT For Dummies,
5th Edition
978-1-118-01259-8

ASVAB For Dummies,
3rd Edition
978-0-470-63760-9

GRE For Dummies,
7th Edition
978-0-470-88921-3

Officer Candidate Tests,
For Dummies
978-0-470-59876-4

Physician's Assistant Exam
For Dummies
978-1-118-11556-5

Series 7 Exam
For Dummies
978-0-470-09932-2

Windows 8

Windows 8 For Dummies
978-1-118-13461-0

Windows 8 For Dummies,
Book + DVD Bundle
978-1-118-27167-4

Windows 8 All-in-One
For Dummies
978-1-118-11920-4

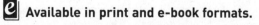 **Available in print and e-book formats.**

Take Dummies with you everywhere you go!

Whether you're excited about e-books, want more from the web, must have your mobile apps, or swept up in social media, Dummies makes everything easier.

Visit Us

Like Us

Follow Us

Watch Us

Join Us

Pin Us

Circle Us

Shop Us